readings from
EDUCATIONAL LEADERSHIP

cooperative learning and the collaborative school

Edited by Ronald S. Brandt

Association for Supervision and Curriculum Development
Alexandria, Virginia

Copyright 1991 by the
Association for Supervision and Curriculum Development

ASCD publications present a variety of viewpoints. The views
expressed or implied in this publication should not be interpreted as
official positions of the Association.

Ronald S. Brandt, *Executive Editor*
Nancy Modrak, *Managing Editor, Books*
Ginger Miller, *Associate Editor*
Cole Tucker, *Editorial Assistant*

ASCD Stock Number: 611-91164
ISBN: 0-87120-186-0
Price: $21.95

Library of Congress Cataloging-in-Publication Data

Cooperative Learning and the Collaborative School: Readings from
    Educational Leadership / edited by Ronald S. Brandt.
    p. cm.
        "The articles in this book were first published in recent issues of
    Educational Leadership"— Introd.
ISBN 0-87120-186-0: $21.95
1. Group work in education. I. Brandt, Ronald S.
LB1032.C593 1991   91-30608
371.3'95—dc20   CIP

Readings from *Educational Leadership* on
Cooperative Learning and the Collaborative School

No one who reads professional journals, goes to conferences, or participates in staff development needs to be told that cooperation and collaboration are major themes in education today. The reasons are evident: research findings on the effectiveness of cooperative learning are among the strongest we have, and people have come to recognize that, in the modern world, almost any endeavor, from construction of a house to negotiation of peace in the Middle East, requires a high degree of cooperation.

Ironically, researchers have found that urbanization is accompanied by a decrease in the kind of "natural" cooperation found in rural areas and traditional societies (Brandt 1989). Our lives are no longer governed by strict conventions dictating how we must deal with one another, and urban anonymity permits blatant competitiveness that would be frowned on in small face-to-face communities. This means that the ability to work constructively with others has joined other aspects of life that at one time were passed on to the young by parents and other elders but are now taught formally in schools.

While this trend may be understandable and probably inescapable in the long run, that does not make implementation any easier. Cooperation in the classroom runs counter to well-established routines and values that nearly all adults—including many educators—take for granted. They do not object to occasional group work, but when it comes to final exams, grade-point averages, and college admissions, they expect education to be a fiercely competitive enterprise.

Our notions of professional excellence are equally individualistic. When most people speak of the expert teacher, they picture the dedicated oddball who demands autonomy so as to teach his or her way. Outstanding principals are said to be strong leaders who heroically buck the system in accord with their personal visions.

Tough as it is to question accepted customs, consider fresh ideas, and try new ways, numerous teachers are doing just that. They are changing the norms of classroom life, helping establish a different set of assumptions, proving that it can be done. Principals and other leaders are encouraging collaboration among adults as well, distributing leadership throughout the school, establishing new sources of collegial support.

Independence, initiative, and personal achievement are obviously very important and will continue to be valued, but in today's schools, they are being balanced with a new emphasis on consideration, sharing, and commitment to group goals. The results include improved student understanding, better relationships among students, and greater teacher satisfaction.

The articles in this book were first published in recent issues of Educational Leadership. We are proud to have contributed to the literature on the collaborative school, and we hope this collection will be useful to educators who sense the historic importance of a fundamental change in the conditions for learning.

Ronald S. Brandt
Editor

Readings from *Educational Leadership* on
Cooperative Learning and the Collaborative School

Introduction

In his lead article, Robert Slavin explains what cooperative learning is, offers his interpretation of research findings, tells why he developed instructional programs in reading and mathematics that incorporate cooperative methods, and describes his conception of the cooperative school. The section also includes a brief article in which I contend that cooperation is not unAmerican, and a conversation with Roger and David Johnson.

Educational Leadership 45 (Nov. 1987): 7-13

— ROBERT E. SLAVIN —

Cooperative Learning and the Cooperative School

The availability of models that can be used in math, reading, and writing at every grade level has made it possible to plan an elementary school around the concept of everyone's working together to improve all aspects of the school.

Photograph by Barbara Bennett

The Age of Cooperation is approaching. From Alaska to California to Florida to New York, from Australia to Britain to Norway to Israel, teachers and administrators are discovering an untapped resource for accelerating students' achievement: the students themselves. There is now substantial evidence that students working together in small cooperative groups can master material presented by the teacher better than can students working on their own.

The idea that people working together toward a common goal can accomplish more than people working by themselves is a well-established principle of social psychology. What is new is that practical cooperative learning strategies for classroom use have been developed, researched, and found to be instructionally effective in elementary and secondary schools. Once thought of primarily as social methods directed at social goals, certain forms of cooperative learning are considerably more effective than traditional methods in increasing basic achievement outcomes, including performance on standardized tests of mathematics, reading, and language (Slavin 1983a, b; Slavin in press a).

"There is now substantial evidence that students working together in small cooperative groups can master material . . . better than can students working on their own."

Recently, a small but growing number of elementary and secondary schools have begun to apply cooperative principles at the school as well as the classroom level, involving teachers in cooperative planning, peer coaching, and team teaching, with these activities directed toward effective implementation of cooperative learning in the classroom. Many of these schools are working toward institutionalization of cooperative principles as the focus of school renewal.

This article reviews the research on cooperative learning methods and presents a vision of the next step in the progression of cooperative learning: the cooperative school.

What Is Cooperative Learning and Why Does It Work?

Cooperative learning refers to a set of instructional methods in which students work in small, mixed-ability learning groups. (See p. 11 for a vignette about one day in the life of a hypothetical cooperative school.) The groups usually have four members—one high achiever, two average achievers, and one low achiever. The students in each group are responsible not only for learning the material being taught in class, but also for helping their groupmates learn. Often, there is some sort of group goal. For example, in the Student Team Learning methods developed at Johns Hopkins University (Slavin 1986), students can earn attractive certificates if group averages exceed a pre-established criterion of excellence.

For example, the simplest form of Student Team Learning, called Student Teams-Achievement Division (STAD), consists of a regular cycle of activities. First, the teacher presents a lesson to the class. Then students, in their four-member mixed-ability teams, work to master the material. Students usually have worksheets or other materials; study strategies within the teams depend on the subject matter. In math,

Students, like teachers, learn by explaining a lesson. When students have to organize their thoughts to communicate ideas to teammates, they engage in cognitive elaboration that enhances their own understanding.

students might work problems and then compare answers, discussing and resolving any discrepancies. In spelling, students might drill one another on spelling lists. In social studies, students might work together to find information in the text relating to key concepts. Regardless of the subject matter, students are encouraged not just to give answers but to explain ideas or skills to one another.

At the end of the team study period, students take brief individual quizzes, on which they cannot help one another. Teachers sum the results of the quizzes to form team scores, using a system that assigns points based on how much individual students have improved over their own past records.

The changes in classroom organization required by STAD are not revolutionary. To review the process, the teacher presents the initial lesson as in traditional instruction. Students then work on worksheets or other practice activities; they happen to work in teams, but otherwise the idea of practice following instruction is hardly new. Finally, students take a brief, individual quiz.

Yet, even though changes in classroom organization are moderate, the effects of cooperative learning on students can be profound. Because one student's success in the traditional classroom makes it more difficult for others to succeed (by raising the curve or raising the teacher's expectations), working hard on academic tasks can cause a student to be labeled as a "nerd" or a "teacher's pet." For this reason, students often express norms to one another that discourage academic work. In contrast, when students are working together toward a common goal, academic work becomes an activity valued by peers. Just as hard work in sports is valued by peers because a team member's success brings credit to the team and the school, so academic work is valued by peers in cooperative learning classes because it helps the team to succeed.

In addition to motivating students to do their best, cooperative learning also motivates students to help one another learn. This is important for several reasons. First, students are of-

ten able to translate the teacher's language into "kid language" for one another. Students who fail to grasp fully a concept the teacher has presented can often profit from discussing the concept with peers who are wrestling with the same questions.

Second, students who explain to one another learn by doing so. Every teacher knows that we learn by teaching. When students have to organize their thoughts to explain ideas to teammates, they must engage in cognitive elaboration that greatly enhances their own understanding (see Dansereau 1985).

Third, students can provide individual attention and assistance to one another. Because they work one-on-one, students can do an excellent job of finding out whether their peers have the idea or need additional explanation. In a traditional classroom, students who don't understand what is going on can scrunch down in their seats and hope the teacher won't call on them. In a cooperative team, there is nowhere to hide; there *is* a helpful, nonthreatening environment in which to try out ideas and ask for assistance. A student who gives an answer in a whole-class lesson risks being laughed at if the answer is wrong; in a cooperative team, the fact that the team has a "we're all in this together" attitude means that, when they don't understand, students are likely to receive help rather than derision.

> ## "Students are often able to translate the teacher's language into 'kid language' for one another."

Under What Conditions Is Cooperative Learning Effective?

Cooperative learning is always fun; it almost always produces gains in social outcomes such as race relations; and it has never been found to reduce student achievement in comparison to traditional methods. However, a substantial body of research has established that two conditions must be fulfilled if cooperative learning is to enhance student achievement substantially. First, students must be working toward a group goal, such as earning certificates or some other recognition. Second, success at achieving this goal must depend on the individual learning of all group members (see Slavin 1983a, b; in press a).

Simply putting students into mixed-ability groups and encouraging them to work together are not enough to produce learning gains: students must have a reason to take one another's achievement seriously, to provide one another with the elaborated explanations that are critical to the achievement effects of cooperative learning (see Webb 1985). If students care about the success of the team, it becomes legitimate for them to ask one another for help and to provide help to each other. Without this team goal, students may feel ashamed to ask peers for help.

Yet team goals are not enough in themselves to enhance student achievement. For example, classroom studies in which students complete a common worksheet or project have not found achievement benefits for such methods.. When the group task is to complete a single product, it may be most efficient to let the smartest or highest achieving students do most of the work. Suggestions or questions from lower-achieving students may be ignored or pushed aside, as they may interfere with efficient completion of the group task. We can all recall being in lab groups in science class or in project groups in social studies in which one or two group members did all the work. To enhance the achievement of all students, then, group success must be based not on a single group product, but on the sum of individual learning performances of all group members.

The group's task in instructionally effective forms of cooperative learning is almost always to prepare group members to succeed on individual assessments. This focuses the group activity on explaining ideas, practicing skills, and assessing all group members to ensure that all will be successful on learning assessments.

When cooperative learning methods provide group goals based on the learning of all members, the effects on student achievement are remarkably consistent. Of 38 studies of at least four weeks' duration comparing cooperative methods of this type to traditional control methods, 33 found significantly greater achievement for the cooperatively taught classes, and 5 found no significant differences (Slavin in press a). In contrast, only 4 of 20 studies that evaluated forms of cooperative learning lacking group goals based on group members' learning found positive achievement effects, and 3 of these are studies by Shlomo Sharan and his colleagues in Israel that incorporated group goals and individual accountability in a different way (see Sharan et al. 1980, Sharan et al. 1984).

Successful studies of cooperative learning have taken place in urban, rural, and suburban schools in the U.S., Canada, Israel, West Germany, and Nigeria, at grade levels from 2 to 12, and in subjects as diverse as mathematics, language arts, writing, reading, social studies, and science. Positive effects have been found on such higher-order objectives as creative writing, reading comprehension, and math problem solving, as well as on such basic skills objectives as language mechanics, math computations, and spelling. In general, achievement effects have been equivalent for high, average, and low achievers, for boys and girls, and for students of various ethnic backgrounds. As noted earlier, positive effects of cooperative learning have also been found on such outcomes as race relations, acceptance of mainstreamed academically handicapped classmates, and student self-

"In a cooperative team, there is nowhere to hide; there *is* a helpful, nonthreatening environment in which to try out ideas and ask for assistance."

esteem and liking of class (see Slavin 1983a).

Comprehensive Cooperative Learning Methods

The cooperative learning methods developed in the 1970s—Student Teams-Achievement Divisions and Teams-Games-Tournaments (Slavin 1986); Jigsaw Teaching (Aronson et al. 1978); the Johnsons' methods (Johnson and Johnson 1986); and Group Investigation (Sharan et al., 1984)—all are generic forms of cooperative learning. They can be used at many grade levels and in many subjects. The broad applicability of these methods partly accounts for their popularity. A one- or two-day workshop given to a mixed group of elementary and secondary teachers of many subjects can get teachers off to a good start in most of the methods, which makes this an ideal focus of staff development.

However, because the early cooperative learning methods are generally applicable across grade levels and subjects, they tend not to be uniquely adapted to any particular subject or grade level. Also, the methods developed earlier are mostly curriculum-free; they rarely replace traditional texts or teaching approaches. As a result, these methods are most often applied as supplements to traditional instruction and rarely bring about fundamental change in classroom practice.

Since 1980, research and development on cooperative learning conducted at Johns Hopkins University has begun to focus on comprehensive cooperative learning methods designed to replace traditional instruction *entirely* in particular subjects and at particular grade levels. Two major programs of this type have been developed and successfully researched: Team Accelerated Instruction (TAI) in mathematics for grades 3–6, and Cooperative Integrated Reading and Composition (CIRC) in reading, writing, and language arts for grades 3–5. The main elements of these programs are described below.

Team Accelerated Instruction (TAI). Team Accelerated Instruction shares with STAD and the other Student Team Learning methods the use of four-member mixed-ability learning teams and certificates for high-performing teams. But where STAD uses a single pace of instruction for the class, TAI combines cooperative learning with individualized instruction. TAI is designed to teach mathematics to students in grades 3–6 (or older students not ready for a full algebra course).

In TAI, students enter an individualized sequence according to a placement test and then proceed at their own rates. In general, team members work on different units. Teammates check each other's work against answer sheets and help one another with any problems. Final unit tests are taken without teammate help and are scored by student monitors. Each week, teachers total the number of units completed by all team members and give certificates or other rewards to teams that exceed a criterion score based on the number of final tests passed, with extra points for perfect papers and completed homework.

Because students are responsible for checking each other's work and managing the flow of materials, the teacher can spend most class time presenting lessons to small groups of students drawn from the various teams who are working at the same point in the mathematics sequence. For example, the teacher might call up a decimals group, present a lesson, and then send the students back to their teams to work on decimal problems. Then the teacher might call the fractions group, and so on.

In TAI, students encourage and help one another to succeed because they want their teams to succeed. Individual accountability is assured because the only score that counts is the final test score, and students take final tests without teammate help. Students have equal opportunities for success because all have been placed according to their level of prior knowledge; it is as easy (or difficult) for a low achiever to complete three subtraction units in a week as it is for a higher-achieving classmate to complete three long division units.

However, the individualization that is part of TAI makes it quite different from STAD. In mathematics, most concepts build on earlier ones. If the earlier concepts were not mastered, the later ones will be difficult or impossible to learn—a student who cannot subtract or multiply will fail to master long division, a student who does not understand fractional concepts will fail to understand what a decimal is, and so on. In TAI, students work at their own levels, so if they lack prerequisite skills they can build a strong foundation before going on. Also, if students can learn more rapidly, they need not wait for the rest of the class.

Individualized mathematics instruction has generally failed to increase student mathematics achievement in the past (see Horak 1981), probably because the teacher's time in earlier models was entirely taken up with checking work and managing materials, leaving little time for actually teaching students. In TAI, students handle the routine checking and management, so the teacher can spend most class time teaching. This difference, plus the motivation and help provided by students within their cooperative teams, probably accounts for the strong positive effects of TAI on student achievement.

Five of six studies found substantially greater learning of mathematics computations in TAI than in control classes, while one study found no differences (Slavin, Leavey, and Madden

A Visit to a Cooperative School

It is Friday morning at "Cooper Elementary School." In Ms. Thompson's third-grade, the students are getting ready for reading. They are sitting in teams at small tables, four or five at each table. As the period begins, Ms. Thompson calls up the "Rockets". Pairs of students from several of the small groups move to a reading group area, while the remaining students continue working at their desks. In Ms. Thompson's class the students at their desks are working together on activities quite different from the usual workbooks. They are taking turns reading aloud to each other; working together to identify the characters, settings, problems, and problem solutions in stories; practicing vocabulary and spelling; and summarizing stories to one another. When Ms. Thompson finishes with the Rockets, they return to their groups and begin working together on the same types of activities. Ms. Thompson listens in on some of the students who are reading to each other and praises teams that are working well. Then she calls up the "Astros," who leave their teams to go to the reading group.

Meanwhile, in Mr. Fisher's fifth-grade, it is math period. Again, students are working in small teams, but in math, each team member is working on different materials depending on his or her performance level. In the teams students are checking one another's work against answer sheets, explaining problems to one another, and answering each other's questions. Mr. Fisher calls up the "Decimals" group for a lesson. Students working on decimals leave their teams and move to the group area for their lesson. When the lesson is over, the students return to their teams and continue working on decimals.

In Mr. Fisher's class there are five learning disabled students, who are distributed among the various teams. The special education resource teacher, Ms. Walters, is teaming with Mr. Fisher. While he is giving lessons, she is moving through the class helping students. At other times, Ms. Walters gives math lessons to groups of students who are having difficulties in math, including her five LD students, while Mr. Fisher works with students in their team areas.

In Mr. Green's fourth-grade class it is writing time. Mr. Green starts the period with a brief lesson on "and disease," the tendency to write long sentences connected by too many "ands." Then the students work on compositions in teams. They cooperatively plan what they will write and then do a draft. The students read their drafts to their teammates and receive feedback on what their teammates heard, what they liked, and what they wanted to hear more about. After revising their drafts, students hold editing conferences with teammates focusing on the mechanics of the composition.

While the students are writing, Mr. Green is moving from team to team, listening in on what they are saying to each other and conferencing with individual students to help them. Also in the class is Ms. Hill, another fourth-grade teacher. She and Mr. Green began using writing process methods at the same time and are coaching each other as they use them in their classes. At the end of the day the two teachers will meet to discuss what happened, and to plan the next steps jointly. On other days, a substitute will cover Mr. Green's class while he visits Ms. Hill's writing class.

All over Cooper Elementary School, students are working in cooperative teams, and teachers are working together cooperatively to help students learn. In the first grades, students are working in pairs taking turns reading to each other. In the sixth grades students are doing team science projects in which each team member is responsible for a part of the team's task. Second-graders are working in teams to master capitalization and punctuation rules.

At the end of the day, teachers award certificates to teams that did outstanding work that week. Those teams that met the highest standards of excellence receive "Superteam" certificates. Throughout the school the sounds of applause can be heard.

After the students have gone home, the school steering committee meets. Chaired by the principal, the committee includes representatives of teachers at several grade levels, plus two parent representatives. The committee discusses the progress they are making toward their goal of becoming a cooperative school. Among other things, the committee decides to hold a school fair to show what the school is doing, to display the students' terrific cooperative work in writing, science, and math; and to encourage parents to volunteer at the school and to support their children's success at home.

—Robert E. Slavin

1984; Slavin, Madden, and Leavey 1984; Slavin and Karweit 1985). Across all six studies, the TAI classes gained an average of twice as many grade equivalents on standardized measures of computation as traditionally taught control classes (Slavin in press b). For example, in one 18-week study in Wilmington, Delaware, the control group gained .6 grade equivalents in mathematics computations, while the TAI classes gained 1.7 grade equivalents (Slavin and Karweit 1985). These experimental-control differences were still substantial (though smaller) a year after the students were in TAI.

Cooperative Integrated Reading and Composition (CIRC). The newest of the Student Team Learning methods is a comprehensive program for teaching reading and writing in the upper elementary grades. In CIRC, teachers use basal readers and reading groups, much as in traditional reading programs. However, students are assigned to teams composed of pairs from two different reading groups. While the teacher is working with one reading group, students in the other groups are working in their pairs on a series of cognitively engaging activities, including reading to one another; making predictions about how narrative stories will come out; summarizing stories to one another; writing responses to stories; and practicing spelling, decoding, and vocabulary. Students also work in teams to master main idea and other comprehension skills. During language arts periods, a structured program based on a writing process model is used. Students plan and write drafts, revise and edit one another's work, and prepare for publication of team books. Lessons on writing skills such as description, organization, use of vivid modifiers, and on language mechanics skills are fully integrated into students' creative writing.

In most CIRC activities, students follow a sequence of teacher instruction, team practice, team pre-assessments, and a quiz. That is, students do not take the quiz until their teammates have determined they are ready. Certificates are given to teams based on the average performance of all team members on all reading and writing activities. Two studies of CIRC (Stevens et al. in press) found substantial positive effects from this method on standardized tests of reading comprehension, reading vocabulary, language expression, language mechanics, and spelling, in comparison to control groups. The CIRC classes gained 30 to 70 percent of a grade equivalent more than control classes on these measures in both studies. Significantly greater achievement on writing samples favoring the CIRC students was also found in both studies.

A New Possibility

The development and successful evaluation of the comprehensive TAI and CIRC models has created an exciting new possibility. With cooperative learning programs capable of being used all year in the 3 Rs, it is now possible to design an elementary school program based upon a radical principle: students, teachers, and administrators can work *cooperatively* to make the school a better place for working and learning.

There are many visions of what a cooperative elementary school might look like, but there is one model that my colleagues and I have begun to work toward in partnership with some innovative practitioners. Its major components are as follows.

1. *Cooperative learning in the classroom.* Clearly, a cooperative elementary school would have cooperative learning methods in use in most classrooms and in more than one subject. Students and teachers should feel that the idea that students can help one another learn is not just applied on

Cooperative learning takes place in reading groups when students practice vocabulary words or summarize stories to one another.

occasion, but is a fundamental principle of classroom organization. Students should see one another as resources for learning, and there should be a schoolwide norm that every student's learning is everyone's responsibility, that every student's success is everyone's success.

2. *Integration of special education and remedial services with the regular program.* In the cooperative elementary school, mainstreaming should be an essential element of school and classroom organization. Special education teachers may team-teach with regular teachers, integrating their students in teams with nonhandicapped students and contributing their expertise in adapting instruction to individual needs to the class as a whole. Similarly, Chapter I or other remedial services should be provided in the regular classroom. If we take seriously the idea that all students are responsible for one another, this goes as much for students with learning problems as for anyone else. Research on use of TAI and CIRC to facilitate mainstreaming and meet the needs of remedial readers has found positive effects on the achievement and social acceptance of these students (see Slavin 1984, Slavin et al. in press).

3. *Peer coaching.* In the cooperative elementary school, teachers should be responsible for helping one another to use cooperative learning methods successfully and to implement other improvements in instructional practice. Peer coaching (Joyce et al. 1983) is perfectly adapted to the philosophy of the cooperative school; teachers learn new methods together

and are given release time to visit one another's classes to give assistance and exchange ideas as they begin using the new programs.

4. *Cooperative planning.* Cooperative activities among teachers should not be restricted to peer coaching. In addition, teachers should be given time to plan goals and strategies together, to prepare common libraries of instructional materials, and to make decisions about cooperative activities involving more than one class.

5. *Building-level steering committee.* In the cooperative elementary school, teachers and administrators should work together to determine the direction the school takes. A steering committee composed of the principal, classroom teacher representatives, representatives of other staff (e.g., special education, Chapter I, aides), and one or more parent representatives meets to discuss the progress the school is making toward its instructional goals and to recommend changes in school policies and practices to achieve these goals.

6. *Cooperation with parents and community members.* The cooperative school should invite the participation of parents and community members. Development of a community sense that children's success in school is everyone's responsibility is an important goal of the cooperative school.

The Cooperative School Today

To my knowledge, there is not yet a school that is implementing all of the program elements listed here, but a few enterprising and committed schools are moving in this direction. In Bay Shore (New York) School District, teachers in two intermediate schools are using CIRC in reading, writing, and language arts, and STAD in math. In Alexandria, Virginia, Mt. Vernon Community School is working with the National Education Association's Mastery in Learning project to build a cooperative school plan. At Mt. Vernon, a building steering committee is planning and helping to implement a gradual phasing in of the TAI math program and CIRC reading, writing, and language arts programs. Several

schools throughout the U.S. that have successfully implemented TAI math are now planning to add CIRC for reading and writing instruction, and are looking toward full-scale implementation of a cooperative school plan. Most schools that have focused school renewal efforts on widespread use of cooperative learning are at the elementary level; but several middle, junior high, and high schools have begun to work in this direction as well.

In a time of limited resources for education, we must learn to make the best use of what we have. Cooperative learning and the cooperative school provide one means of helping students, teachers, and administrators work together to make meaningful improvements in the learning of all students.□

References

Aronson, E., N. Blaney, C. Stephan, J. Sikes, and M. Snapp. *The Jigsaw Classroom.* Beverly Hills, Calif.: Sage, 1978.

Dansereau, D. F. "Learning Strategy Research." In *Thinking and Learning Skills: Relating Instruction to Basic Research, Vol. 1*, edited by J. Segal, S. Chipman, and R. Glaser. Hillsdale, N.J.: Erlbaum, 1985.

Horak, V. M. "A Meta-analysis of Research Findings on Individualized Instruction in Mathematics." *Journal of Educational Research* 74 (1981): 249–253.

Johnson, D. W., and R. T. Johnson. *Learning Together and Alone.* 2d ed. Englewood Cliffs, N.J.: Prentice-Hall, 1986.

Joyce, B. R., R. H. Hersh, and M. McKibbin. *The Structure of School Improvement.* New York: Longman, 1983.

Sharan, S., R. Hertz-Lazarowitz, and Z. Ackerman. "Academic Achievement of Elementary School Children in Small-Group vs. Whole Class Instruction." *Journal of Experimental Education* 48 (1980): 125–129.

Sharan, S., P. Kussell, R. Hertz-Lazarowitz, Y. Bejarano, S. Raviv, and Y. Sharan. *Cooperative Learning in the Classroom: Research in Desegregated Schools.* Hillsdale, N.J.: Erlbaum, 1984.

Slavin, R. E. *Cooperative Learning.* New York: Longman, 1983a.

Slavin, R. E. "When Does Cooperative Learning Increase Student Achievement?" *Psychological Bulletin* 94 (1983b): 429–445.

Slavin, R. E. "Team Assisted Individualization: Cooperative Learning and Individualized Instruction in the Mainstreamed Classroom." *Remedial and Special Education* 5, 6 (1984): 33–42.

Slavin, R. E. *Using Student Team Learning.* 3d ed. Baltimore, Md.: Center for Research on Elementary and Middle Schools, Johns Hopkins University, 1986.

Slavin, R. E. "Cooperative Learning: A Best-Evidence Synthesis." In *School and Classroom Organization*, edited by R. E. Slavin. Hillsdale, N.J.: Erlbaum. In press a.

Slavin, R. E. "Combining Cooperative Learning and Individualized Instruction." *Arithmetic Teacher.* In press b.

Slavin, R. E., and N. L. Karweit. "Effects of Whole-Class, Ability Grouped, and Individualized Instruction on Mathematics Achievement." *American Educational Research Journal* 22 (1985): 351–367.

Slavin, R. E., M. Leavey, and N. A. Madden. "Combining Cooperative Learning and Individualized Instruction: Effects on Student Mathematics Achievement, Attitudes, and Behaviors." *Elementary School Journal* 84 (1984): 409–422.

Slavin, R. E., N. A. Madden, and M. Leavey. "Effects of Team Assisted Individualization on the Mathematics Achievement of Academically Handicapped and Nonhandicapped Students." *Journal of Educational Psychology* 76 (1984): 813–819.

Slavin, R. E., R. J. Stevens, and N. A. Madden. "Accommodating Student Diversity in Reading and Writing Instruction: A Cooperative Learning Approach." *Remedial and Special Education.* In press.

Stevens, R. J., N. A. Madden, R. E. Slavin, and A. M. Farnish. "Cooperative Integrated Reading and Composition: Two Field Experiments." *Reading Research Quarterly.* In press.

Webb, N. "Student Interaction and Learning in Small Groups: A Research Summary." In *Learning to Cooperate, Cooperating to Learn*, edited by R. E. Slavin, S. Sharan, S. Kagan, R. Hertz-Lazarowitz, C. Webb, and R. Schmuck. New York: Plenum, 1985.

Author's note: This article was written under funding from the Office of Educational Research and Improvement, U.S. Department of Education (Grant No. OERI-G-86–006). However, the opinions expressed are mine and do not necessarily reflect OERI positions or policy.

Robert E. Slavin is Director of the Elementary School Program at the Center for Research on Elementary and Middle Schools, Johns Hopkins University, 3505 N. Charles St., Baltimore, MD 21218.

RON BRANDT

Overview

Is Cooperation Un-American?

We Americans like to think of ourselves as rugged individualists, but few of us resemble our self-sufficient ancestors. Instead, we work in complex organizations where, to get things done, we must collaborate with others.

Unfortunately, because schools still retain organizational patterns and practices developed more than a century ago, they probably do not prepare students very well for today's team-oriented world. There are notable exceptions, of course—talented, gregarious kids who take part in athletics, musical groups, and school clubs—but the majority of ordinary "shy persons," whose school experiences are confined mostly to classrooms, miss out.

In exemplary schools across the country, that is beginning to change. Students in regular academic classes are joining forces to "sink or swim together." The reason, say advocates such as Robert Slavin (p. 7) and David and Roger Johnson (p. 14), is that group work not only develops social skills, it is also a powerful tool for learning. In last month's issue Bruce Joyce and his co-authors (1987) reported, as part of their recent meta-analysis on a variety of teaching strategies, that research on cooperative learning is "overwhelmingly positive" (p. 17).

That should not be surprising. People understand and remember things much better if they talk about them with others; the cognitive processing helps transfer information from short-term to long-term memory.

Another plus for cooperative learning is its potential for influencing peer pressure, a force that severely limits achievement in many schools. When students compete individually, mainstream students make up for their lack of success by scorning the "nerd" who works hard and thereby makes them look bad. In cooperative classrooms, students encourage their teammates to do well, because they also benefit.

Cooperation pays off not only for young people but also for adults. In this issue we report numerous examples of professional collegiality, ranging from voluntary teacher support groups (p. 36) to peer coaching (p. 40) to inservice programs for principals (p. 70).

But are these trends contrary to basic American values? Is it fair that students should benefit from each other's efforts and share responsibility for what others do or don't do? Ask doctors, who more and more engage in group practice, consulting with one another on difficult cases. Ask ministers, who depend on volunteer committees for much of the work of their churches. Ask military officers, who train young men and women in intricate maneuvers. Ask members of work teams in automated factories. Ask executives involved in team management.

If these typical citizens recognize the role of cooperation in their own lives, they will support the use of cooperative learning in schools. Americans have always prized individuality, and we will continue to, but in the modern world we also need teamwork.□

Reference

Joyce, Bruce, Beverly Showers, and Carol Rolheiser-Bennett. "Staff Development and Student Learning: A Synthesis of Research on Models of Teaching." *Educational Leadership* 45 (October 1987): 11–23.

Educational Leadership 45 (Nov. 1987): 14-19

On Cooperation in Schools: A Conversation with David and Roger Johnson

David and Roger Johnson, articulate proponents of cooperative learning and authors of ASCD's popular *Circles of Learning,* believe that developing cooperative structures at all levels will contribute to overall effectiveness in a district.

Roger Johnson

David Johnson

For several years the two of you have promoted cooperative learning among students. Now there seems to be a trend toward more cooperation at the professional level.

David: Yes, we're seeing not only more cooperative learning in classrooms, but collegial support groups of teachers and administrators at the building, and sometimes the district, level. Cooperation needs to start at the classroom level because that determines the organizational climate and atmosphere in the district. If teachers spend five to seven hours a day advocating a competitive, individualistic approach—telling students, "Do your own work. Don't talk to your neighbor, don't share, don't help, don't care about each other; just try to be better," those are the values the teachers are going to have in their relationships with colleagues and their administrators.

On the other hand, if teachers spend five to seven hours a day saying, "Help each other. Share, work together, discuss the material, explain," and make it clear that "you're responsible not only for your own learning but for the learning of your peers"—if they promote cooperation among students—they will look at their colleagues as potential cooperators.

How widespread is cooperative learning at the classroom level?

Roger: In certain areas it's getting very popular: on the East and West

Ronald S. Brandt

coasts—in California especially—and in parts of the Midwest. It's taking hold primarily in suburban upper-middle-class advanced districts, where parents want their children to do well in college.

So parents support it?

Roger: Yes, especially upper-middle-class parents. For example, when I talked to a PTA in a suburban district in the New York area a couple of years ago, a father stood up and said, "I know exactly what you're talking about: it's management training, the same thing we're getting at the First Bank. You mean my kid learns math and gets management training at the same time?" The parents in that district see cooperative learning as a bonus because their children are getting the training in leadership, group decision making, and conflict management they'll need to be successful in later life.

But is there evidence that cooperative learning in fact pays off?

David: Yes. If there's any one educational technique that has firm empirical support, it's cooperative learning. The research in this area is the oldest research tradition in American social psychology. The first study was done in 1897; we've had 90 years of research, hundreds of studies. There is probably more evidence validating the use of cooperative learning than there is for any other aspect of education—more than for lecturing, age grouping, starting reading at age six, departmentalization, or the 50-minute period. And the research applies as much to teachers as it does to students.

There's research on that as well?

David: Yes, in fact most of the work done up to 1970 was on adult cooperation; it was only in the '70s that much research was done in elementary and secondary schools. But from both types of studies it's clear that cooperation increases productivity. At the adult level, cooperation among adult teachers increases teaching effectiveness, while at the classroom level, cooperation increases each individual student's achievement.

"What you want for every child—but especially for those with a lot of ability—is a cheering section urging that student to work to maximal capacity."

There are two possible bases for making those kinds of statements. One is to infer that findings of research done in other settings apply to schools. Madeline Hunter has done that very well with the psychological research on learning. Another way is to apply the research in the new situation and test whether it actually produces the intended effects. Which approach are you citing?

David: Both. We believe the first requirement for a good school practice is a solid theory. The theory for cooperation was developed by Morton Deutsch in the late 1940s. Second, you need research to validate the theory, to determine the conditions under which it's valid, and so on. Third, you have to operationalize it so it can be used in practice. That's basically an engineering issue; if the theory is valid, it's a matter of varying and modifying the system until it works in the classroom and school the way the theory says it should.

There's been a lot of theoretical research establishing that cooperative learning *should* work. I suppose that's the Madeline Hunter approach, and actually it's our approach too. We say, "Here's a conceptual system; now look at the characteristics of your situation, of your group of students, and design a system that works in your classroom with your students." But other researchers—such as Spencer Kagan at Riverside, California; Schlomo Sharan in Israel; David Devries and Robert Slavin at Johns Hopkins—have developed detailed curriculum approaches and have tested and validated them.

One reason I would expect cooperative learning to be effective is its use of positive peer pressure. In conventional school organization, peer pressure seems to restrict students' learning.

Roger: Yes. What you want for every child—but especially for those with a lot of ability—is a cheering section urging that student to work to maximal capacity. You can have high, medium, and low kids in the same group with the low kid cheering the high one on and saying, "Rene, we need you to top out the test and get an absolutely perfect score, so don't watch TV tonight, study!" And you can get the high kid saying to the low kid, "Look, if you get six right we're okay. Last week you only had three, but you've really got to get up to six. I'm behind you all the way." The cooperative system encourages everybody to work to top capacity.

David: And the same is true at the building level with teachers. What you want is teachers cheering each other on so that if a teacher has a particular strength or plans a new unit or comes in with new materials, the other teachers say, "That's terrific."

So there's evidence that cooperative learning is effective—but as we all know, that doesn't necessarily mean that schools will use it. For teachers to use it, research evidence probably is not enough. It has to pay off for them with kids in a way they consider beneficial.

12

Roger: When teachers use cooperative learning they get a whole variety of outcomes. Achievement goes up—for high, medium, and low students—but they also get higher-level processing, deeper-level understanding, critical thinking, and long-term retention. When students get engaged in discussing material and explaining it to each other, their brains respond differently than if they were only reading and listening.

But another plus is a sense of interdependence. Students learn to care about and get committed to each other's success as well as their own. In a competitive classroom, students really have a stake in other students' failure. The worse other students do, the easier it is to get an A. In an individualistic classroom, students have no stake in other students whatsoever. Each student works independently on his or her own against set criteria. What happens to others is irrelevant. Within a cooperative group students have a vested interest in making sure that other people do well. They start to celebrate when other people learn. Anything they can do to help their groupmates learn the material better, retain it longer, get a better grade on the test, benefits them too. That produces committed relationships in which students really care about each other and provide assistance and help when needed. It promotes more positive peer relationships, better social skills, more social support, and, partly for that reason, higher self-esteem. Students like the class better, they like school better, they're more interested in the subject.

You mentioned social support. Why is that so important?

Roger: In today's schools we're expecting more and more of students and staff. When there's an increase in pressure, there should be an increase in social support at the same time. When students are expected to learn more complex material faster and more thoroughly, they need more social support. When teachers are told to work harder or do a better job, they should have lots of social support.

> "and . . . what you want is teachers cheering each other on so that if a teacher has a particular strength or plans a new unit or comes in with new materials, the other teachers say, 'That's terrific.'"

David: As a psychotherapist I may talk with someone who says, "One of my parents just died, I have a child in the hospital in critical condition, my spouse just left with all the money, and I'm destitute"; but if that person has a set of caring, committed friends that he or she can confide in and talk to, the person may be coping better than an isolated, alienated person who has only—say, lost his job. The point is that the ability to cope is determined not by the amount of stress a person is under, but by the balance between the stress and the support. And much of that support has to come from peers. In the classroom that means other students. In the school it means there must be strong, caring, supportive relationships among teachers. There's no alternative.

In ASCD our emphasis has long been on supervision. We assume that the principal or some other official person is responsible—

David: Yes, but the supervisor's job is not to *be* the support system but to *manage* the support system. A supervisor can't provide all the support and caring that a teacher needs on a day-to-day, minute-by-minute basis. A principal can't be in every teacher's classroom two or three times a day providing help. A colleague can.

I'm sure it's true that a supervisor can't do it all, but now there are moves to create middle-level roles for teachers: mentor teachers and so on. Even leaders of teacher organizations are in favor of having "lead teachers."

David: From the research in social psychology I have to say that such differentiation is a mistake. It's based on a parental model that, to be meaningful, social support and assistance have to come from your superior. Good, constructive, helpful, committed support can come from peers and subordinates as well as from superiors. And in many ways it's better coming from peers than from anyone else.

That may be true, but you also know how important it is in this society to make teaching a more prestigious and rewarding profession, and these programs offer promise of doing that.

David: I can only advise that if a district decides to have master teachers, one of the main criteria for their selection should be the ability to establish collegial relationships with other teachers. I believe that creating hierarchies among teachers can create divisiveness. What most principals want is a cooperative staff that pulls together.

Let's get back to the classroom level. What does it take to make cooperative learning work?

Roger: Five basic elements. The first is what we call "positive interdependence." The students really have to believe they're in it together, sink or swim. They have to care about each other's learning.

Second is a lot of verbal, face-to-face interaction. Students have to explain, argue, elaborate, and tie in the material they learn today with what they had last week.

The third element is individual accountability. It must be clear that every member of the group has to learn, that there's no hitchhiking. No one can sit on the outside and let others do the work; everyone has to be in there pulling his or her own weight.

The fourth element is social skills. Students need to be taught appropriate leadership, communication, trust building, and conflict resolution skills so they can operate effectively. To say it slightly differently, if students have not developed social skills, a lot of the benefits of cooperative learning are lost.

The fifth element is what we call "group processing." Periodically the groups have to assess how well they are working together and how they could do even better.

Getting all that to happen surely isn't easy. We have a history of innovations of one sort or another in schools that can be sustained for a few years by asking teachers to work extra hard. Eventually people wear out and the innovation disappears. Is cooperative learning like that?

Roger: I don't think so. Let me explain why. A workshop or course teaches teachers *about* cooperative learning, but it doesn't teach them *how* to do it. The only way teachers can learn the "how" is in their own classrooms, doing it. That means there must be a support system to provide advice and assistance when the teacher needs it. If a teacher goes to a workshop, goes back to the classroom and has no support, then the first time the approach doesn't work, the teacher will drop it and go back to what he or she was doing before. When that happens, the money and effort invested in the workshop have been wasted.

David: The best support system, obviously, is colleagues. So if you train a team of three, four, or five teachers from the same building, they get established as a collegial support group to sustain one another's efforts; and there's a very good chance that cooperative learning will be there forever.

"**Good, constructive, helpful, committed support can come from peers and subordinates as well as from superiors. And in many ways it's better coming from peers than from anyone else.**"

I can see that an administrator might encourage teachers to attend cooperative learning training, but many administrators would probably be reluctant to do more than that. We generally think of classroom organization as a matter for teachers to decide for themselves without outside interference.

David: Insisting that teachers use cooperative learning certainly wouldn't work and would be inconsistent with the ultimate purpose. Roger and I like a "grassroots up" system; we first give a general awareness presentation on cooperative learning to the whole staff—building or district. Then we begin working with some of the better teachers who get interested and volunteer, training them as a team and building a collegial support group within the building. After that we train new groups in concentric circles: teachers are sent by their colleagues so they can get started doing cooperative learning and join one of the collegial groups.

The principal may want every teacher in the building to be involved in a support group, but we know that to be successful such groups must have a clear purpose, and they must be help-

ful to teachers in a day-to-day, nitty-gritty way. So a focus on learning to use cooperative learning is a reason for having support groups that teachers can buy into.

If eventually every teacher in the building is a member of such a group, the principal can then run the building the same way a teacher runs a cooperative classroom. His or her responsibility is to make sure that the support groups have those same five elements. Again they are—first, positive interdependence: the teachers care about each other's productivity and well-being. Second, a lot of face-to-face interaction among the teachers: they talk to each other about professional practice. Third, individual accountability: no freeloading or hitchhiking. Fourth, the teachers have the social skills, the leadership, the group decision making, the conflict management skills they need in order to operate together. And fifth, that periodically the teams review how well they are doing.

You mentioned the need for teachers to have group process skills. That can't be taken for granted.

Roger: No. A critical moment of truth in a collegial support group is when two teachers disagree strongly with each other and argue. Within an organizational climate that's primarily competitive or individualistic, such conflicts turn very destructive: teachers feel angry toward each other, they avoid each other, there's a lot of acrimony and divisiveness among the staff.

When teachers in a cooperative group disagree, they must have the skills to manage the conflict constructively. So the issue becomes: How do you teach teachers the basic collaborative skills they need to be good colleagues? There are two approaches, one direct and the other indirect. We prefer the indirect: by teaching their students how to provide leadership for the learning groups—how to disagree in constructive and helpful ways, how to build and maintain trust within the learning group, how to make group decisions—the teachers learn those social skills themselves and see when and how they should be used with their colleagues.

Our experience has been that if you just walk in on a faculty and say, "We're going to teach you how to resolve conflicts better," many teachers don't see the need for it. They think, "I seldom talk to my colleagues. Why do I need to know how to resolve conflicts?" The same is true at the principal-principal level, by the way. When principals begin running collegial support groups within their buildings, ensuring that teachers have the collaborative skills they need to be good colleagues, they begin to look at other principals differently. And in training teachers how to collaborate effectively the principals develop skills themselves to use with their colleagues. This is important because it's not unusual in many school districts for superintendents to place principals in direct competition with each other. A superintendent may say, "There are five elementary schools, but we have only three special ed. teachers. Every-

body write a proposal; the three best proposals will get the special ed. teachers." In that situation it is in each principal's best interest that other principals do poorly.

If the superintendent wants to build more collegiality among principals, more peer support, he or she does it with the five basic elements: deliberately structure sink-or-swim-together, get a lot of face-to-face interaction among principals in small decision-making groups, have clear individual accountability, make sure the social skills are there, and make sure that the groups think constructively about how well they are operating and how they might do better in the future.

So those five elements apply at every level?

David: Yes. And where a district builds that structure—cooperative learning in classrooms, collegial teacher support groups in buildings, colle-

gial administrative relationships within the district—the whole school district functions better: morale goes way up, absenteeism and divisiveness go down. People are more committed, have more energy for their jobs, there are all sorts of positive outcomes. And it puts student cooperative learning in the appropriate context.□

Reference

Deutsch, M. "Cooperation and Trust: Some Theoretical Notes." In *Nebraska Symposium on Motivation*, edited by M. R. Jones. Lincoln: University of Nebraska Press, 1962, 275–319.

David W. Johnson is Professor of Educational Psychology, and **Roger T. Johnson** is Professor of Curriculum and Instruction; both are Co-Directors of the Cooperative Learning Center, University of Minnesota, 202 Pattee Hall, 150 Pillsbury Dr., S.E., Minneapolis, MN 55455. **Ron Brandt** is ASCD's Executive Editor.

Models

The articles in this section portray selected models of cooperative learning. Robert Slavin and his colleagues write about TAI and CIRC, programs developed at The Johns Hopkins University that teach mathematics and language arts using cooperative methods. Spencer Kagan explains his concept of cooperative structures. Neil Davidson and Pat Wilson O'Leary show that cooperative learning is compatible with Madeline Hunter's Mastery Teaching. Yael and Shlomo Sharan describe their Group Investigation model.

Educational Leadership 47 (Dec. 1989-Jan. 1990) 22-28

ROBERT E. SLAVIN, NANCY A. MADDEN, AND ROBERT J. STEVENS

Cooperative Learning Models for the 3 R's

Cooperative learning can be used successfully
as the primary instructional method
in reading, writing, and mathematics.

In 1980 at Johns Hopkins University we began to develop and evaluate cooperative learning programs designed specifically for particular subjects and grade levels. We set out with several critical objectives. First, we wanted to use what we had learned about cooperative learning to try to solve fundamental problems of instruction, such as accommodating individual differences in reading and math. In particular, we wanted to design programs that could be used in heterogeneous classes, to reduce the need for special education or tracking. Second, we wanted to design cooperative learning programs that could be used all year, not just from time to time as part of a teacher's bag of tricks. Third, we wanted to incorporate knowledge about curriculum- and domain-specific learning into our cooperative approaches, such as the teaching of story grammar and summarizing in reading, or the writing process in writing.

The programs we developed, Team Assisted Individualization (TAI) in mathematics and Cooperative Integrated Reading and Composition (CIRC), are among the best researched and most effective of all cooperative learning methods. This article describes TAI and CIRC and the research on them.

Team Assisted Individualization

The first comprehensive cooperative learning model we developed and researched was Team Assisted Individualization—Mathematics,[1] a program that combines cooperative learning with individualized instruction to meet the needs of diverse classrooms (Slavin 1985b).

We developed TAI for several reasons. First, we hoped TAI would provide a means of combining the motivational power and peer assistance of cooperative learning with an individualized instructional program—one

> **TAI was developed to apply cooperative learning techniques to solve many of the problems of individualized instruction.**

that would provide all students with materials appropriate to their levels of skill and allow them to proceed through these materials at their own rates. Second, TAI was developed to apply cooperative learning techniques to solve many of the problems of individualized instruction.

In the 1960s, individualized instruction and related methods had been expected to revolutionize instruction, especially in mathematics. However, reviews of the research on these instruction methods in mathematics have consistently concluded that these methods are no more effective than traditional instruction (see, for example, Miller 1976, Horak 1981). Several problems inherent in programmed instruction have been cited as contributing to these disappointing findings: too much time spent on management rather than teaching, too little incentive for students to progress rapidly through the programmed materials, and excessive reliance on written instruction rather than instruction from a teacher.

We felt that by combining programmed instruction with cooperative learning and turning most of the management functions (for example, scoring answers, locating and filing materials, keeping records, assigning new work) over to the students themselves, these problems could be solved. If students could handle most of the checking and management, the teacher would be free to teach individuals and small homogeneous teaching groups. Students working in learning teams toward a cooperative goal could help one another study, provide instant feedback to one another, and encourage one another to proceed rapidly and accurately through the materials.

Finally, TAI was developed as a means of producing the well-documented social effects characteristic of cooperative learning (Slavin in press) while meeting diverse needs. Our principal concern here was mainstreaming. We felt that mainstreaming of academically handicapped students in mathematics was limited by the belief of regular class teachers that they were unprepared to accommodate the instructional needs of these students (see Gickling and Theobald 1975). Further, studies of attitudes toward academically handicapped students had consistently found that these students are not well accepted by their nonhandicapped classmates (see Gottlieb and Leyser 1981).

Since cooperative learning methods have had positive effects on social relations of all kinds, specifically on relationships between handicapped and nonhandicapped students (Madden and Slavin 1983), we felt that the best possible mathematics program for the mainstreamed classroom would be one that combined cooperative learning with individualized instruction (see Madden and Slavin 1983). Recently, as many districts have moved away from tracking toward heterogeneous classes, the need for effective programs that can accommodate mathematics instruction to diverse needs has increased.

Principal Features of TAI. TAI is designed primarily for grades 3–6, but it has been used at higher grade levels (up to the community college level) for groups of students not ready for a full algebra course. It is almost always used without aides, volunteers, or other assistance. The principal elements of TAI are as follows (adapted from Slavin et al. 1986):

If students handle most of the checking and management, the teacher is free to teach individuals and small homogeneous groups.

Teams. Students are assigned to four- to five-member teams. Each team has a mix of high, average, and low achievers, boys and girls, and students of any ethnic groups in the class. Every eight weeks, students are reassigned to new teams.

Placement test. At the beginning of the program, students are pretested on mathematics operations. They are placed at the appropriate point in the individualized program based on their performance on the placement test.

Curriculum materials. Following instruction from the teacher (see "Teaching groups," below), students work in their teams on self-instructional curriculum materials covering addition, subtraction, multiplication, division, numeration, decimals, fractions, word problems, statistics, and algebra. The units are in the form of books. Each unit has the following parts:

● a guide page that reviews the teacher's lesson, explaining the skill to be mastered and giving a step-by-step method for solving the problems;

● several skill practice pages, each consisting of 16 problems. Each skill practice page introduces a subskill that leads to a final mastery of the entire skill;

● formative tests A and B (two parallel 10-item sets);

● a unit test of 15 items;

● answer sheets for the skill practice pages and formative tests (located at the back of student books) and answers for unit tests (located in a separate "monitor book").

Word problems are emphasized throughout the materials.

Teaching groups. Every day, the teacher teaches lessons to small groups of students (drawn from the heterogeneous teams) who are at the same point in the curriculum. Teachers use specific concept lessons provided as part of the program. The purpose of these sessions is to introduce major concepts to the students. Teachers make extensive use of manipulatives, diagrams, and demonstrations. The lessons are designed to help students understand the connection between the mathematics they are doing and familiar real-life problems.

While the teacher works with a teaching group, the other students continue to work in their teams on their self-instructional units. This direct instruction to teaching groups is possible because students take responsibility for almost all checking, handling of materials, and routing.

Team study method. Following the placement test, the students are given a starting place in the sequence of mathematics units. They work on their units in their teams, using the following steps:

1. Students locate their units within their books and read the guide page, asking teammates or the teacher for help if necessary. Then the students begin with the first skill practice page in their unit.

2. Each student works the first four problems on his or her own skill practice page and then has a teammate check the answers against an answer sheet printed upside-down at the back of each student book. If all four are correct, the student may go on to the next skill practice page. If any are incorrect, the student must try the next four problems, and so on, until he or she gets one block of four problems correct. If they run into difficulties at this stage, students are encouraged to ask for help within their teams before asking the teacher for help.

3. When a student gets four in a row correct on the last skill practice page, he or she takes Formative Test A, a 10-item quiz that resembles the last skill practice page. Students work alone on the test until they are finished. A teammate scores the formative test. If the student gets 8 or more of the 10 problems correct, the teammate signs the student's paper to indicate that the student is certified by the team to take the unit test. If the student does not get 8 correct (this is rare), the teacher is called in to respond to any problems the student is having. The teacher would diagnose the student's problem and briefly reteach the skill, possibly asking the student to work again on certain skill practice items. The student then takes Formative Test B, a second 10-item test comparable in content and difficulty to Formative Test A.

4. When a student passes Formative Test A or B, he or she takes the test paper to a student monitor from a different team to get the appropriate unit test. The student then completes the unit test, and the monitor scores it. Two different students serve as monitors each day. If the student gets at least 12 items correct (out of 15), the monitor posts the score on the student's Team Summary sheet. Otherwise, the test is examined by the teacher, who meets with the student to diagnose and remediate the student's problems. Again, because students have already shown mastery on the skill practice pages and formative tests, they rarely fail a unit test.

Team scores and team recognition. At the end of each week, the teacher computes a team score. This score is based on the average number of units covered by each team member and the accuracy of the unit tests. Criteria are established for team performance. A high criterion is set for a team to be a "superteam," a moderate criterion is set for a team to be a "greatteam," and a minimum criterion is set for a team to be a "goodteam." The teams meeting the "superteam" and "greatteam" criteria receive attractive certificates.

Facts tests. Twice each week, the students are given three-minute facts tests (usually multiplication or division facts). The students are given fact sheets to study at home to prepare for these tests.

Whole-class units. Every three weeks, the teacher stops the individualized program and spends a week teaching lessons to the entire class covering such skills as geometry, measurement, sets, and problem-solving strategies.

Research on TAI. Seven field experiments have evaluated the effects of TAI on student achievement, attitudes, and behavior (see Slavin 1985a). Academic achievement outcomes were assessed in six of the seven studies. In five of these, TAI students significantly[2] exceeded control students on standardized (CTBS or CAT) Math Computations scales. Similar effects were found for Concepts and Applications in only one of the four studies in which this variable was assessed; but in all four studies, means for Concepts and Applications favored the TAI group. In the five studies in which the treatment effects for Computations were statistically significant, they were also quite large; on average, TAI classes gained twice as many grade equivalents as did control students. Effects of TAI were equally positive for

In five of six studies, TAI students significantly exceeded control students on standardized Math Computation scales.

high, average, and low achievers, and for academically handicapped as well as nonhandicapped students. Positive effects of TAI have also been found on such outcomes as self-concept in math, liking for math class, classroom behavior, race relations, and acceptance of mainstreamed academically handicapped students (Slavin 1985a).

Cooperative Integrated Reading and Composition

Following the success of the TAI mathematics program, we turned to reading and writing/language arts, the two subjects that, with mathematics, constitute the core of the elementary school program. Because these subjects are very different from mathematics, our approach to applying cooperative learning to them was very different. For one thing, reading, writing, and language arts include subskills that each demand different approaches. For example, optimal procedures for teaching reading comprehension or vocabulary would certainly be different from those for teaching decoding, spelling, writing, or language mechanics.

The program we ultimately developed and researched is called Cooperative Integrated Reading and Composition, or CIRC (Madden et al. 1986a). Our development plan focused on using cooperative learning as a vehicle to introduce practices identified in recent research on reading and writing into routine classroom practice, and to embed cooperative learning within the fabric of the elementary reading and writing program (see Stevens et al. 1987).

Principal Features of CIRC. The CIRC program includes three principal elements: basal-related activities, direct instruction in reading comprehension, and integrated language arts/writing. In all of these activities, students work in heterogeneous learning teams.

Reading groups. Students are assigned to two or three reading groups (8–15 students per group) according to their reading level, as determined by their teachers.

Teams. Students are assigned to pairs (or triads) within their reading

The CIRC program includes three principal elements: basal-related activities, direct instruction in reading comprehension, and integrated language arts/writing.

groups. The pairs are then assigned to teams composed of partnerships from two different reading groups. For example, a team might be composed of two students from the top reading group and two from the low group. Mainstreamed academically handicapped and remedial reading (for example, Chapter I) students are distributed among the teams.

Many of the activities within the teams are done in pairs, while others involve the whole team; even during pair activities, however, the other pair is available for assistance and encouragement. Most of the time, the teams work independently of the teacher, while the teacher either teaches reading groups drawn from the various teams or works with individuals.

Students' scores on all quizzes, compositions, and book reports contribute to a team score. Teams that meet an average criterion of 90 percent on all activities in a given week are designated "superteams" and receive attractive certificates; those that meet an average criterion of 80–89

percent are designated "greatteams" and receive less elaborate certificates.

Basal-related activities. Students use their regular basal readers (or whatever texts or reading materials are used in the school). Stories are introduced and discussed in teacher-led reading groups that meet for approximately 20 minutes each day. During these sessions, teachers set a purpose for reading, introduce new vocabulary, review old vocabulary, discuss the story after students have read it,

Cooperative Learning in Elementary School Science

Michael R. Hannigan

Science for Life and Living: Integrating Science, Technology, and Health is a new science program for elementary schools developed by the Biological Sciences Curriculum Study (BSCS) (Bybee and Landes 1988; in press). The program emphasizes concrete experiences; it gives students opportunities to observe phenomena, to record their observations, and to discuss them with other students. Cooperative learning is a central strategy of the program, for several reasons.

First, the Johnsons' research (1984, 1987a, 1987b) shows that cooperative learning enhances children's ability to construct knowledge. Working in groups gives children time to think and talk about what they are learning; they can carefully construct their knowledge of the world around them. In cooperative groups of two or three, each student can share experiences and thoughts with teammates; learning becomes more personal than in the traditional classroom.

Second, cooperative learning helps teachers with classroom management. Hands-on science requires that students interact with materials; and cooperative learning is structured so that students, not teachers, manage those materials. In a cooperative learning classroom, students help each other with assignments and problems, which alleviates some of the stress on the teacher to maintain order and to keep students on task.

A third benefit of cooperative learning is improved self-confidence for many students. Because many students do not feel comfortable taking the risk of being wrong in front of the entire class, they often say nothing at all. When working in small groups, however, more students risk speaking out. They then discover they have something important to contribute and that their ideas can be useful to others.

Fourth, science and technology are cooperative enterprises. Neil Armstrong was the first person to walk on the moon, but thousands of people in research, engineering, and industry labored for a decade to get him there. Cooperative learning reflects the way scientists themselves work in teams.

Of course, cooperative learning is not a magic wand to wave over students, but it can provide an effective framework for teaching about science, technology, and health. That is why it holds a prominent place in the new BSCS science curriculum.

References

Bybee, R., and N. Landes. (May 1988). "Science for Life and Living: Integrating Science, Technology, and Health." *Science and Children* 25, 8: 36–37.

Bybee, R., and N. Landes. (In press). "Elementary School Science Programs: The New Generation." *School Science and Mathematics.*

Johnson, D., and R. Johnson. (1984). *Cooperation in the Classroom.* Edina, Minn.: Interaction Book Company.

Johnson, D., and R. Johnson. (1987a). *Learning Together and Alone: Cooperative, Competitive, and Individualistic Learning.* 2nd ed. Englewood Cliffs, N.J.: Prentice Hall.

Johnson, D., R. Johnson, and E. Holubec. (1987b). *Circles of Learning: Cooperation in the Classroom.* Edina, Minn.: Interaction Book Company.

Michael R. Hannigan is Staff Associate, BSCS, 830 N. Tejon St., Ste. 405, Colorado Springs, CO 80903.

and so on. Presentation methods for each segment of the lesson are structured. For example, teachers are taught to use a vocabulary presentation procedure that requires a demonstration of understanding of word meaning by each individual, a review of methods of word attack, repetitive oral reading of vocabulary to achieve automaticity, and use of the meanings of the vocabulary words to help introduce the content of the story. Story discussions are structured to emphasize such skills as making and supporting predictions about the story and understanding major structural components of the story (for example, problem and solution in a narrative).

After the stories are introduced, the students are given a series of activities to do in their teams when they are not working with the teacher in a reading group. The sequence of activities is as follows:

1. *Partner reading*. First, students read the story silently, then take turns reading the story aloud with their partners, alternating readers after each paragraph. As his or her partner reads, the listener follows along and corrects any errors the reader makes.

2. *Story structure and story-related writing*. Students are given questions related to each narrative that emphasize story grammar. Halfway through the story, they are instructed to stop reading and to identify the characters, the setting, and the problem in the story, and to predict how the problem will be resolved. At the end of the story, students respond to the story as a whole and write a few paragraphs on a topic related to the story (for example, they might be asked to write a different ending to the story).

3. *Words out loud*. Students are given a list of new or difficult words used in the story, which they must be able to read correctly in any order without hesitating or stumbling. These words are presented by the teacher in the reading group, and then students practice their lists with their partners or other teammates until they can read them smoothly.

4. *Word meaning*. Students are given a list of story words that are new

in their speaking vocabularies. They look them up in a dictionary, paraphrase the definitions, and write a sentence for each that shows the meaning of the word (i.e., "An *octopus* grabbed the swimmer with its eight long legs," not "I have an *octopus*").

5. *Story retell*. After reading the story and discussing it in their reading groups, students summarize the main points of the story to their partners. The partners have a list of essential story elements, which they use to check the completeness of the story summaries.

6. *Spelling*. Students pretest one another on a list of spelling words each week, and then work over the course of the week to help one another master the list. Students use a "disappearing list" strategy in which they make new lists of missed words after each assessment until the list disappears and they can go back to the full list, repeating the process as many times as necessary.

Partner checking. After students complete the activities listed above,

> **One key concern in the design of the CIRC program was to fully integrate the activities of special education and remedial reading teachers with those of regular classroom teachers.**

their partners initial a student assignment form indicating that they have completed or achieved criterion on that task. Students are given daily expectations as to the number of activities to be completed, but they can go at their own rate and complete the activities earlier if they wish, creating additional time for independent reading (see below).

Tests. At the end of three class periods, students are given a comprehension test on the story, are asked to write meaningful sentences for each vocabulary word, and are asked to read the word list aloud to the teacher. Students are not permitted to help one another on these tests. The test scores and evaluations of the story-related writing are major components of students' weekly team scores.

Direct instruction in reading comprehension. One day each week, students receive direct instruction from the teacher in reading comprehension skills such as identifying main ideas, drawing conclusions, and comparing and contrasting ideas. A special curriculum was designed for this purpose. After each lesson, students work on reading comprehension worksheets or games as a whole team, first gaining consensus on one set of worksheet items, then practicing independently, assessing one another's work, and discussing any remaining problems on a second set of items.

Independent reading. Students are asked to read a trade book of their choice every evening for at least 20 minutes. Parents initial forms indicating that students have read for the required time, and students contribute points to their teams if they submit a completed form each week. Students complete at least one book report every two weeks, for which they also receive team points. Independent reading and book reports replace all other homework in reading and language arts. If students complete their basal-related activities or other activities early, they may also read their independent reading books in class.

Integrated language arts and writing. During language arts periods, teachers use a specific language arts/

writing curriculum developed for the project. Students work on language arts in the same teams as in reading. During three one-hour sessions each week, students participate in a writers' workshop (Graves 1983), writing at their own pace on topics of their choice. Teachers present 10-minute mini-lessons at the beginning of each period on the writing process, style, or mechanics; for example, brainstorming for topics, conducting a peer revision conference, eliminating run-on sentences, or using quotations. Students spend the main part of the period planning, drafting, revising, editing, or publishing their writing.

Informal and formal peer and teacher conferences are held during this time. Ten minutes at the end of the hour are reserved for sharing and "celebration" of student writing. Teacher-directed lessons on specific aspects of writing, such as organizing a narrative or a descriptive paragraph, using specific sensory words in a description, and ensuring noun-verb agreement, are conducted during two periods each week, and students practice and master these skills in their teams.

Involvement of special education resource teachers and reading teachers. One key concern in the design of the CIRC program was to fully integrate the activities of special education resource teachers and remedial reading teachers (such as Chapter I teachers) with those of regular classroom teachers. This integration was done differently in the two evaluations of the full CIRC program. In the 12-week pilot study (Madden et al. 1986b), resource and remedial reading teachers removed students from their reading classes for part or all of the reading period and implemented the CIRC program in separate areas. However, in a 24-week full-scale evaluation (Stevens et al. 1987, Madden et. al. 1986b), the schools scheduled resource and remedial reading pullouts at times other than reading or language arts/writing periods. Special and remedial reading teachers attended the CIRC training sessions but did not use CIRC methods or materials in their pullout programs, except that they occasion-

> **Cooperative learning is not only an innovation in itself, but also a catalyst for other needed changes in curriculum and instruction.**

ally helped students with problems they were encountering in the CIRC program used in the regular class.

Research on CIRC. As of this writing, two studies have evaluated the impact of the full CIRC program. The first study (Madden et al. 1986b, Stevens et al. 1987) evaluated the full CIRC program over a 12-week period. Overall, the effects of the CIRC program on student achievement were quite positive. CIRC classes gained 30 to 36 percent of a grade equivalent more than control students in reading comprehension and reading vocabulary, 52 percent of a grade equivalent more in language expression, 25 percent of a grade equivalent more in language mechanics, and 72 percent of a grade equivalent more in spelling. On writing samples, CIRC students outperformed control students on ratings of organization, ideas, and mechanics. The effects of CIRC were equal for students at all levels of prior achievement: high, average, and low.

The second study (Stevens et al. 1987) was designed to evaluate the CIRC program in 3rd and 4th grade classes over a full school year, incorporating changes suggested by the pilot study. For the total samples involved, the results of Study 2 were even more positive than those of Study

1. On the reading comprehension, language expression, and language mechanics scales of the California Achievement Test, CIRC students gained significantly more than control students, averaging gains of almost two-thirds of a grade equivalent more than control students. Differences of 20 percent of a grade equivalent on reading vocabulary were not significant, however. On writing samples, CIRC students again outperformed control students on organization, ideas, and mechanics ratings.

Study 2 added informal reading inventories as measures of students' oral reading skills. CIRC students scored significantly higher than control students on word recognition, word analysis, fluency, error rate, and grade placement measures of the Durrell Informal Reading Inventory, with effect sizes ranging from 44 percent to 64 percent of a standard deviation. As in Study 1, the CIRC program produced equal gains for students initially high, average, and low in reading skills, although mainstreamed academically handicapped students made particularly impressive gains (Slavin et al. 1988).

A Primary Instructional Method

Research on TAI and CIRC has clearly supported the idea that complex, comprehensive approaches that combine cooperative learning with other instructional elements can be effective in increasing the achievement of all students in heterogeneous classes. Studies demonstrate that cooperative learning programs can be used as the primary instructional method in reading, writing, and mathematics—not just is an additional strategy to add to teachers' repertoires.

One important possibility opened up by the development of TAI and CIRC is the use of cooperative learning as the unifying element of *school* reform. Cooperative learning methods are critical elements of the cooperative school (Slavin 1987), a school-level change model that incorporates widespread use of cooperative learning, peer coaching, comprehensive mainstreaming, and teacher involvement in decision making.

Comprehensive cooperative learning models can also serve as a vehicle for introducing developments from the fields of curriculum and educational psychology into routine classroom use. Cooperative learning provides a structure for incorporating identification of story elements, prediction, summarization, direct instruction in reading comprehension, and integration of reading and writing within the reading period. It provides a structure that can enhance the effectiveness and practicality of writing process methods or of adapting instruction to individual needs in mathematics. Thus cooperative learning is not only an innovation in itself, but also a catalyst for other needed changes in curriculum and instruction.

If educational methods are to effect major changes in student achievement, they must address many elements of classroom organization and instruction at the same time. TAI and CIRC are two examples of what the future may hold in applying the best knowledge we have to improving instruction methodology.□

[1]TAI is currently published under the title "Team Accelerated Instruction" by Charlesbridge Publishing, 85 Main St., Watertown, MA 02171.

[2]We use *significant* in the sense of *statistically significant* throughout this paper.

References

Gickling, E., and J. Theobold. (1975). "Mainstreaming: Affect or Effect." *Journal of Special Education* 9: 317–328.

Gottlieb, J., and Y. Leyser. (1981). "Friendship Between Mentally Retarded and Nonretarded Children." In *The Development of Children's Friendships*, edited by S. Asher and J. Gottman. Cambridge: Cambridge University Press.

Graves, D. (1983). *Writing: Teachers and Children at Work*. Exeter, N.H.: Heinemann.

Horak, V.M. (1981). "A Meta-Analysis of Research Findings on Individualized Instruction in Mathematics." *Journal of Educational Research* 74: 249–253.

Madden, N.A., and R.E. Slavin. (1983). "Mainstreaming Students with Mild Academic Handicaps: Academic and Social Outcomes." *Review of Educational Research* 53: 519–569.

Madden, N.A., R.E. Slavin, and R.J. Stevens. (1986a). *Cooperative Integrated Reading and Composition: Teacher's Manual*. Baltimore, Md.: Center for Research on Elementary and Middle Schools, Johns Hopkins University.

Madden, N.A., R.J. Stevens, and R.E. Slavin. (1986b). *Reading Instruction in the Mainstream: A Cooperative Learning Approach*. (Technical Report No. 5). Baltimore, Md.: Center for Research on Elementary and Middle Schools, Johns Hopkins University.

Miller, R.L. (1976). "Individualized Instruction in Mathematics: A Review of Research." *The Mathematics Teacher* 69: 345–351.

Slavin, R.E. (1985a). "Cooperative Learning: Applying Contact Theory in Desegregated Schools." *Journal of Social Issues* 41, 3: 45–62.

Slavin, R.E. (1985b). "Team Assisted Individualization: Combining Cooperative Learning and Individualized Instruction in Mathematics." In *Learning to Cooperate, Cooperating to Learn*, edited by R.E. Slavin, S. Sharan, S. Kagan, R. Hertz-Lazarowitz, C. Webb, and R. Schmuck. New York: Plenum.

Slavin, R.E. (1987). "Cooperative Learning and the Cooperative School." *Educational Leadership* 45, 3: 7–13.

Slavin, R.E. (In press). *Cooperative Learning: Theory, Research, and Practice*. Englewood Cliffs, N.J.: Prentice-Hall.

Slavin, R.E., M.B. Leavey, and N.A. Madden. (1986). *Team Accelerated Instruction—Mathematics*. Watertown, Mass.: Mastery Education Corporation.

Slavin, R.E., R.J. Stevens, and N.A. Madden. (1988). "Accommodating Student Diversity in Reading and Writing Instruction: A Cooperative Learning Approach." *Remedial and Special Education* 9, 1: 60–66.

Stevens, R.J., N.A. Madden, R.E. Slavin, and A.M. Farnish. (1987). "Cooperative Integrated Reading and Composition: Two Field Experiments." *Reading Research Quarterly* 22: 433–454.

Authors' note: Preparation of this article was supported by a grant from the Office of Educational Research and Improvement, U.S. Department of Education (No. OERI-G-86-0006). However, any opinions expressed are ours, and do not represent Department of Education policy.

Robert E. Slavin is Director, Elementary School Program, Center for Research on Elementary and Middle Schools (CREMS), The Johns Hopkins University, 3505 N. Charles St., Baltimore, MD 21218. **Nancy A. Madden** and **Robert J. Stevens** are Research Scientists at CREMS.

Educational Leadership 47 (Dec. 1989-Jan. 1990) 12-15

SPENCER KAGAN

The Structural Approach to Cooperative Learning

Teachers who are well versed in a variety of team structures can create skillful lessons that engage and enlighten their students.

The structural approach to cooperative learning is based on the creation, analysis, and systematic application of *structures*, or content-free ways of organizing social interaction in the classroom. Structures usually involve a series of steps, with proscribed behavior at each step. An important cornerstone of the approach is the distinction between "structures" and "activities."

To illustrate, teachers can design many excellent cooperative *activities*, such as making a team mural or a quilt. Such activities almost always have a specific content-bound objective and, thus, cannot be used to deliver a range of academic content. In contrast, *structures* may be used repeatedly with almost any subject matter, at a wide range of grade levels, and at various points in a lesson plan. To illustrate further, if a teacher new to cooperative learning learns five activities, he or she might well report back after a week, "Those worked well, but what should I do next week?" If, instead, the teacher learns five structures, he or she could meaningfully include cooperative learning in lessons all year to further the academic progress of students in any subject matter.

Structures differ in their usefulness in the academic, cognitive, and social domains, as well as in their usefulness in different steps of a lesson plan.

Accordingly, structures can be combined to form "multistructural" lessons in which each structure—or building block—provides a learning experience upon which subsequent structures expand, leading toward predetermined academic, cognitive, and social objectives.

Competitive vs. Cooperative Structures

In teaching, new structures continue to be developed, and old structures continue to evolve. They are based on distinct philosophies of education and lead to variations in types of learning and cooperation, student roles and communication patterns, teacher roles, and evaluation (Kagan 1985). There are several dozen distinct structures, some with adaptations, such as the half dozen major variations on Jigsaw (Kagan 1989). Among the most well-known structures are Jigsaw (Aronson et al. 1978); Student-Teams Achievement-Divisions, or STAD (Slavin 1980); Think-Pair-Share (Lyman 1987); and Group-Investigation (Sharan and Hertz-Lazarowitz 1980).

One of the most common structures teachers use is a competitive structure called Whole-Class Question-Answer (see fig. 1). In this arrangement, students vie for the teacher's attention and praise, creating negative interdependence among them. That is, when the teacher calls

Fig. 1. Whole-Class Question-Answer

1. The teacher asks a question.
2. Students who wish to respond raise their hands.
3. The teacher calls on one student.
4. The student attempts to state the correct answer.

25

Fig. 2. Numbered Heads Together

1. The teacher has students number off within groups, so that each student has a number: 1, 2, 3, or 4.
2. The teacher asks a question.
3. The teacher tells the students to "put their heads together" to make sure that everyone on the team knows the answer.
4. The teacher calls a number (1, 2, 3, or 4), and students with that number can raise their hands to respond.

on one student, the others lose their chance to answer; a failure by one student to give a correct response increases the chances for other students to receive attention and praise. Thus, students are set against each other, creating poor social relations and peer norms against achievement.

In contrast to the competitive Whole-Class Question-Answer structure stands Numbered Heads Together, a simple four-step cooperative structure (see fig. 2). Numbered Heads includes teams, positive interdependence, and individual accountability, all of which lead to cooperative interaction among students. Positive interdependence is built into the structure: if any student knows the answer, the ability of each student is increased. Individual accountability is also built in: all the helping is confined to the heads together step; students know that once a number is called, each student is on his or her own. The high achievers share answers because they know their number might not be called, and they want their team to do well. The lower achievers listen carefully because they know their number might be called. Numbered Heads Together is quite a contrast to Whole-Class Question-Answer in which only the high achievers need participate and the low achievers can (and often do) tune out.

Why So Many Structures?

As I mentioned, there are a number of different structures, as well as variations among them. This variety is necessary because the structures have different functions or domains of usefulness.

To illustrate, let's contrast two similar simple structures, Group Discussion and Three-Step Interview (see fig. 3). In Group Discussion, there is no individual accountability; in some groups some individuals may participate little or not at all. Also, there is no assurance that team members will listen to each other: in some groups all the individuals may be talking while none are listening. Further, at any one moment, if one person at a time is speaking, one-fourth of the class is involved in language production.

In contrast, in Three-Step Interview, each person must produce and receive language; there is equal participation; there is individual accountability for listening, because in the third step each student shares what he or she has heard; and for the first two steps, students interact in pairs, so one-half rather than one-fourth of the class is involved in language production at any one time.

Thus, there are profound differences between apparently similar simple cooperative structures. Group Discussion is the structure of choice for brainstorming and for reaching group consensus; Three-Step Interview is far better for developing language and listening skills as well as promoting equal participation. When the teacher is aware of the effects of different structures, he or she can design lessons with predetermined outcomes.

Turning to more complex structures, the differences are even greater. For example, Co-op Co-op (Kagan 1985a) is a 10-step structure in which students in teams produce a project that fosters the learning of students in other teams. Each student has his or her mini-topic, and each team makes a distinct contribution toward the class goal. The structure involves higher-level thinking skills, including analysis and synthesis of materials. Like all structures, however, Co-op Co-op is content-free. For example, when it is used in university classrooms, students may work 10 weeks to complete a sophisticated audiovisual presentation, whereas in a kindergarten classroom, a project might culminate in a 20-minute presentation in which each student on a team shares with the class one or two new facts he or she learned about the team animal. Whether the projects are brief or extended, the content complex or simple, the students in kindergarten or college, the 10 steps of Co-op Co-op remain the same.

Likewise, different structures are useful for distinct objectives such as teambuilding, classbuilding, communication building, mastery, and concept development. Among those structures used for mastery, there are further important distinctions. For example, Color-Coded Co-op Cards are designed for efficient memory of basic facts; Pairs Check is effective for mastery of basic skills; and Numbered

---

Fig. 3. Group Discussion vs. Three-Step Interview

Group Discussion	Three-Step Interview
Steps in the Process:	
1. The teacher asks a low-consensus question.	1. Students form two pairs within their teams of four and conduct a one-way interview in pairs.
2. Students talk it over in groups.	2. Students reverse roles: interviewers become the interviewees.
	3. Students roundrobin: each student takes a turn sharing information learned in the interview.
Characteristics:	
• Unequal participation	• Equal participation
• Not all participate	• All participate
• No individual accountability	• Individual accountability
• 1/4 of class talking at a time	• 1/2 of class talking at a time

Fig. 4. Overview of Selected Structures

Structure	Brief Description	Functions Academic & *Social*
Teambuilding		
Roundrobin	Each student in turn shares something with his or her teammates.	Expressing ideas and opinions, creation of stories. *Equal participation, getting acquainted with teammates.*
Classbuilding		
Corners	Each student moves to a corner of the room representing a teacher-determined alternative. Students discuss within corners, then listen to and paraphrase ideas from other corners.	Seeing alternative hypotheses, values, problem-solving approaches. *Knowing and respecting different points of view, meeting classmates.*
Communication Building		
Match Mine	Students attempt to match the arrangement of objects on a grid of another student using oral communication only.	Vocabulary development. *Communication skills, role-taking ability.*
Mastery		
Numbered Heads Together	The teacher asks a question, students consult to make sure everyone knows the answer, then one student is called upon to answer.	Review, checking for knowledge, comprehension. *Tutoring.*
Color-Coded Co-op Cards	Students memorize facts using a flash card game. The game is structured so that there is a maximum probability of success at each step, moving from short-term to long-term memory. Scoring is based on improvement.	Memorizing facts. *Helping, praising.*
Pairs Check	Students work in pairs within groups of four. Within pairs students alternate—one solves a problem while the other coaches. After every two problems the pair checks to see if they have the same answers as the other pair.	Practicing skills. *Helping, praising.*
Concept Development		
Three-Step Interview	Students interview each other in pairs, first one way, then the other. Students each share with the group information they learned in the interview.	Sharing personal information such as hypotheses, reactions to a poem, conclusions from a unit. *Participation, listening.*
Think-Pair-Share	Students think to themselves on a topic provided by the teacher; they pair up with another student to discuss it; they then share their thoughts with the class.	Generating and revising hypotheses, inductive reasoning, deductive reasoning, application. *Participation, involvement.*
Team Word-Webbing	Students write simultaneously on a piece of chart paper, drawing main concepts, supporting elements, and bridges representing the relation of ideas in a concept.	Analysis of concepts into components, understanding multiple relations among ideas, differentiating concepts. *Role-taking.*
Multifunctional		
Roundtable	Each student in turn writes one answer as a paper and a pencil are passed around the group. With Simultaneous Roundtable more than one pencil and paper are used at once.	Assessing prior knowledge, practicing skills, recalling information, creating cooperative art. *Teambuilding, participation of all.*
Inside-Outside Circle	Students stand in pairs in two concentric circles. The inside circle faces out; the outside circle faces in. Students use flash cards or respond to teacher questions as they rotate to each new partner.	Checking for understanding, review, processing, helping. *Tutoring, sharing, meeting classmates.*
Partners	Students work in pairs to create or master content. They consult with partners from other teams. They then share their products or understanding with the other partner pair in their team.	Mastery and presentation of new material, concept development. *Presentation and communication skills.*
Jigsaw	Each student on the team becomes an "expert" on one topic by working with members from other teams assigned the corresponding expert topic. Upon returning to their teams, each one in turn teaches the group; and students are all assessed on all aspects of the topic.	Acquisition and presentation of new material, review, informed debate. *Interdependence, status equalization.*
Co-op Co-op	Students work in groups to produce a particular group product to share with the whole class; each student makes a particular contribution to the group.	Learning and sharing complex material, often with multiple sources; evaluation; application; analysis; synthesis. *Conflict resolution, presentation skills.*

Heads Together is designed for review or checking for comprehension. A list of major structures and their functions is presented in Figure 4 (See Kagan 1989 for details about the structures in the figure as well as others).

Structures differ also in their usefulness in the academic, cognitive, and social domains, as well as in their usefulness in different steps of a lesson plan. The most important considerations when determining the domain of usefulness of a structure are:

1. What kind of cognitive and academic development does it foster?

2. What kind of social development does it foster?

3. Where in a lesson plan does it best fit?

To illustrate the distinct domains of usefulness of different structures, let's contrast Color-Coded Co-op Cards and Three-Step Interview (see fig. 5). Color-Coded Co-op Cards work well for convergent thinking (knowledge-level thinking), such as when the academic goal is memorization of many distinct facts; the Co-op Cards promote helping and are most often used for practice. Three-Step Interview does not serve any of those goals well. In contrast, Three-Step but not the Co-op Cards is most often used for divergent thinking (evaluation, analysis, synthesis, and application-level thinking), such as when the academic goal is promoting thought as part of participation in the scientific inquiry process or as part of the writing process; Three-Step Interview promotes listening skills and serves well to provide an anticipatory set for the lesson ("What would you most like to learn about . . . ?" or "What do you now know about . . . ?") or to obtain closure ("What is the most important thing you have learned about . . . ?" "If we had more time, what aspect of . . . would you like to study further?").

Because each structure has distinct domains of usefulness and can more efficiently reach some but not other cognitive, academic, and social goals, the efficient design of lessons involves using a variety of structures, each chosen for the goals it best accomplishes. Reliance on any one structure limits the cognitive and social learning of students.

The Multistructural Lesson

A cooperative learning teacher fluent

Fig. 5. Contrasting Domains of Usefulness

	Color-Coded Co-op Cards	Three-Step Interview
Academic & Cognitive	Memory of basic facts and information	Evaluation, analysis, synthesis, application
Social	Helping, praising	Listening
Steps in Lesson Plan	Practice	Anticipatory set, closure

in many structures can competently move in and out of them as needed to reach certain learning objectives. Such a multistructural lesson, for example, might begin with content-related class-building using a Line-up, followed by content-related teambuilding using Round Table. The lesson might then move into Direct Instruction, followed by Partners for information input. To check for comprehension and emphasize key concepts, the teacher would shift into Numbered Heads Together. Next might come Group Discussion or Team Word-Webbing for concept development, followed by a Cooperative Project. No one structure is most efficient for all objectives, so the most efficient way of reaching all objectives in a lesson is a multistructural lesson.[1]

Whether the objective is to create a poem, write an autobiography, or learn the relationship of experimental and theoretical probability, the teacher's ability to use a range of structures increases the range of learning experiences for students, resulting in lesson designs that are richer in the academic, cognitive, and social domains. By building on the outcomes of the previous structures, the teacher is, thus, able to orchestrate dynamic learning experiences for students.

All Together, a Structure a Month

For schools and districts conducting training for cooperative learning, there are advantages in the structural approach. Whereas it can be quite overwhelming for teachers to master "cooperative learning," it is a relatively easy task to master one structure at a time.

Many schools and districts have adopted a "structure of the month" strategy in which site-level trainers introduce the structure, provide demon-

stration lessons, and lead participants in planning how to adapt the structure to their own classroom needs. When many teachers at a site are all working to learn the same structure, there is a common base of experience, promoting formal and informal collegial coaching and support.□

[1]Two recent books illustrate how teachers can use multistructural lessons to reach a wide range of academic objectives: B. Andrini, (1989), *Cooperative Learning and Math: A Multi-Structural Approach* (San Juan Capistrano, Calif.: Resources for Teachers); and J.M. Stone, (1989), *Cooperative Learning and Language Arts: A Multi-Structural Approach* (San Juan Capistrano, Calif.: Resources for Teachers).

References

Aronson, E., N. Blaney, C. Stephan, J. Sikes, and M. Snapp. (1978). *The Jigsaw Classroom.* Beverly Hills, Calif.: Sage.

Kagan, S. (1989). *Cooperative Learning Resources for Teachers.* San Juan Capistrano, Calif.: Resources for Teachers.

Kagan, S. (1985). "Dimensions of Cooperative Classroom Structures." In *Learning to Cooperate, Cooperating to Learn,* edited by R. Slavin, S. Sharan, S. Kagan, R. Hertz Lazarowitz, C. Webb, and R. Schmuck. New York: Plenum.

Lyman, F. (1987). "Think-Pair-Share: An Expanding Teaching Technique." *MAA-CIE Cooperative News* 1, 1: 1–2.

Sharan, S., and R. Hertz-Lazarowitz. (1980). "A Group-Investigation Method of Cooperative Learning in the Classroom." In *Cooperation in Education,* edited by S. Sharan, P. Hare, C. Webb, and R. Hertz-Lazarowitz. Provo, Utah: Brigham Young University Press.

Slavin, R. (1980). *Using Student Team Learning.* Baltimore: The Center for Social Organization of Schools, The Johns Hopkins University.

Spencer Kagan is Director, Resources for Teachers, 27134 Paseo Espada, #202, San Juan Capistrano, CA 92675.

Educational Leadership 47 (Dec. 1989-Jan. 1990) 8-11

RON BRANDT

On Cooperative Learning: A Conversation with Spencer Kagan

First as a graduate student at UCLA and later as Professor of Psychology and faculty member in the School of Education at the University of California–Riverside, Spencer Kagan has been researching the development of cooperation since 1967. Recently he has devoted full time to conducting training institutes and writing about his structural approach to cooperative learning, which he describes here, including its effects on competitive behavior and racial relations and the ways it differs from other cooperative methods.

What do you mean by a "structural" approach to cooperative learning?

There are a variety of classroom structures—ways of organizing the social interaction among students. The most common structure is for students to sit passively while teachers talk at them. Then a second structure is often used to check for comprehension: Whole-Class Question-Answer. The teacher asks the question, the students who think they know the answer raise their hands, and the teacher calls on one of them. We've all seen it many times: when one student is called on, the other students who have their hands up register their disappointment with a little "Oh." It's a structure that sets the kids against each other.

So you favor the use of different structures?

Yes. That Whole-Class Question-Answer structure is used primarily to review or check for comprehension. If that were my goal, I'd use "Numbered Heads Together." I'd have the students sitting in heterogeneous teams with one high-, two middle-, and one low-achieving students on a team. Each student would have a number—*one*, *two*, *three*, or *four*. I'd ask a question as I normally would but then say, "Put your heads together and make sure everybody knows." After the students had a chance to make sure everybody on the team knew the answer, I'd call a number: "Number three's, what's the answer?" Now, with that structure, when a question is asked there is a buzz of participation among all students in the classroom. And instead of feeling bad when someone else is called on, students are glad that another student knows the answer.

—unless the student is a member of another team.

Well, we can use other structures to set up a cooperative classroom, in which a team doing well actually makes others feel good because all the teams can be gaining points toward a class goal or contributing to a class project.

That, too, is just a matter of structure, then?

Yes, we're talking about positive versus negative interdependence. When a student makes a mistake in the traditional classroom—misses a question, for example—the other students are happy. They begin waving their hands, and they feel good because now they've got a second chance to be recognized.

In contrast, students in the cooperative classroom are positively interde-

Photograph by Freeborn-Jones and Assoc.

pendent. For example, you might have a class thermometer on which you post points earned by all the teams. When the class reaches a certain class goal, we all spend a little time celebrating that. Another way to create positive interdependence among teams is to have each team do one part of a class project.

It sounds as though this idea of structure goes beyond just another new method of teaching.

It's grounded in a tradition of research and thought that says our behaviors are determined to a large extent by the situations we're in. People tend to underestimate the power of situational variables. We look at someone who's behaving cooperatively or competitively and say, "She's a cooperative person" or "He's very competitive" without realizing that the person's behavior is greatly influenced by the situation.

For example, if a group of us were caught in a room with sirens outside

and smoke coming under the door and the only way we could get out of the room would be to pull together, we would all be very cooperative. But if someone walked into the room and threw out a bunch of gold coins and said, "Whoever gets them, they're yours," we'd suddenly be very competitive. The same individuals will be quite cooperative or quite competitive in different situations.

How do you know how a particular structure will affect people's behavior?

We've conducted quite a bit of research on that. I personally began looking at the influence of various situations on cooperative and competitive behavior among children back in 1967. I've conducted an extensive series of research studies on that issue.

So even though your ideas are presented as practical suggestions, they've derived from a body of scholarly theory and research.

That's right. My interest in cooperation began when I was an undergraduate at UCLA. I studied with Professor Millard Madsen, who had done some research in Mexico. Madsen had developed a device with four strings on it. The idea was that to obtain toys, children could either compete by pulling against each other or could coordinate their efforts. He found that children in rural Mexico were far more cooperative than those in more urban parts of Mexico.

I became interested and began designing games and other methods for assessing the cooperativeness and competitiveness of children, both their behaviors and their motives. We discovered certain rather universal findings, including that competition increases with urbanization. We found that to be true worldwide; it didn't matter what continent or what subcultural group we went to; children were more competitive in more urban settings. If you couple that finding with the fact that the whole world is rapidly becoming more urban, you can see what our future social character will be unless we somehow intervene.

That was one of the reasons I became interested in the question of whether we could influence the competitiveness of children. One of our findings was that when we used cooperative teams in the classroom, we were able to reverse the tendency toward increasing competitiveness with age.

You're saying these were not just casual observations; you had objective measures of cooperativeness.

Yes, both behavioral and paper-and-pencil measures—in over 20 published research studies—documenting that cooperative learning leads to a more pro-social orientation among students.

Apparently your interests have turned from research to practice.

Yes, I began using cooperative learning methods in 1972 in my own classes at the University of California–Riverside. As we experimented with those methods and found positive results among student teachers, I got more and more involved in teacher training in general and so began going into classrooms and working with students from kindergarten on up.

The turning point for me was an experiment we conducted in 1980. Irving Balow, Dean of the School of Education at UC–Riverside, gave me permission to conduct a large-scale research project with the student teachers at the school of education. That year we randomly assigned the student teachers to teach using either cooperative methods or more traditional methods. The 50 student teachers had some 2,000 pupils, and we assessed the results as broadly as we could: we had measures of ethnic relations, self-esteem, role-taking abilities, classroom climate, cooperativeness, and of course standardized achievement tests. We collected close to a million bits of data in that one research project.

One of the more important findings was a tremendous improvement in racial relations among students as a result of cooperative learning. But in the classrooms of the student teachers who were randomly assigned to use traditional methods, we found that race relations patterns were as they generally are in schools: at or near entry to school there was no self-segregation among students; by 3rd grade there emerged a slight segregation, and by 6th grade students chose as friends those of the same race. But in the classrooms where cooperative learning was used, students' highest levels of intimacy choices were their teammates—and, because we had integrated teams, we essentially eliminated self-segregation among students. Race of the other students was not a significant predictor of friendship choices.

That's fascinating.

Yes, and since that study there've been a couple of dozen very good studies supporting that general finding. We've had court-mandated desegregation in this country for some time, but it hasn't served to improve race relations, because students quickly

When you create heterogeneous teams and make them heterogeneous not only by achievement but by race, you get strong improvement in race relations.

self-segregate; we have desegregation without integration. With cooperative learning there is true integration because students become friends with their teammates. Several of the studies suggest that these are not trivial findings; there's generalization to cafeteria seating patterns and playground play patterns, even to friendship choices the following school year, when students are no longer in the same cooperative learning teams. When you create heterogeneous teams and make them heterogeneous not only by achievement but by race, you get strong improvement in race relations.

There are, of course, different formulations of cooperative learning. They aren't necessarily opposed to one another, but they are somewhat different. Will you contrast your approach with those of Roger and David Johnson and of Robert Slavin?

Sure. The structural approach shares with David and Roger Johnson's approach the idea of giving teachers new methods so they can teach whatever they want to teach more successfully. It's curriculum free; the choice of a structure does not involve choice of any particular curriculum or curriculum materials; in fact, the structures can be used from kindergarten through university across the curriculum.

That is in contrast, of course, to the curriculum-specific approach that Robert Slavin and the Johns Hopkins group has favored recently. On the other hand, the structural approach shares with the Johns Hopkins approaches an emphasis on specific behaviors among teachers rather than giving them general principles and leaving it up to them to decide how to structure the classroom.

We've worked hard, though, to try to incorporate the most important principles—positive interdependence and individual accountability—into the various structures. For example, if a teacher used "Numbered Heads Together," there's positive interdependence at the point where students are working together in step 3. There's individual accountability in the last step, because the teacher calls on one student and none of the other students is allowed to help.

Teachers trained in the structural approach teach quite differently from those trained only by the Johnsons or only in the Johns Hopkins approaches. Both of those approaches train the teachers in relatively few structures and don't emphasize "domains of usefulness"—when to use each. In contrast, teachers trained in the structural approach learn a great many structures and when to use them. They don't have to design ways to create positive interdependence or individual accountability—that's built into the structures. They also don't follow detailed prescriptions of what and how to teach. They concentrate on choosing the appropriate set of structures for a given academic or social goal. As teachers become fluent in the structures, they move from one to another through a lesson. The structures are tools, and the teachers use the tools to design dynamic lessons. Part of the art of teaching is choosing an appropriate structure for whatever goal you have.

You specify structures for various purposes. Are there some educational purposes for which a cooperative approach is not appropriate?

Cooperative learning methods are very powerful; they allow us to reach our objectives more efficiently. But there are some objectives we shouldn't be trying to reach, some curriculums we shouldn't be trying to deliver. In California we've gone through a time when students have been memorizing algorithms in mathematics classes without understanding the algorithms and without having a meaningful context for working those kinds of problems. The new math framework has rightly challenged that. We have, for example, Color-Coded Co-op Cards that can be used to help students memorize math facts very efficiently. But if they're memorizing those facts without understanding, then something's wrong. That structure, which is an efficient memory structure, is only appropriate if used in conjunction with other structures that provide meaning and context for the memory work.

It's probably true that schools sometimes teach some things that shouldn't be delivered with or without cooperation, but that isn't what I had in mind. What I meant to ask is: are there legitimate objectives that should not be taught cooperatively?

Absolutely. Students need to learn to compete; they need to be able to work alone. An individualistic orientation is often very adaptive. But they also need to work together. The problem I have with the traditional approach is not that it's too competitive or too individualistic; it's that it almost never includes *any* cooperative activities.

And the structural approach helps us recognize that the conventional structure, the one most adults grew up with, is very one-sided.

Yes. Each structure has its benefits and its limits. To rely exclusively on any one structure is to limit the range of experience of students and leave them less prepared for the kind of world they'll be living in.□

Spencer Kagan is Director, Resources for Teachers, 27134 Paseo Espada, #202, San Juan Capistrano, CA 92675. **Ron Brandt** is ASCD's Executive Editor.

Educational Leadership 47 (Feb. 1990) 30-33

NEIL DAVIDSON AND PAT WILSON O'LEARY

How Cooperative Learning Can Enhance Mastery Teaching

When you add the harmony of cooperative learning to the melody of mastery teaching, you produce a richer sound in the classroom.

Recent controversies in *Educational Leadership* have highlighted the relative merits of cooperative learning and of Hunter's mastery teaching model. Here we attempt to transform the debate into a dialogue by illustrating how the versatility, flexibility, and powerful social motivation of cooperative learning add to direct instruction à la Hunter. After all, the two models address different aspects of the teaching-learning process, and each model makes its own distinct contributions. But, first, let's review each model and its merits separately.

The Basics of Mastery Teaching

The premise of Hunter's model—sometimes called the UCLA model or ITIP (Instructional Theory into Practice)—is that effective teaching is a constant chain of deliberate professional decisions in the following categories:

1. *Content*: what to teach (including objectives, task analysis, and diagnosis).

2. *Learner behavior*: what the student will do or say to learn and to demonstrate his or her learning (input-output modalities).

3. *Teacher behavior*: what the teacher can do to increase learning based upon principles of motivation, retention, transfer, rate and degree of learning, practice, reinforcement, and modeling.

Hunter's design provides teachers a comprehensive framework of decisions to consider in lesson planning. Nevertheless, many implementors have missed the flexibility Hunter intended in her "recipe for a basic white sauce" (Hunter 1984) by "Hunterizing" (Slavin 1987, Hunter 1987) their staff members, rather than allowing them the freedom to decide for themselves which elements to include, repeat, or delete.

Hunter's design provides teachers a comprehensive framework of decisions to consider in lesson planning.

When implemented properly, however, the model has many merits. For example, mastery teaching:

● emphasizes planning by objectives (the teacher's objectives are to be very clear, whether or not they are stated for the students);

● improves teachers' presentation skills;

● is based on psychological principles that have achieved widespread, if not universal, acceptance;

● emphasizes checking for understanding, which is crucial for learning.

Further, the step-by-step task analysis and careful giving of directions in mastery teaching are crucial to the success of many experiential learning activities (except for open-ended explorations and possibly group investigations with goals and procedures chosen by students). In addition, teacher exposition related to experiential learning activities helps students see the big picture. Finally, Hunter's language (or labeling) system is useful for analyzing and developing a common vocabulary for talking about the act of teaching.

Principles of Cooperative Learning

There is a large repertoire of cooperative learning strategies (Kagan 1989), also called methods, models, structures, or procedures, based on several common ideas. For example:

• The class is divided into small groups (typically with two to five members each), who work together cooperatively to discuss and complete an academic task.

• Tasks can be given at various levels of intellectual complexity: facts, skills, concepts, principles, problem solving, and creative thinking. A teacher presentation may or may not precede the group activities.

• The teacher states guidelines to foster cooperation and mutual interdependence within each group, circulating from group to group and noting progress and problems for later processing.

In working together, students use a variety of social skills; these are explicitly taught in some cooperative models but not in others. To illustrate how cooperative groups operate, we will briefly describe three well-known structures: Think-Pair-Share, Co-op Co-op, and Jigsaw.

1. In *Think-Pair-Share*, the teacher poses a question to the students in the class, who are sitting in pairs. Students *think* of a response individually for a given period of time, then *pair* with their partners to discuss the question and reach consensus. The teacher next asks students to *share* their agreed-upon answers with the rest of the class.

2. *Co-op Co-op* is a highly structured version of Sharan and Sharan's (1989) group investigation model. Elements of Co-op Co-op include: (a) student-centered class discussion; (b) selection of student learning teams; (c) teambuilding; (d) team topic selection; (e) mini-topic selection, preparation, and presentation; (f) preparation of team presentations; (g) team presentations; and (h) evaluation.

3. The elements of *Jigsaw* include:

a. Task division: A task or passage of text material is divided into several component parts (or topics).

b. Home groups: Each group member is given a topic on which to become an expert.

Proponents of combining the two models sometimes promote group work as guided practice, but we suggest there are many other opportunities for combination.

c. Expert groups: Students who have the same topics meet in expert groups to discuss the topics, master them, and plan how to teach them.

d. Home groups: Students return to their original groups and teach what they have learned to their group members.

Note: If steps e and f are used, the method is called Jigsaw II.

e. Quiz: The quiz is taken individually.

f. Team recognition.

Enhancing Lesson Design

Now let's look at some ways that cooperative learning can add to mastery teaching. Proponents of combining these models sometimes promote group work as guided practice, but we suggest there are many other opportunities for combination. Here we will expand each category of lesson design

by adding contributions from cooperative learning.

• *Anticipatory set* may occur in cooperative brainstorming or in group discussions. Students can learn to pose key questions such as: What is this topic all about? Why would I wish to learn it? How would it be interesting or useful for me? What do I know about this already?

• Students in groups can talk about the lesson's *objective and purpose* to clarify the task, remind each other of why it's worth doing, and identify specific uses of the skill or learning outcomes.

• In addition to the teacher, text, or instructional media, the students become sources of *input* when they contribute ideas to the discussion in language familiar to their peers.

• After the teacher demonstrates his or her best modeling, the students themselves can also serve as *models*. Research in social learning (Johnson and Johnson 1989) shows the effectiveness of peer models (if properly validated). For example, the expert groups in Jigsaw help students learn effective modeling behaviors to use in their home groups.

• The teacher can *check for understanding* within each group and can also show students how to do so within their own groups, for example, by using the think-pair-share process. Peers often offer immediate feedback not readily available from the teacher.

• *Guided practice* is highly effective in small groups, as demonstrated by research on STAD, TGT, and TAI (Slavin 1983, Slavin et al. 1985). Additional cooperative strategies that can stimulate practice include color-coded co-op cards, pairs check, roundtable, and numbered heads together (Kagan 1989).

• *Independent practice* takes place in the context of the group, for example, as students practice individually in their groups and periodically check each other's responses for accuracy.

• *Closure* occurs in a group sum-

Mastery teaching synthesizes the most rewarding aspects of expository instruction and clarifies what the best traditional teachers do so well, and cooperative learning breathes creative life into that teaching by inviting students to become coproducers of ideas with their teachers.

mary or synthesis, addressing questions such as, "What are the key ideas we learned today?" "What social skills did we do well on today?" "Which skills do we need to improve?" Responses can be shared within groups, between groups, or with the whole class.

Strengthening the Learning Principles

In addition to enhancing lesson design, cooperative learning can contribute to a teacher's use of Hunter's categories of learning principles. We will examine each category.

1. *Motivation.* As Glasser (1986) and others have shown, students have strong needs to affiliate; they often come to school primarily to be with their friends. In a cooperative group, they may develop higher levels of trust, feel less vulnerable to taking risks, and feel more comfortable than in the class as a whole. Group work may even reassure the overly anxious student and energize the unconcerned one.

Cooperative groups provide a variety of sources of motivation. Intrinsic motives such as interest, curiosity, and desire for understanding often arise in group explorations. Social motives are shown by statements such as: "We're all in this together" and "I want to do my part well and not let the group down." When group members acknowledge, recognize, or praise each other's contributions, ego-integrative motives come into play. Students in groups often develop a sense of competence in their own abilities to reason and to solve problems. As group members learn to nurture and support one another, they also begin to develop mutual respect across the boundaries of race, ethnicity, and social class. Further, cooperative groups foster active participation, which in itself is motivating for many students.

2. *Practice.* Research on cooperative learning shows strong effects of peer practice models, and a variety of structures is available for practice, including color-coded co-op cards, pairs check, roundtable, and numbered heads together (Kagan 1989).

3. *Retention.* The retention of information is closely linked with formation of concepts and schemata. Concepts and schemata can be formed and modified via communication with others in a group discussion. Vygotsky (1962) asserts that cognitive functions appear first on the social level, then on the individual level. Further, cognitive rehearsal strategies can increase retention, and these readily take place in small groups. In fact, students frequently attest to the benefits; for example, one student remarked, "I remember the story much better when I talk it over with my group than if I just read it by myself."

4. *Transfer.* Small-group tasks are often designed explicitly to require and facilitate transfer of ideas from one setting to another. The processing of social skills provides transfer to other school and nonschool settings.

5. *Learning styles.* Cooperative groups accommodate a wide variety of learning styles and modalities. For example, small groups can benefit introverted as well as extraverted learners (Emley and Davidson, in press). Methods such

as think-pair-share, which involve wait-time for silent thinking, benefit all students, especially reflective ones. In addition, through concrete manipulative materials and structured movement activities, small groups employ auditory and verbally expressive modalities, visual modalities (graphs, diagrams, nonverbal cues), and tactile/kinesthetic modalities.

6. *Extending students' thinking.* Small group tasks can be designed at all levels of Bloom's taxonomy: knowledge, comprehension, application, analysis, synthesis, and evaluation. Group investigation (Sharan and Sharan 1989) and its variation, Co-op Co-op (Kagan 1989), involve extended group study requiring higher cognitive levels. Research on small-group inquiry/discovery and problem solving in mathematics (Davidson 1990) and science (Lazarowitz 1985) is aimed at higher-order outcomes. In addition, the processing of social skills in some models of cooperative learning elicits higher-order thinking (Johnson and Johnson 1987, Dishon and Wilson O'Leary 1984, Solomon and Solomon 1987). Further, the exposure to multiple perspectives inherent in group work fosters analysis, synthesis, and evaluation.

Research on cooperative learning (Slavin 1983, Johnson and Johnson 1989,

In addition to enhancing lesson design, cooperative learning can contribute to a teacher's use of Hunter's categories of learning principles.

Sharan 1980) shows positive effects in the areas of academic achievement, self-esteem as a learner, cross-race friendships, social acceptance of mainstreamed children, and social skill development (if social skills are taught and practiced). In addition, the fact that the research base for both academic and social outcomes is stronger for cooperative learning than for mastery teaching (Slavin 1987) may prompt mastery teaching practitioners to add cooperative learning to their repertoire.

Cooperative learning shows the power of divergent thinking and learning. When teachers release some of their control over learning situations and share the responsibility with students, a dramatic release of creative potential can occur for both.

Combining Melody and Harmony

To use a musical analogy, mastery teaching provides the basic scales and

Cooperative learning shows the power of divergent thinking and learning.

traditional melodies in the repertoire of teaching strategies, while cooperative learning brings in the harmonies, tonal colors, rhythms, variations, and

point/counterpoint. That is, mastery teaching synthesizes the most rewarding aspects of expository instruction and clarifies what the best traditional teachers do so well, and cooperative learning breathes creative life into that teaching by inviting students to become coproducers of ideas with their teachers. The result? The teacher's role changes from solo performer and practice master in the Hunter model to conductor of a choir or an orchestra of cooperative learning groups.□

References

Davidson, N. (1990). *Cooperative Learning in Mathematics: A Handbook for Teachers*. Menlo Park, Calif.: Addison-Wesley Innovative Division.

Dishon, D., and P.W. O'Leary. (1984). *A Guidebook for Cooperative Learning: A Technique for Creating More Effective Schools*. Holmes Beach, Fla.: Learning Publications, Inc.

Emley, W., and N. Davidson. (In press). *Collegians Cooperate Too: TAI in Remedial Mathematics*.

Glasser, W. (1986). *Control Theory in the Classroom*. New York: Harper and Row.

Hunter, M. (April 1987). "The Hunterization of America's Schools." *Instructor*: 60.

Hunter, M. (1984 Yearbook). "Knowing, Teaching, and Supervising." *Using What We Know About Teaching*. Alexandria, Va.: Association for Supervision and Curriculum Development. p. 175.

Johnson, D.W., and R.T. Johnson. (1987). *Learning Together and Alone: Cooperation, Competition, and Individualization*. Englewood Cliffs, N.J.: Prentice-Hall.

Johnson, D.W., and R.T. Johnson. (1989). *Cooperation and Competition: Theory and Research*. Edina, Minn.: Interaction Book Company.

Kagan, S. (1989). *Cooperative Learning Resources for Teachers*. San Juan Capistrano, Calif.: Resources for Teachers.

Lazarowitz, R., et al. (1985). "The Effects of Modified Jigsaw on Achievement, Classroom Social Climate, and Self-Esteem in High School Science Classes." In *Learning to Cooperate, Cooperating to Learn*, edited by R.E. Slavin et al. New York: Plenum Press.

Sharan, S. (1980). "Cooperative Learning in Small Groups: Recent Methods and Effects on Achievement, Attitudes, and Ethnic Relations." *Review of Educational Research* 50: 241–271.

Sharan, S., and Y. Sharan. (December 1989/January 1990). "Group Investigation Expands Cooperative Learning." *Educational Leadership* 47:17–21.

Slavin, R.E. (1983). *Cooperative Learning*. New York: Longman.

Slavin, R.E. (April 1987). "The Hunterization of America's Schools." *Instructor*: 56–58.

Slavin, R.E., et al., eds. (1985). *Learning to Cooperate, Cooperating To Learn*. New York: Plenum Press.

Solomon, R., and E. Solomon. (1987). *The Handbook for the Fourth R: Relationship Skills*. Columbia, Md.: National Institute for Relationship Training.

Vygotsky, L.S. (1962). *Thought and Language*. Cambridge, Mass.: MIT Press.

Neil Davidson is Associate Professor of Curriculum and Instruction, University of Maryland, Benjamin Bldg., College Park, MD 20742. He serves as President of the Mid-Atlantic Association for Cooperation in Education and is President-Elect of the International Association for the Study of Cooperation in Education. **Pat Wilson O'Leary** is a staff development speaker, consultant, and university lecturer. She may be contacted at Cooperation Unlimited, P.O. Box 68, Portage, MI 49081.

Educational Leadership 47 (Dec. 1989-Jan. 1990) 17-22

YAEL SHARAN AND SHLOMO SHARAN

Group Investigation Expands Cooperative Learning

Group Investigation harnesses students' individual interests and gives them even more control over their learning than other cooperative learning methods do.

In Group Investigation, students take an active part in planning what they will study and how. They form cooperative groups according to common interest in a topic. All group members help plan how to research their topic. Then they divide the work among themselves, and each group member carries out his or her part of the investigation. Finally, the group synthesizes and summarizes its work and presents these findings to the class (Joyce and Weil 1972, Sharan and Hertz-Lazarowitz 1980, Miel 1952, Sharan and Sharan 1976).

This method grew out of our interest in Thelen's (1960) group investigation model, "which attempts to combine in one teaching strategy the form and dynamics of the democratic process and the process of academic inquiry" (Joyce and Weil 1972). The basic features of Group Investigation are presented, in an early form, as "small group teaching" (Sharan and Sharan 1976). Sharan and Hertz-Lazarowitz (1980) refined the method and shaped its present form.

Stages of Implementation

Group Investigation is an effective organizational medium for encouraging and guiding students' involvement in learning. Students actively share in influencing the nature of events in their classroom. Also, by communicating freely and cooperating in planning and carrying out their chosen topic of investigation, they can achieve more than they would as individuals. The final result of the group's work reflects each member's contribution, but it is intellectually richer than work done individually by the same students.

In planning and carrying out Group Investigation, students progress through six consecutive stages. These stages can be compressed into a week or two, or they can be carried out over several weeks or even months, depending on the scope of the topic under investigation and the skillfulness of the students and the teacher.

The topic should be a multifaceted one, so that it will trigger a variety of reactions from the students.

Stage 1. *Identifying the topic to be investigated and organizing students into research groups.*

STEP 1. This exploratory step may take two or three class periods. The teacher presents a broad topic to the whole class. The topic may be part of the curriculum or may stem from the students' interest or from a timely issue. Teachers should phrase the topic as a question: instead of presenting the topic "Arizona Indians," for example, the teacher should ask, "What can we learn from Arizona Indians?" or "How do Arizona Indians differ from Indians in other states?" This phrasing serves two purposes: it helps to define the scope of the investigation, and it sets the tone for inquiry.

The topic should be a multifaceted one, so that it will trigger a variety of reactions from the students. At this point, students are not expected to show what they know but what they *want* to know. Some students will ask questions based on their reading; others may ask questions related to their past experiences. If the teacher encourages diverse reactions, everyone will participate. Teachers should avoid imposing their own suggestions or rejecting students' questions.

The teacher can further stimulate inquiry by having students scan a variety of sources: films, texts, picture books, magazines, articles, and so on. These materials might be displayed on a table so that students can examine them whenever they have free time. Perhaps a lecture on the subject or a visit to a particular site would be helpful—anything to acquaint students with the subject and stimulate their interest.

STEP 2. Now the students are ready to formulate and select various subtopics for inquiry. The teacher writes the general topic on the board and asks: "Now that you've looked at some of the references about this topic, what do you think you want to investigate in order to understand it better?" Selection of subtopics is done by cooperative planning, which can proceed in one of several ways (Gorman 1969, Miel 1952, Sharan and Sharan 1976):

• Each student raises questions that he or she would like to investigate. The teacher writes each suggestion on the board; or

• Students meet in buzz groups (four or five per group), and each group member expresses his or her ideas about what to investigate. Recorders in each group write down each idea and then report them to the whole class. A short class discussion results in a shared list; or

• Each student writes down his or her questions. Then planning continues in progressively larger groups, from pairs to quartets to groups of eight. At each step students compare their lists, eliminate repetitions, and compile a single list. The final list represents the interests of all participants.

STEP 3. The teacher makes all the suggestions available to the whole class, either by writing them on the board or by duplicating them and distributing a copy to each student.

STEP 4. The next step is to classify everyone's questions into several categories. This can be done by adapting one of the three methods outlined in Step 2. The categories are then presented as the subtopics for separate groups to investigate.

STEP 5. The titles of the subtopics are presented to the whole class. Then each student joins the group studying the subtopic of his or her choice. The

Through discussion, group members exchange views about the scope of their inquiry. They clarify exactly what it is they want to investigate.

teacher may wish to limit the number of students in a group or, if a particular subtopic is very popular, to form two or more groups that will investigate it.

Stage 2. *Planning the investigation in groups*. Upon joining their respective groups, the students turn their attention to the subtopic of their choice. Together they formulate a researchable problem and plan their course of action. Group members determine which aspect of the subtopic each one of them, singly or in pairs, will investigate. In effect, each group has to devote an hour or two to its internal organization. Members have to decide how to proceed and what resources they will need to carry out their investigation.

As the teacher circulates among the groups, he or she can offer help to those who need it. Perhaps one group is unhappy with their original plan. Instead of insisting that the group stick to a plan that has proven uninteresting to them, the teacher can discuss alternatives and help them redirect their goal. Another group may have planned to tackle too many questions. Again, the teacher can help them formulate a more realistic plan.

Through discussion, group members exchange views about the scope of their inquiry. They clarify exactly what it is they want to investigate. One group member will serve as recorder and write down everyone's questions. The first time a class undertakes Group Investigation the procedure at this stage may be somewhat schematic. If there are four students in the group, there may be eight questions, which the students then divide among themselves. As the class becomes more comfortable with the process, it is not unusual for the group to start off with one idea and end up with quite another. Many teachers find it useful to have groups fill out a worksheet that structures the steps of this planning stage. Figure 1 is an example of such a worksheet.

Generally, groups find it helpful to have one member serve as recorder to organize their work. The recorder reminds group members what their roles are and what the deadline is for

---

Fig. 1. Sample Worksheet

Our Research Topic:
    How did the different Indian tribes adapt their dwellings to their environment?

Group Members:
    Bob, Spencer, Billie Jean, Shel, and Nancy

Roles:
    Bob—coordinator; Billie Jean and Nancy—resource persons; Spencer—steering committee; Shel—recorder

What do we want to find out?
    Bob and Nancy—How did the nomadic Apaches design their shelters?
    Spencer and Billie Jean—In what way did hogans suit the Navajo way of life?
    Shel—What kind of dwellings did the ancient Indians design?

What are our resources?
    Under this heading the recorder will list the books to be read, the people to be interviewed, and the sites to be visited. Perhaps all five members of this subgroup will visit the same site and interview the same people, but each one will prepare specific questions and may turn to different reference material.

reporting back to the group. The recorder may also keep a record of everyone's progress. A coordinator (or chair) serves as leader during group discussions when everyone shares information and makes plans. The coordinator also encourages everyone to contribute to the group's effort.

A copy of each group's worksheet should be posted. In addition to serving as a reminder of what each group is doing, this display shows how the whole class works as a "group of groups." Each student contributes to the small group's investigation, and each group contributes to the whole class's study of the larger topic.

Stage 3. *Carrying out the investigation.* In this stage, each group carries out the plans decided on in Stage 2. Group members gather information from a variety of sources, analyze and evaluate the data, reach conclusions, and apply their share of new knowledge to "solving" the group's research problem. Each class period at this stage begins with the teacher's reviewing with each group what it plans to do that day. One or two group members may spend some time in the library, others may summarize their visit to a museum, while a few may interview a resource person inside the school. Or they may all view a filmstrip or read a relevant article. Group members discuss their work and help one another.

Groups may choose to have the recorder note their tentative conclusions, or each member may present a written summary of his or her findings. Groups carrying out their first investigations, especially in the lower grades, may simply have each member present a short summary or answer to the question that he or she investigated. With experience, this intergroup summary becomes a problem-solving discussion: the students continue to share information but go on to compare their respective findings and search for ways to apply them to their research problem. At this point experienced students will often "discover" a new problem that evolves from their discussion of their findings.

Stage 4. *Preparing a final report.* This stage serves as a transition from data gathering and clarification to the

How Effective Is Group Investigation?

Over the past 12 years, we have evaluated the effectiveness of Group Investigation in a series of 10 large-scale experiments. These studies encompassed many classrooms and hundreds of pupils and were conducted at different grade levels with different subject matter. Most of these studies required several years for training, implementation, and evaluation to be completed. By this thoroughness, we hoped to avoid the artificial character of many short-term classroom experiments whose results have limited applicability to real classroom situations. Here we highlight the main features of these studies and refer the reader to the relevant publications.

All of the research we carried out had to begin from scratch. Our aim was to implement cooperative learning in general, and Group Investigation in particular, as well as study various effects of the implementation. We first had to train the participating teachers in the principles and procedures of cooperative learning, because they were accustomed almost exclusively to whole-class instruction. In each study, we took steps to help teachers cope with their doubts and fear of failure, as well as with their need to change basic attitudes and skills. For instance, we set up small teams of teachers to provide mutual assistance in planning lessons in detail, observing each other's lessons, and giving each other objective feedback on what happened during the lesson. These "self-help" units proved invaluable for the teachers.

Academic achievement. Five of the studies assessed pupils' achievement. At both the elementary and secondary levels, students from the Group Investigation classes generally demonstrated a higher level of academic achievement than did their peers taught with the whole-class method. Moreover, students who experienced Group Investigation did better on questions assessing high-level learning, although on occasion they did only just as well as students from the traditional method on questions evaluating the acquisition of information (Lazarowitz and Karsenty 1989, Sharan et al. 1984a, Sharan et al. 1980, Sharan and Shachar 1988, Sharan and Shaulov 1989). Of particular interest are the findings from a study that analyzed pupils' spoken language (Sharan and Shachar 1988). Three groups of pupils (with six pupils per group) from each of nine 8th grade classes were formed at random and asked to conduct two discussions of 15 minutes each, one on a topic from their study of geography, the other on a topic from their history classes. The discussions were videotaped and analyzed by judges.

When they studied in Group Investigation classes, pupils from both ethnic groups in Israel (those whose families are from Western countries and those from Middle Eastern countries) used more words per turn of speech than did their ethnic peers taught with the whole-class method. Moreover, the lower-class Middle Eastern children (often considered to have limited language) who had studied in Group Investigation classes used as many words per turn during the discussions as did the middle-class Western students in the groups taught with the whole-class method. Pupils from both ethnic groups who had studied in Group Investigation classes participated with equal frequency in the discussions, but in those groups from classes taught with the whole-class method, the Western middle-class students dominated the discussions.

Social interaction. Data gathered on pupils' social interaction leave no doubt that whole-class teaching stimulates a great deal of competition among students while Group Investigation promotes cooperation and mutual assistance among them. Group Investigation even promotes positive social interaction among classmates from different ethnic groups (Hertz-Lazarowitz et al. 1980, Sharan in press, Sharan et al. 1984b, Sharan and Rich 1984, Sharan and Shachar 1988).

Group Investigation and teachers. One of our studies reported an in-depth analysis of teachers' reactions to an instructional change program to implement cooperative learning in three elementary schools (Sharan and Hertz-Lazarowitz 1982). Teachers expressed more positive attitudes toward their work following participation in the project: they perceived their schools as having a more positive climate, and they expressed less need to control their students' behavior all the time.

Another study examined the effects of Group Investigation on teachers' language when interacting with their students (Hertz-Lazarowitz and Shachar 1989). Twenty-seven teachers of 1st through 6th grade were tape-recorded several times during the first half of the year when they employed the whole-class method exclusively and several times during the second half of the year when they taught with the Group Investigation method. The researchers found that, during use of the whole-class method, the teachers tended to deliver long lectures, give students orders, ask questions that required short answers, use collective disciplinary measures, and praise the entire class as a unit in general terms. All in all, their speech was quite formal, even rigid, in nature. By contrast, when these same teachers used Group Investigation, their speech was more intimate; they expressed support for student initiative, encouraged communication among the students, gave students feedback about their academic work, and praised individuals for specific activities.

—Yael Sharan and Shlomo Sharan

presentation of the most significant results of the inquiry. It is primarily an organizational stage, yet it entails such intellectual activities as abstracting the main idea of the group's project, pulling together all the parts into an integrated whole, and planning a presentation that will be both instructive and appealing. Presentations can take the form of an exhibit, a model, a learning center, a written report, a dramatic presentation, a guided tour, or a slide presentation, to mention only a few options.

Some groups decide what their final report will be when they begin their work. Other groups plan their report in Stage 4. For still others, the report begins to take shape while they're involved in their investigation. A group studying the dwellings of Indian tribes, for example, constructed an Indian village as part of their inquiry and then presented it to the class. Students in a group inquiring into the life of an author waited until all their data were collected in order to prepare a short skit on the most important period of her life.

During the planning that groups conduct at this stage, students assume a new role—that of teacher. True, all along group members have been telling each other about their work and continually discussing what they did or did not understand; they have been tutoring each other every step of the way. But now they begin to plan how to teach their classmates, in an organized way, the essence of what they've learned.

When the teacher notes that the groups are nearing the end of their investigations, it is time to convene the members of the steering committee (who were chosen in Stage 2). The committee hears each group's plan for its report. The teacher writes down each group's requests for special materials and coordinates the schedule. With the teacher's guidance, the committee members make sure that the ideas for presentation are varied and clear and can indeed be carried out. The teacher continues in the role of advisor, helping the committee where

In assessing learning in Group Investigation, the teacher evaluates students' higher-level thinking about the topic they studied.

needed, and reminding them that each group's plan should involve all its members.

Stage 5. *Presenting the final report.* The groups are now prepared to present their final reports to the class. At this stage, all the groups meet and reconstitute the whole class as a social unit. The schedule of presentations is posted, and each group knows how much time it has for its presentation. After each group's turn, the members of the "audience" voice their reactions to what they saw and heard.

Stage 6. *Evaluation.* Group Investigation exposes students to constant evaluation, by both peers and teacher. The discussions among group members at every stage of their work, as well as the meetings with the teacher, make students' grasp of their topic and of their work visible at all times. During the entire course of the inquiry, the teacher has many opportunities to form reliable judgments on the basis of frequent conversations and observations of the students' academic and social activity (Sharan and Hertz-Lazarowitz 1980).

In assessing learning in Group Investigation, the teacher evaluates students' higher-level thinking about the topic they studied. Evaluation focuses on the application of knowledge to new problems, the use of inferences, and the drawing of conclusions. In addition, the teacher evaluates the investigation process itself.

Alternatively, teachers and students can collaborate in order to evaluate learning. Each group can submit questions about the most important aspects of their subtopic. In a class of seven groups, for example, each group might suggest two questions. The final exam then consists of 14 questions. Each student answers 12 questions, excluding the two contributed by his or her group. After the exam, the teacher may ask each group to correct everyone's answers to the two questions it submitted. In this way the group serves as a committee of experts who evaluate their classmates' learning.

Students' affective experiences during their investigation are also part of the evaluation. Students should reflect on how they feel about the topic they investigated as well as about how they carried out their investigation. The teacher might ask the students to write a short summary of what they felt they learned about the topic and about how to increase their effectiveness as investigators. Or the teacher could conduct discussions in small groups to allow students to express their feelings about the content they learned and the process of learning.

Studying What Interests One Most

Why is Group Investigation so effective? First and foremost, it gives students more control over their learning than other teaching methods—even other cooperative learning methods —do. Students inquire into those aspects of a subject that interest *them* most. They raise questions that reflect their different interests, backgrounds, values, and abilities. These differences are the group's greatest asset: they ensure a wide range of knowledge and skills. The Group Investigation method provides an excellent structure for harnessing both these skills and students' individual interests for fruitful academic inquiry. □

Authors' note: This article is based on a chapter from our forthcoming book of similar title.

References

Gorman, A. (1969). *Teachers and Learners: The Interactive Process of Education*. Boston, Mass.: Allyn and Bacon.

Hertz-Lazarowitz, R., and H. Shachar. (1989). "Teachers' Verbal Behavior in Cooperative and Whole-Class Instruction." In *Cooperative Learning: Theory and Research*, edited by by S. Sharan. New York: Praeger Publishing Co.

Hertz-Lazarowitz, R., S. Sharan, and R. Steinberg. (1980). "Classroom Learning Style and Cooperative Behavior of Elementary School Children." In *Journal of Educational Psychology* 73: 97–104.

Joyce, B., and M. Weil. (1972). *Models of Teaching*. Englewood Cliffs, N.J.: Prentice Hall.

Lazarowitz, R., and G. Karsenty. (1989). "Cooperative Learning and Students' Academic Achievement, Process Skills, Learning Environment and Self-Esteem in Tenth Grade Biology Classrooms." In *Cooperative Learning: Theory and Practice*, edited by S. Sharan. New York: Praeger Publishing Co.

Miel, A. (1952). *Cooperative Procedures in Learning*. New York: Teachers College, Columbia University.

Sharan, S. (In press). "Cooperative Learning and Helping Behavior in the Multi-Ethnic Classroom." In *Children Helping Children*, edited by H. Foot et al. London: John Wiley and Sons.

Sharan, D., and R. Hertz-Lazarowitz. (1980). "A Group Investigation Method of Cooperative Learning in the Classroom." In *Cooperation in Education*, edited by S. Sharan et al. Provo, Utah: Brigham Young University Press.

Sharan, S., and R. Hertz-Lazarowitz. (1982). "Effects of an Instructional Change Program on Teachers' Behavior, Attitudes, and Perceptions." In *The Journal of Applied Behavorial Science* 18: 185–201.

Sharan, S., R. Hertz-Lazarowitz, and Z. Ackerman. (1980). "Academic Achievement of Elementary School Children in Small Group Versus Whole-class Instruction." *Journal of Experimental Education* 48: 125–129.

Sharan, S., Y. Bejarano, P. Kussell, and R. Peleg. (1984a). "Achievement in English Language and Literature." In *Cooperative Learning in the Classroom: Research in Desegrated Schools*, edited by S. Sharan et al., pp. 46–72. Hillsdale, N.J.: Lawrence Erlbaum Associates.

Sharan, S., S. Raviv, P. Kussell, and R. Hertz-Lazarowitz. (1984b). "Cooperative and Competitive Behavior." In *Cooperative Learning in the Classroom: Research in Desegrated Schools*, edited by S. Sharan et al., pp. 73–106. Hillsdale, N.J.: Lawrence Erlbaum Associates.

Sharan, S., and Y. Rich. (1984). "Field Experiments on Ethnic Integration in Israeli Schools." In *School Desegregation*, edited by Y. Amir and S. Sharan, pp. 189–217. Hillsdale, N.J.: Lawrence Erlbaum Associates.

Sharan, S., and H. Shachar. (1988). *Language and Learning in the Cooperative Classroom*. New York: Springer Publishing Co.

Sharan, S., and Y. Sharan. (1976). *Small Group Teaching*. Englewood Cliffs, N.J.: Edcational Technology Publications.

Sharan, S., and A. Shaulov. (1989). "Cooperative Learning, Motivation to Learn and Academic Achievement." In *Cooperative Learning: Theory and Research*, edited by S. Sharan. New York: Praeger Publishing Co.

Thelen, H. (1960). *Education and the Human Quest*. New York: Harper & Row.

Yael Sharan is Coordinator of Teacher Training, Israel Educational Television Center, Tel-Aviv, Israel. **Shlomo Sharan** is Professor of Educational Psychology, School of Education, Tel-Aviv University, Israel. Their home address is 12 Oppenheimer St., Tel Aviv, Israel.

Implementation

Beginning with Robert Slavin's editorial warning against superficial implementation but affirming his belief that cooperative learning is here to stay, this section has several interesting commentaries. Dianne Augustine and her fellow teachers testify that "Cooperation Works!" Another teacher, James Schultz, agrees, but admits that he learned a few things through experience, including the need to teach social skills. David and Roger Johnson offer authoritative advice about how social skills can be taught. Laura Carson and Sharon Hoyle reinforce the need to teach such skills explicitly.

GUEST EDITORIAL

HERE TO STAY—OR GONE TOMORROW?

ROBERT E. SLAVIN

Cooperative learning seems to be an extraordinary success. It has an excellent research base, many viable and successful forms, and hundreds of thousands of enthusiastic adherents. Yet every innovation in education carries within it the seeds of its own downfall, and cooperative learning is no different in this regard.

One danger inherent in the widespread adoption of cooperative learning is that large numbers of teachers with half-knowledge may use ineffective forms of the approach and experience failure and frustration. Cooperative learning appeals particularly to humanistic teachers who feel uncomfortable with a great deal of structure and with providing rewards or other "extrinsic" incentives to students. Yet research consistently finds that the successful forms of cooperative learning are those that provide a good deal of structure as well as rewards or recognition based on group performance.

At worst, some teachers hear about cooperative learning and believe that students can simply be placed in groups, given some interesting materials or problems to solve, and allowed to discover information or skills. Others may allow groups to work together to produce a single product or solution. Research clearly does not support either of these uses of the approach. Successful models always include plain old good instruction; the cooperative activities *supplement* but do not replace direct instruction (what they do replace is individual seatwork). Moreover, they always include individual accountability, in that group success depends on the sum of all group members' quiz scores or particular contributions to a team task.

Another danger inherent in the success of cooperative learning is that the methods will be oversold and undertrained. It is being promoted as an alternative to tracking and within-class grouping, as a means of mainstreaming academically handicapped students, as a means of improving race relations in desegregated schools, as a solution to the problems of students at risk, as a means of increasing prosocial behavior among children, as well as a method for simply increasing the achievement of all students. Cooperative learning can in fact accomplish this staggering array of objectives, but not as a result of a single three-hour inservice session.

Real and lasting success with the approach requires in-class follow-up over time from peer coaches or expert coaches, unambiguous administrative support, and the availability of materials designed for cooperative learning or time to adapt existing materials to this purpose. It also requires using the right methods for the right objectives. For example, Student Teams-Achievement Divisions (STAD) and Teams-Games-Tournaments (TGT) are excellent for teaching skills or objectives with one right answer, from calculus to spelling to geography (Slavin 1986). I'm often depressed, however, to see these methods applied to subjects that lend themselves more to discussion and controversy.

The future of cooperative learning is difficult to predict. My hope is that even when cooperative learning is no longer the "hot" new method, schools and teachers will continue to use it as a routine part of instruction. My fear is that cooperative learning will largely disappear as a result of the faddism so common in American education.

However, I have several reasons to believe that cooperative learning is here to stay. First, it has a vastly better research base than most innovations, so it is likely to be found successful when school districts evaluate it. Second, the nature of cooperative learning makes it a method unlikely to be forced on unwilling teachers. Making mandatory such methods as mastery learning and Madeline Hunter's models, for example, has probably undermined the longevity of these methods. Third, cooperative learning appears to be becoming a standard element of preservice education, so a generation of teachers is likely to have been exposed to the idea. Finally, cooperative learning makes life more pleasant for teachers as well as for students. Students love to work together, and their enthusiasm makes teaching more fun. Long after something else is the novelty, teachers will continue to use cooperative methods because they can see the effects with their own eyes.□

Reference

Slavin, R.E. (1986). *Using Student Team Learning.* 3rd ed. Baltimore, Md.: Center for Research on Elementary and Middle Schools, The Johns Hopkins University.

Robert E. Slavin is Director, Elementary School Program, Center for Research on Elementary and Middle Schools, The Johns Hopkins University, 3505 N. Charles St., Baltimore, MD 21218.

Educational Leadership 47 (Dec. 1989-Jan. 1990) 4-7

—— DIANNE K. AUGUSTINE, KRISTIN D. GRUBER, AND LYNDA R. HANSON ——

Cooperation Works!

Cooperative learning can benefit
all students, even those who are
low-achieving, gifted, or mainstreamed.

With a combined total of 48 years in the classroom and 23 years using cooperative learning strategies, we are confident that cooperation works: it promotes higher achievement, develops social skills, and puts the responsibility for learning on the learner.

The three of us come from the ranks of the more than 30,000 teachers trained by Roger and David Johnson in the Cooperative Learning Center at the University of Minnesota. We have used cooperative learning in our 3rd, 4th, and 6th grade classrooms for many years, as do many of the teachers in our open-space elementary school. We also collaborate to train other teachers throughout the state of Minnesota in the use of the Johnsons' cooperative learning model.

Effects on Achievement

Each year, as we use cooperative learning in our own classrooms, we see improved achievement in a variety of curriculum areas. For example, Kristin has used heterogeneous cooperative groups in 3rd grade spelling for more than 10 years, and individual and class spelling scores have improved consistently over that time (see "Cooperative Spelling Groups").

In one case, Andy, a low-achieving student who received LD services, was failing social studies, health, and language early in the year. He needed constant supervision just to stay on task, paid little attention to classroom discussions, and seldom completed assignments. With a cooperative group to support and encourage him, however, Andy completed many assignments during class and brought back homework consistently. Soon he earned a "B" in health, a "C" in language, and his social studies average went up markedly. By mid-February, he was passing every subject; and he was able to maintain his grades for the rest of the year. From a dejected, isolated child at the beginning of the year, Andy became a cheerful, confident child whose achievement had improved dramatically by the end of the year.

Teachers Dianne Augustine, Kristin Gruber, and Lynda Hanson (left to right) believe strongly in the cooperative concept. They apply it in their work together and individually in their 6th (opposite page), 3rd (center), and 4th grade (right) classrooms at Dayton Elementary School in Minnesota.

Photographs by Eric Augustine

Mainstreamed Students

Many mainstreamed students lack social skills and have low self-esteem. When they are placed in small heterogeneous cooperative groups and assigned specific roles, their achievement generally increases and their psychological health improves.

In one instance, Dianne placed Susan, a mainstreamed child, in a co-

Cooperative Spelling Groups

Here is a procedure we recommend for using cooperative groups to teach spelling.

First, in order to collect data on individual spelling abilities, teach spelling in a traditional individualistic setting for three or four weeks. Then form heterogeneous triads including one high-, one average-, and one low-scoring speller. Triads then work together to study spelling for the rest of the year in the following fashion:

Day 1—Pretest. As teams sit together to take the pretest, they reach consensus on how to spell each word. Teams self-correct their pretests and note any troublesome words.

Day 2—Spelling games and activities. Teams choose from a variety of activities to study the unit words. For example, if teams "jigsaw" the words (Aronson et al. 1978), they divide word cards for the spelling unit equally among team members. Each student is responsible for studying his or her words and devising a strategy to teach the others how to remember those words.

Any spelling games or activities are appropriate—as long as the students perceive a group goal. Everyone must learn to spell all the words, and everyone must understand that she or he will be held individually accountable on the test.

Day 3—Practice test. Teams spend 5 minutes coaching each other in preparation for the test. Students take the practice test individually. After the test, teams reconvene (without pencils) to compare test papers. Teams tutor teammates who have misspelled words, then celebrate accurate papers.

Day 4—Study or free day. If all team members within a team have accurate practice tests, that team earns free time. If any team member(s) misspelled a word, the entire team uses this time to tutor the student(s).

Day 5—Final test. Teams spend 5 minutes coaching members who misspelled words on the practice test. These students retake the test individually. After the test, the entire team reconvenes (without pencils) to check test papers and praise each other's work.

Teams in which every member masters his or her required number of words receive a reward. If one team member fails to reach mastery, the team does not earn the reward. This reward system promotes positive interdependence: a feeling of "we're in this together, sink or swim" (Johnson et al. 1988). The combination of peer pressure and peer support creates an environment where students feel accountable to each other for learning spelling. In this motivated atmosphere, individual spelling scores have always improved in our classes—in some cases increasing from 40 percent accuracy to 100 percent accuracy.

—Dianne K. Augustine, Kristin D. Gruber, and Lynda R. Hanson

When mainstreamed students are placed in small cooperative groups, their achievement generally increases and their psychological health improves.

operative group to prepare for a social studies chapter test. The children understood that each member of the group needed to do well on the test: the group score would be the average of their four individual scores. Susan was having difficulty learning the information for her modified test. When the study time was over and Susan still had not mastered the material, her group members asked if they could stay in during recess to work with her until she was prepared. The next day, Dianne observed them quizzing Susan as soon as she arrived at school. When the tests were corrected, Susan and her teammates all received 100 percent. The children shouted for joy and complimented each other on their success.

Angela learned to be tactful with her classmates and made significant progress in sharing ideas and respecting others' opinions.

Gifted Students

Of course, gifted students and their parents are often skeptical of the benefits of cooperation. Let's look at a few situations that occurred in Lynda's 4th grade "gifted cluster" classroom.

Lynda's classroom is divided into five base groups. There are three pairs of students in each group. Lynda chooses the pairs very carefully, putting a high-achieving student with a lower-achieving student. Because students are paired, when an assignment is structured cooperatively, there are ready-made partners. Or Lynda can divide the six members of each base group into two triads, with heterogeneity assured. The base groups are kept together four to five weeks before being reassigned.

Some very unlikely friendships have come out of these partnerships. In one instance, Amy, a gifted student, and Scott, an average student, were assigned to one another. Theirs was a rocky relationship from the start. They insisted they hated each other, couldn't possibly work together, and even if they could, they wouldn't. Lynda decided to leave the pair together for an extended period.

Leaving pairs together has proved a very effective way of dealing with reluctant partners. The two students involved may not become the best of friends, but that's not necessary. Almost always, however, they develop respect for each other and an awareness of how to work together. Amy and Scott became good friends. When Scott's family moved during the third quarter of the year, Amy was so upset she cried.

In another case, Angela, a gifted student, had always enjoyed school immensely. Early in the year, however, her parents contacted the school to question why Angela was being put into groups in which each person was dependent on the others to complete assignments. Angela was upset by these groups. She knew she could do the work faster alone. The parents' first concern was Angela's unhappiness. Why was she having trouble?

Lynda explained that Angela was having problems interacting with others when working in a cooperative pair or triad. Angela's father observed that Angela had always been successful at everything she'd attempted: she was a superior student and was outstanding in piano, gymnastics, and dance. But Angela had never found it necessary to work *with* anyone. He thought Angela had discovered something she did not excel at, and it made her uncomfortable. The parents agreed it would be to their daughter's benefit to learn how to interact in a positive way, even though she could admittedly do the assignments alone. They were also enthusiastic about the critical thinking the groups stimulated. They assured Lynda they would support her efforts; then they let Angela know they thought success in cooperative groups was important. As a result, Angela learned to be tactful with her classmates and made significant progress in sharing ideas and respecting others' ideas and opinions.

Jenny, another high-achieving student, was concerned that her grades might suffer because of the group work. Lynda offered to delete the cooperative scores from Jenny's average and give her the average of her individual scores. The results surprised both Jenny and her parents. Her average with all included was 97 percent, while her individual average, excluding the cooperative scores, was only 96 percent. (This is a typical result. Very seldom do cooperative assignments have a negative effect on student averages.)

But Jenny was uncomfortable with group work. When someone disagreed with her answer, she was afraid to speak up, fearing she might hurt their feelings. She simply allowed an incorrect answer to be recorded. Jenny's parents had originally asked that their daughter be excluded from cooperative groups because the experience was too traumatic for her. Eventually, however, they supported cooperative groups and agreed that being assertive enough to explain one's answers and stand up for one's point of view was a valuable skill to develop. Jenny learned, in the context of a cooperative group, to manage conflicts within her group more effectively.

Dramatic Changes

Implementing cooperative learning has dramatically changed our perception of teaching and learning. We now expect to see students in small heterogeneous groups discussing topics, using effective social skills, and—what's most important—caring about each other's learning.

If other educators believe as we do that higher achievement, increased acceptance of differences, improved attitudes toward school, and enhanced self-esteem are valuable goals for all children, then we all need to promote the continued use of cooperative learning. □

References

Aronson, E., N. Blaney, C. Stephan, J. Sikes, and M. Snapp. (1978). *The Jigsaw Classroom*. Beverly Hills, Calif.: Sage Publications.
Johnson, D.W., R.T. Johnson, and E. Holubec. (1988). *Cooperation in the Classroom*. Edina, Minn.: Interaction Book Company.

Dianne K. Augustine, **Kristin D. Gruber**, and **Lynda R. Hanson** are teachers of grades 6, 3, and 4 respectively at Dayton Elementary School in the Anoka-Hennepin School District, 12000 S. Diamond Lake Rd., Dayton, MN 55327.

Educational Leadership 47 (Dec. 1989-Jan. 1990) 43-45

JAMES L. SCHULTZ

Cooperative Learning: Refining the Process

Teachers must give adequate attention to monitoring and teaching social skills if they are to introduce cooperative learning successfully.

"Where's the teacher?" asked the secretary from the main office as she entered my classroom. She had instinctively looked to the front of the classroom for me. I raised my hand from the midst of four students selecting their own topics for a paper. Cooperative learning had taken me from the center stage of the classroom and made me a facilitator within the learning process.

When I began teaching, methodology in colleges still fostered the teacher/sergeant image. I was sorry to see "day in, day out, low achievers get negative feedback on their academic efforts," as Slavin observed (1986, p. 8). I was equally depressed that high-achieving students were saying that school was not stimulating or fun. I started asking my students what was missing, what they would change, what they wanted. Universally, they told me that they wanted to be active, to work with others, and to have more control.

William Glasser, in a *Phi Delta Kappan* interview, showed me that everyone is motivated internally by needs for power, freedom, love, and fun (Gough 1987). In a survey, students had told Glasser that their favorite subjects were band, journalism, and physical education; in each of these group activities,

their needs were being met. My students' needs were not being met; they felt helpless, controlled, and bored. Many performed only for external motivators: parents, college admissions, charismatic teachers.

I believed cooperative learning could give my students more satisfying experiences. By working cooperatively, they would take an active role in their learning; they would work with others toward success; they would enjoy an equal chance for recognition.

So the desks in my room started to have a different orientation: students were facing each other. I waited for the radiant smiles of free, enlightened students to brighten my day, as Slavin had promised. Instead, student jour-

> **My students told me that they wanted to be active, to work with others, and to have more control.**

nals about our experience showed negative reactions: "I wouldn't want to do this again," and "As long as I pay attention in class so that I'm able to pass with an 80 percent, I don't bother doing the homework." I came to realize that I had inadvertently taught my students a damaging lesson: to be dependent on me for their learning.

Preparation and Social Skills

Through my reading, I determined two major flaws in my approach. First, I had not adequately prepared my students for cooperative learning. They had 11 years of independent and competitive lessons to unlearn; they and I both needed to be trained in cooperative methods. Second, I needed to focus on the differences between group work and cooperative work; the latter requires positive interdependence, face-to-face interaction, individual accountability, group processing, and interpersonal skills (Johnson et al. 1984).

Of these components, the most important was the last: interpersonal skills. My students had few social skills for working together. They had been taught repeatedly to keep their eyes on their own papers, not to share homework, and to be responsible for their own grades. I had asked them in one assignment to overcome those values and to work together; I had asked for too much, too soon.

My Next Attempt

As I considered my next cooperative venture, I concentrated on start-up procedures. Several authors suggested that social skills had to be taught before the group could function effectively. For example, Smith (1987) suggests teaching students to make eye contact while speaking, to praise others' responses, and to convey disagreement without hostility. Teaching these skills was one step I had omitted from my first try.

This time, I started by grouping my 9th grade English students into writing groups of three, to work with a journal they had already written in the persona of a character from *To Kill a Mockingbird*. I focused on the instructional objective of selecting clues to the character of the persona and on the collaborative goal of accepting another person's ideas about one's work. (Johnson repeatedly states that the collaborative goals must be articulated for the students; they cannot merely be implied in the unit.) To ensure that social skills were being practiced, each group selected a coordinator, whose task was to encourage each member to contribute, and a recorder, whose function was to provide a record of comments for sharing with the entire class.

The results of this lesson were encouraging. The recorders' reports provided a means for identifying and modeling appropriate interactions. The reports showed that my students had begun to develop the interpersonal skills that would ensure the success of future cooperative projects.

Monitoring

The other important factor in cooperative learning that had been weak in my first attempt was monitoring: checking for total team involvement and appropriate social interactions. According to Johnson, frequent monitoring is essential. Most sources I read mentioned the negative effect of sarcasm or put-downs on group dynamics. The difference between "Your idea

is dumb," and "I don't understand your idea; could you explain it in more detail?" can mean the difference between bonding and dysfunction. Monitoring can be as simple as asking the group to write down two things they did well as a group and one area on which they need to work. Teachers who use oral monitoring should be specific about which behaviors are appropriate and which are not. In addition to oral checks, I had my groups evaluate their group efforts with a grade, which I then included as part of their overall grade. Monitoring can also be done by a student observer or, as several authors suggested, by the team itself.

If persistent problems are identified in the monitoring process, several solutions are available. One is to present the problem to the group as an exercise in problem solving, thereby shifting responsibility to the owner of the problem—the group—and also providing another opportunity to reinforce social skills. Sometimes a problem can be corrected by making one of the group members the monitor for a day. Upon returning to the group the next day, the monitor often has a heightened awareness of the problem and subsequently moves to correct it.

If the problem is a particular group member with whom no one wants to interact, David Johnson suggested many options to me at a recent workshop. First, select group members for inclusion in his group carefully. If he is shy, select your most supportive students to work with him. If he is hyperactive, select your most assertive. Second, give that student a highly structured role such as recorder. Third, try to "get your foot in the door" by asking him to do only one small task. If that is successful, add one small additional task at a time.

Improved Attitudes

Thanks to cooperative learning, my students are now satisfying some of their needs for freedom and love or at least for fellowship and fun. The most significant improvement I have observed is in their attitude toward learning. When authors suggested that co-

operative learning would eliminate control problems and increase on-task time, I had been skeptical. An incident with my Latin I class, however, has convinced me.

This class had been divided into five groups of four, with each member responsible for a different component of the unit. Students had scheduled a Monday when I was to be away at a conference as a group sharing day. When I returned, I learned that my substitute teacher had been half an hour late but that she had found the class busily sharing ideas when she arrived. Obviously, my students were motivated enough to direct their own time with or without an authority.

In the short time that I have been trying cooperative learning units, I have felt a huge weight lifted from my pedagogical shoulders. As Popp (1987) says, "The teacher's authority has shifted from being 'in authority' to being 'an authority'." I no longer feel like a worker trying to "sand, polish, and paint students into educated objects" (Gough 1987), but rather like a facilitator working with people who are discussing a book together, researching a topic together, evaluating a project together—working in the way they will work in the world outside school.□

References

Gough, P. (May 1987). "The Key to Improving Schools: An Interview with William Glasser." *Phi Delta Kappan*: 656–662.
Johnson, D., R. Johnson, E. Holubec, and P. Roy. (1984). *Circles of Learning*. Alexandria, Va.: ASCD.
Popp, J. (Spring 1987). "If You See John Dewey, Tell Him We Did It." *Educational Theory*: 145–152.
Slavin, R. (Summer 1986). "Learning Together." *American Educator*: 6–13.
Smith, R. (May 1987). "A Teacher's Views on Cooperative Learning." *Phi Delta Kappan*: 663–666.

James L. Schultz is K-12 Language Arts District Department Head, Burnt Hills-Ballston Lake Schools, Lakehill Rd., Burnt Hills, NY 12027.

Educational Leadership 47 (Dec. 1989-Jan. 1990) 29-33

DAVID W. JOHNSON AND ROGER T. JOHNSON

Social Skills for Successful Group Work

Interpersonal and small-group skills are vital to the success of cooperative learning.

Photograph by W. Spencer

Social skills—like other skills—must be learned. But once learned, the abilities to cooperate and to work effectively with others will serve students well in school and later on in their careers.

In a 4th grade classroom the teacher is trying out learning groups. "This is a mess," she thinks. In one group, students are bickering over who is going to do the writing. In another group, one child sits quietly, too shy to participate. Two members of a third group are talking about football while the third member works on the assignment. "My students do not know how to work cooperatively," she sighs.

What is a teacher to do in such a situation? Simply placing students in groups and telling them to work together does not, in and of itself, produce cooperation—and certainly not the higher achievement and positive social outcomes that can result from cooperative learning groups. The reason? Traditional group efforts may go wrong in many ways. Group members sometimes seek a free ride on others' work by "leaving it to George" to complete the group's tasks. Students who are stuck doing all the work sometimes decrease their efforts to avoid being suckers. High-ability group members may take over in ways that benefit themselves at the expense of lower achieving group members (the "rich get richer" effect). Pressures to conform may suppress individual efforts. Or group work may break down because of divisive conflicts and power struggles.

Only under certain conditions can we expect cooperative efforts to increase students' efforts to achieve and improve the quality of their relationships with classmates and their psychological health. These conditions are positive interdependence, face-to-face (promotive) interaction, individual accountability, social skills, and group processing (Johnson and Johnson 1987, Johnson et al. 1988). Each of these elements mediates the relationship between cooperation and its outcomes (Johnson and Johnson 1989). And they are all interrelated. Using social skills, for example, makes sense only when there is positive interdependence. In competitive and individualistic situations, trust and empathy are inappropriate.

Teaching Cooperative Skills

People do not know instinctively how to interact effectively with others. Nor do interpersonal and group skills magically appear when they are needed. Students must be taught these skills and be motivated to use them. If group members lack the interpersonal and small-group skills to cooperate effectively, cooperative groups will not be productive.

To achieve mutual goals, students must communicate accurately and resolve conflicts constructively.

Fig. 1. T-Chart	
Encouraging Participation	
Looks Like	**Sounds Like**
Smiles	What is your idea?
Eye contact	Awesome!
Thumbs up	Good idea!
Pat on back	That's interesting.

In order to coordinate efforts to achieve mutual goals, students must (1) get to know and trust one another, (2) communicate accurately and unambiguously, (3) accept and support one another, and (4) resolve conflicts constructively (Johnson 1986, Johnson and Johnson 1987). Interpersonal and small-group skills make possible the basic nexus among students; and if students are to work together productively and cope with the stresses of doing so, they must have at least a modicum of these skills.

Teachers can follow a series of steps in teaching students interpersonal and small-group skills. First, students must see the need to use the skill. To want to learn the skill, students must believe that they will be better off if they know it. Teachers can highlight the need for the skill by explaining why it is important, displaying what it looks like on posters and bulletin boards, and informing students they will be rewarded for using it.

Second, students must understand what the skill is and when it should be used. This information is most commonly conveyed through a "T-Chart" (Johnson et al. 1988) and through modeling the skill. (See Figure 1 for an example of a T-Chart.) The teacher lists the skill (e.g., encouraging participation) and then asks the class, "What would this skill look like?" After several nonverbal behaviors are generated, the teacher asks, "What would this skill sound like?" Several phrases are listed. The teacher then models the skill until the students have a clear idea of what the skill sounds and looks like.

Third, to master a social skill, students must practice it again and again. Immediately after defining the skill, the teacher should ask students to role-play the skill several times with the persons sitting next to them. The social skill may also be assigned to students as a role to be engaged in during group meetings. For example, the teacher could assign the roles of reader, encourager, summarizer, and elaboration-seeker to the members of a cooperative group. The roles could be rotated daily until every student has been responsible for each role several times. At the end of each cooperative lesson, teachers can announce how many times the skill was observed. New skills need to be cued consistently and reinforced for some time. Teachers should be relentless in encouraging prolonged use of cooperative skills.

Fourth, students must process how frequently and how well they are using the skill. Students need to discuss, describe, and reflect on their use of the skill in order to improve their performance. To ensure that they do so, teachers should provide a regular time for group processing and give students group processing procedures to follow. A standard processing task is, "Name three things your group did well, and name one thing your group could do better next time." Such group processing will not only increase students' interpersonal and small-group skills, it will also increase achievement (Johnson et al. in press, Yager et al. 1985) and the quality of the relationships developed among students (Putnam et al. 1989).

Fifth, students must persevere in practicing the skill. Students have to practice cooperative skills long enough to go through the stages of awkward enactment, phony (role-playing) enactment, and mechanical use of the skill to automatic, routine use where the skill is fully internalized. Ways to ensure that the students persevere include continuing to assign the skill as a group role, continuing to give students feedback as to how frequently and how well they are performing the skill, and rewarding the groups when members use the skill.

Students learn more social skills and engage in them more frequently when the group is given bonus points for their doing so.

Using Bonus Points

Many teachers want to use a structured program to teach students the interpersonal and small-group skills they need. Such a program will give students the opportunity to earn bonus points for their groups by using targeted cooperative skills. We have found that students, even socially isolated and withdrawn ones, learn more social skills and engage in them more frequently when the group is given bonus points for their doing so (Lew et al. 1986a, 1986b). Bonus points can be accumulated for academic credit or for special rewards, such as free time or minutes listening to one's own choice of music. We recommend the following procedure:

1. Identify, define, and teach a social skill you want students to use in working cooperatively with one another. This skill becomes a target for mastery. Skills include staying with the group, using quiet voices, giving direction to the group's work, encouraging participation, explaining answers, relating present learning to past learning, criticizing ideas without criticizing people, asking probing questions, and requesting further rationale (Johnson et al. 1988).

2. Use group points and group rewards to increase the use of the cooperative skill:

   a. Each time a student engages in the targeted skill, the student's group receives a point.

   b. Points may be awarded only for positive behavior.

   c. Points are added and never taken away. All points are permanently earned.

3. Summarize total points daily. Emphasize daily progress toward the goal. Use a visual display such as a graph or chart.

4. Develop an observational system that samples each group for the same amount of time. In addition, use student observers to record the frequency of students' use of the targeted skills.

5. Set a reasonable number of points for earning the reward. Rewards can be both social and tangible. A social reward is having the teacher say, "That shows thought, " "I like the way you explained it, " "That's a good way of putting it," "Remarkably well done." The points earned can be traded in for a tangible reward: free time, computer time, library time, time to a play a game, extra recess time, and any other activity that students value.

6. In addition to group points, class points may be awarded. For example, the teacher might say, "Eighteen people are ready to begin and helped the class earn a reward," or "I noticed 12 people worked the last 25 minutes." Class points may be recorded with a number line, beans in a jar, or checks on the chalkboard.

7. In addition to social skills, potential target behaviors include following directions, completing assigned tasks, handing in homework, behaving appropriately in out-of-class settings such as lunch or assemblies, or helping substitute teachers.

Long-Term Outcomes

Teaching students interpersonal and small-group skills produces both short-term and long-term outcomes (Johnson and Johnson 1989). Short-term outcomes include greater learning, retention, and critical thinking. Long-term outcomes include greater employability and career success.

Most people realize that a college education or vocational training improves their career opportunities, but many are less aware that interpersonal skills may be the set of skills most important to their employability, productivity, and career success. Employers typically value verbal communication, responsibility, initiative, and interpersonal and decision-making skills. A question all employers have in mind when they interview a job applicant is, "Can this person get along with other people?" Having a high degree of technical competence is not enough to ensure a successful career. A person also has to have a high degree of interpersonal competence.

For example, in 1982 the Center for Public Resources published "Basic Skills in the U.S. Workforce," a nationwide survey of businesses, labor unions, and educational institutions. The Center found that 90 percent of the respondents who had been fired from their jobs were fired for poor job attitudes, poor interpersonal relationships, and inappropriate behavior. Being fired for lack of basic and technical skills was infrequent. Even in high-tech jobs, the ability to work effectively with other personnel is essential, as is the ability to communicate and work with people from other professions to solve interdisciplinary problems.

In the real world of work, the heart of most jobs—especially higher-paying, more interesting jobs—is getting others to cooperate, leading others, coping with complex problems of power and influence, and helping solve people's problems in working together. Millions of technical, professional, and managerial jobs today require much more than technical competence and professional expertise. Such jobs also require leadership. More and more, employees are asked to get things done by influencing a large and diverse group of people (bosses, subordinates, peers, customers, and others), despite lacking much or any formal control over them and despite their general disinterest in cooperating. Employees are expected to motivate others, negotiate and mediate, get decisions implemented, exercise authority, and develop credibility—all tasks that require interpersonal and small-group skills. Thus, the skills developed within cooperative efforts in school are important contributors to personal employability and career success. In addition, social skills are directly related to building and maintaining positive relationships and to keeping psychological health. Main-

Interpersonal skills may be the set of skills most important to one's employability, productivity, and career success.

taining a set of good friends, being a caring parent, maintaining a loving relationship with your spouse—all directly relate to how interpersonally skilled you are. One's quality of life as an adult depends largely on one's social skills. Furthermore, the more socially skilled people are, the healthier they tend to be psychologically. For these and many other reasons, we should teach students the skills necessary to build and maintain cooperative relationships with others.

As Important as Academic Content

If the potential of cooperative learning is to be realized, students must have the prerequisite interpersonal and small-group skills and be motivated to use them. These skills should be taught just as systematically as mathematics, social studies, or any subject. Doing so requires that teachers communicate to students the need for social skills, define and model these skills, have students practice them over and over again, process how effectively students perform the skills, and ensure that students persevere until the skills are fully integrated into their behavioral repertoires. If teachers do so, they will not only increase student achievement, they will also increase students' future employability, career success, quality of relationships, and psychological health.□

References

Johnson, D.W. (1986). *Reaching Out: Interpersonal Effectiveness and Self-Actualization*. Englewood Cliffs, N.J: Prentice Hall.

Johnson, D.W., and F. Johnson. (1987). *Joining Together: Group Theory and Group Skills*. Englewood Cliffs, N.J.: Prentice Hall.

Johnson, D.W., and R. Johnson. (1989). *Cooperation and Competition: Theory and Research*. Edina, Minn.: Interaction Book Company.

Johnson, D.W., R. Johnson, and E. Holubec. (1988). *Cooperation in the Classroom*. Edina, Minn.: Interaction Book Company.

Johnson, D.W., R. Johnson, M. Stanne, and A. Garibaldi. (In press). "The Impact of Leader and Member Group Processing on Achievement in Cooperative Groups." *Journal of Social Psychology*.

Lew, M., D. Mesch, D.W. Johnson, and R. Johnson. (1986a). "Positive Interdependence, Academic and Collaborative-Skills Group Contingencies and Isolated Students." *American Educational Research Journal* 23: 476–488.

Lew, M., D. Mesch, D.W. Johnson, and R. Johnson. (1986b). "Components of Cooperative Learning: Effects of Collaborative Skills and Academic Group Contingencies on Achievement and Mainstreaming." *Contemporary Educational Psychology* 11: 229–239.

Putnan, J., R. Johnson, J. Rynders, and D.W. Johnson. (1989). "Effects of Cooperative Skill Instruction on Promoting Positive Interpersonal Interactions Between Moderately-Severely Mentally Handicapped and Nonhandicapped Children." Submitted for publication.

Yager, S., D.W. Johnson, R. Johnson, and B. Snider. (1985). "The Effect of Cooperative and Individualistic Learning Experiences on Positive and Negative Cross-Handicap Relationships." *Contemporary Educational Psychology* 10: 127–138.

David W. Johnson is Professor of Educational Psychology and **Roger T. Johnson** is Professor of Curriculum and Instruction, both at the University of Minnesota, 202 Pattee Hall, Minneapolis, MN 55455.

Teaching Social Skills: A View from the Classroom

Laura Carson and Sharon Hoyle

After cooperative learning training, I (Laura Carson) entered fall semester with high goals for using cooperative groups in my high school home economics classroom. I was determined to reap full advantage of the benefits by beginning early in the year, so I targeted the third day of Career Investigation class for my first cooperative lesson.

When the day arrived, I explained to my 29 students that they would be working in groups to teach each other vocabulary, using the social skills *encouraging* and *checking for understanding*. I also explained why those skills were important when working with others. As a class, we brainstormed and listed examples of what the skills would look and sound like in a group. Then I explained my role as observer, assigned students to groups, and anxiously awaited what I knew would be a successful and enjoyable experience for both the students and me.

However, as I monitored the groups, I quickly became frustrated. In several groups I saw students who weren't helping each other but who were merely trading their vocabulary lists. Other groups were interacting but not using the social skills. As the end of class drew near, I announced that we would spend the rest of the period discussing the use of the social skills. When I asked students what they had done to encourage each other or check for understanding, I got either no response or direct quotes from the examples on our list. As I had been unable to observe any use of the social skills, when I gave the students my feedback, many groups received observation sheets with nothing on them. We were all discouraged.

On reflection, I realized that I had expected my students to go too far too fast, without knowing *how* to work together. Most of my students had probably gone years without having to work with others. I also realized that I had given my students too many new things to focus on at once. They were not accustomed to sitting and working together, being responsible for teaching each other, or consciously practicing social skills, and I had asked them to do all of these—while concentrating on learning new content. No wonder we were all feeling disheartened.

I resolved to start again and ease my class into working in groups and practicing social skills. I planned frequent brief group activities without assigning social skills, to allow students to acclimate themselves to working and sitting together. I decided to keep students in the same groups for a while so they could get to know each other, and I assigned familiar tasks such as memorizing or completing worksheets to minimize the number of new skills being practiced at one time.

Two weeks later I reintroduced the concept of social skills. I decided to start with one skill—*encouraging*—instead of two. We again brainstormed reasons to use *encouraging*, along with what it would sound and look like. I paired the skill with a familiar task to allow students to focus on the use of the social skill. This time there was definite improvement in the amount of encouraging I observed in the groups, and yet a number of individuals still did not use the skill. I struggled to determine what was needed to fill the gap.

I concluded that some students still needed better models of the skill to relate to; listing examples of *encouraging* was not enough for them. So, over the next two weeks, I planned different ways to model the skill. On one day I asked two students who I knew were displaying the skill to role-play an assignment with me in which we demonstrated acceptable ways to encourage each other. On another day, students went through a "dry run" to practice the skill. For five minutes they sat with their groups and took turns saying encouraging phrases while displaying encouraging actions. There was no task involved. For a few of my students, it was the first time I had seen or heard any evidence of the skill.

When we returned to completing tasks, I altered my method of recording students' use of social skills during group work. Instead of recording words and actions used as a group, I began listing them for each individual. As an incentive for all, I began to offer a reward to groups in which I was able to observe each individual use at least two encouraging words and two encouraging actions. With this, I began to hear students encouraging each other to encourage! At last success was ours.

Laura Carson and **Sharon Hoyle** are Mastery Learning Specialists, Keystone Project, Fort Worth Independent School District, 3320 W. Cantey, Fort Worth, TX 76109.

A Caring Community

Mara Sapon-Shevin and Nancy Schniedewind join in celebrating the virtues of cooperative learning, but entreat educators not to interpret the idea too narrowly. Instead, they propose to "examine all aspects of school policy, philosophy, and practice, making these consistent with a belief in the value and educability of all students and a sense of the mutual responsibility that creates communities." Eric Schaps and Daniel Solomon of the Developmental Studies Center tell how their Child Development Project in San Ramon, California incorporates cooperation in their program designed to create "a caring community within each school and each classroom." A brief piece by Susan Sherwood recounts how her 1st grade students welcomed a multiply handicapped child into their caring community.

Educational Leadership 47 (Dec. 1989-Jan. 1990) 63-65

MARA SAPON-SHEVIN AND NANCY SCHNIEDEWIND

Selling Cooperative Learning Without Selling It Short

Cooperative learning has the potential
to transform our schools, our communities,
and ultimately our society.

Cooperative learning is being marketed as one of the patent medicines of the '80s and '90s—good for whatever ails the schools. It's the answer to everything from mainstreaming to classroom management, from motivating students to raising standardized test scores.

As early proponents and implementers of cooperative learning, we believe strongly in its potential to transform classrooms, schools, and, ultimately, society, by creating communities of caring and support, which, in turn, engender high levels of achievement in many domains. Working together, communicating, sharing, finding common goals and the common ground—these are central values for us and ones that we believe can be realized in classrooms through cooperative learning. And we are delighted by the attention finally being given to this approach and by the recognition that cooperative learning has tremendous potential.

We are not, however, always happy about the nature of the discourse or the sometimes unreflective enthusiasm with which cooperative learning is advocated. Discussions and debates about cooperative learning often focus around questions like:

- "Which form of cooperative learning is best for raising student achievement?" (with no consideration given to the other outcomes of cooperative learning)
- "What cooperative learning strategies are most effective for classroom management?" (assuming that teacher control of a classroom is normative and desirable)

We must examine how cooperative learning either conflicts with or enhances other classroom values or teacher intentions.

- "How can we compare the relative efficacy of various cooperative learning models using standardized test scores?" (neglecting long-term, qualitative measures of intrinsic learning or critical thinking).[1]

Other, more penetrating questions need to be asked. While cooperative learning has encouraged us to reexamine *one* aspect of our educational system—how students are asked to relate to one another in classrooms—other aspects of classroom practice and schooling have gone largely unquestioned.[2] Thinking about and implementing cooperative learning can provide us a wonderful opportunity: as we think more carefully about the reward structures of classrooms, we can also step back and look at the structures and functions of schooling that we accept as givens. Next let us consider some opportunities for realizing the power of cooperative learning.

Reflecting on Content
Some advocates stress that cooperative learning is a teaching technique that can be used for whatever a teacher would typically teach. True, but this

may be a good time to ask ourselves about the *value* of what we ask students to learn (either competitively or cooperatively). Simply because a lesson is implemented cooperatively does not assure its value. Using cooperative techniques to have students cover the same boring, inconsequential, or biased material or to have them "get through" worksheets with more efficiency doesn't demonstrate the approach's full potential for changing what goes on in schools. Rather, let's use this time of restructuring the *ways* in which we teach to examine *what* we teach as well, weighing carefully the value and relative merit of every aspect of the curriculum.

Making Content and Process Compatible

We can certainly use heterogeneous learning groups to learn about World War I, but why not use such groups to explore the role of competition in causing wars and, alternately, cooperative methods of conflict resolution? When we use the Jigsaw method[3] to learn about famous people (each person learning and teaching about a different person of accomplishment), we can ask students to focus on how these people cooperated with others to make positive contributions or to build a better world. Let's broaden our list of "Who's Famous?" and encourage students to think about *which* famous people we usually talk about and why people of color and women are sometimes excluded from our lists and our learning. Further, we can use cooperative learning to help students learn *about* cooperation,[4] using cooperative teaching strategies to help students understand the things that divide us, that keep us from seeing one another as full human beings, including racism, sexism, and discrimination based on age or physical condition.

Coordinating the Approach with Other Classroom Values

While teachers can start implementing cooperative learning in small bits and pieces, we must also examine how the approach either conflicts with or enhances other classroom values or teacher intentions. For example, using a cooperative group for social studies when that lesson is preceded by the weekly spelling bee and followed by the teacher's choosing the "row of the week" for an award may lead to confusion for students and to limited success for teachers. At a recent cooperative learning workshop, a teacher confessed to one of us that she caught herself yelling at a group of students, "Stop helping each other; we're not doing cooperative learning now!" She reflected, with honest embarrassment, that there was no reason why her students shouldn't help each other most, if not all, of the time.

Teachers also need to be empowered to look at all aspects of their classrooms, rather than just being asked to implement a cooperative learning group for a portion of the day. Because cooperative learning is often packaged and taught as some expert's "nine-step model" to be followed precisely, teachers are not encouraged to think about how the model fits in with the rest of what they do. For example, a key step in many models is "processing," in which students discuss how they functioned as a group and work further on their interpersonal skills. Processing *is* very important, but "processing" should also

We can use the principles of cooperative learning to allow teachers to assume major responsibility—and credit—for thinking about what they want to teach and how they want to teach it.

be conceptualized as going beyond the five minutes that follow the lesson. Processing happens in the class all the time, as students learn to trust and respect one another, as they learn to work together, as they gather formal and tacit messages that the ways they relate to one another are important and of interest to the teacher and to the smooth functioning of the class.

Giving Teachers and Students a Voice

If students and teachers can begin to redefine their roles in decision making about the classroom and the school, cooperative learning can become a potent model of empowerment. In some instances, however, teachers who implement the approach are not really empowered but rather are asked to implement models brought in from outside, planned and organized by outside experts, and evaluated by others using standard norm-referenced evaluation tools. An alternative would be to use the principles of cooperative learning to allow teachers to assume major responsibility—and credit—for thinking about what they want to teach and how they want to teach it.

Similarly, in some instances, cooperative learning has been used primarily as a classroom management strategy, as a way to get students to do what teachers want them to do. This is a far cry from sharing more responsibility for learning *with* students, involving them in decisions that affect their lives, including what they want to learn, how they want to organize themselves, and, ultimately, how they should be evaluated. Ideally, cooperative learning can lead to both student and teacher empowerment, can help schools become models of democracy, allowing all participants in the classroom and the school to have a voice in what happens and to learn how to make and implement fair and reasonable choices.

Eliminating Competition

One of the central premises of cooperative learning is that students will understand that by working together they can be smarter and more powerful than by working alone. What, then, does cooperative learning in teams—with posted awards and prizes—really teach students about the value of cooperation? If we use cooperation only to foster a higher level of competition, then we are sending mixed messages. Do we want to teach students that there are intrinsic values to cooperation, or is it simply another, better way to get ahead of other people? Similarly, when we use rewards and prizes as part of cooperative learning, what do we teach students about the satisfactions of working together? Instead, we could use cooperative learning to model what *inclusive communities* might look like, classroom communities in which everyone helps everyone else, no one is left behind, and satisfaction derives from overcoming obstacles together.

Promoting Cooperative Learning Appropriately

Within the last month, one of us heard both a leading cooperative learning researcher and a prominent teacher educator explain that the approach is easy to sell to teachers because it doesn't make them change that much of what they do. The researcher explained that teachers still present material (generally in lecture format) and still test students individually—the only thing different is that the *practice* portion of the lesson is done in heterogeneous small groups. Perhaps this makes cooperative learning easy to sell, but it sells short both teachers and the process and potential of cooperative learning.

Instead of assuming that teachers will only "buy into" something that isn't too challenging or different from what they already do, we need to trust that teachers are truly interested in and capable of reflecting about classroom practice and the consistency between their long-term goals and their methods—and encourage that reflectivity. In doing so, we can promote cooperative learning *not* because it is similar to our typical ways of operating, but precisely because it is so *different*. We can engage teachers and

When we use rewards and prizes as part of cooperative learning, what do we teach students about the satisfactions of working together?

school districts with the notion that instead of business as usual with cooperative learning added on, we can employ the issues and values raised by cooperative learning to reconsider and change *many* aspects of classroom instruction and organization.

Cooperative learning can help us to re-think much of what goes on in classrooms. What could a focus on cooperation teach us, for example, about how we label and separate students identified "learning disabled" or "gifted"? How compatible is a school's focus on cooperative learning with an equally strong focus on a highly competitive athletic program in which only a few students who excel have continuing and consistent opportunities to participate in sports and physical activity? What is the purpose of grading, and how does one handle evaluation if one is committed to concepts of diversity, heterogeneity, and cooperation? Learning about and implementing cooperative learning can provide schools an opportunity to examine *all* aspects of school policy, philosophy, and practice, making these consistent with a belief in the value and educability of all students and a sense of the mutual responsibility that creates communities.

Cooperating for a Better World

The future of cooperative learning is rich in possibilities. We have not yet come close to a full understanding of what schools built on a model of cooperation might look like and what power they might unleash for students and teachers alike. Let's become critical consumers and critical practitioners, seeing beyond labels—simply calling something "cooperative learning" doesn't make it the best practice. If we use the principles of cooperative learning and the values of cooperation—empowering teachers and students, valuing cooperation as both process and content, and affirming interpersonal relations—we can create schools that are truly cooperative and a society in which people really do work together for shared, equitable goals.□

[1] See, for example, R. Slavin, (Fall 1988), "Cooperation Beats the Competition," *School and Community* LXVV, 1: 16–19.

[2] For an exploration of the extent to which competition colors society, see A. Kohn, (1986), *No Contest: The Case Against Competition* (Boston: Houghton Mifflin).

[3] For an explanation of this technique, see E. Aronson, (1978), *The Jigsaw Classroom* (Beverly Hills, Calif.: Sage Publishers).

[4] See N. Schniedewind and E. Davidson, (1987), *Cooperative Learning, Cooperative Lives: A Sourcebook of Learning Activities for Building a Peaceful World* (Dubuque, Iowa: William C. Brown) for specific activities that enable students to learn about cooperation and to make connections between the classroom and broader societal issues.

Mara Sapon-Shevin is Associate Professor, Elementary and Special Education, University of North Dakota, Center for Teaching and Learning, Box 8158, University Station, Grand Forks, ND 58202; she is also Board Member of the International Association for the Study of Cooperation in Education. **Nancy Schniedewind** is Professor of Educational Studies, State University of New York at New Paltz, New Paltz, NY 12561; she is also Chair of the New York Cooperative Learning Association.

Educational Leadership 48 (Nov. 1990) 38-42

ERIC SCHAPS AND DANIEL SOLOMON

Schools and Classrooms as Caring Communities

When students feel they are valued members of the school family, the school becomes more effective at fostering all aspects of their development—intellectual, social, and moral.

How can schools encourage social responsibility in their students? They can teach the behaviors that constitute being "socially responsible," but social responsibility is more than a set of learned skills or acquired habits—it is anchored in the development of deeply personal commitments to such core social values as justice, tolerance, and concern for others. We cannot expect our children to develop commitments of this kind in a vacuum. They must be able to see and experience these values in action in their daily lives, including their lives in school. This is why schools must strive to become "caring communities," imbued with these values, in which all children become contributing, valued members.

Creating such communities has not, unfortunately, been a priority in American education, but a few schools are succeeding at developing them. We would like to describe a program presently in place in seven elementary schools in two California districts.[1] This program, the Child Development Project (CDP), fosters the creation of a caring community within each school and each classroom.

Toward More Optimistic Assumptions

Although students spend their academic careers in groups, schools often ignore the potential benefits of this group life. Teachers and administrators, when they organize students to work individualistically or competitively, actually undermine a sense of community. An emphasis on competition guarantees that school life will become a series of contests, with some students winners and some losers. And the current enthusiasm for "time-on-task" often condemns students to spend inordinate amounts of time working alone on narrowly defined cognitive exercises.

In our view, the assumptions about student learning and motivation that underlie these approaches are misguided. We view students as partly self-interested, of course, but also as

Photograph by Jim Ketsdever of students at Longwood School, Hayward, California

well intentioned and concerned about their fellows, curious and interested, and capable of using and responding to reason.

The Child Development Project is based on these optimistic assumptions. We designed it to promote children's *prosocial development*: their kindness and considerateness, concern for others, interpersonal awareness and understanding, and their ability and inclination to balance consideration of their own needs with consideration for the needs of others. What we have tried to do is to structure conditions in schools and classrooms that bring out the best in teachers, administrators, and students alike.

The CDP classroom contains three major elements that work together to foster prosocial development: cooperative learning, "developmental discipline," and a literature-based approach to reading instruction. The CDP version of cooperative learning emphasizes:

● extensive interaction among group members;

● collaboration toward group goals;

● division of labor among group members;

● mutual helping;

● use of reason and explanation;

● explicit consideration and discussion of values relevant to the group activity.

This approach stresses two major types of experience that we consider essential for promoting children's prosocial development: collaboration and adult guidance. It is through their collaboration with equal-status peers that children learn the importance of attending to others, supporting them, and working out compromises. Then, because peer interaction is not *always* equal-status, collaborative, and benevolent, the teachers act as values advocates, pointing out the importance and relevance of helpfulness, fairness, concern and respect for others, and responsibility. They show students the meaning of doing one's best, one's part, one's fair share, and how these values can be effectively applied in their group work. In "setting up" cooperative activities and in

"processing" them with the students afterwards, teachers routinely lead discussions about the relevant values and their applications, after first focusing on the academic task at hand.

"Developmental discipline" is a classroom management approach that encourages children to take an active role in classroom governance, including participating in the development of classroom rules. They meet periodically to discuss issues of general concern, enjoy as much autonomy as is appropriate for their age level, and work collaboratively with the teacher to develop solutions to discipline problems. The teachers treat the children with respect—as capable people who can respond to reason. They help students to think about and understand the importance of common values, rather than imposing values by virtue of their authority or power. Further, these teachers avoid extrinsic incentives (rewards as well as punishments) so that children will develop their own reasons for positive actions other than "what's in it for me." Teachers work to help children develop and tap their own intrinsic motivation by emphasizing the inherent interest in and importance of the academic activities.

We want each student to feel that the school is a large family and that he or she is an important and valued member. It is the feeling of belonging and contributing that motivates children to abide by and uphold the norms and values that the school community has decided are important.

We try to ensure that students' emerging sense of community is not achieved through a process of isolating and distancing their communities from others. To discourage such isolation, we change the membership within class groups, so that by the end of the year each student will have worked in groups with most, if not all, the other students in the class. And in the school at large, students often work outside their own particular classrooms, particularly in the "buddies" program. For this program, classes of older students are paired with classes of younger students for activities such as reading to each

other, planting a vegetable garden, or holding a bake sale to raise money for an earthquake relief fund.

As with other literature-based reading programs, ours is designed to help students become more skilled in reading and more inclined to read. Ours is also designed to develop children's understanding of prosocial values and how those values play out in daily life. In much the way that cuisinaire rods provide examples of mathematical processes, good literature shows how values "work." For example, the touching story *The Hundred Dresses* by Eleanor Estes (about a poor girl who claims to have 100 dresses at home) helps children to see how damaging and hurtful teasing can be. Similarly, other stories and books show concretely and vividly how such values as fairness and kindness make the world a better place. Still others reveal the inner lives of people from other cultures, ages, and circumstances as they deal with universal issues and concerns— they help children to empathize with people who are both like them and not like them and to see the commonalities that underly diversity.

Encouraging Results

To find out how well the program was actually implemented in the project classrooms and what effects it had on participating students—to see whether what *should* work in theory actually works in practice—we conducted a comprehensive evaluation of the project. Our evaluation has followed a cohort of children who participated in the project from kindergarten through 6th grade.[2]

Our findings show that the project was well implemented in most participating classrooms and that it produced a broad range of positive effects on students. It helped them to improve in social competence, interpersonal behavior in the classroom, interpersonal understanding, endorsement of democratic values, and higher-level reading comprehension. They also reported themselves to be significantly less lonely in class and less socially anxious. Overall, we believe the program is fostering a healthy balance between children's tendencies to attend to their own needs and to attend to the needs and rights of others.

In this article, we want to focus on our attempt to assess students' perceptions of their classrooms as caring communities and the impact of such perceptions. We included a measure of this perception in questionnaires that we administered to project students when they were in the 4th, 5th, and 6th grades. This instrument included items representing two major components in our conception of the sense of community: (1) students' perceptions that they and their classmates care about and are supportive of one another and (2) their feeling that they have an important role in classroom decision making and direction.

The first of these components was represented by 7 items, including: *Students in my class work together to solve problems, My class is like a family,* and *The children in this class really care about each other.* The second component was measured by 10 items, including: *In my class the teacher and students plan together what we will do, In my class the teacher and students decide together what the rules will be,* and *The teacher in my class asks the students to help decide what the class should do.* Students in the three project schools scored significantly higher on this combined measure than those in three comparison schools each year of the three years we administered the questionnaires. Thus, as we had hoped, the program was successful in creating caring communities in the classrooms, at least as seen by the students in those classrooms.

We also found, in general, that the greater the sense of community among the students in a program class, the more favorable their outcomes on measures of prosocial values, helping, conflict resolution skill, responses to transgressions, motivation to help others learn, and intrinsic motivation.

These findings indicate that the program produces its best effects on students when it succeeds in creating caring communities in classrooms. We believe that students who feel themselves to be part of such communities are strongly motivated to abide by the norms of the communities, as they see them. When these norms include the maintenance of prosocial values and the development of and reliance on intrinsic motivation, these are the characteristics that children in such classrooms will display.

Creating Caring Communities

Because of fundamental changes in American family and community life, today's children often lack close, stable relationships with caring adults. Schools cannot ignore this reality—it cuts across all class and ethnic categories, and it shows no sign of abating—nor can they avoid the problems it causes. Schools have little choice but to compensate by becoming caring communities, by becoming more like supportive families.

Our experience in the Child Development Project shows that, with effort and dedication, schools *can* become such communities. What's more, when they do, they become measurably more effective at promoting all aspects of children's development—intellectual, social, and moral.

All too often, meeting children's needs for belonging and contributing is the missing variable in the school improvement equation. Systematic attention to their human needs holds high promise for both children and society, as children and adults thrive in caring communities and develop their personal commitments to each other, to the world around them, and to abiding human values.□

[1] In the San Ramon Valley Unified School District, the project schools are Neil Arm-

strong, Bollinger Canyon, Country Club, Walt Disney, and Rancho Romero; in the Hayward Unified School District, the project schools are Longwood and Ruus.

[2] The research described here was conducted in six schools, three that implemented the program and three "comparison" schools in the same district. We have focused on a cohort of children who began kindergarten in the fall of 1982 and finished 6th grade in the spring of 1989. During each of these years we have conducted classroom observations to assess program implementation and student behavior and have assessed characteristics of the children with interviews, questionnaires, and small-group activities. From 300 to 350 students have taken part in our research assessments each year. For further information about our findings, see Watson et al. 1989, Solomon et al. 1990, and Battistich et al. in press.

References

Battistich, V., M. Watson, D. Solomon, E. Schaps, and J. Solomon. (In press). "The Child Development Project: A Comprehensive Program for the Development of Prosocial Character." In *Handbook of Moral Behavior and Development: Vol. 3. Application,* edited by W. M. Kurtines and J. L. Gewirtz. Hillsdale, N.J.: Erlbaum.

Solomon, D., M. Watson, E. Schaps, V. Battistich, and J. Solomon. (1990). "Cooperative Learning as Part of a Comprehensive Classroom Program Designed to Promote Prosocial Development." In *Cooperative Learning: Theory and Research,* edited by S. Sharan. New York: Praeger.

Watson, M., D. Solomon, V. Battistich, E. Schaps, and J. Solomon. (1989). "The Child Development Project: Combining Traditional and Developmental Approaches to Values Education." In *Moral Development and Character Education,* edited by L. Nucci. Berkeley, Calif.: McCutchan.

Eric Schaps is President, and **Daniel Solomon** is Director of Research, Developmental Studies Center, 111 Deerwood Pl., Suite 165, San Ramon, CA 94583.

A Circle of Friends in a 1st Grade Classroom

Susan K. Sherwood

Ann. Age 6. Severe multiple disabilities. Birth trauma. Head injured. Moderate to severe mental disabilities. Hemiplegia to right side of body but ambulatory. No right field vision. Small amount of left peripheral and central vision. Color-blind. Verbal.

Pacing back and forth in the entryway, I pondered the details in my mind. As I anticipated Ann's arrival on the area agency education bus, I vacillated between calm conviction and near panic. Three days before, the special education teacher had greeted me with a request for a full-time integration placement. In light of my conviction to meet the needs of all students, my answer was instantaneous. Now I wasn't quite so sure.

As a teacher of young children for 18 years, I know that *every* class has a wide range of abilities and problems. This particular group of 21 students was no different. Their intelligence range, as measured by the Cognitive Abilities Test was 137–68 (excluding Ann's evaluation). Shane was reading at the 8th grade level; Sara had been diagnosed as learning disabled, James as hyperactive; Mike was adept at mathematics problem solving; Erica was a 6-year-old in puberty; and so on. Indeed, Ann was not so different. *All* needed to belong to our classroom community and to accept their own strengths and limitations before they could freely accept others. To develop confidence, instill love of learning, and enhance self-concept, the teacher builds on each child's uniqueness— creating a motivating and challenging atmosphere where all children are free to work cooperatively, learn from mistakes, take risks, and rejoice in accomplishments. Such a classroom community is a support system for each of its members.

Special educators coined the term "a circle of friends" to describe the framework of peers, friends, and adults in the natural environment that surrounds a child with severe multiple disabilities and offers mainstream support (Perske 1988, Stainbeck and Stainbeck 1987). Only the term itself, however, is new to the classroom teacher who has worked to build these relationships in his or her classroom all along.

Just as circles of friends draw the lives of children together, networking within the classroom links special educators and regular educators together in common goals. Our objectives for Ann were to help her (1) develop normal relationships and friendships with her peers; (2) build functional skills through normal 1st grade routines; and (3) continue work at her level toward functional academic life skills.

In social interactions, nonhandicapped children are good role models. By observing what they see, the handicapped imitate appropriate social behaviors and engage in fewer inappropriate ones (Donder and Nietupski 1981, Stainbeck et al. 1983). I was amazed at the ability of my students to provide structure for Ann's activities in the absence of an adult aide. For example, when Mike noticed that Ann needed assistance, he would gather the necessary materials, quietly approach her, and firmly direct her task. On one occasion, when she flatly refused to participate, he unemotionally prodded her, "You have to because you're a 1st grader, and these are the things 1st graders do." Then, without a pause, with the same sense of purpose as an adult, he directed her to trace the letters.

Of course, to promote Ann's independence, we had to adapt basic 1st grade materials to enable her to follow directions and participate routinely. For example, to allow her easy access to her supplies, we affixed a wooden block to the top of her desk to hold pencils, crayons, and her name stamp in an upright position.

On some academic tasks, such as rote counting by one's and five's to one hundred, Ann was capable of full participation. At other times, we struggled creatively to supply her with parallel activities so that she could still feel part of the group.

We also initiated the "facilitator of learning" role for each supporting adult on our classroom team. This means that their primary purpose was to assist Ann's integration; however, each team member was to support *any* child when not directly involved with Ann. In this way, the other children did not perceive Ann as having a special helper.

As I reflect on this past year, I know that Ann's life has been touched in many ways by her peers and teachers because she was afforded a free and public education in a regular classroom. Yet the integration process isn't easy. At times, it can become all-consuming. With no right answers, however, we cannot allow ourselves to be constrained by past practice. Don't be afraid to try. We can capitalize on mistakes and transform them into learning experiences and opportunities to creatively solve problems. My vision for education is students, parents, educators, and administrators working cooperatively to make learning positive and empowering for each student within a *regular* classroom.

References

Donder, D., and J. Nietupski. (1981). "Nonhandicapped Adolescents Teaching Playground Skills to Their Mentally Retarded Peers: Toward a Less Restrictive Middle School Environment." *Education and Training of the Mentally Retarded* 16: 270–276.

Perske, R. (1988). *Circles of Friends.* Nashville: Abingdon Press.

Stainbeck, W., and S. Stainbeck. (1987). "Educating All Students In Regular Education." *The Association for Persons with Severe Handicaps Newsletter* 13, 14: 1, 7.

Stainbeck, S. B., W. C. Stainbeck, and C. W. Hatcher. (1983). "Nonhandicapped Peer Involvement in the Education of Severely Handicapped Students." *The Journal of the Association for Persons With Severe Handicaps* 8: 39–42.

Susan K. Sherwood taught 1st grade for 18 years at Hansen Elementary in Cedar Falls, Iowa. She is presently instructor in the Education Department at Wartburg College, 222 - 9th St. NW, Waverly, IA 50677.

Getting Started

The articles in this section will be especially useful to those planning staff development programs in cooperative learning. Susan Ellis recounts her extensive experience in the Greenwich, Connecticut, Public Schools. Yael and Shlomo Sharan recommend the experiential approach they have used successfully in Israel and other countries. Two Oklahoma teachers, Claudia Edwards and Judy Stout, review the factors that helped make them successful in their first year of cooperative learning.

Educational Leadership 47 (Dec. 1989-Jan. 1990) 34-37

SUSAN S. ELLIS

Introducing Cooperative Learning

Six years' experience with cooperative learning
has taught one district some
valuable—and surprising—lessons.

The Greenwich, Connecticut, Public Schools have been providing training in cooperative learning to interested staff members since October 1983. Our original training design followed six steps (Ellis 1985):

1. Before asking teachers to commit themselves to an extensive training program, we offered them an overview of the theory and research behind cooperative learning and gave them practical, hands-on experience using the new strategy as well.

2. For those who elected to learn the new strategy, we provided training at regular intervals during the school year, on work time.

3. We ensured that in-school support from at least one peer and one administrator was available for each participant during and after initial training.

4. We provided visible and continuous district-level support (funds, coaching, encouragement) throughout training, implementation, and maintenance of the innovation.

5. As interest grew, we made expanded training opportunities available.

6. We developed training expertise within the school system.

Our six years of experience have taught us how best to follow these steps in practice—and have provided a few surprises.

> **Our experience with follow-up support suggests that many options can be effective.**

Training and Support

We have found that teachers who elect to become trained in cooperative learning are already convinced of the value of the strategy and wish to jump into practical, how-to sessions immediately. Because we believe teachers should have a good understanding of the theory and research behind cooperative learning, we have not simply dispensed with that part of the training. Instead, we have incorporated that information into experiential sessions that simultaneously teach participants how to use the strategy.

Training schedules. During our six years, we have experimented with a variety of training schedules. When training sessions occurred two months apart, the sense of urgency was lost, and teachers put off practicing their new skills until shortly before they were to reconvene with the trainer. Half-days of training did not provide enough hands-on practice to give all participants sufficient confidence to try new skills in their classrooms. Two or three consecutive days of training

Teachers have told us that working with peers has made a crucial difference in their ability to learn to use cooperative learning.

overwhelmed some participants and left them feeling unable to assimilate all the new knowledge.

What has worked best for our initial training in cooperative learning is a total of four full days of released time with sessions occurring three or four weeks apart (Sparks 1983). This schedule provides a manageable "chunk" of new information, allows teachers sufficient time for practice between training sessions, and keeps enthusiasm and momentum high.

Follow-up support. While we recommend providing initial training on a particular schedule, our experience with follow-up support suggests that many options can be effective, including:

● half-day released time training sessions throughout the year,

● occasional after-school sharing and problem-solving sessions,

● visits to observe cooperative learning in action in other classrooms,

● a consultant's or colleague's observation of a teacher's use of cooperative learning, with feedback,

● planning or team-teaching a cooperative learning lesson with another teacher,

● access to a notebook of cooperative learning lessons developed by peers,

● paid time (during vacations) to develop cooperative learning lessons collaboratively with a colleague.

Not all participants have used all of

these options; teachers select those that meet their needs or learning styles.

Local Support
Our original plan called for local support from two sources: a peer and the principal. Teachers came to the training in pairs or groups, so that each participant had at least one colleague with whom to share plans, problems, and successes. Each training session ended with time for the pairs or trios

to plan how to support each other back at their school. Teachers have told us that working with peers has made a crucial difference in their ability to learn to use cooperative learning.

Principals and central office administrators attended training sessions that described what they should look for when observing cooperative learning lessons, how to provide positive feedback to teachers, and how to model cooperative learning in meetings. They also participated in the

Photographs by Deborah B. Wright

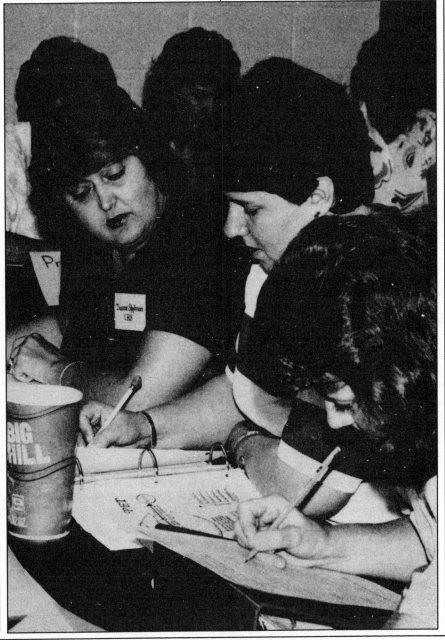

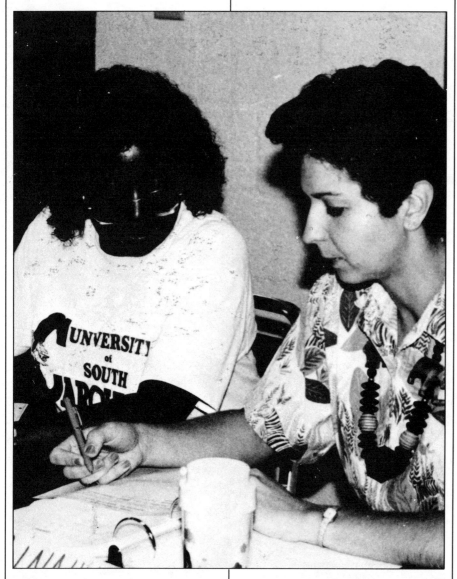

central office and building administrators as people outside the district began to ask to observe cooperative learning in action. During the past four years, we have entertained editors from a variety of publications, teachers and administrators from as far away as Alaska and Arizona, and a videotaping crew from ASCD.

The time required to arrange these visits is justified, however, by the benefits our teachers derive from them. As one teacher observed, "Having visitors really keeps me on my toes and reminds me of all the elements of cooperative learning." And, of course, being complimented by visitors on their use of cooperative learning validates teachers' efforts to incorporate this strategy into their repertoires.

Expanded Opportunities for Training

When we began this project, we planned to offer training each year for three years, assuming that by then we would have reached everyone who was interested. Our biggest surprise has been the very gradual but continuous development of interest in cooperative learning among our staff members—so that we are still providing the basic training course seven years later!

A number of events have stimulated this interest, particularly the calls from researchers in many disciplines for the use of teaching strategies that promote

One pleasant surprise has been the emergence of leadership in some teachers who had not previously sought that role.

training sessions for teachers. Not surprisingly, in those schools where principals took an active role in promoting the use of cooperative learning, more teachers acquired the strategy, and more now use it regularly.

District-Level Support
To provide ongoing district-level support, we have sought to ensure:
• funds for consultants and for released time,
• identification of cooperative learning as an effective teaching practice to be pursued as a board of education priority,

• regular articles in the monthly staff development newsletter highlighting successful uses of cooperative learning,
• participation of central office administrators in training,
• encouragement from central office administrators, both to teachers using cooperative learning and to principals supporting it in their schools,
• use of cooperative learning groups by central office administrators in their own meetings.

What we did not anticipate was the logistical support needed from both students' active engagement in their learning. For example, the new standards from the National Council of Teachers of Mathematics specifically advocate putting students into groups to do mathematics. Accordingly, five math teachers at Greenwich High School requested a training program in cooperative learning for the 1988–89 school year and persuaded most of their colleagues in the math department to join them.

Many teaching strategies designed to improve students' abilities to read and write—such as writing workshop, readers' workshop, or reciprocal teaching—also emphasize the importance of having students work together. As our teachers receive training in these strategies, those who have not studied cooperative learning recognize the need to participate in that training as well.

Finally, our transition to a middle school model has sparked interest in cooperative learning among former junior high teachers who see value in both the academic and the social skills that cooperative learning promotes. Moreover, our 7th grade interdisciplinary units are built on the concept of "interdependence"; several call for students to work in cooperative groups and to analyze both their effectiveness at working collaboratively and the advantages they derive from solving problems together.

In-District Expertise

While we had always planned to develop our own cooperative learning trainers, one pleasant surprise has been the emergence of leadership in some teachers who had not previously sought that role. Because we provide a variety of leadership opportunities (including facilitating sharing sessions, publishing lesson plans, and running workshops), many teachers have been able to earn recognition for their successes with cooperative learning. Some have elected to attend the Johnsons' Leadership Training Course and now provide week-long summer training sessions for the State of Connecticut as well as shorter sessions for schools in Greenwich and other districts.

Another Surprise

Initially we had been prepared for parental concern about cooperative learning. When a few parents questioned whether learning to cooperate would render their children unable to compete in the real world, we provided two evening workshops on cooperative learning for parents, explaining the importance of cooperative skills in the workplace and the need for students to acquire those skills in school.

Much to our surprise, six years later parental concern has surfaced again. (This time the questions tend to be, "Shouldn't the teacher be doing more teaching?" "How can my child learn from the other students?") Some parents of gifted children express fear that their youngsters will be held back by slower students in their groups. So once again we are providing a series of meetings for parents—with the advantage now of being able to use the ASCD videotapes about cooperative learning, two of which were made in our classrooms (see "New 'Cooperative Learning' Videotape").

The Most Important Lesson

The most important lesson we have learned over these six years is that cooperative learning is a valuable teaching strategy that more than repays teachers for the time and effort they must invest in learning to use it. The benefits for students, both academically and socially, can be great. We hope other educators will learn from our experiences and make their own implementations of cooperative learning even more effective than ours has been.□

References

Ellis, S. (1985). "Introducing Cooperative Learning Groups: A District-Wide Effort." *Journal of Staff Development* VI: 52–59.
Sparks, G.M. (November 1983). "Synthesis of Research on Staff Development for Effective Teaching." *Educational Leadership* 43: 46–53.

Susan S. Ellis is Teacher Leader, Staff Development Center, Greenwich Public Schools, Havemeyer Bldg., Greenwich Ave., Greenwich, CT 06830.

Tips on Implementing Cooperative Learning

Our major discoveries from our long-term investment in cooperative learning are simple:
- Once the idea takes hold, teachers want practical, how-to instruction. They prefer theory and research to be built into the hands-on sessions, not imposed up front.
- Teachers need regular released-time training and continued follow-up support if they are to acquire and use this complex new teaching strategy.
- The more follow-up support teachers have, the more they use the new techniques.
- Success can lead to fame, which can lead to lots of visitors. Arranging for visitors takes time, but the gains in teacher self-confidence and commitment to the new strategy are worth the time spent.
- "Stars" will emerge where you may not expect them.
- Voluntary change can take twice as long as you think it will—or more.
- Parents need training, too.

—Susan S. Ellis

Educational Leadership 45 (Nov. 1987) 20-25

YAEL SHARAN AND SHLOMO SHARAN

Training Teachers for Cooperative Learning

Creating a cooperative classroom for themselves
in a workshop setting is valuable preparation for
teachers who wish to foster norms of helping
and sharing among their students.

A teacher shares his observations of a cooperative learning simulation game with the rest of the "class."

Cooperative learning encompasses a wide range of strategies for promoting academic learning through peer cooperation and communication. As the term "cooperative learning" implies, students help each other learn, share ideas and resources, and plan cooperatively what and how to study. The teacher does not dictate specific instructions but rather allows students varying degrees of choice as to the substance and goals of their learning activities, thus making students active participants in the process of acquiring knowledge.

Teachers learn their role in cooperative learning from practice over time, as do students. First and foremost, the teacher must model the social and communication skills expected from the students. Cooperative learning in the classroom requires that helping, sharing, and cooperating become classroom norms. The gradual introduction of cooperative games, learning tasks, and activities helps teacher and students alike acquire communication and helping skills and the rudiments of small-group organization (Slavin et al. 1985, Sharan 1984, Sharan and Hertz-Lazarowitz 1980). A comprehensive overview of games and learning activities, and of the cognitive and social skills these activities seek to develop, can be found in many sources (Cohen 1987; Graves and Graves 1985; Johnson and Johnson 1987; Kagan 1985; Orlick 1978, 1982; Sharan and Sharan 1976; Slavin 1986).

The Experiential Learning Model

Cooperative learning differs considerably in theory and in practice from traditional whole-class instruction and requires a different approach to teacher training. Cooperative learning does not involve production-type tasks, where every element is specifiable and where outcomes are largely predictable. While the discussion skills and helping behaviors required for cooperative learning are indeed specifiable, we cannot always stipulate their outcomes.

Cooperative learning encourages, and is in fact built upon, the contributions of group members. Even in the most highly structured cooperative learning situation, such as students' tutoring one another in a vocabulary list, their interaction cannot be controlled. The teacher, therefore, must be comfortable with varying degrees of uncertainty as to what each group member will contribute. He or she must be willing to acknowledge diversity among pupils in interests, talents, and pace of work.

Prospective teachers of cooperative learning must make independent decisions as to how to balance cooperative behaviors and academic skills and goals. Their training, therefore, should focus on developing skills for organizing cooperative learning as well as skills for analyzing and evaluating the lessons in terms of their effects on children's cooperative behaviors and

on their academic learning. A learning model based on Kolb's (1975, 1986) experiential learning theory is particularly appropriate for such training. Kolb presents a "holistic integrative perspective on learning that combines experience, perception, cognition, and behavior" (1986, p. 21). This model is rooted in John Dewey's philosophy of education and in Kurt Lewin's integration of scientific inquiry and social problem solving. Both Dewey and Lewin viewed learning as based on personal experience, provided the learner has the tools with which to observe and analyze the effects of experience.

Within the experiential learning model, concrete experience is the catalyst for learning (fig. 1). Learners participate in activities that serve as a basis for observation of the process as well as reflection on the effects of the experience. Their reflections are organized into general principles about the topic being studied and are assimilated into generalizations that direct their application in new situations. Chickering (1977) sums up the four different capabilities fostered by this learning model:

The learners must be able to enter new experiences openly and fully without bias; they must be able to stand back from these experiences, observe them with some detachment, and reflect on their significance; they must be able to develop a logic, a theory, a conceptual framework that gives some order to the observation; and they must be able to use these concepts to make

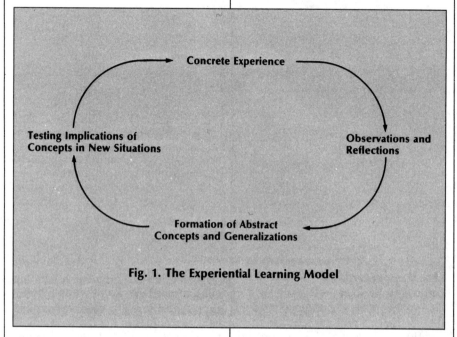

Fig. 1. The Experiential Learning Model

decisions, to solve problems, to take action (p. 18).

The new action then becomes a new concrete experience that generates new observations, and so forth, as the cycle repeats.

A Cooperative Learning Experiential Workshop

Each stage of the experiential learning model has an application when we train teachers to use cooperative learning methods. Advocates of experiential learning have developed a pool of tasks, exercises, and games that simulate cooperative learning for teachers and involve them directly in cooperative interactions with their peers. The activities challenge teachers' thinking about learning and teaching and generate insight into the basic features of learning cooperatively.

Stage 1: Concrete Experience. Cooperative learning training workshops employ a variety of experiences that are particularly suited to adult learners of different ages with diverse backgrounds and interests. (In fact, diversity is essential for developing cooperation.) Workshop groups are formed randomly, and each teacher is encouraged to make a unique contribution to the group's cooperative effort. Thus,

from the onset of the workshop, teachers experience one of the basic elements of cooperative learning: acknowledgment and acceptance of other people's ideas and viewpoints.

This principle is illustrated by one of many activities suitable for the opening session of a workshop: preparing a group poster. The trainer gives groups of four or five teachers magazines, tag board, felt markers, scissors, and paste and asks them to create a group poster. The only specific requirement is that the product must reflect the ideas of every member of the group.

Creating a poster exposes teachers to a rich constellation of cooperative procedures. In order to decide which form the poster will take, teachers must exchange ideas and share feelings about their understanding of the assignment and about how to organize their work. They also share their feelings about the procedure. Some teachers may express frustration at the lack of specific directions for carrying out the task, while others may feel more comfortable precisely because the directions give them an opportunity to act independently and make their own decisions. Involvement in the discussion as well as in the actual preparation of the poster illustrates an essen-

tial feature of cooperative work: individual group members helping each other plan and achieve their collective goal.

After completing the posters, each group presents its product to the class. Each poster is unique because it emerged from the combined input of that particular group's members. Later, the groups report how their posters evolved, illustrating similarities as well as differences in how each group organized its work. By listening to the reports, the trainer gains information about the teachers' knowledge, opinions, and skills and thus can informally assess their familiarity with cooperative learning. Finally, hanging the posters on the wall creates a sense of belonging to the group and to the class as a whole.

An activity appropriate for a later workshop session is a "fishbowl" discussion in which teachers form two concentric circles. Teachers in the inner circle discuss a previously determined topic. Those in the outer circle, who serve as observers, complete a short questionnaire on how often the observed teachers participated in the discussion, whether the speaker's remarks were relevant to the topic, and so on, depending on the particular discussion skills the trainer seeks to develop. After the observers report on the discussion process, the participants conduct another discussion, refining certain behaviors accordingly. At the next opportunity, observers and participants reverse roles.

In addition to giving participants actual practice in communication skills (e.g., discussion and feedback), this "fishbowl" exercise demonstrates that cooperative learning skills are amenable to development. As they practice these skills, the teachers also increase their awareness of how to cultivate the skills among their students.

To sum up stage one of the model, in the course of the workshop the trainer conducts a series of games, exercises, and simulations that illustrate different ways of organizing groups, a variety of cooperative learning tasks, and a wide range of communication skills. In effect, these experiences are the "content" of the workshop. Instead of learning *about* a cooperative classroom, the teachers *create* one for themselves, by themselves. Effective transfer from the workshop to the classroom depends on the next three stages.

Stage 2: Observations and reflections. During the next stage learners reflect on the experience's significance for them both personally and professionally. Reflection is the bridge between the concrete experience and the formal learning of relevant concepts. Teachers share their reactions to the events that occurred during the concrete experience.

Observations and reflections are generally shared during a discussion, which can be conducted first in "buzz" groups or in pairs, followed by quartets and then classwide. Sometimes trainers will suggest that teachers write down individual reactions to the exercise before sharing them.

It is useful from time to time to have teachers take turns as observers of the experience. Their reactions supply another source of perception and point of view. This role will enhance teachers' awareness of the complexities of interaction within a group.

Three questions (Pearson and Smith 1985) lend structure to the process of observation and reflection: What happened? How did the participants feel? What does it mean?

What happened? A common starting point is for teachers to help each other reconstruct the event. Sharing perceptions becomes a vivid reminder that not everyone perceives the same event in the same way—a fact we all know but often forget! Teachers do not try to recall every detail of what happened; rather they are instructed to emphasize the general sequence of events and how group members contributed to the process.

How did the participants feel? After clarifying their personal and collective perceptions of the exercise, teachers reflect upon positive as well as negative feelings evoked by the experience. The trainer must establish an atmosphere of trust and acceptance so

that teachers will be willing to "risk" exposing their feelings without censure.

What does it mean? Next, teachers explore the meaning of the experience and of the feelings it aroused. From personal meanings they construct generalizations about cooperative activities. For example, how did they feel about a loosely structured activity? Did some teachers find it easier to assume leadership roles when there was no designated leader? Did paraphrasing another's remarks require unusual amounts of concentration?

With time and practice, teachers integrate seemingly disconnected features of cooperative learning activities into a meaningful whole, making the connections between particular tasks and social skills. Group members begin to associate cooperative learning activities with the corresponding cooperative behaviors.

Stage 3: Formation of abstract concepts and generalizations. During the next stage, the teachers organize the outcomes of observation and reflection into concepts, formulating them according to the terminology of the cooperative learning field. This creates a common professional vocabulary for all participants. In this stage the trainer's role is more direct than heretofore. Now he or she functions as "the interpreter of a field of knowledge and a guide to ... the manipulation of terms and concepts" (Kolb and Lewis 1986, p. 101). The trainer may at this time assign readings to be done during the workshop or at home.

After debriefing several activities, teachers begin to recognize the essential features of a cooperative learning task, concluding that some tasks call for sharing and exchanging ideas, for planning together, or for solving problems and making decisions. These findings may be posted on a chart for future reference. Other activities will familiarize teachers with more features of cooperative learning, and the list can be expanded. When teachers have experienced, reflected upon, and clarified different types of tasks, they will be able to formulate a typology of

"Instead of learning *about* a cooperative classroom, the teachers *create* one for themselves, by themselves."

> "Reflection is the bridge between the concrete experience and the formal learning of relevant concepts."

cooperative learning tasks.

The same process takes place in relation to communication skills. As a result of repeated activities and debriefings, teachers become familiar with an array of skills required for smooth group functioning. In addition to generalizing about the various skills themselves (e.g., listening, paraphrasing, giving feedback), teachers match the skills with appropriate tasks. A "Jigsaw" task, for instance, calls for listening, sharing ideas, and reaching consensus. On the other hand, a "buzz" group discussion, prior to a classwide deliberation, remains open-ended and requires no consensus. Similarly, teachers analyze other features of cooperative learning, such as which tasks call for a group product and how the product reflects the group effort.

Stage 4: Testing applications of concepts in new situations. Activities per-

formed in this stage help teachers apply knowledge and skills gained in the previous stages to their own lesson planning. At first they may plan isolated tasks that emphasize only one or two cooperative learning elements. As their ability to integrate the variety of factors that constitute cooperative learning increases, their plans become more complex.

At this stage the trainer may group teachers by grade level and content area to facilitate practical application of their planning. Together, teachers choose a unit of study and decide which aspect of the unit is appropriate for cooperative learning. Each group determines the goal of the cooperative lesson, the types of tasks that will achieve the goal, and the kind of product the student group will create. They focus on formulating clear instructions for students that correspond to the teacher's objectives.

ORGANIZATION How many in group? What or who determines group composition?	TASK Describe task.	GOAL Group or individual?	COOPERATIVE SKILLS Communication, interaction.	PRODUCT Group or individual?
SESSION I 1. 5-6, random composition, by choice.	**CONCRETE EXPERIENCE:** Create a poster that will represent your group.	Group goal—all members must contribute (positive interdependence).	Cooperative planning; sharing ideas; decision making; group members determine their own organization of the task.	Group product— poster.
2. Individual, then pairs, then quartets.	**OBSERVATIONS AND REFLECTIONS:** Conduct discussion: debrief how group organized its work and the interaction that took place.	Share ideas and feelings.	Listening; taking turns; exchanging and synthesizing ideas.	Combined list of processes that group experienced.
3. Classwide organization (class is group of groups).	**FORMULATING GENERALIZATIONS:** a. Representative from each group reports on its list of findings. b. Whole class categorizes basic principles of small-group work.	Exchange ideas; synthesize ideas; generalize principles.	Listening; taking turns; accepting diversity.	Combined list of principles of group work (chart posted on wall).
4. 4-5, by grade level.	**PLANNING IMPLEMENTATION:** Plan learning task for students that requires cooperative planning.	Group goal.	Listening; sharing, exchanging, and synthesizing ideas.	Group lesson plan that incorporates cooperative planning.
5. 4-5, by grade level.	Two groups compare tasks; evaluate according to list of principles formulated in activity #3.	Group goal.	Listening; sharing, exchanging, and synthesizing ideas.	Combined lesson plan based on intergroup cooperation.

Fig. 2. Cooperative Learning Experiential Workshop

> "With time and practice, teachers ... associate cooperative learning activities with the corresponding cooperative behaviors."

The trainer at this stage becomes a coach, reminding the teachers of basic principles learned in previous stages and encouraging them to evaluate their plans. Indeed, a lively discussion of what is and isn't appropriate for a cooperative learning lesson usually occurs during this activity. Teachers have yet another opportunity to clarify and integrate the elements of cooperative learning acquired in the workshop. The plans they design together validate their learning.

Throughout the training teachers have had ample opportunity for subjective experiences as well as objective ones (in the first three stages) with cooperative learning. In this fourth stage, while designing cooperative learning situations for the real world of their classrooms, teachers recreate their learnings by synthesizing their subjective preferences with the method's objective requirements. Trainers can facilitate the transition from planning to classroom implementation by having teachers "rehearse" the experience in the relatively safe environment of the workshop setting. Whether teachers experiment in the workshop or in their own classrooms, these applications become new concrete experiences. Time is then set aside for teachers to reflect upon the experience, draw conclusions, and modify plans for future implementation. Figure 2 illustrates the four stages of an experiential workshop in cooperative learning.

Something to Take Back

By following the stages of the experiential learning model, teachers become active participants in the process of acquiring cooperative learning skills and concepts. The workshop is particularly effective if teachers from the same school attend. Together they acquire a common technical vocabulary and establish norms of behavior that facilitate the continuing development of cooperative learning in their school (Little 1982).

If the teachers are trained together and continue to function as members of small groups or teams, and if the teams are devoted to mutual assistance in the trial of new strategies, cooperative learning will be sustained in a school (Joyce and Showers 1987, Sharan and Hertz-Lazarowitz 1982).

Our goal is to train teachers who can use a variety of cooperative learning strategies and then analyze their efforts. We also hope that teachers may come to see each other as valued resources for both implementing and evaluating their own modifications of cooperative learning strategies.□

References

Chickering. A. *Experience and Learning*. Rochelle, N.Y.: Change Magazine Press, 1977.

Cohen, E. *Designing Groupwork*. New York: Teacher's College, Columbia University, 1987.

Graves, N., and T. Graves. "Creating a Cooperative Learning Environment: An Ecological Approach." In *Learning to Cooperate, Cooperating to Learn*, edited by R. Slavin, et al. New York: Plenum Publishing Corp., 1985.

Johnson, D., and R. Johnson. *Learning Together and Alone*. Englewood Cliffs, N.J.: Prentice Hall, Inc., 1987.

Joyce, B., and B. Showers. *Student Achievement Through Staff Development*. New York: Longman, Inc., 1987.

Kagan, S. *Cooperative Learning Resources for Teachers*. Riverside, Calif.: University of California Department of Psychology, 1985.

Kolb, D., and R. Fry. "Towards an Applied Theory of Experiential Learning." In *Theories of Group Processes*, edited by C. Cooper. London: John Wiley, 1975.

Kolb, D., and L. Lewis. "Facilitating Experiential Learning: Observation and Reflection." In *Experiential and Simulation Techniques for Teaching Adults*, edited by L. Lewis. San Francisco: Jossey-Bass, Inc., 1986.

Little, J. "Norms of Collegiality and Experimentation. *American Educational Research Journal* 19 (1982): 325–340.

Orlick, J. *The Cooperative Sports and Games Book*. New York: Pantheon Books, 1978.

Orlick, J. *The Second Cooperative Sports and Games Book*. New York: Pantheon Books, 1982.

Pearson, M., and D. Smith. "Debriefing in Experience-Based Learning." In *Reflection: Turning Experience into Learning*, edited by D. Boud, et al. London: Kogan Page, 1985.

Sharan, S. *Cooperative Learning in the Classroom: Research in Desegregated Schools*. Hillsdale, N.J.: Lawrence Erlbaum, Publisher, 1984.

Sharan, S., and R. Hertz-Lazarowitz. "A Group Investigation Method of Cooperative Learning in the Classroom." In *Cooperation in Education*, edited by S. Sharan, et al. Provo, Utah: Brigham Young University Press, 1980.

Sharan, S., and R. Hertz-Lazarowitz. "Effects of an Instructional Change Program on Teachers' Behavior, Attitudes, and Perceptions." *The Journal of Applied Behavioral Science* 18, 2 (1982): 185–201.

Sharan, S., and Y. Sharan. *Small Group Teaching*. Englewood Cliffs, N.J.: Educational Technology Publications, 1976.

Slavin, R. *Using Student Team Learning*, 3d ed. Baltimore, Md.: Center for Research on Elementary and Middle Schools, The Johns Hopkins University Press, 1986.

Slavin, R., S. Sharan, S. Kagan, R. Lazarowitz, C. Webb, and R. Schmuck, eds. *Learning to Cooperate, Cooperating to Learn*. New York: Plenum Publishing Corp., 1985.

Yael Sharan is National Coordinator of Teacher Training, Israel Educational Television Center, Pre-service Teacher Training, Kibbutz Teachers College, Tel Aviv, Israel. **Shlomo Sharan** is Associate Professor of Educational Psychology, School of Education, Tel Aviv University, Tel Aviv, Israel.

Educational Leadership 47 (Dec. 1989-Jan. 1990) 38-41

CLAUDIA EDWARDS AND JUDY STOUT

Cooperative Learning: The First Year

A group of Oklahoma teachers who have learned by experience how to implement cooperative learning offer their advice to other educators.

ASCD photograph

A one-day training session with David and Roger Johnson in the summer of 1987 excited and challenged our three classroom teachers who attended. The presentation convinced us that cooperative experiences would be overwhelmingly beneficial to our students. We were ready to dive into cooperative learning.

So we took the plunge, and soon we found ourselves treading water—floundering even—from time to time. Fortunately, we've come a long way since then. We hope this article will help other teachers make a smoother transition to the successful use of a cooperative learning program. We believe three components are vital to success: commitment, pacing, and support.

Vital Components

Commitment. So many times, each of us had jumped on a bandwagon only to face what seemed to be insurmountable difficulties. Then we had given up because of lack of commitment. On our way home from the Johnson and Johnson training session, however, we promised ourselves to use cooperative learning for a minimum of one year—and we took that promise seriously. Our commitment to the program and to the district has helped us see the cooperative learning project through the rough times.

Pacing the program. The Johnsons told us that it takes teachers two to three years to incorporate cooperative learning fully into their present teaching styles and to use it the recommended 60 percent of the teaching day. Our enthusiasm temporarily blinded us to this fact, however, and we began too quickly. We immediately planned different groups for each subject area and too often neglected the direct teaching of social skills. As a result, our foundations were not well established, and our first year's experiences were more difficult than necessary.

We recommend that teachers start with one lesson in a subject with which they feel comfortable. They should continue in this area until the cooperative process goes smoothly—both socially and academically. Then they can add other subjects as competence develops and add social skills as the need arises. Some teachers may spend considerable time teaching and modeling social skills first. These skills are then firmly in place before the groups begin their academic assignments. Every teacher must internalize cooperative learning, and adapt it to his or her own teaching style. Feeling comfortable and secure takes time, and no two classrooms will be identical.

When introducing students to cooperative learning activities, we first decide on a class name, then on names for each group—quite a lesson in give-and-take! We have learned that lots of modeling must also occur as we move into academic experiences. Younger children in particular must see what they are expected to do.

Support. Just as positive interdependence is vital to a cooperative learning lesson, it is vital for the teachers who use it as well. At first, every day at least one of us was ready to give up. But because there were others with whom to share difficulties and triumphs, we persevered.

Our group started with only three members. It now includes 17 of 19 staff members, all of whom use cooperative learning in some way. Our support group meets monthly, with

In our enthusiasm, we immediately planned different groups for each subject area and too often neglected the direct teaching of social skills.

interested teachers and administrators from across the district in attendance. Today at these meetings, those of us who were involved from the beginning still learn from others. Many of us have developed close friendships, and our commitment is stronger than ever.

Practical Suggestions
The following suggestions can help any classroom teacher use cooperative learning more easily. Some of these ideas we have discovered through the "learn-by-your-mistake" method. Others we have discovered through books, articles, and newsletters (see, for example, Johnson et al. 1986).

Arrange groups efficiently. We simply leave desks in group clusters all day. Students face the front during instruction or independent activities, then rotate their desks to face each other for group work. If there is too

Photograph by Betty Clanton

This page: *The Park Lane Elementary cooperative learning support group meets monthly to share difficulties as well as successes. Shown here are some of the members (left to right): Marcia Easton and Bobbie Dunham (teachers), Ken Baden (principal), and Judy Stout, Judi Priest, and Claudia Edwards (teachers).*

Opposite page: *When forming cooperative learning groups, teachers of younger students may want to start small—with groups of two.*

much socializing during independent work, some teachers arrange desks so that group members are back to back. Other teachers may prefer students in rows but arrange desks so that group members are easily moved together. Teachers must keep experimenting until they find what works best in their classrooms. The best arrangement may vary from group to group and from year to year.

Determine group size. When in doubt, start small. Remember, the more members in a group the more input, but the more personalities with which to deal. Pairing students may be the easiest way for both teachers and students to begin cooperative learning. Teachers of younger students typically use groups of two, as these children are at a more self-centered stage of development. When there is one real "troublemaker" in the class, pair-

The bottom line for inducing students to work cooperatively: a base group must realize that its members will stay together until they can work well together.

ing him or her with just one other child eliminates excessive distraction. Teachers should experiment with different numbers until they find what works best for them.

Decide how long groups stay together. Our teachers in grades 3–5 have students stay in groups for four to six weeks, depending on the length of the unit studied. This amount of time seems to work well for secondary teachers, also. Kindergarten, transition, and 1st grade teachers often pair students for only one lesson, one day, or one week. A special education teacher reported that her goal was to get the same two students to make it through one short assignment per day for a week. The bottom line for inducing students to work cooperatively: a base group must realize that its members will stay together until they can work well together.

Form new groups. Each time new groups are formed, teachers should provide activities for students to get acquainted. These activities may include trading phone numbers, telling about themselves, discovering similarities and differences, and choosing team names. For most situations, we have found that groups composed of different ability levels work best for students. Nevertheless, even when classes are already arranged according to ability (honors classes, reading groups, learning disabilities), cooperative learning concepts are still viable.

Divide group responsibilities. Putting a different symbol on each desk is a handy way to divide group responsibilities. For instance, teachers can give each student a star of a different color. Today the Red Star reads, the Blue Star writes, and so on. With our primary students, we have each student read and explain only one problem or question on a page rather than the whole page. This system allows the teacher to determine whether each student understands the concept. It also avoids taking the amount of time that slower students may need to struggle through the entire page.

Encourage responsibility. Peer pressure works well for discipline. Teachers can give groups rewards for

achieving desired criteria. For example, teachers can make a chart with each group's team name listed. Every group that fulfills expectations—such as working quietly, praising members, bringing back completed homework, and returning office notes—earns a point. Then the teacher gives appropriate rewards for attaining a certain number of points.

Teachers should give teams, rather than individuals, classroom responsibilities: for instance, one group keeps the library organized this week; another group cleans the boards. This system works especially well with elementary children; it allows everyone to contribute rather than just the ones who finish first.

Each team can have a leader for the week. Each member shows his or her work, when completed, to the leader. The leader checks for completion and marks the assignment off by the student's name. This system can reduce the number of late papers and, in elementary classrooms, can even help get names on papers. Next week, a different group member can be the leader, so that everyone shares the responsibility.

Decide when to use cooperative learning. We always use cooperative learning when practicing a new concept, so we can make sure each student has a solid understanding. For instance, when the class is just beginning subtraction with regrouping or algebraic equations, each student must take turns solving the problem aloud, explaining each step. If the student is wrong, the teacher will catch the mistake immediately, rather than later when checking a page of 25 problems worked incorrectly.

Whenever an assignment requires discussion and higher-order thinking skills, cooperative learning is appropriate. It also provides a perfect setting for small-group brainstorming: quiet voices are not lost or shouted down in this situation, and there is less risk in sharing with two or three others than with the whole class. Cooperative learning also lends itself well to art activities, storytelling, and peer editing.

The Sound of Learning

A rise in the noise level of the classroom may pose a serious threat to the use of cooperative learning. Do not let it! "Using quiet voices" is a social skill that teachers should have students work on early and often—and quiet groups should be rewarded appropriately. Remember, monitoring determines the success of cooperative learning. When teachers listen to what is being discussed in groups, rather than to the general noise level, they can assess students' understanding and progress. What we hear during cooperative learning assignments is the sound of children learning—and that is what we are here for.

But it's almost impossible to implement alone. There must be someone with whom to share ideas, successes, and failures. So get a friend and start slowly. Read, share, experiment, and share and share and share!□

Authors' note: The authors gratefully acknowledge the contributions of Bobbie Dunham, Marcia Easton, Judi Priest, and Ken Baden to this article.

"Using quiet voices" is a social skill that teachers should have students work on early and often—and quiet groups should be rewarded appropriately.

Reference

Johnson, D.W., R.T. Johnson, and E.J. Holubec. (1986). *Circles of Learning: Cooperation in the Classroom*. Rev. ed. Edina, Minn.: Interaction Book Company.

Claudia Edwards and Judy Stout are classroom teachers at Park Lane Elementary School, 4912 Avalon, Lawton, OK 73501.

Research and Controversy

This section contains articles reviewing research on cooperative learning. It begins with a recent synthesis by Robert Slavin which, because of the selection criteria he insists upon, emphasizes his own findings. That piece is followed by an exchange between Slavin and Roger and David Johnson over the validity of some of the research cited by the Johnson brothers, along with a later article in which Slavin attempts to clarify their disagreements and stresses points on which they agree.

Next is an exchange between Alfie Kohn, who cites psychological research showing that extrinsic rewards decrease motivation and Slavin, who cites educational research in support of his contention that extrinsic rewards are essential to the effectiveness of cooperative learning. Ted Graves, executive editor of *Cooperative Learning* magazine, summarizes the controversy and suggests a balanced position.

A third dispute with Slavin is launched by Susan Allan, consultant on education of the gifted, who claims that Slavin's research reviews on ability grouping and cooperative learning are misleading because they cause educators to oppose separate programs for the gifted. Slavin and Bruce Joyce reply.

Educational Leadership 48 (Feb. 1991) 71-82

ROBERT E. SLAVIN

Synthesis of Research on Cooperative Learning

The use of cooperative learning strategies results in improvements both in the achievement of students and in the quality of their interpersonal relationships.

There was once a time when it was taken for granted that a quiet class was a learning class, when principals walked down the hall expecting to be able to hear a pin drop. Today, however, many schools are using programs that foster the hum of voices in classrooms. These programs, called *cooperative learning*, encourage students to discuss, debate, disagree, and ultimately to teach one another.

Cooperative learning has been suggested as the solution for an astonishing array of educational problems: it is often cited as a means of emphasizing thinking skills and increasing higher-order learning; as an alternative to ability grouping, remediation, or special education; as a means of improving race relations and acceptance of mainstreamed students; and as a way to prepare students for an increasingly collaborative work force. How many of these claims are justified? What effects do the various cooperative learning methods have on student achievement and other outcomes? Which forms of cooperative learning are most effective, and what components must be in place for cooperative learning to work?

To answer these questions, I've synthesized in this article the findings of studies of cooperative learning in elementary and secondary schools that have compared cooperative learning to traditionally taught control groups studying the same objectives over a period of at least four weeks (and up to a full school year or more). Here I present a brief summary of the effects of cooperative learning on achievement and noncognitive outcomes; for a more extensive review, see *Cooperative Learning: Theory, Research, and Practice* (Slavin 1990).

Cooperative Learning Methods

There are many quite different forms of cooperative learning, but all of them involve having students work in small groups or teams to help one another learn academic material. Cooperative learning usually supplements the teacher's instruction by giv-

Highlights of Research on Cooperative Learning

In cooperative learning, students work in small groups to help one another master academic material. There are many quite different forms of cooperative learning, and the effectiveness of cooperative learning (particularly for achievement outcomes) depends on the particular approach used.

• For enhancing student achievement, the most successful approaches have incorporated two key elements: group goals and individual accountability. That is, groups are rewarded based on the individual learning of all group members.

• When group goals and individual accountability are used, achievement effects of cooperative learning are consistently positive; 37 of 44 experimental/control comparisons of at least four weeks' duration have found significantly positive effects, and none have favored traditional methods.

• Achievement effects of cooperative learning have been found to about the same degree at all grade levels (2–12), in all major subjects, and in urban, rural, and suburban schools. Effects are equally positive for high, average, and low achievers.

• Positive effects of cooperative learning have been consistently found on such diverse outcomes as self-esteem, intergroup relations, acceptance of academically handicapped students, attitudes toward school, and ability to work cooperatively.

—Robert E. Slavin

ing students an opportunity to discuss information or practice skills originally presented by the teacher; sometimes cooperative methods require students to find or discover information on their own. Cooperative learning has been used—and investigated—in every imaginable subject in grades 2–12, and is increasingly used in college.

Small-scale laboratory research on cooperation dates back to the 1920s (see Deutsch 1949; Slavin 1977a); research on specific applications of cooperative learning to the classroom began in the early 1970s. At that time, four research groups, one in Israel and three in the U.S., began independently to develop and study cooperative learning methods in classroom settings.

Now researchers all over the world are studying practical applications of cooperative learning principles, and many cooperative learning methods have been evaluated in one or more experimental/control comparisons. The best evaluated of the cooperative models are described below (adapted from Slavin 1990). These include four Student Team Learning variations, Jigsaw, Learning Together, and Group Investigation.

Student Team Learning

Student Team Learning (STL) techniques were developed and researched at Johns Hopkins University. More than half of all experimental studies of practical cooperative learning methods involve STL methods.

All cooperative learning methods share the idea that students work together to learn and are responsible for one another's learning as well as their own. STL methods, in addition to this idea, emphasize the use of team goals and team success, which can only be achieved if all members of the team learn the objectives being taught. That is, in Student Team Learning the students' tasks are not to *do* something as a team but to *learn* something as a team.

Three concepts are central to all Student Team Learning methods: *team rewards, individual accountability,* and *equal opportunities for success.* Using STL techniques, teams earn certificates or other team rewards if they achieve above a designated criterion. The teams are not in competition to earn scarce rewards; all (or none) of the teams may achieve the criterion in a given week. *Individual accountability* means that the team's success depends on the individual learning of all team members. This focuses the activity of the team members on explaining concepts to one another and making sure that everyone on the team is ready for a quiz or other assessment that they will take without teammate help. *Equal opportunities for success* means that students contribute to their teams by improving over their own past performances. This ensures that high, average, and low achievers are equally challenged to do their best and that the contributions of all team members will be valued.

The findings of these experimental studies (summarized in this section) indicate that team rewards and individual accountability are essential elements for producing basic skills achievement (Slavin 1983a, 1983b, 1990). It is not enough to simply tell students to work together. They must have a reason to take one another's achievement seriously. Further, if students are rewarded for doing better than they have in the past, they will be more motivated to achieve than if they are rewarded based on their performance in comparison to others, because rewards for improvement make success neither too difficult nor too easy for students to achieve (Slavin 1980).

Four principal Student Team Learning methods have been extensively developed and researched. Two are general cooperative learning methods adaptable to most subjects and grade levels: Student Teams-Achievement Divisions (STAD) and Teams-Games-Tournament (TGT). The remaining two are comprehensive curriculums designed for use in particular subjects at particular grade levels: Team Assisted Individualization (TAI) for mathematics in grades 3–6 and Cooperative Integrated Reading and Composition (CIRC) for reading and writing instruction in grades 3–5.

Student Teams-Achievement Divisions (STAD)

In STAD (Slavin 1978, 1986), students are assigned to four-member learning teams mixed in performance level, sex, and ethnicity. The teacher presents a lesson, and then students work within their teams to make sure that all team members have mastered the lesson. Finally, all students take individual quizzes on the material, at which time they may *not* help one another.

Students' quiz scores are compared to their own past averages, and points are awarded based on the degree to which students can meet or exceed their own earlier performances. These points are then summed to form team scores, and teams that meet certain criteria earn certificates or other rewards. The whole cycle of activities, from teacher presentation to team

Cooperative learning usually supplements the teacher's instruction by giving students an opportunity to discuss information or practice skills originally presented by the teacher.

practice to quiz, usually takes three to five class periods.

STAD has been used in a wide variety of subjects, from mathematics to language arts and social studies. It has been used from grade 2 through college. STAD is most appropriate for teaching well-defined objectives with single right answers, such as mathematical computations and applications, language usage and mechanics, geography and map skills, and science facts and concepts.

Teams-Games-Tournament (TGT)

Teams-Games-Tournament (DeVries and Slavin 1978; Slavin 1986) was the first of the Johns Hopkins cooperative learning methods. It uses the same teacher presentations and teamwork as in STAD, but replaces the quizzes with weekly tournaments. In these, students compete with members of other teams to contribute points to their team scores. Students compete at three-person "tournament tables" against others with similar past records in mathematics. A "bumping" procedure changes table assignments to keep the competition fair. The winner at each tournament table brings the same number of points to his or her team, regardless of which table it is; this means that low achievers (competing with other low achievers) and high achievers (competing with other high achievers) have equal opportunities for success. As in STAD, high-performing teams earn certificates or other forms of team rewards. TGT is appropriate for the same types of objectives as STAD.

Team Assisted Individualization (TAI)

Team Assisted Individualization (TAI; Slavin et al. 1986) shares with STAD and TGT the use of four-member mixed ability learning teams and certificates for high-performing teams. But where STAD and TGT use a single pace of instruction for the class, TAI combines cooperative learning with individualized instruction. Also, where STAD and TGT apply to most subjects and grade levels, TAI is specifically designed to teach mathematics to students in grades 3–6 (or older students not ready for a full algebra course).

In TAI, students enter an individualized sequence according to a placement test and then proceed at their own rates. In general, team members work on different units. Teammates check each others' work against answer sheets and help one another with any problems. Final unit tests are taken without teammate help and are scored by student monitors. Each week, teachers total the number of units completed by all team members and give certificates or other team rewards to teams that exceed a criterion score based on the number of final tests passed, with extra points for perfect papers and completed homework.

Because students take responsibility for checking each others' work and managing the flow of materials, the teacher can spend most of the class time presenting lessons to small groups of students drawn from the various teams who are working at the same point in the mathematics sequence. For example, the teacher might call up a decimals group, present a lesson, and then send the students back to their teams to work on problems. Then the teacher might call the fractions group, and so on.

Cooperative Integrated Reading and Composition (CIRC)

The newest of the Student Team Learning methods is a comprehensive program for teaching reading and writing in the upper elementary grades called Cooperative Integrated Reading and Composition (CIRC) (Stevens et al. 1987). In CIRC, teachers use basal or literature-based readers and reading groups, much as in traditional reading programs. However, all students are assigned to teams composed of two pairs from two different reading groups. For example, a team might have two "Bluebirds" and two "Redbirds." While the teacher is working with one reading group, the paired students in the other groups are working on a series of cognitively engaging activities, including reading to one another, making predictions about how narrative stories will come out, summarizing stories to one another, writing responses to stories, and

practicing spelling, decoding, and vocabulary. If the reading class is not divided into homogeneous reading groups, all students in the teams work with one another. Students work as a total team to master "main idea" and other comprehension skills. During language arts periods, students engage in writing drafts, revising and editing one another's work, and preparing for "publication" of team books.

In most CIRC activities, students follow a sequence of teacher instruction, team practice, team pre-assessments, and quizzes. That is, students do not take the quiz until their teammates have determined that they are ready. Certificates are given to teams based on the average performance of all team members on all reading and writing activities.

Other Cooperative Learning Methods

Jigsaw

Jigsaw was originally designed by Elliot Aronson and his colleagues (1978). In Aronson's Jigsaw method, students are assigned to six-member teams to work on academic material that has been broken down into sections. For example, a biography might be divided into early life, first accomplishments, major setbacks, later life, and impact on history. Each team member reads his or her section. Next, members of different teams who have studied the same sections meet in "expert groups" to discuss their sections. Then the students return to their teams and take turns teaching their teammates about their sections. Since the only way students can learn sections other than their own is to listen carefully to their teammates, they are motivated to support and show interest in one another's work.

Slavin (1986) developed a modification of Jigsaw at Johns Hopkins University and then incorporated it in the Student Team Learning program. In this method, called Jigsaw II, students work in four- or five-member teams as in TGT and STAD. Instead of each student's being assigned a particular section of text, all students read a common narrative, such as a book

> **All cooperative learning methods share the idea that students work together to learn and are responsible for one another's learning as well as their own.**

chapter, a short story, or a biography. However, each student receives a topic (such as "climate" in a unit on France) on which to become an expert. Students with the same topics meet in expert groups to discuss them, after which they return to their teams to teach what they have learned to their teammates. Then students take individual quizzes, which result in team scores based on the improvement score system of STAD. Teams that meet preset standards earn certificates. Jigsaw is primarily used in social studies and other subjects where learning from text is important.

Learning Together
David Johnson and Roger Johnson at the University of Minnesota developed the Learning Together models of cooperative learning (Johnson and Johnson 1987). The methods they have researched involve students working on assignment sheets in four- or five-member heterogeneous groups. The groups hand in a single sheet and receive praise and rewards based on the group product. Their methods emphasize team-building activities before students begin working together and regular discussions within groups about how well they are working together.

Group Investigation
Group Investigation, developed by Shlomo Sharan and Yael Sharan at the University of Tel-Aviv, is a general classroom organization plan in which students work in small groups using cooperative inquiry, group discussion, and cooperative planning and projects (Sharan and Sharan 1976). In this method, students form their own two-to six-member groups. After choosing subtopics from a unit being studied by the entire class, the groups further break their subtopics into individual tasks and carry out the activities necessary to prepare group reports. Each group then makes a presentation or display to communicate its findings to the entire class.

Research on Cooperative Learning
Cooperative learning methods are among the most extensively evaluated alternatives to traditional instruction in use today. Outcome evaluations include:

- academic achievement,
- intergroup relations,
- mainstreaming,
- self-esteem,
- others.

Academic Achievement
More than 70 high-quality studies have evaluated various cooperative learning methods over periods of at least four weeks in regular elementary and secondary schools; 67 of these have measured effects on student achievement (see Slavin 1990). All these studies compared the effects of cooperative learning to those of traditionally taught control groups on measures of the same objectives pursued in all classes. Teachers and classes were either randomly assigned to cooperative or control conditions or matched on pretest achievement level and other factors.

Overall, of 67 studies of the achievement effects of cooperative learning, 41 (61 percent) found significantly greater achievement in cooperative than in control classes. Twenty-five (37 percent) found no differences, and in only one study did the control group outperform the experimental group. However, the effects of cooperative learning vary considerably according to the particular methods used. As noted earlier, two elements must be present if cooperative learning is to be effective: *group goals* and *individual accountability* (Slavin 1983a, 1983b, 1990). That is, groups must be working to achieve some goal or to earn rewards or recognition, and the success of the group must depend on the individual learning of every group member.

In studies of methods such as STAD, TGT, TAI, and CIRC, effects on achievement have been consistently positive; 37 out of 44 such studies (84 percent) found significant positive achievement effects. In contrast, only 4 of 23 studies (17 percent) lacking group goals and individual accountability found positive effects on student achievement. Two of these positive effects were found in studies of Group Investigation in Israel (Sharan et al. 1984; Sharan and Shachar 1988). In Group Investigation, students in each group are responsible for one unique part of the group's overall task, ensuring individual accountability. Then the group's overall performance is evaluated. Even though there are no specific group rewards, the group evaluation probably serves the same purpose.

Why are group goals and individual accountability so important? To understand this, consider the alternatives. In some forms of cooperative learning, students work together to complete a single worksheet or to solve one problem together. In such methods, there is little reason for more able students to take time to explain what is going on to their less able groupmates or to ask their opinions. When the group task is to *do* something, rather than to *learn* something, the participation of less able students may be seen as interference rather than help. It may be easier in this circumstance for students to give each other answers than to explain concepts or skills to one another.

In contrast, when the group's task

is to ensure that every group member *learns* something, it is in the interests of every group member to spend time explaining concepts to his or her groupmates. Studies of students' behaviors within cooperative groups have consistently found that the students who gain most from cooperative work are those who give and receive elaborated explanations (Webb 1985). In contrast, Webb found that giving and receiving answers without explanations were *negatively* related to achievement gain. What group goals and individual accountability do is to motivate students to give explanations and to take one another's learning seriously, instead of simply giving answers.

Cooperative learning methods generally work equally well for all types of students. While occasional studies find particular advantages for high or low achievers, boys or girls, and so on, the great majority find equal benefits for all types of students. Sometimes teachers or parents worry that cooperative learning will hold back high achievers. The research provides absolutely no support for this claim; high achievers gain from cooperative learning (relative to high achievers in traditional classes) just as much as do low and average achievers (see Slavin, this issue, p. 63).

Research on the achievement effects of cooperative learning has more often taken place in grades 3–9 than 10–12. Studies at the senior high school level are about as positive as

Cooperative learning methods have been equally successful in urban, rural, and suburban schools and with students of different ethnic groups.

those at earlier grade levels, but there is a need for more research at that level. Cooperative learning methods have been equally successful in urban, rural, and suburban schools and with students of different ethnic groups (although a few studies have found particularly positive effects for black students; see Slavin and Oickle 1981).

Among the cooperative learning methods, the Student Team Learning programs have been most extensively researched and most often found instructionally effective. Of 14 studies of STAD and closely related methods, 11 found significantly higher achievement for this method than for traditional instruction, and two found no differences. For example, Slavin and Karweit (1984) evaluated STAD over an entire school year in inner-city Philadelphia 9th grade mathematics classes. Student performance on a standardized mathematics test increased significantly more than in either a mastery learning group or a control group using the same materials. Substantial differences favoring STAD have been found in such diverse subjects as social studies (e.g., Allen and Van Sickle 1984), language arts (Slavin and Karweit 1981), reading comprehension (Stevens, Slavin, Farnish, and Madden 1988), mathematics (Sherman and Thomas 1986), and science (Okebukola 1985). Nine of 11 studies of TGT found similar results (DeVries and Slavin 1978).

The largest effects of Student Team Learning methods have been found in studies of TAI. Five of six studies found substantially greater learning of mathematics computations in TAI than in control classes, while one study found no differences (see Slavin 1985b). Experimental control differences were still substantial (though smaller) a year after the students were in TAI (Slavin and Karweit 1985). In mathematics concepts and applications, one of three studies (Slavin et al. 1984) found significantly greater gains in TAI than control methods, while two found no significant differences (Slavin and Karweit 1985).

In comparison with traditional control groups, three experimental studies of CIRC have found substantial positive

Cooperative learning methods are among the most extensively evaluated alternatives to traditional instruction in use in schools today.

effects on scores from standardized tests of reading comprehension, reading vocabulary, language expression, language mechanics, and spelling (Madden et al. 1986, Stevens et al. 1987, Stevens et al. 1990). Significantly greater achievement on writing samples was also found favoring the CIRC students in the two studies which assessed writing.

Other than STL methods, the most consistently successful model for increasing student achievement is Group Investigation (Sharan and Sharan 1976). One study of this method (Sharan et al. 1984) found that it increased the learning of English as a foreign language, while Sharan and Shachar (1988) found positive effects of Group Investigation on the learning of history and geography. A third study of only three weeks' duration (Sharan et al. 1980) also found positive effects on social studies achievement, particularly on higher-level concepts. The Learning Together methods (Johnson and Johnson 1987) have been found instructionally effective when they include the assignment of group grades based on the average of group members' individual quiz scores (e.g., Humphreys et al. 1982, Yager et al. 1985). Studies of the original Jigsaw method have not generally supported this approach (e.g., Moskowitz et al. 1983); but studies of Jigsaw II, which uses group goals and individual accountability, have shown positive effects (Mattingly and VanSickle 1990, Ziegler 1981).

Intergroup Relations

In the laboratory research on cooperation, one of the earliest and strongest findings was that people who cooperate learn to like one another (Slavin 1977b). Not surprisingly, the cooperative learning classroom studies have found quite consistently that students express greater liking for their classmates in general as a result of participating in a cooperative learning method (see Slavin 1983a, 1990). This is important in itself and even more important when the students have different ethnic backgrounds. After all, there is substantial evidence that, left alone, ethnic separateness in schools does not naturally diminish over time (Gerard and Miller 1975).

Social scientists have long advocated interethnic cooperation as a means of ensuring positive intergroup relations in desegregated settings. Contact Theory (Allport 1954), which is in the U.S. the dominant theory of intergroup relations, predicted that positive intergroup relations would arise from school desegregation if and only if students participated in cooperative, equal-status interaction sanctioned by the school. Research on cooperative learning methods has borne out the predictions of Contact Theory. These techniques emphasize cooperative, equal-status interaction between students of different ethnic backgrounds sanctioned by the school (Slavin 1985a).

In most of the research on intergroup relations, students were asked to list their best friends at the beginning of the study and again at the end. The number of friendship choices students made outside their own ethnic groups was the measure of intergroup relations.

Positive effects on intergroup relations have been found for STAD, TGT, TAI, Jigsaw, Learning Together, and Group Investigation models (Slavin 1985b). Two of these studies, one on STAD (Slavin 1979) and one on Jigsaw II (Ziegler 1981), included follow-ups of intergroup friendships several

months after the end of the studies. Both found that students who had been in cooperative learning classes still named significantly more friends outside their own ethnic groups than did students who had been in control classes. Two studies of Group Investigation (Sharan et al. 1984, Sharan and Shachar 1988) found that students' improved attitudes and behaviors toward classmates of different ethnic backgrounds extended to classmates who had never been in the same groups, and a study of TAI (Oishi 1983) found positive effects of this method on cross-ethnic interactions outside as well as in class. The U.S. studies of cooperative learning and intergroup relations involved black, white, and (in a few cases) Mexican-American students. A study of Jigsaw II by Ziegler (1981) took place in Toronto, where the major ethnic groups were Anglo-Canadians and children of recent European immigrants. The Sharan (Sharan et al. 1984, Sharan and Shachar 1988) studies of Group Investigation took place in Israel and involved friendships between Jews of both European and Middle Eastern backgrounds.

Mainstreaming

Although ethnicity is a major barrier to friendship, it is not so large as the one between physically or mentally handicapped children and their normal-progress peers. Mainstreaming, an unprecedented opportunity for handicapped children to take their place in the school and society, has created enormous practical problems for classroom teachers, and it often leads to social rejection of the handicapped children. Because cooperative learning methods have been successful in improving relationships across the ethnicity barrier—which somewhat resembles the barrier between mainstreamed and normal-progress students—these methods have also been applied to increase the acceptance of the mainstreamed student.

The research on cooperative learning and mainstreaming has focused on the academically handicapped child. In one study, STAD was used to attempt to

integrate students performing two years or more below the level of their peers into the social structure of the classroom. The use of STAD significantly reduced the degree to which the normal-progress students rejected their mainstreamed classmates and increased the academic achievement and self-esteem of all students, mainstreamed as well as normal-progress (Madden and Slavin 1983). Similar effects have been found for TAI (Slavin et al. 1984), and other research using cooperative teams has also shown significant improvements in relationships between mainstreamed academically handicapped students and their normal-progress peers (Ballard et al. 1977, Cooper et al. 1980).

In addition, one study in a self-contained school for emotionally disturbed adolescents found that the use of TGT increased positive interactions and friendships among students (Slavin 1977a). Five months after the study ended, these positive interactions were still found more often in the former TGT classes than in the control classes. In a study in a similar setting, Janke (1978) found that the emotionally disturbed students were more on-task, were better behaved, and had better attendance in TGT classes than in control classes.

In the laboratory research on cooperation, one of the earliest and strongest findings was that people who cooperate learn to like one another.

Self-Esteem

One of the most important aspects of a child's personality is his or her self-esteem. Several researchers working on cooperative learning techniques have found that these methods do increase students' self-esteem. These improvements in self-esteem have been found for TGT and STAD (Slavin 1990), for Jigsaw (Blaney et al. 1977), and for the three methods combined (Slavin and Karweit 1981). Improvements in student self-concepts have also been found for TAI (Slavin et al. 1984).

Other Outcomes

In addition to effects on achievement, positive intergroup relations, greater acceptance of mainstreamed students, and self-esteem, effects of cooperative learning have been found on a variety of other important educational outcomes. These include liking school, development of peer norms in favor of doing well academically, feelings of individual control over the student's own fate in school, and cooperativeness and altruism (see Slavin 1983a, 1990). TGT (DeVries and Slavin 1978) and STAD (Slavin 1978, Janke 1978) have been found to have positive effects on students' time-on-task. One study found that lower socioeconomic status students at risk of becoming delinquent who worked in cooperative groups in 6th grade had better attendance, fewer contacts with the police, and higher behavioral ratings by teachers in grades 7–11 than did control students (Hartley 1976). Another study implemented forms of cooperative learning beginning in kindergarten and continuing through the 4th grade (Solomon et al. 1990). This study found that the students who had been taught cooperatively were significantly higher than control students on measures of supportive, friendly, and prosocial behavior; were better at resolving conflicts; and expressed more support for democratic values.

Useful Strategies

Returning to the questions at the beginning of this article, we now see the usefulness of cooperative learning strategies for improving such diverse outcomes as student achievement at a

> **What group goals and individual accountability do is to motivate students to give explanations and to take one another's learning seriously, instead of simply giving answers.**

variety of grade levels and in many subjects, intergroup relations, relationships between mainstreamed and normal-progress students, and student self-esteem. Further, their widespread and growing use demonstrates that cooperative learning methods are practical and attractive to teachers. The history of the development, evaluation, and dissemination of cooperative learning is an outstanding example of the use of educational research to create programs that have improved the educational experience of thousands of students and will continue to affect thousands more.□

Author's note. This article was written under funding from the Office of Educational Research and Improvement, U.S. Department of Education (Grant No. OERI-R-117-R90002). However, any opinions expressed are mine and do not represent OERI positions or policy.

References

Allen, W.H., and R.L. Van Sickle. (1984). "Learning Teams and Low Achievers." *Social Education*: 60–64.

Allport, G. (1954). *The Nature of Prejudice*. Cambridge, Mass.: Addison-Wesley.

Aronson, E., N. Blaney, C. Stephan, J. Sikes, and M. Snapp. (1978). *The Jigsaw Classroom*. Beverly Hills, Calif.: Sage.

Ballard, M., L. Corman, J. Gottlieb, and M. Kauffman. (1977). "Improving the Social Status of Mainstreamed Retarded Children." *Journal of Educational Psychology* 69: 605–611.

Blaney, N.T., S. Stephan, D. Rosenfeld, E. Aronson, and J. Sikes. (1977). "Interdependence in the Classroom: A Field Study." *Journal of Educational Psychology* 69: 121–128.

Cooper, L., D.W. Johnson, R. Johnson, and F. Wilderson. (1980). "Effects of Cooperative, Competitive, and Individualistic Experiences on Interpersonal Attraction Among Heterogeneous Peers." *Journal of Social Psychology* 111: 243–252.

Deutsch, M. (1949). "A Theory of Cooperation and Competition." *Human Relations* 2: 129–152.

DeVries, D.L., and R.E. Slavin. (1978). "Teams-Games-Tournament (TGT): Review of Ten Classroom Experiments." *Journal of Research and Development in Education* 12: 28–38.

Gerard, H.B., and N. Miller. (1975). *School Desegregation: A Long-Range Study*. New York: Plenum.

Hartley, W. (1976). *Prevention Outcomes of Small Group Education with School Children: An Epidemiologic Follow-Up of the Kansas City School Behavior Project*. Kansas City: University of Kansas Medical Center.

Humphreys, B., R. Johnson, and D.W. Johnson. (1982). "Effects of Cooperative, Competitive, and Individualistic Learning on Students' Achievement in Science Class." *Journal of Research in Science Teaching* 19: 351–356.

Janke, R. (April 1978). "The Teams-Games-Tournament (TGT) Method and the Behavioral Adjustment and Academic Achievement of Emotionally Impaired Adolescents." Paper presented at the annual convention of the American Educational Research Association, Toronto.

Johnson, D.W., and R.T. Johnson. (1987). *Learning Together and Alone*. 2nd ed. Englewood Cliffs, N.J.: Prentice-Hall.

Madden, N.A., and R.E. Slavin. (1983). "Cooperative Learning and Social Acceptance of Mainstreamed Academically Handicapped Students." *Journal of Special Education* 17: 171–182.

Madden, N.A., R.J. Stevens, and R.E. Slavin. (1986). *A Comprehensive Cooperative Learning Approach to Elementary Reading and Writing: Effects on Student Achievement*. Report No. 2. Baltimore, Md.: Center for Research on Elementary and Middle Schools, Johns Hopkins University.

Mattingly, R.M., and R.L. VanSickle. (1990). *Jigsaw II in Secondary Social Studies: An Experiment*. Athens, Ga.: University of Georgia.

Moskowitz, J.M., J.H. Malvin, G.A. Schaeffer, and E. Schaps. (1983). "Evaluation of a Cooperative Learning Strategy." *Ameri-*

can *Educational Research Journal* 20: 687–696.

Oishi, S. (1983). "Effects of Team-Assisted Individualization in Mathematics on Cross-Race Interactions of Elementary School Children." Doctoral diss., University of Maryland.

Okebukola, P.A. (1985). "The Relative Effectiveness of Cooperative and Competitive Interaction Techniques in Strengthening Students' Performance in Science Classes." *Science Education* 69: 501–509.

Sharan, S., and C. Shachar. (1988). *Language and Learning in the Cooperative Classroom*. New York: Springer.

Sharan, S., and Y. Sharan. (1976). *Small-group Teaching*. Englewood Cliffs, N.J.: Educational Technology Publications.

Sharan, S., R. Hertz-Lazarowitz, and Z. Ackerman. (1980). "Academic Achievement of Elementary School Children in Small-group vs. Whole Class Instruction." *Journal of Experimental Education* 48: 125–129.

Sharan, S., P. Kussell, R. Hertz-Lazarowitz, Y. Bejarano, S. Raviv, and Y. Sharan. (1984). *Cooperative Learning in the Classroom: Research in Desegregated Schools*. Hillsdale, N.J.: Erlbaum.

Sherman, L.W., and M. Thomas. (1986). "Mathematics Achievement in Cooperative Versus Individualistic Goal-structured High School Classrooms." *Journal of Educational Research* 79: 169–172.

Slavin, R.E. (1977a). "A Student Team Approach to Teaching Adolescents with Special Emotional and Behavioral Needs." *Psychology in the Schools* 14: 77–84.

Slavin, R.E. (1977b). "Classroom Reward Structure: An Analytical and Practical Review." *Review of Educational Research* 47: 633–650.

Slavin, R.E. (1978). "Student Teams and Achievement Divisions." *Journal of Research and Development in Education* 12: 39–49.

Slavin, R.E. (1979). "Effects of Biracial Learning Teams on Cross-Racial Friendships." *Journal of Educational Psychology* 71: 381–387.

Slavin, R.E. (1983a). *Cooperative Learning*. New York: Longman.

Slavin, R.E. (1983b). "When Does Cooperative Learning Increase Student Achieve-

ment?" *Psychological Bulletin* 94: 429–445.

Slavin, R.E. (March 1985a). "Cooperative Learning: Applying Contact Theory in Desegregated Schools." *Journal of Social Issues* 41: 45–62.

Slavin, R.E. (1985b). "Team Assisted Individualization: A Cooperative Learning Solution for Adaptive Instruction in Mathematics." In *Adapting Instruction to Individual Differences*, edited by M.Wang and H. Walberg. Berkeley, Calif.: McCutchan.

Slavin, R.E. (1986). *Using Student Team Learning*. 3rd ed. Baltimore, Md.: Center for Research on Elementary and Middle Schools, Johns Hopkins University.

Slavin, R.E. (1990). *Cooperative Learning: Theory, Research, and Practice*. Englewood Cliffs, N.J.: Prentice-Hall.

Slavin, R.E. (February 1991). "Are Cooperative Learning and 'Untracking' Harmful to the Gifted?" *Educational Leadership* 48: 63–74.

Slavin, R.E., and N. Karweit. (1981). "Cognitive and Affective Outcomes of an Intensive Student Team Learning Experience." *Journal of Experimental Education* 50: 29–35.

Slavin, R.E., and N. Karweit. (1984). "Mastery Learning and Student Teams: A Factorial Experiment in Urban General Mathematics Classes." *American Educational Research Journal* 21: 725–736.

Slavin, R.E., and N.L. Karweit. (1985). "Effects of Whole-Class, Ability Grouped, and Individualized Instruction on Mathematics Achievement." *American Educational Research Journal* 22: 351–367.

Slavin, R.E., M. Leavey, and N.A. Madden. (1984). "Combining Cooperative Learning and Individualized Instruction: Effects on Student Mathematics Achievement Attitudes and Behaviors." *Elementary School Journal* 84: 409–422.

Slavin, R.E., M.B. Leavey, and N.A. Madden. (1986). *Team Accelerated Instruction-Mathematics*. Watertown, Mass.: Mastery Education Corporation.

Slavin, R.E., N.A. Madden, and M.B. Leavey. (1984). "Effects of Team Assisted Individualization on the Mathematics Achievement of Academically Handicapped and Nonhandicapped Students." *Journal of Educational Psychology* 76: 813–819.

Slavin, R.E., and E. Oickle. (1981). "Effects

of Cooperative Learning Teams on Student Achievement and Race Relations: Treatment x Race Interactions." *Sociology of Education* 54: 174–180.

Solomon, D., M. Watson, E. Schaps, V. Battistich, and J. Solomon. (1990). "Cooperative Learning as Part of a Comprehensive Classroom Program Designed to Promote Prosocial Development." In *Current Research on Cooperative Learning*, edited by S. Sharan, New York: Praeger.

Stevens, R.J., N.A. Madden, R.E. Slavin, and A.M. Farnish. (1987). "Cooperative Integrated Reading and Composition: Two Field Experiments." *Reading Research Quarterly* 22: 433–454.

Stevens, R.J., R.E. Slavin, and A.M. Farnish. (April 1990). "A Cooperative Learning Approach to Elementary Reading and Writing Instruction: Long-Term Effects." Paper presented at the annual convention of the American Educational Research Association, Boston.

Stevens, R.J., R.E. Slavin, A.M. Farnish, and N.A. Madden. (April 1988). "The Effects of Cooperative Learning and Direct Instruction in Reading Comprehension Strategies on Main Idea Identification." Paper presented at the annual convention of the American Educational Research Association, New Orleans.

Webb, N. (1985). "Student Interaction and Learning in Small Groups: A Research Summary." In *Learning to Cooperate, Cooperating to Learn*, edited by R. Slavin, S. Sharan, S. Kagan, R. Hertz-Lazarowitz, C. Webb, and R. Schmuck. New York: Plenum.

Yager, S., D.W. Johnson, and R.T. Johnson. (1985). "Oral Discussion, Group-to-Individual Transfer, and Achievement in Cooperative Learning Groups." *Journal of Educational Psychology* 77: 60–66.

Ziegler, S. (1981). "The Effectiveness of Cooperative Learning Teams for Increasing Cross-Ethnic Friendship: Additional Evidence." *Human Organization* 40: 264–268.

Robert E. Slavin is Director of the Elementary School Program, Center for Research on Effective Schooling for Disadvantaged Students, The Johns Hopkins University, 3505 N. Charles St., Baltimore, MD 21218.

Educational Leadership 46 (Oct. 1988) 31-33

ROBERT E. SLAVIN

Cooperative Learning and Student Achievement

Remarkable claims are made about cooperative learning, many of them true, but the research tells us that to produce achievement gains, these methods must include both a group goal and individual accountability.

In recent years, cooperative learning has been proposed as a solution to a staggering array of problems. Cooperative learning methods have been offered as an alternative to ability grouping, special programs for the gifted, Chapter I pull-outs, and special education. They have been suggested as a means of introducing higher-level skills into the curriculum, of ensuring students an adequate level of basic skills, of mainstreaming academically handicapped students, and of giving students the collaborative skills necessary in an increasingly interdependent society. Further, cooperative learning methods have been proposed as a major component of bilingual and ESL programs and as a way to improve relationships among students of different racial or ethnic backgrounds.

There is evidence that cooperative learning can in fact, under certain circumstances, accomplish many of these goals. However, I am becoming increasingly concerned about a widespread belief that *all* forms of cooperative learning are instructionally effective. This is emphatically not the case.

Two Essential Conditions

Two conditions are essential if the achievement effects of cooperative learning are to be realized. First, the cooperating groups must have a *group goal* that is important to them. For example, groups may be working to earn certificates or other recognition, to receive a few minutes extra of re-

I am becoming increasingly concerned about a widespread belief that *all* forms of cooperative learning are instructionally effective. This is emphatically not the case.

cess, or to earn bonus points on their grades (although I am philosophically opposed to having grades largely determined by team performance). Second, the success of the group must depend on the individual learning of all group members. That is, there must be *individual accountability* as well as group accountability. For example, groups might be rewarded based on the average of their members' individual quiz scores.

We can only hypothesize reasons that group goals and individual accountability are essential to the achievement effects of cooperative learning. Some plausible explanations are that group goals are necessary to motivate students to help one another learn; they give students a stake in one another's success. Without group goals, students are not likely to engage in the elaborate explanations that have been found to be essential to the achievement effects of cooperative learning (Webb 1985). Further, group goals may help students overcome their reluctance to ask for help or provide help to one another; that is, without an overriding group goal, they may be embarrassed to ask for

	Median Effect Size	No. of Studies
Group Goals and Individual Accountability	+.30	32
Group Goals Only	+.04	8
Individual Accountability Only (Task Specialization)	+.12	9
No Group Goals or Individual Accountability	+.05	2

Note: Effect sizes are the difference between cooperative learning and control classes on achievement measures divided by the post-test standard deviation. Only methodologically adequate studies of at least four weeks' duration are included.

Fig. 1. Achievement Effects of Alternative Forms of Cooperative Learning

or offer help. In addition, without individual accountability, one or two group members may do all the work; group members perceived to be low achievers may be ignored if they contribute ideas or ask for help.

Achievement Effects of Various Methods

Figure 1 presents data from a recent review of the cooperative learning literature (Slavin 1988). In the studies from which the figure was derived, cooperative learning groups were compared to randomly selected or matched control groups on fair measures of the objectives pursued equally by both groups. Study durations were at least four weeks, with a median length of 10 weeks.

Figure 1 shows that the success of cooperative learning in increasing student achievement depends substantially on the provision of group goals and individual accountability. Methods that incorporate group goals and individual accountability include Student Teams-Achievement Divisions (Slavin 1986), Teams-Games-Tournament (DeVries and Slavin 1978), Cooperative Integrated Reading and Composition (Stevens et al. 1987), and Team Assisted Individualization–Mathematics (Slavin et al. 1984).

In contrast to the relatively positive effects of methods that use both group goals and individual accountability, those that use group goals but not individual accountability have been ineffective in increasing student achievement. For example, in Johnson and Johnson's (1987) Learning Together methods, students work together to complete a single worksheet and are praised, rewarded, and/or graded on the basis of this common worksheet. On fair measures of achievement these methods have produced no better achievement than individualistic or traditional methods (e.g., Johnson et al. 1978). Two studies did find positive achievement effects for a form of this approach in which students were graded not on the basis of one worksheet, but on the average of individual quiz scores, which ensures individual accountability (Humphreys et al. 1982,

Yager et al. 1986). However, it is important to note that these studies are highly artificial experiments in which teachers did not present lessons to students. Rather, teachers only helped individuals with worksheets, so that in the "individualistic" control groups students had no resources other than the worksheets to help them understand the material.

Another major category of cooperative learning methods uses task specialization, which means that each student has a unique task within an overall group objective. For example, Jigsaw Teaching (Aronson et al. 1978) assigns each student a topic on which he or she is to become an "expert." This method has not generally been instructionally effective. A much more effective form of cooperative learning that uses task specialization is Group Investigation (Sharan and Shachar in press), in which students take on subtasks within an overall group task. In contrast to Jigsaw, Group Investigation bases individuals' evaluations on the group's product or report, so this method may in actuality be an instance of group goals and individual accountability.

Finally, studies of methods that provide neither group goals nor individual accountability find few achievement benefits for this approach. One example is the Groups of Four mathematics program in which students work together to solve complex math problems (Burns 1981).

Comparing the achievement effects of the various cooperative learning

methods, we see that those incorporating both group goals and individual accountability are considerably more effective than other methods (see, for example, the following reviews of the literature: Slavin 1983a, b; Davidson 1985; Newmann and Thompson 1987). The misconception that all forms of cooperative learning are equally effective can perhaps be attributed to a meta-analysis by Johnson and colleagues (1981) that claimed that 122 studies supported the effectiveness of cooperative learning in all its forms. However, this meta-analysis was not restricted to *school* achievement; it included playing golf, card playing, swimming, block stacking, solving mazes, and other performance outcomes. Most of these were laboratory studies of a few hours' duration, and most allowed the groups to work together on the task that constituted the outcome measure while the "individualistic" students had to work alone. Obviously, individuals will score better when they can give each other answers than when they work in isolation, but they may or may not *learn* more from the experience (see Slavin 1984).

Consider the Research

I'm delighted to see the enthusiasm with which school districts have embraced cooperative learning. Regardless of its effects on achievement, cooperative learning has many positive effects, for example, on self-esteem, intergroup relations, and the ability to work with others (see Slavin 1983a). However, when schools adopt cooperative learning methods with the primary intention of increasing student achievement, they must take the research into account. There is no reason to expect that if teachers simply allow students to work together or reward them based on a single group product or task, they will learn more than will students taught traditionally.

Future research may identify effective forms of cooperative learning that do not require group goals and individual accountability; but schools that use such programs now must do so with a clear understanding that, at present, nothing in the literature promises that they will increase student achievement.□

References

Aronson, E., N. Blaney, C. Stephan, J. Sikes, and M. Snapp. *The Jigsaw Classroom.* Beverly Hills, Calif.: Sage, 1978.

Burns, M. "Groups of Four: Solving the Management Problem." *Learning* (September 1981): 46-51.

Davidson, N. "Small-Group Learning and Teaching in Mathematics: A Selective Review of the Research." In *Learning to Cooperate, Cooperating to Learn*, edited by R. E. Slavin, S. Sharan, S. Kagan, R. Hertz-Lazarowitz, C. Webb, and R. Schmuck. New York: Plenum, 1985.

DeVries, D.L., and R. E. Slavin. "Teams-Games-Tournament (TGT): Review of Ten Classroom Experiments." *Journal of Research and Development in Education* 12 (1978): 28-38.

Humphreys, B., R. Johnson, and D. W. Johnson. "Effects of Cooperative, Competitive, and Individualistic Learning on Students' Achievement in Science Class." *Journal of Research in Science Teaching* 19 (1982): 351-356.

Johnson, D. W., and R. T. Johnson. *Learning Together and Alone.* 2nd ed. Englewood Cliffs, N.J.: Prentice Hall, 1987.

Johnson, D. W., R. T. Johnson, and L. Scott. "The Effects of Cooperative and Individualized Instruction on Student Attitudes and Achievement." *Journal of Social Psychology* 104 (1978): 207-216.

Johnson, D. W., G. Maruyama, R. Johnson, D. Nelson, and L. Skon. "Effects of Cooperative, Competitive, and Individualistic Goal Structures on Achievement: A Meta-Analysis." *Psychological Bulletin* 89 (1981): 47-62.

Newmann, F. M., and J. Thompson. *Effects of Cooperative Learning on Achievement in Secondary Schools: A Summary of Research.* Madison, Wis.: University of Wisconsin, National Center on Effective Secondary Schools, 1987.

Sharan, S., and H. Shachar. *Language and Learning in the Cooperative Classroom.* New York: Springer-Verlag, in press.

Slavin, R. E. *Cooperative Learning.* New York: Longman, 1983a.

Slavin, R. E. "When Does Cooperative Learning Increase Student Achievement?" *Psychological Bulletin* 94 (1983b): 429-445.

Slavin, R. E. "Meta-Analysis in Education: How Has It Been Used?" *Educational Researcher* 13, 8 (1984): 6-15, 24-27.

Slavin, R. E. *Using Student Team Learning.* 3rd ed. Baltimore: Center for Research on Elementary and Middle Schools, Johns Hopkins University, 1986.

Slavin, R. E. "Cooperative Learning and Student Achievement." In *School and Classroom Organization*, edited by R. E. Slavin. Hillsdale, N.J.: Erlbaum, 1988.

Slavin, R. E., N. A. Madden, and M. Leavey. "Effects of Team Assisted Individualization on the Mathematics Achievement of Academically Handicapped Students and Nonhandicapped Students." *Journal of Educational Psychology* 76 (1984): 813-819.

Stevens, R. J., N. A. Madden, R. E. Slavin, and A. M. Farnish. "Cooperative Integrated Reading and Composition: Two Field Experiments." *Reading Research Quarterly* 22 (1987): 433-454.

Webb, N. "Student Interaction and Learning in Small Groups: A Research Summary." In *Learning to Cooperate, Cooperating to Learn*, edited by R. E. Slavin, S. Sharan, S. Kagan, R. Hertz-Lazarowitz, C. Webb, and R. Schmuck, 147-172. New York: Plenum, 1985.

Yager, S., R. T. Johnson, D. W. Johnson, B. Snider. "The Impact of Group Processing on Achievement in Cooperative Learning." *Journal of Social Psychology* 126 (1986): 389-397.

Author's note: This paper was written under funding from the Office of Educational Research and Improvement, U.S. Department of Education (No. OERI-G-86-0006). However, any opinions expressed are mine and do not represent OERI positions or policy.

Robert E. Slavin is Director, Elementary School Program, Center for Research on Elementary and Middle Schools, The Johns Hopkins University, 3505 N. Charles St., Baltimore, MD 21218.

Educational Leadership 46 (April 1989) 80-81

DAVID W. JOHNSON AND ROGER T. JOHNSON

Toward a *Cooperative* Effort: A Response to Slavin

In his recent article, Slavin inaccurately depicts our approach to cooperative learning and omits crucial information about our research.

We would like to clarify Robert Slavin's description of our approach to cooperative learning and of our research in his recent article, "Cooperative Learning and Student Achievement" (October 1988 issue). He describes our approach as having groups of students complete a single worksheet while the teacher rewards them on the basis of the single product. Contrary to what Slavin stated, we do *not* recommend this procedure, *except* under a very special set of conditions.

Five Basic Elements

Our approach to cooperative learning emphasizes five basic elements that must be included within each lesson:

- *positive interdependence*— students must believe that they are responsible for both their own learning and the learning of the other members of their group;

- *face-to-face promotive interaction*—students must have the opportunity to explain what they are learning to each other and to help each other understand and complete assignments;

- *individual accountability*—each student must demonstrate mastery of the assigned work;

Our approach to cooperative learning emphasizes five basic elements that must be included within each lesson.

- *social skills*—each student must communicate effectively, provide leadership for the group's work, build and maintain trust among group members, and resolve conflicts within the group constructively;

- *group processing*—groups must stop periodically and assess how well they are working and how their effectiveness may be improved (Johnson 1970; Johnson and Johnson 1975, 1987).

Further, Slavin goes on to state that our research does not provide evidence that cooperative learning produces higher achievement than individualistic or traditional learning, citing one study to support his claim. He discounts two of our other studies based on a misrepresentation of the individualistic condition: contrary to what Slavin states, the material *was* taught in the individualistic conditions.

93

Controlled Studies

What Slavin does not tell the reader is that over the past 12 years we have published 43 studies comparing the relative impact of cooperative, competitive, and individualistic learning on achievement. In our studies, primarily field-experimental, students were randomly assigned to conditions, teachers were rotated across conditions, the same curriculum was used in all conditions, and the conditions were observed daily to ensure that they were appropriately implemented. These criteria make them some of the best controlled studies in the field. They took place in primary (8 studies), intermediate (20 studies), junior high (7 studies), high school (4 studies), and college (4 studies) classes. They were conducted on a wide variety of subject areas (some were conducted on more than one subject area): math (11 studies), social studies (11 studies), science (10 studies), reading and language arts (6 studies), geography/mapping (4 studies), physical education (2 studies), music education (1 study), and foreign languages (1 study).

Of our 43 studies, 10 compared cooperative and competitive learning; from these studies effect sizes weighted (1) to control for the number of findings in the study and (2) to minimize the variance of the effect size could be computed (see fig. 1). The effect size is 0.95. The effect size for the 6 studies that lasted for less than two weeks is 0.92, and the effect size for the 4 studies that lasted for two weeks or more is 1.01. The weighted effect size for the 29 studies that compared cooperative and individualistic learning is 1.02. Of the 29 studies, for the 9 that lasted less than two weeks, the effect size is 0.98; and for the 20 that lasted for two weeks or more, the effect size is 1.05. For 4 studies, no effect size could be computed, as a result of nonexperimental design or small sample size. The results of all 4 studies favor cooperation over competitive or individualistic learning (voting method).

Slavin criticized our 1981 meta-analysis because we included all available studies *before* we conducted subanal-yses on the methodologically superior studies. He insists that physical education and the use of manipulatives (such as blocks and mazes) in math are not legitimate educational tasks. We disagree. Learning how to swim or play golf, furthermore, represent "procedural learning," whereby students not only have to learn conceptually the nature of swimming but also have to be able to perform it. Since most adult learning is of a procedural nature, studying procedural learning in the schools is an important enterprise.

A Fatal Flaw

Slavin's summary of the research on cooperative learning and achievement suffers from a fatal flaw. He takes the position that field-experimental studies that lasted *less* than 20 days—but did test theoretical propositions, include random assignment of students to conditions, rotate teachers across conditions, use the same curriculum in all conditions, check daily to ensure that the independent variable was being operationalized adequately, and use a well-conceptualized and well-defined control condition—are inferior to nontheoretical curriculum evaluation studies that *did* last 20 days but did not meet these criteria for experimental design. This emphasis on length of operationalization over methodological quality does the field a disservice.

A Cooperative Effort

It is time researchers stop competing over whose cooperative learning method is best and start focusing on conducting theoretical research that enhances our knowledge of the basic dynamics of cooperative efforts. There is room for all approaches. We invite Slavin to join in a cooperative effort to better understand the conditions under which cooperative, competitive, and individualistic efforts are effective and *how* and *why* cooperative efforts are so powerful.□

References

Johnson, D.W. (1970). *Social Psychology of Education*. New York: Holt, Rinehart, and Winston.

Johnson, D.W., and R. Johnson. (1975 and 1987). *Learning Together and Alone: Cooperative, Competitive, and Individualistic Learning*. Englewood Cliffs, N.J.: Prentice-Hall.

David W. Johnson is Professor of Educational Psychology, and **Roger T. Johnson** is Professor of Curriculum and Instruction, both at the University of Minnesota, Cooperative Learning Center, 202 Pattee Hall, 150 Pillsbury Dr., S.E., Minneapolis, MN 55455. For a list of the meta-analysis references, contact the Cooperative Learning Center.

Slavin Replies

David and Roger Johnson are among the most articulate spokespersons for cooperative learning, and I have few problems with their methods or with the five "basic elements" they propose. I do, however, have serious differences with them on what the research says. They claim effects of cooperative learning on achievement that are larger than the effects typical of one-to-one tutoring. I wish they were right. However, the research they cite to support this claim has little or nothing to do with classroom practice. Most of it shows that, for example, two or more students can solve a maze or figure out a math problem better than one student can. This is both obvious and uninteresting. In the Johnsons' own research, at least one achievement measure usually involves scores on a worksheet or test that the cooperative groups completed *together* but that the competitive or individualistic students took by themselves. Of course the cooperative groups do better; if nothing else, students can tell each other the answers.

What is important for classroom practice, however, is how much *individual* students learn from a cooperative experience, as shown on a test they take by themselves. These are the only data considered in my reviews. I also think few educators would disagree with my contention that studies of less than four weeks' duration have little direct relevance for practice. Cooperative learning still succeeds under these more stringent and meaningful conditions, but the effects are (obviously) smaller and appear only when the methods incorporate group goals and individual accountability.

Robert E. Slavin is Director, Elementary School Program, Center for Research on Elementary and Middle Schools, The Johns Hopkins University, 3505 N. Charles St., Baltimore, MD 21218.

Educational Leadership 47 (Dec. 1989-Jan. 1990) 52-54

ROBERT E. SLAVIN

Research on Cooperative Learning: Consensus and Controversy

Researchers agree that cooperative learning can produce positive effects on achievement but disagree on the conditions under which the approach is effective.

Cooperative learning is one of the most thoroughly researched of all instructional methods. In a recent review (Slavin 1989a), I identified 60 studies that contrasted the achievement outcomes of cooperative learning and traditional methods in elementary and secondary schools. To be included in my review, studies had to have lasted at least four weeks, and experimental and control classes had to take the same achievement tests under the same conditions. Using different inclusion criteria, Johnson and colleagues (1981) identified 122 achievement studies. Most of these studies also measured many outcomes in addition to achievement.

With so many studies, one would imagine that a consensus would emerge about the nature and size of the effects of cooperative learning; and, in fact, the areas of agreement among cooperative learning researchers far outweigh the areas of disagreement. Yet there remain several key points of controversy among researchers and reviewers that concern the conditions under which cooperative learning is instructionally effective. This article briefly summarizes the main areas of consensus and controversy in research on cooperative learning.

The areas of agreement among cooperative learning researchers far outweigh the areas of disagreement.

Cooperative Learning and Student Achievement

Consensus. There is wide agreement among reviewers of the cooperative learning literature that cooperative methods can and usually do have a positive effect on student achievement. Further, there is almost as strong a consensus that the achievement effects are not seen for all forms of cooperative learning but depend on two essential features, at least at the elementary and secondary levels. One of these features is *group goals*, or positive interdependence: the cooperative groups must work together to earn recognition, grades, rewards, and other indicators of group success. Simply asking students to work together is not enough. The second essential feature is *individual accountability*: the group's success must depend on the individual learning of all group members. For example, group success might depend on the sum of members' quiz scores or on evaluation of a report in which each group member contributed his or her own chapter. In contrast, studies of methods in which students work together to prepare a single worksheet or project without differentiated tasks hardly ever find achievement benefits (Slavin 1989a).

The degree of consensus on the achievement effects of cooperative learning methods that use group goals and individual accountability is considerable. I am aware of four full-scale reviews by different authors on this topic. My own reviews (Slavin 1983, 1989a, in press) have focused on elementary and secondary schools. Reviews by the Johnsons (Johnson et al. 1981) have included all levels, including college. Newmann and Thompson (1987) have focused on secondary schools (middle, junior, and high schools), and Davidson (1985) has reviewed research on cooperative learning in mathematics.

The findings of the four reviews were similar. My own concluded, "Cooperative learning can be an effective means of increasing student achievement, but only if group goals and individual accountability are incorporated in the cooperative methods" (Slavin 1989a, p. 151). Newmann and Thompson (1987, pp. 11–12) came to similar conclusions:

A review of the research on cooperative learning and achievement in grades 7–12 produced 27 reports of high-quality studies, including 37 comparisons of cooperative versus control methods. Twenty-five (68 percent) of these favored a cooperative learning method at the .05 level of significance. . . . The pattern of results supports the importance not only of a cooperative task structure, but also of group rewards, of individual accountability, and probably of group competition as well.

Davidson (1985, p. 224) wrote: "If the term *achievement* refers to computational skills, simple concepts, and simple application problems, the studies at the elementary and secondary levels support Slavin's (1983) conclusions. . . . 'Cooperative learning methods that use group rewards and individual accountability consistently increase student achievement more than control methods in . . . elementary and secondary classrooms.' " All four reviews mentioned group goals and individual

accountability as essential elements of cooperative learning.

Controversy. While no reviewer has yet expressed doubt that there is a broad set of conditions under which cooperative learning will increase student achievement, there is controversy about the specific conditions under which positive effects will be found.

One focus of controversy has been a debate between David and Roger Johnson and me that has more to do with different views on what constitutes adequate research than on questions of the essential elements of cooperative learning. The main elements of this debate have been covered in earlier issues of *Educational Leadership* (see Slavin 1988, Johnson and Johnson 1989, Slavin 1989b).

In addition to the controversy between the Johnsons and me, several other issues have been raised by various writers and reviewers. One issue is whether cooperative learning is effective at all grade levels. Newmann and Thompson (1987) question whether cooperative learning is effective in senior high school (grades 10–12). There is ample evidence that these methods are instructionally effective in grades 2–9, but relatively few studies examine grades 10–12. More research is needed in this area.

> **There is ample evidence that cooperative methods are instructionally effective in grades 2–9, but relatively few studies examine grades 10–12.**

Another issue is the effects of cooperative learning at the college level. Again, there are relatively few studies at this level, and the results are not as consistent as those from elementary and junior high/middle schools. However, there are several examples of positive achievement effects of cooperative learning in senior high school and college settings (see, for example, Sherman and Thomas 1986, Fraser et al. 1977).

Another question being debated is the appropriateness of cooperative learning for higher-order conceptual learning. Most cooperative learning studies have focused on basic skills (mathematics, language arts, reading), but several have successfully taught such higher-order skills as creative writing (Stevens et al. 1987) and identification of main idea and inference in reading (Stevens et al. 1988). Studies of Sharan's Group Investigation method (see, for example, Sharan et al. 1980) and of the Johnsons' constructive controversy methods (see, for example, Smith et al. 1981) have reported particularly strong effects on higher-order understanding in social studies.

Davidson (1985) has questioned whether group goals and individual accountability are necessary at the college level, and there is some evidence that they may not be. Studies of pair learning of text comprehension strategies by Dansereau (1988), as well as some of the mathematics studies cited by Davidson (1985), provide examples of successful use of cooperative learning at the college level without group goals or individual accountability.

Outcomes Other than Achievement
In areas other than achievement, there is even broader consensus about the effects of cooperative learning. One of the most consistent of these is the effect on intergroup relations (see Slavin 1985, Johnson et al. 1983). When students of different racial or ethnic backgrounds work together toward a common goal, they gain in liking and respect for one another. Cooperative learning also improves the social acceptance of mainstreamed

Outcomes seen in many studies of cooperative learning include gains in self-esteem, liking of school, time-on-task, and attendance.

academically handicapped students by their classmates (Madden and Slavin 1983, Johnson et al. 1983), as well as increasing friendships among students in general (Slavin in press).

Other outcomes seen in many studies of cooperative learning include gains in self-esteem, liking of school and of the subject being studied, time-on-task, and attendance (Slavin in press). Studies by Sharan and colleagues (1984) have shown that extended experiences with cooperative learning can increase the ability to work effectively with others.

Basic Agreement
In every area of research there are debates about what the research means. Cooperative learning, a topic studied by many researchers from different research traditions, is certainly no exception. However, after nearly two decades of research and scores of studies, a considerable degree of consensus has emerged. There is agreement that—at least in elementary and middle/junior high schools and with basic skills objectives—cooperative methods that incorporate group goals and individual accountability accelerate student learning considerably. Further, there is agreement that these methods have positive effects on a wide array of affective outcomes, such as intergroup relations, acceptance of mainstreamed students, and self-esteem.

Research must continue to test the limits of cooperative learning, to broaden our understanding of *why* and *how* cooperative learning produces its various effects (see Bossert 1988–89). Yet what we know already is more than enough to justify expanded use of cooperative learning as a routine and central feature of instruction.□

Author's note: Preparation of this article was supported by a grant from the Office of Educational Research and Improvement, U.S. Department of Education (No. OERI-G-86–0006). However, any opinions expressed are mine and do not represent OERI positions or policy.

References

Bossert, S.T. (1988–89). "Cooperative Activities in the Classroom." In *Review of Research in Education* (vol. 15), edited by E.Z. Rothkopf. Washington, D.C.: American Educational Research Association.

Dansereau, D.F. (1988). "Cooperative Learning Strategies." In *Learning and Study Strategies: Issues in Assessment, Instruction, and Evaluation*, edited by E.E. Weinstein, E.T. Goetz, and P.A. Alexander. New York: Academic Press.

Davidson, N. (1985). "Small-Group Learning and Teaching in Mathematics: A Selective Review of the Research." In *Learning to Cooperate, Cooperating to Learn*, edited by R.E. Slavin, S. Sharan, S. Kagan, R. Hertz-Lazarowitz, C. Webb, and R. Schmuck. New York: Plenum.

Fraser, S.C., A.L. Beaman, E. Diener, and R.T. Kelem. (1977). "Two, Three, or Four Heads Are Better Than One: Modification of College Performance by Peer Monitoring." *Journal of Educational Psychology* 69, 2: 101–108.

Johnson, D.W., and R.T. Johnson. (1989). "Toward a Cooperative Effort: A Response to Slavin." *Educational Leadership* 46, 7: 80–81.

Johnson, D.W., R.T. Johnson, and G. Maruyama. (1983). "Interdependence and Interpersonal Attraction Among Heterogeneous and Homogeneous Individuals: A Theoretical Formulation and a Meta-Analysis of the Research." *Review of Educational Research* 53: 5–54.

Johnson, D.W., G. Maruyama, R. Johnson, D. Nelson, and L. Skon. (1981). "Effects of Cooperative, Competitive, and Individualistic Goal Structures on Achievement: A Meta-Analysis." *Psychological Bulletin* 89: 47–62.

Madden, N.A., and R.E. Slavin. (1983). "Mainstreaming Students with Mild Academic Handicaps: Academic and Social Outcomes." *Review of Educational Research* 53: 519–569.

Newmann, F.M., and J. Thompson. (1987). *Effects of Cooperative Learning on Achievement in Secondary Schools: A Summary of Research*. Madison, Wisc.: University of Wisconsin, National Center on Effective Secondary Schools.

Sharan, S., R. Hertz-Lazarowitz, and Z. Ackerman. (1980). "Academic Achievement of Elementary School Children in Small-Group vs. Whole Class Instruction." *Journal of Experimental Education* 48: 125–129.

Sharan, S., P. Kussell, R. Hertz-Lazarowitz, Y. Bejarano, S. Raviv, and Y. Sharan. (1984). *Cooperative Learning in the Classroom: Research in Desegregated Schools*. Hillsdale, N.J.: Erlbaum.

Sherman, L.W., and M. Thomas. (1986). "Mathematics Achievement in Cooperative Versus Individualistic Goal-Structured High School Classrooms." *Journal of Educational Research* 79: 169–172.

Slavin, R.E. (1983). "When Does Cooperative Learning Increase Student Achievement?" *Psychological Bulletin* 94: 429–445.

Slavin, R.E. (1985). "Cooperative Learning: Applying Contact Theory in Desegregated Schools." *Journal of Social Issues* 41, 3: 45–62.

Slavin, R.E. (1988). "Cooperative Learning and Student Achievement." *Educational Leadership* 45, 2: 31–33.

Slavin, R.E. (1989a). "Cooperative Learning and Student Achievement." In *School and Classroom Organization*, edited by R.E. Slavin. Hillsdale, N.J.: Erlbaum.

Slavin, R.E. (1989b). "Slavin Replies." *Educational Leadership* 46, 7: 81.

Slavin, R.E. (In press). *Cooperative Learning: Theory, Research, and Practice*. Englewood Cliffs, N.J.: Prentice-Hall.

Smith, K.A., D.W. Johnson, and R.T. Johnson. (1981). "Can Conflict Be Constructive? Controversy Versus Concurrence Seeking in Learning Groups." *Journal of Educational Psychology* 73: 651–663.

Stevens, R.J., N.A. Madden, R.E. Slavin, and A.M. Farnish. (1987). "Cooperative Integrated Reading and Composition: Two Field Experiments." *Reading Research Quarterly* 22: 433–454.

Stevens, R.J., R.E. Slavin, A.M. Farnish, and N.A. Madden. (April 1988). "The Effects of Cooperative Learning and Direct Instruction in Reading Comprehension Strategies on Main Idea Identification." Paper presented at the annual convention of the American Educational Research Association, New Orleans.

Robert E. Slavin is Director, Elementary School Program, Center for Research on Elementary and Middle Schools, The Johns Hopkins University, 3505 N. Charles St., Baltimore, MD 21218.

Educational Leadership 48 (Feb. 1991) 83-87

ALFIE KOHN

Group Grade Grubbing versus Cooperative *Learning*

The perils of using rewards to bribe students to work together include decreased motivation and lower levels of performance.

Even before the recent surge of interest in cooperative learning (CL), researchers and practitioners were already staking out positions on precisely what the term denotes and how the idea should be implemented. Constructive controversies (or, less charitably, factional disputes) have arisen with respect to almost every aspect of CL theory and practice. Everyone in the field agrees that students benefit when they can help each other learn instead of having to work against each other or apart from each other; beyond this, unanimity is in short supply.

What should be one of the central areas of discussion, however, has not yet received the attention it deserves. I refer to the prominent role assigned to grades, awards, certificates, and other rewards in many of the CL models now being offered to teachers. While some approaches incorporate these rewards without calling attention to that fact, others assert that rewards are the linchpin of cooperation. Some writers even go so far as to use the phrases "cooperative goals" and "cooperative reward structures" interchangeably.

Most researchers would agree, I think, that effective CL depends on helping students to develop what the social psychologist Morton Deutsch (1949) called "promotive interdependence," in which the goals of group members are positively linked and their interactions are characterized by mutual facilitation. (Counterbalancing this in most versions of CL is some feature to assure individual account-

ability so that each student is held responsible to an external source for participating in the process and for learning.) But the assumption that interdependence is best achieved—or even, as some would have it, that it can *only* be achieved—by the use of rewards is a claim that demands critical examination. An impressive body of research in social psychology has shown that rewards are not only surprisingly limited in their effectiveness but also tend to undermine interest in the task. Over the long run, they may actually reduce the quality of many kinds of performance.

Hidden Costs of Rewards
In terms of motivational power, no artificial inducement can match the strength of intrinsic interest in a task. Think of someone whom you regard as extraordinarily good at what he or she does for a living; then ask yourself whether this individual is concerned primarily with collecting a paycheck. Most people who reach for excellence truly enjoy what they do. The same is true of students in the classroom.

Rewards have been described as the "enemies of exploration."

But the "hidden costs of rewards" (Lepper and Greene 1978) have to do not only with their relative lack of efficacy but with their corrosive effects on both attitude and performance. The psychologist Robert J. Sternberg (1990) recently summarized what a growing number of motivation researchers now concede: "Nothing tends to undermine creativity quite like extrinsic motivators do. They also undermine intrinsic motivation: when you give extrinsic rewards for certain kinds of behavior, you tend to reduce children's interest in performing those behaviors for their own sake" (p. 144). More succinctly, rewards have been described as the "enemies of exploration" (Condry 1977).

Despite the continuing influence of Skinnerian psychology on education and on lay thinking, this phenomenon is not entirely counterintuitive. The following three-step sequence of events will sound all too familiar to many of us: (1) we engage in some activity simply because it is pleasurable, (2) we get paid for doing it, and (3) we suddenly find ourselves unwilling to do it unless we are paid. We have come to see ourselves as working in order to receive the reward—in this case, money—with the result that our interest in the activity has mysteriously evaporated along the way.

This effect has been documented repeatedly, beginning in the early 1970s with the research of Mark Lepper at Stanford University (for an early summary, see Lepper and Greene 1975), Edward Deci at the University of Rochester (Deci and Ryan 1985), and their respective students. Since then, other researchers replicating and clarifying the phenomenon include John Nicholls (1989), Judith M. Harackiewicz and associates (1984), Mark Morgan in Ireland (1983, 1984), and Ruth Butler in Israel (Butler and Nisan 1986; Butler 1987, 1988, 1989). Their experiments have shown, *inter alia*, that:

• preschoolers who are told they will receive an award for drawing with felt-tip markers subsequently show less interest in using them (Greene and Lepper 1974);

• college students competing to solve a puzzle are less likely to continue working on such puzzles than are those who had not competed (Deci et al. 1981);

• merely watching someone else get rewarded for doing a task is enough to reduce one's own motivation to do it (Morgan 1983);

• the expectation of being evaluated distracts one from the task at hand and interferes with involvement and interest in it (Harackiewicz et al. 1984);

• not only grades but even some kinds of praise (as opposed to purely informational feedback) can undermine interest in an activity (Ryan 1982, Butler 1987).

In addition to these studies, whose dependent variable is motivation, Teresa Amabile at Brandeis University and other researchers have shown that rewards often lead to lower performance, particularly at creative tasks. For example,

• Students promised a reward if they were effective at tutoring younger children took longer to communicate ideas, got frustrated more easily, and ended up with pupils who didn't understand as well as a group of children whose tutors were promised no reward (Garbarino 1975);

• Children and undergraduates who expected to receive a prize for making collages or telling stories proved to be less imaginative at both tasks than those who received nothing (Amabile et al. 1986);

• When creative writers were asked to spend a few minutes reflecting on extrinsic reasons for writing—making money, impressing teachers, and so forth—their poetry dropped in quality

and also was judged to be worse than the poems written by people who weren't thinking about these things (Amabile 1985);

• Teenagers offered a reward for remembering details about a newspaper story they had recently read had poorer recall than those who received nothing for their efforts; moreover, they also scored lower on two measures of creativity (Kruglanski et al. 1971).

All of these studies have direct implications for classroom learning, but other research has shown that the destructive effects of rewards extend to other spheres: They are counterproductive for promoting generosity and other prosocial behavior (see a review in Kohn 1990), for eliciting love toward one's romantic partner (Seligman et al. 1980), and for motivating employees to use seat belts (Geller et al. 1987). In short, the conclusion offered for one experiment seems an apt summary of an entire body of research: "The more salient the reward, the more undermining of performance [is] observed" (Condry 1977, p. 464).

Several explanations have been proposed to account for these remarkably consistent findings. First, people who think of themselves as working for a reward feel controlled by it, and this lack of self-determination interferes with creativity (Deci and Ryan 1985). Second, rewards encourage "ego involvement" to the exclusion of "task involvement," and the latter is more

> **People who think of themselves as working for a reward feel controlled by it, and this lack of self-determination interferes with creativity.**

predictive of achievement (Nicholls 1989). Third, the promise of a reward is "tantamount to declaring that the activity is not worth doing for its own sake" (A. S. Neill, quoted in Morgan 1984); indeed, anything construed as a prerequisite to some other goal will likely be devalued as a result (Lepper et al. 1982).

Taking Away What's Been Given

All of these explanations account for reduced performance on the basis of how rewards reduce interest in the given task. But the decline of interest and the decline in performance are distinct phenomena, each significant in itself. The reduction in motivation also has undesirable effects on "self-esteem, perceived cognitive competence, and sense of control" (Ryan et al. 1985, p. 45); it is undesirable apart from its achievement effects. Conversely, extrinsic inducements may also reduce creativity for a reason having nothing to do with intrinsic motivation: they encourage students to work as quickly as possible, take few risks, and focus narrowly on a task. A reward-driven child (or adult) is after the goodie, and this mental set is hardly conducive to the playful encounter with words or numbers or ideas that characterizes true creativity (Amabile 1983).

It should not be surprising, then, that students for whom rewards are salient—even high-achieving students—will choose the easiest possible tasks (Harter 1978, Greene and Lepper 1974). Commenting on "Book It!," a program sponsored by the Pizza Hut restaurant chain that dangles free pizza before children to induce them to read, John Nicholls says the likely long-term consequence is "a lot of fat kids who don't like to read" (personal communication, 1989). Children are likely to pick books that are short and simple, the aim being to plow through them fast rather than coming to appreciate the pleasures of reading. The same is true with respect to inedible extrinsics as well. Thus, if the question is *Do rewards motivate students?*, the answer is *Absolutely—they motivate students to get rewarded*. Unfortunately, such motivation is often at the expense of interest in, or excellence at, whatever it is they are doing.

All of this prompts several disconcerting questions for anyone committed to CL. If bribing individuals to learn is so demonstrably ineffective and disadvantageous, what makes us think that bribing groups to learn is productive and benign? Why, in other words, should CL be exempt from the principle that emerges from this research—namely, the less salient grades and other rewards are for students, the better? Might it not be naive, in light of the corrosive effect of extrinsics, to assume that we can simply remove the rewards "as soon as the intrinsic motivation inherent in cooperative learning groups becomes apparent" (Johnson et al. 1986, p. 63)?

Alternatively, we could frame the challenge this way: many of us were drawn to CL because of the manifest failure of competition as a pedagogical tool. One of the reasons for competition's failure is precisely its status as an extrinsic motivator (Deci and Ryan 1985, Kohn 1986, Nicholls 1989). So could it not be said that the use of grades and other rewards to ensure cooperation takes away with one hand what has been given with the other?

To answer these questions definitively, we first need to consider the evidence offered in support of reward-driven CL by such careful researchers as Robert Slavin. His review of the data has persuaded him that "cooperative learning methods that use specific group rewards based on group members' individual learning consistently increase achievement more than control methods" (1983, p. 53). I believe, however, that the force and relevance of this conclusion is sharply limited by several factors.

First, many, if not most, of the measures in the studies to which Slavin refers are tasks that require only the straightforward application of a known principle (that is, algorithmic or convergent tasks), and these are less vulnerable to the destructive effects of extrinsics than are more open-ended (heuristic or divergent) tasks. Teachers who care about stimulating creativity and curiosity will not take much comfort from the fact that the promise of a certificate may prompt students to

How do children who are repeatedly bribed to learn come to view the process of learning months or years later?

memorize more facts. That striving for a reward may enhance performance on a boring task may be less important than the finding that rewards, from a students' perspective, turn interesting tasks into boring ones.

Second, while Slavin's notion of methodological adequacy turns in part on whether an experiment lasted for several weeks or several days, we also need to attend to the very long term. It is true that the toxicity of rewards typically manifests itself with alarming rapidity: in many of the studies cited above, a single trial—that is, one presentation of an extrinsic reward—was sufficient to undermine performance and interest. But how do children who are repeatedly bribed to learn come to view the process of learning months or years later? Specifically, how do they view a given subject when no one is around to reward them? A temporary performance gain on routine classroom assignments may mask a chronic shift in students' attitude that will have long-term negative effects on learning. We already know that "children become increasingly more extrinsically oriented over the school years" (Harter, paraphrased in Barrett and Boggiano 1988; see also Ryan et al. 1985)—an occurrence that Slavin presumably finds as troubling as I. It appears likely that the widespread use of extrinsics (mostly by people who have never even heard of cooperative learning) has something to do with this. Continuing to use extrinsics at the level of the group would seem to be ill-advised.

Third, we need to ask what exactly is being contrasted with reward-driven CL in the studies that find a perfor-

mance advantage. My impression is that the control condition typically consists of either (a) a "traditional" classroom, which, as I have just noted, is also characterized by reward-based motivation, or (b) some loose, unstructured arrangement ("Why don't you four work together on this ditto sheet?") that scarcely qualifies as CL. The first comparison tells us nothing about the effects of rewards *per se*—only about rewarding individuals versus groups. The second comparison does nothing to discredit the possibility of carefully structured, non-reward-based approaches to CL.

A Proposal for Success
When Slavin says, as he did in this journal ("Cooperative Learning and Student Achievement," October 1988), that "the cooperating groups must have a group goal that is important to them," I heartily agree. The problem is that he goes on in the very next sentence to operationalize the concept of group goals in terms of "working to earn certificates or other recognition, to receive a few minutes extra of recess, or to earn bonus points on their grades."

Those of us who are both persuaded and disturbed by all the evidence indicating that such rewards are counterproductive will want to turn to (or create) models of CL that can claim all the familiar advantages—but without relying on extrinsics. I would propose three key components of successful CL: curriculum, autonomy, and relationship.

Curriculum obviously matters in many respects, but the point to be emphasized here is that the perceived need to bribe children often tells us more about what they are being asked to learn (namely, that it lacks any intrinsic appeal) than about how learning per se takes place. While some proponents have proudly described CL as a method that can be used to teach anything—which implies that teachers who adopt it need not ask difficult questions about the value of what they are requiring students to do—others have challenged the value of "using cooperative techniques to have students cover the same boring, inconsequential, or biased material or to have them 'get through' worksheets with more efficiency" (Sapon-Shevin and Schniedewind 1989/1990, p. 64). I sympathize with the latter point of view.

Autonomy is vital for producing intrinsic motivation because people are more likely to find a task interesting when they have had a role in deciding what they are to do and how they are to do it (Nicholls 1989, Deci and Ryan 1985, Amabile and Gitomer 1984). Rewards are destructive, in the view of Deci and others, primarily because they restrict autonomy. But teachers should not only minimize extrinsic motivators, they should affirmatively help students to become responsible for their own education. A child who can make (teacher-guided) choices about what happens in his or her classroom is a child who will be less likely to require artificial inducements to learn.

Relationship refers to the specific trainable social skills that already play a part in some models of CL (for example, Johnson et al. 1986) as well as to a broader emphasis on caring for others. Explicit attention to the value (and intrinsic appeal) of prosocial behavior may encourage students to view others in their group as collaborators rather than as obstacles to their own success. By contrast, a certain cynicism inheres in the assumption that students will work together only on the basis of self-interest (Kohn 1990)—that is, that no classroom environment could possibly develop norms leading to cooperation without the use of rewards.

Several models of CL already emphasize these things. First, "if the task is challenging and interesting, and if students are sufficiently prepared for skills in group process, students will experience the process of groupwork itself as highly rewarding," as Cohen (1986, p. 69) has written. Similarly, the scores of lessons and activities offered in Schniedewind and Davidson's (1987) introduction to CL are based on the idea that *what* gets taught not only matters as much as *how* it is taught but actually can be the central impetus for learning. Second, autonomy is key to the Group Investigation approach: Achievement comes chiefly from giving "students more control over their learning" (Sharan and Sharan 1989/

It is time to set about trying to maximize the benefits of cooperative learning in the absence of rewards.

1990, p. 20), not from waving a gradebook at them.

Finally, relationship, and specifically the idea of creating a community within the classroom, is the primary feature of the program developed by the Child Development Project in San Ramon, California. For that matter, the project also places special emphasis on the quality of the curriculum and on helping students to take responsibility for their learning—all of which have moved the project developers away from relying on punishments or rewards (Solomon et al. 1990).

In sum, my hypothesis is that a carefully structured cooperative environment that offers challenging learning tasks, that allows students to make key decisions about how they perform those tasks, and that emphasizes the value (and skills) of helping each other to learn constitutes an alternative to extrinsic motivators, an alternative both more effective over the long haul and more consistent with the ideals of educators.

But even if we lack certainty about how to make CL work—even if subsequent research modifies this preliminary three-part formulation—it is time to abandon the project of trying to fine-tune a system of grades and other extrinsic motivators and instead to set about trying to maximize the benefits of CL in the absence of rewards.□

References

Amabile, T. M. (1983). *The Social Psychology of Creativity*. New York: Springer-Verlag.

Amabile, T. M. (1985). "Motivation and Creativity: Effects of Motivational Orientation on Creative Writers." *Journal of Personality and Social Psychology* 48: 393–399.

Amabile, T. M., and J. Gitomer. (1984). "Children's Artistic Creativity: Effects of Choice in Task Materials." *Personality and Social Psychology Bulletin* 10: 209–215.

Amabile, T. M., B. A. Hennessey, and B. S. Grossman. (1986). "Social Influences on Creativity: The Effects of Contracted-for Reward." *Journal of Personality and Social Psychology* 50: 14–23.

Barrett, M., and A. K. Boggiano. (1988). "Fostering Extrinsic Orientations: Use of Reward Strategies to Motivate Children." *Journal of Social and Clinical Psychology* 6: 293–309.

Butler, R. (1987). "Task-Involving and Ego-Involving Properties of Evaluation: Effects of Different Feedback Conditions on Motivational Perceptions, Interest, and Performance." *Journal of Educational Psychology* 79: 474–482.

Butler, R. (1988). "Enhancing and Undermining Intrinsic Motivation: The Effects of Task-Involving and Ego-Involving Evaluation on Interest and Performance." *British Journal of Educational Psychology* 58: 1–14.

Butler, R. (1989). "Interest in the Task and Interest in Peers' Work in Competitive and Noncompetitive Conditions: A Developmental Study." *Child Development* 60: 562–570.

Butler, R., and M. Nisan. (1986). "Effects of No Feedback, Task-Related Comments, and Grades on Intrinsic Motivation and Performance." *Journal of Educational Psychology* 78: 210–216.

Cohen, E. G. (1986). *Designing Groupwork: Strategies for the Heterogeneous Classroom*. New York: Teachers College Press.

Condry, J. (1977). "Enemies of Exploration: Self-Initiated Versus Other-Initiated Learning." *Journal of Personality and Social Psychology* 35: 459–477.

Deci, E. L., G. Betley, J. Kahle, L. Abrams, and J. Porac. (1981). "When Trying to Win: Competition and Intrinsic Motivation." *Personality and Social Psychology Bulletin* 7: 79–83.

Deci, E. L., and R. M. Ryan. (1985). *Intrinsic Motivation and Self-Determination in Human Behavior*. New York: Plenum Press.

Deutsch, M. (1949). "A Theory of Cooperation and Competition." *Human Relations* 2: 129–152.

Garbarino, J. (1975). "The Impact of Anticipated Reward Upon Cross-Age Tutoring." *Journal of Personality and Social Psychology* 32: 421–28.

Geller, E. S., J. R. Rudd, M. J. Kalsher, F. M. Streff, and G. R. Lehman. (1987). "Employer-Based Programs to Motivate

Safety Belt Use: A Review of Short-Term and Long-Term Effects." *Journal of Safety Research* 18: 1–17.

Greene, D., and M. R. Lepper. (1974). "Effects of Extrinsic Rewards on Children's Subsequent Intrinsic Interest." *Child Development* 45: 1141–1145.

Harackiewicz, J. M., G. Manderlink, and C. Sansone. (1984). "Rewarding Pinball Wizardry: Effects of Evaluation and Cue Value on Intrinsic Interest." *Journal of Personality and Social Psychology* 47: 287–300.

Harter, S. (1978). "Pleasure Derived from Challenge and the Effects of Receiving Grades on Children's Difficulty Level Choices." *Child Development* 49: 788–799.

Johnson, D. W., R. T. Johnson, and E. J. Holubec. (1986). *Circles of Learning: Cooperation in the Classroom*, rev. ed. Edina, Minn.: Interaction Book Co.

Kohn, A. (1986). *No Contest: The Case Against Competition*. Boston: Houghton Mifflin.

Kohn, A. (1990). *The Brighter Side of Human Nature: Altruism and Empathy in Everyday Life*. New York: Basic Books.

Kruglanski, A. W., I. Friedman, and G. Zeevi. (1971). "The Effects of Extrinsic Incentive on Some Qualitative Aspects of Task Performance." *Journal of Personality* 39: 606–617.

Lepper, M. R., and D. Greene. (April 1975). "When Two Rewards Are Worse Than One: Effects of Extrinsic Rewards on Intrinsic Motivation." *Phi Delta Kappan*: 565–566.

Lepper, M., and D. Greene, eds. (1978). *The Hidden Costs of Reward*. Hillsdale, N.J.: Lawrence Erlbaum Associates.

Lepper, M. R., G. Sagotsky, J. L. Dafoe, and D. Greene. (1982). "Consequences of Superfluous Social Constraints: Effects on Young Children's Social Inferences and Subsequent Intrinsic Interest." *Journal of Personality and Social Psychology* 42: 51–65.

Morgan, M. (1983). "Decrements in Intrinsic Motivation Among Rewarded and Observer Subjects." *Child Development* 54: 636–644.

Morgan, M. (1984). "Reward-Induced Decrements and Increments in Intrinsic Motivation." *Review of Educational Research* 54: 5–30.

Nicholls, J. G. (1989). *The Competitive Ethos and Democratic Education*. Cambridge, Mass.: Harvard University Press.

Ryan, R. M. (1982). "Control and Information in the Intrapersonal Sphere: An Extension of Cognitive Evaluation Theory." *Journal of Personality and Social Psychology* 43: 450–461.

Ryan, R. M., J. P. Connell, and E. L. Deci. (1985). "A Motivational Analysis of Self-Determination and Self-Regulation in Education." In *Research on Motivation in Education, vol. 2, The Classroom Milieu*, edited by C. Ames and R. Ames. Orlando, Fla.: Academic Press.

Sapon-Shevin, M., and N. Schniedewind. (December 1989/January 1990). "Selling Cooperative Learning Without Selling It Short." *Educational Leadership* 47,4: 63–65.

Schniedewind, N., and E. Davidson. (1987). *Cooperative Learning, Cooperative Lives: A Sourcebook of Learning Activities for Building a Peaceful World*. Dubuque, Iowa: William C. Brown Co.

Seligman, C., R. H. Fazio, and M. P. Zanna. (1980). "Effects of Salience of Extrinsic Rewards on Liking and Loving." *Journal of Personality and Social Psychology* 38: 453–460.

Sharan, Y., and S. Sharan. (December 1989/January 1990). "Group Investigation Expands Cooperative Learning." *Educational Leadership* 47, 4: 17–21.

Slavin, R. E. (1983). *Cooperative Learning*. New York: Longman.

Slavin, R.E. (October 1988). "Cooperative Learning and Student Achievement." *Educational Leadership* 46, 2: 31–33.

Solomon, D., M. Watson, E. Schaps, V. Battistich, and J. Solomon. (1990). "Cooperative Learning as Part of a Comprehensive Classroom Program Designed to Promote Prosocial Development." In *Cooperative Learning: Theory and Research*, edited by S. Sharan. New York: Praeger.

Sternberg, R. J. (1990). "Prototypes of Competence and Incompetence." In *Competence Considered*, edited by R.J. Sternberg and J. Kolligian, Jr. New Haven: Yale University Press.

Author's note: I wish to thank Eric Schaps and Marilyn Watson for their helpful comments on an earlier draft of this article.

Alfie Kohn lectures widely on cooperative learning and other educational issues. He is the author of *The Brighter Side of Human Nature: Altruism and Empathy in Everyday Life* (Basic Books 1990) and *No Contest: The Case Against Competition* (Houghton Mifflin 1986). His address is 3 Sacramento Place, Cambridge, MA 02138.

Educational Leadership 48 (Feb. 1991) 89-91

ROBERT E. SLAVIN

Group Rewards Make Groupwork Work

Response to Kohn

Teachers should try to make what they teach cooperative learning groups intrinsically motivating, but if they want to encourage students to expend the effort to truly master a subject, they should use rewards.

One of the poignant ironies of the cooperative learning movement is that the educators and researchers most often drawn to such a humanistic, prosocial form of instruction are the very people most likely to be ideologically opposed to the use of rewards for learning. Yet classroom research over two decades has consistently found that in elementary and secondary schools, the positive effects of cooperative learning on student achievement depend on the use of group rewards based in the individual learning of group members (see Slavin 1988, 1989/90, 1990; Newmann and Thompson 1987; Davidson 1985; Johnson and Johnson 1989). There are a few exceptions, but almost every study of cooperative learning in which the cooperative classes achieved more than traditional control groups used some sort of group reward.

For example, in our own research this reward usually consists of certificates for teams whose average performance on individual assessments exceeds a pre-established standard of excellence (Slavin 1986). The methods of Spencer Kagan (1989) employ similar rewards. David and Roger Johnson (1987) often recommend giving grades on the basis of group performance (a practice I oppose on ethical grounds, but that's another story). Shlomo Sharan and his colleagues (Sharan and Shachar 1988) evaluate group projects to determine which group members contributed unique elements—an appraisal that can be seen as a type of reward.

Nintendo versus Shakespeare

In this issue Alfie Kohn (p. 83) makes a case against the use of cooperative rewards. This case rests on two major arguments. The first is that extrinsic rewards undermine intrinsic interest

> **Almost every study of cooperative learning in which the cooperative classes achieved more than traditional control groups used some sort of group reward.**

and that this effect is likely to apply to cooperative learning. The second is that there are effective alternatives to the use of group rewards; thus, they are unnecessary.

Kohn's reading of research on the "undermining" effect of rewards is extremely narrow and therefore misleading. He is correct in saying there are many studies that demonstrate this undermining effect, but he fails to note there are at least as many studies that show just the opposite: that rewards *enhance* continuing motivation or that they have no effect on continuing motivation.

In the classic experiment in this area, preschoolers who freely selected drawing with felt-tipped markers from among a choice of activities were rewarded for drawing with the markers. Afterwards, these students were less likely to choose a drawing activity than were similar students who were never rewarded (Lepper et al. 1973). This experiment, which has been replicated many times, does show that rewards can undermine intrinsic interest. However, the experiment involves a very short time period (usually about an hour), preschool children, an artificial setting, and a task unlike most school tasks. Does the undermining effect apply in situations more like typical elementary and secondary classrooms? Scores of studies have been done to test the limits of this finding, and the results certainly do not support the simplistic view that rewards are bad. Perhaps the most important counterevidence is the consistent finding that rewards *increase* motivation when the task involved is one that students would not do on their own without rewards (Bates 1979, Morgan 1984, Lepper and Greene 1978).

I don't know many students who would put away their Nintendo games to do complex math problems, to write reports on the economy of Brazil, to write essays comparing Shakespeare and Molière, or to learn to use the subjunctive case in French. Students will productively fool around with science equipment or learn from visits to museums, and there is no reason to reward such intrinsically motivating activities. There is also a need for teachers to try to make everything they teach as intrinsically interesting as possible. But students are unlikely to exert the sustained, systematic effort needed to truly master a subject without some kind of reward, such as praise, grades, or recognition. Besides, try to imagine a highly motivated scientist who has not been rewarded for doing science, a singer who has not been rewarded for singing, an inventor who has not been rewarded for inventing. Outstanding achievement always produces extrinsic rewards of some kind; how else, then, do outstanding achievers maintain their motivation?

Many other aspects of the undermining effect show how little it is likely to apply to real school situations. One is the finding that rewards given over a period of days or weeks do not diminish intrinsic motivation (for example, see Vasta et al. 1978). Other studies find that rewards enhance intrinsic motivation if they convey information on performance relative to others (e.g., Boggiano et al. 1982) or if they are social rather than tangible (Lepper and Greene 1978, Deci and Ryan 1985).

It is clear, then, that the undermining effect of rewards on continuing motivation exists, but it is equally clear that it operates in a narrow set of

> **Outstanding achievement always produces extrinsic rewards of some kind; how else, then, do outstanding achievers maintain their motivation?**

circumstances; it applies only to activities students would engage in without rewards, to short-term reward situations, and to concrete rather than social rewards. No study has ever shown an undermining effect of rewards in a cooperative learning context. At least one study (Hom et al. 1990) found that cooperative learning enhanced intrinsic motivation. There is no reason to expect that cooperative learning would undermine intrinsic interest.

Ensuring Success

Can cooperative learning be successful without rewards? The research cited earlier suggests that this is unlikely, although Kohn mentions the Child Development Project in San Ramon, California, as an example of how cooperative learning can work without cooperative rewards. This study has indeed fastidiously avoided the use of group rewards. Studies of the program have shown that after five years of cooperative learning (from kindergarten through 4th grade), students performed academically no better than did students in traditionally organized schools (Solomon et al. 1990). This contrasts with the results of 35 studies of cooperative methods that used group rewards and individual accountability, in which cooperative classes achieved a median of 32 percent of a standard deviation more than tradi-

tional classes on achievement measures (see Slavin 1990). Overall, the median difference in achievement between forms of cooperative learning that used neither group goals nor individual accountability and traditional methods was a trivial 5 percent of a standard deviation. Cooperative methods without group rewards have been successful in enhancing outcomes other than achievement, but the need for rewards in increasing achievement is clear.

Why are group rewards necessary in cooperative learning? Evidence points to several factors. First, a key explanation for the effects of cooperative learning on achievement is that it creates peer norms favoring achievement (see Slavin 1983). That is, students in cooperative learning say that their groupmates' achievement is important to them. Without group rewards, why should a groupmate's achievement be important? Cooperative learning works (for achievement) only when students are actively explaining ideas to each other, not simply giving each other answers (Webb 1985). An altruistic student is likely to "help" a partner by giving answers, but to do the much tougher (and less friendly) job of *teaching*, the partner's learning must be important to his or her teammate. Without group rewards based on the learning of all group members, cooperative learning can degenerate into answer-sharing. At the same time, many students are reluctant to ask a fellow student for help (Newman and Goldin 1990). The fact that all students are striving toward a common goal helps students overcome this reluctance, since the student asking for help knows it is in the interests of the student giving help to do so.

The idea that group rewards are alternatives to no rewards is, of course, absurd. With the possible exception of Summerhill, just about every school in the world uses grades, praise, recognition, and other rewards to maintain student motivation. Cooperative learning simply focuses the classroom reward system on helping others learn (as well as on one's own learning).

Celebrating Good Work

Perhaps someday someone will come up with a form of cooperative learning that will work without cooperative rewards. Sharan and Shachar (1988) have a successful program that deemphasizes group rewards and solves the answer-sharing problem by giving each student a unique task in a group investigation, but this program has been used successfully only for social studies projects (and only in Israel). For the bulk of the elementary and secondary curriculum, however, the idea that cooperative rewards can be dispensed with in cooperative learning is wishful thinking, and the idea that such rewards will undermine intrinsic interest or continuing motivation is unproven and unlikely.

Remember, the rewards we're talking about are generally paper certificates (current street value: $.02). Kohn (and others) would oppose rewards on ideological grounds, regardless of their achievement effects. But to me it just doesn't seem excessive to give kids a fancy certificate if they've done a good job as a team. All it does is make tangible the teacher's pride and satisfaction with their cooperative efforts. Is that so terrible? □

References

Bates, J. A. (1979). "Extrinsic Reward and Intrinsic Motivation: A Review With Implications for the Classroom." *Review of Educational Research* 19: 557–576.

Boggiano, A. K., D.N. Ruble, and T.S. Pittman. (1982). "The Mastery Hypothesis and the Overjustification Effect." *Social Cognition* 1: 38–49.

Davidson, N. (1985). "Small-Group Learning and Teaching in Mathematics: A Selective Review of the Research." In *Learning to Cooperate, Cooperating to Learn*, edited by R. E. Slavin, S. Sharan, S. Kagan, R. Hertz-Lazarowitz, C. Webb, and R. Schmuck. pp. 221–230. New York: Plenum. .

Deci, E. L., and R.M. Ryan. (1985). *Intrinsic Motivation and Self-Determination in Human Behavior*. New York: Plenum.

Hom, H. L., M. Berger, M. Duncan, A. Miller, and A. Blevin. (1990). *The Influence of Cooperative Reward Structures on Intrinsic Motivation*. Springfield, Mo.: Southwestern Missouri State University.

Johnson, D. W., and R.T. Johnson (1987). *Learning Together and Alone*. Englewood Cliffs, N.J.: Prentice-Hall.

Johnson, D. W., and R.T. Johnson (1989). *Cooperation and Competition: Theory and Research*. Edina, Minn.: Interaction Book Co.

Kagan, S. (1989). *Cooperative Learning Resources for Teachers*. San Juan Capistrano, Calif.: Resources for Teachers.

Lepper, M. R., and D. Greene (1978). *The Hidden Costs of Reward*. Hillsdale, N.J.: Erlbaum.

Lepper, M. R., D. Greene, and R.E. Nisbett. (1973). "Undermining Children's Intrinsic Interest With Extrinsic Rewards: A Test of the Overjustification Hypothesis." *Journal of Personality and Social Psychology* 28: 129–137.

Morgan, M. (1984). "Reward-Induced Decrements and Increments in Intrinsic Motivation." *Review of Educational Research* 54: 5–30.

Newman,. R. S., and L. Goldin. (1990). "Children's Reluctance to Seek Help With Schoolwork." *Journal of Educational Psychology* 82: 92–100.

Newmann, F. M., and J. Thompson. (1987). *Effects of Cooperative Learning on Achievement in Secondary Schools: A Summary of Research*. Madison, Wis.: University of Wisconsin, National Center on Effective Secondary Schools.

Sharan, S., and C. Shachar. (1988). *Language and Learning in the Cooperative Classroom*. New York: Springer.

Slavin, R. E. (1983). *Cooperative Learning*. New York: Longman.

Slavin, R. E. (1986). *Using Student Team Learning*. Baltimore: Center for Research on Elementary and Middle Schools, The Johns Hopkins University.

Slavin, R. E. (1988). "Cooperative Learning and Student Achievement." *Educational Leadership* 45, 2: 31–33.

Slavin, R. E. (1989/90). "Research on Cooperative Learning: Consensus and Controversy." *Educational Leadership* 47,4: 52–54.

Slavin, R. E. (1990). *Cooperative Learning: Theory, Research, and Practice*. Englewood, N.J.: Prentice-Hall.

Solomon, D., M. Watson, E. Schaps, V. Battistich, and J. Solomon. (1990). "Cooperative Learning as Part of a Comprehensive Classroom Program Designed to Promote Prosocial Development." In *Recent Research on Cooperative Learning*, edited by S. Sharan. New York: Praeger.

Vasta, R., D.E. Andrews, A.M. McLaughlin, L.A. Stirpe, and C. Comfort. (1978). "Reinforcement Effects on Intrinsic Interest: A Classroom Analog." *Journal of School Psychology* 16: 161–166.

Webb, N. (1985). "Student Interaction and Learning in Small Groups: A Research Summary." In *Learning to Cooperative, Cooperating to Learn*, edited by R. E. Slavin, S. Sharan, S. Kagan, R. Hertz-Lazarowitz, C. Webb, and R. Schmuck. pp. 147–172. New York: Plenum.

Author's note: This article was written under funding from the Office of Educational Research and Improvement, U.S. Department of Education (Grant No. OERI-R117-R90002). However, any opinions expressed do not necessarily represent the positions or policies of OERI.

Robert E. Slavin is Director of the Elementary School Program, Center for Research on Effective Schooling for Disadvantaged Students, The Johns Hopkins University, 3505 N. Charles St., Baltimore, MD 21218.

Educational Leadership 48 (Feb. 1991) 93-94

ALFIE KOHN

Don't Spoil the Promise of Cooperative Learning

Response to Slavin

Where is the evidence that rewards improve motivation at all, much less for any meaningful amount of time?

Photograph by Randy Wyant. Courtesy of Fairfax County Public Schools

Cooperative learning can help children learn together, but using rewards and extrinsic motivators undermines their creativity.

If bribing students with rewards undermines their interest in learning and, in the long run, reduces the quality of their work, then, yes, we would have to conclude it *is* "so terrible"—even though this is hardly the result that Slavin (or teachers) intend.

The question is whether extrinsic motivators really do have this effect.

If students are unmotivated to begin with—perhaps because they have been assigned mind-numbing worksheets and drills—then Slavin is quite right to suggest that rewards may "have no effect on continuing motivation." After all, their motivation can't drop any lower. But where are the studies he alludes to that ostensibly refute the work of Deci, Lepper, Amabile, Nicholls, and others by showing that motivation is *enhanced* by rewards—

and that it stays high even after there is no teacher to hand out an *A* or a gold star for doing the task? I can't find them.

Reward or Penalty?

A closer look at the research Slavin does cite raises more doubts about his argument than it allays. Because my space is limited here, I will mention only four examples. First, and most telling, his opening paragraph cites the work of David Johnson and Roger Johnson, and Neil Davidson in support of the idea that cooperative learning boosts achievement only if group rewards are used. But in fact, David Johnson (1990) says, "For achievement gains to occur, positive *goal* interdependence has to be present. Group rewards are optional." And Davidson (1990) says, "Several recent studies suggest that rewards are not always necessary to increase student achievement on problem-solving and reasoning tasks."

Second, Slavin invokes the names of Deci and Ryan (1985) to support his claim that social (as opposed to tangible) rewards can boost intrinsic motivation. But in fact, their research suggests that positive feedback will have

> **Slavin may be correct that few non-reward-based classrooms now exist in the U.S., but this hardly demonstrates that the best alternative to bribing individuals is to bribe groups.**

precisely the same motivation-killing effects as money or grades if it is experienced as controlling. Indeed, Butler (1987, p. 481) found that "subsequent performance declined after both grades and praise" and that "praise did not yield higher subsequent intrinsic motivation than grades."

Third, Slavin dismisses the Child Development Project's (1990) experience with non-reward-based cooperative learning on the grounds that these students did not outperform their peers. But in fact, when 6th graders were given an essay exam to measure higher-order reading comprehension, children in the program did significantly better than the carefully matched comparison students (effect size .34). (Slavin may have been unaware of these very recent findings from the project).

Fourth, the only evidence Slavin cites on the question of cooperative learning and intrinsic motivation is an unpublished paper by Harry Hom and his colleagues (1990). This study, however, merely compared individual rewards with group rewards; it tells us nothing about non-extrinsic cooperative learning. Moreover, reward-driven cooperative learning failed to produce higher intrinsic motivation on one of the two behavioral measures that Hom used *or* on the self-report measure.

Chasing Trophies

Slavin may be correct that few non-reward-based classrooms now exist in the U.S., but this hardly demonstrates that the best, let alone the only, alternative to bribing individuals is to bribe groups. And if the only studies he can cite simply compare these two versions of education-by-extrinsics, then he has failed to demonstrate his central thesis: that cooperative learning won't work unless it is shot through with artificial incentives. When presented with a success story for cooperative learning without extrinsics, such as the Group Investigation method, he mysteriously tries to claim it as further substantiation for his behaviorist approach.

If we offer children rewards for eating an unfamiliar food, they will probably like that food *less* as a result

> **If we offer children rewards for learning, they will like learning less.**

(Birch et al. 1984). If we offer children rewards for learning, they will like learning less. Let's not spoil the promise of cooperative learning by turning it into yet another exercise in chasing rewards.□

References

Birch, L.L., D.W. Marlin, and J. Rotter. (1984). "Eating as the 'Means' Activity in a Contingency." *Child Development* 55:431–439.

Butler, R. (1987). "Task-Involving and Ego-Involving Properties of Evaluation." *Journal of Educational Psychology* 79: 474–482.

Davidson, N. (1990). Personal communication.

Deci, E.L., and R.M. Ryan. (1985). *Intrinsic Motivation and Self-Determination in Human Behavior.* New York: Plenum.

Developmental Studies Center. (April 1990). "Evaluation of the Child Development Project: Summary of Findings to Date." Unpublished manuscript. San Ramone, Calif.: DSC.

Hom, H. L., M. Berger, M. Duncan, A. Miller, and A. Blevin. (1990). *The Influence of Cooperative Reward Structures on Intrinsic Motivation.* Springfield, Mo.: Southwestern Missouri State University.

Johnson, D. (1990). Personal communication.

Alfie Kohn lectures widely on cooperative learning and other educational issues. He is the author of *The Brighter Side of Human Nature: Altruism and Empathy in Everyday Life* (Basic Books 1990) and *No Contest: The Case Against Competition* (Houghton Mifflin 1986). His address is 3 Sacramento Place, Cambridge, MA 02138.

Educational Leadership 48 (April 1991) 77-79

TED GRAVES

The Controversy over Group Rewards in Cooperative Classrooms

While the debate over the value of
extrinsic rewards persists, teachers can follow
a few guidelines now to help them use
extrinsic rewards appropriately, while building
intrinsic interest into their curriculums.

Academic controversy can be constructive and useful when the parties involved conduct a dialogue with the goal of understanding each other and arriving at a synthesis that takes all points of view into consideration. This requires listening carefully to each other's arguments and looking for their strengths rather than their weaknesses (as in a debate), the value of their insights, and the purposes they are trying to achieve. The recent exchange between Alfie Kohn and Robert Slavin concerning the use of group rewards in cooperative learning, published in the February issue of *Educational Leadership* (Kohn 1991a and 1991b, and Slavin 1991a and 1991b), represents only the first stage in this process.

A constructive controversy around this topic has been going on in the pages of *Cooperative Learning* magazine (Kohn 1990a, Slavin 1990, Schaps 1990) for several months, culminating last July in a roundtable session at the convention of the International Association for the Study of Cooperation in Education (IASCE) in Baltimore.[1] A summary of that session was published in the December 1990 issue of *Cooperative Learning* (Graves 1990). My purpose here is to carry that discussion another step forward, to discuss its applications for practitioners.

Polar Positions

Slavin and Kohn represent polar positions on the issue of group rewards. Slavin is concerned with increasing student achievement, and he believes the only demonstrably effective cooperative learning strategies are those that use group rewards based on the individual achievement of each group member (Slavin 1989, 1990, 1991a, 1991b). Kohn is concerned with fostering love of learning among students, and he believes that external rewards should never be used because they will undermine students'

The "social rewards" of working cooperatively probably enhance intrinsic motivation, and are among the great advantages of using cooperative learning strategies.

intrinsic motivation to learn (Kohn 1990a, 1990b, 1991a, 1991b).

From his reading of the research (much of which he has conducted himself), Slavin sees little evidence that achievement gains through cooperative learning are possible without the use of group rewards, although he acknowledges a few important exceptions, most notably Sharan's use of Group Investigation (Slavin 1989 and 1991a). In the roundtable last July, the Child Development Project and the program of "complex instruction" at Stanford were cited as additional examples (Graves 1990). In both cases, educators have made deliberate efforts to foster intrinsic motivation among students to work hard and to help their teammates, by using appealing curriculum materials, by establishing student norms for achievement and for helping others achieve, and by teaching students the appropriate skills to achieve those norms. This process is difficult and costly, however, and the research evidence for its success is still weak.

To bolster his arguments against the use of group rewards, Kohn cites a body of research evidence showing that extrinsic rewards undermine intrinsic motivation (Kohn 1990a, 1991a, 1991b). Unfortunately, this evidence is mixed and subject to alternative interpretations. A careful meta-analysis and best-evidence synthesis of this literature is still needed. The best approximation I know of at this time is Lepper (1988).

Three Questions to Guide Practice

Obviously these issues need to be settled. In the meantime, however, the business of schooling must go on, and classroom teachers need the best guidance we can give based on available evidence and practical experience. Accordingly, we will consider these three questions that broaden this debate concerning the use of extrinsic rewards in the classroom:

1. Are there forms of group rewards that minimize possible negative effects on intrinsic motivation?

2. Under what conditions will reliance on intrinsic motivation be most likely to achieve our academic goals?

3. Under what conditions may extrinsic group rewards continue to be necessary and useful?

Minimizing negative effects. Extrinsic rewards appear to have their most damaging effects on intrinsic motivation under two conditions:

1. When students would be willing to engage in the activities without the use of these rewards;

2. When the rewards may be seen by students as an attempt to manipulate and control their behavior.

Extrinsic rewards appear to have their least damaging effect on intrinsic motivation (and may actually enhance it) under the following conditions:

1. When the tasks are ones students would be unwilling to do on their own;

2. When the rewards are largely symbolic in form, serving more to communicate to students how well they are doing and their teachers' pride in their accomplishments, than as "payment" for their performance;

3. When the rewards are social rather than tangible;

4. When they are unanticipated.

A number of practical recommendations for the classroom follow from these observations. As Slavin correctly points out, however, the vast majority of tasks we expect students to perform are not ones they would be motivated to do on their own. When students are

unmotivated and the tasks are routine, some forms of group rewards may be helpful.

When extrinsic incentives seem necessary, try using symbolic rewards such as certificates of group achievement, stars, and smiley stickers, which communicate your pleasure in and appreciation of your students' efforts, rather than tangible rewards, such as small gifts and treats, which are more likely to become the focus of their attention.

Avoid the appearance of manipulation. Behavior modification is a powerful psychological tool and there are classroom situations so chaotic that its use may be justified to create sufficient order for learning to occur. But try to involve students as much as possible in setting their own goals and reward them for achieving these. Encouraging students to pursue their own goals is a form of social reward likely to increase their intrinsic motivation to learn.

Most students find the pleasure of working together in cooperative groups a reward in itself. The "social rewards" of working cooperatively probably enhance intrinsic motivation, and are among the great advantages of using cooperative learning strategies. Many teachers find that after awhile students no longer seem to need the group certificates and other external incentives that induced them to work together effectively. Kohn is skeptical that students can be weaned away from extrinsic rewards once these have been used. But the practical experience of many teachers suggests it is really quite easy. In fact, it may be more difficult to wean *teachers* away from routinely using these rewards even when they are no longer necessary.

Finally, unanticipated rewards, whether simply in the form of teacher recognition, a class party, or free time at the end of the day for pure fun after the class has worked hard and effectively, are powerful tools for enhancing student motivation.

Using intrinsic rewards. Group rewards do serve to motivate students to undertake routine academic tasks, such as basic skills acquisition. Increasingly, however, educators are urging discovery and problem solving approaches in science and math,

whole language learning, and simulations and role plays in social studies. With these approaches, basic skills are acquired in context, while students undertake engaging activities. Clearly, we need to make our lessons as intrinsically interesting as possible and be alert for whether their inherent fascination is sufficient to motivate our students. A continuing need for extrinsic rewards may serve as a useful indicator that our curriculum requires further examination in this regard.

Slavin (1991b) is justly concerned that in group situations the more able students may do most of the work or simply share answers with their teammates. Group rewards based on the individual achievement of each group member is one way to ensure that able students take the trouble to help their teammates really learn and not just complete their group project or worksheet. Such rewards may also serve to "give permission" to students to ask for help when they need it, since otherwise they might let down their teammates.

Without group rewards, we would need to find some other means to accomplish these goals. Fostering internalized norms for high quality academic performance and helping others is a slow and difficult task, but this behavior should transfer to other situations where group rewards are not provided. The Child Development Project (Solomon 1990) and the Stanford Program for Complex Instruction (Cohen 1986) provide models for how to proceed.

Teaching students the skills to help each other effectively is also necessary—and something that Slavin's Student Team Learning approach (Slavin 1989) does not include. Good helping behavior is not automatic; it needs to be defined, modeled, and practiced. But it is a skill that will particularly benefit and challenge the more able students—and it is one they would not be likely to acquire in special programs for the gifted.

Conditions that call for extrinsic rewards. All our efforts to improve our curriculums may still leave us with a large portion of school activities students may be reluctant to engage in without some form of extrinsic reward. This is true for most adult jobs;

why should we expect school to be different? The use of cooperative learning groups, with small, largely symbolic certificates of group achievement based on the individual achievement of each group member, will usually increase student scores on standardized tests; and these learning teams can make the effort more fun. When improved test scores are our goal, we now have a proven means to attain them.

But many of us aspire to much more for our students. Slavin's Student Team Learning strategies are ideal for non-contextual basic skills acquisition. They are not ideally suited for whole language learning, mathematics problem solving, and the development of higher-order thinking skills in science and social studies. Other cooperative learning strategies are available for these purposes, however, such as Group Investigation (S. Sharan 1990, Y. Sharan 1990) and jigsaw modifications developed mainly by Australian and Canadian educators that involve groups in synthesizing and applying the information their members teach each other (Clarke et al. 1990, Kagan 1985, Reid et al. 1989). Research conducted by Shlomo Sharan and his colleagues (Sharan and Shachar 1988) with Group Investigation, in which they carefully measured higher-order thinking skills, verbal fluency, and other rich intellectual outcomes, amply demonstrates the effectiveness of this approach. There is almost no formal research on achievement outcomes from the variety of other cooperative/ collaborative learning strategies available, but teachers almost universally report their students are thinking more deeply as a result of their use. These informal observations, though unreported in the research journals, should not be ignored—they probably carry more weight with teachers than formal research findings.

A Shared Vision

Many of the differences between Slavin and Kohn are a matter of where they stand along a pragmatic/idealistic continuum. Both share a vision of what education should be: not simply the acquisition of knowledge, but the development of intellectual curiosity,

creativity, and problem-solving skills. By systematically using group rewards based on the individual achievement of each group member, Slavin has developed and refined cooperative learning strategies that work successfully for the vast majority of learning tasks he finds teachers giving their students. Kohn fears that this very success may detract from our efforts to develop a richer and intrinsically motivating curriculum and to expect more from our students than good test scores. The contrast between Kohn's and Slavin's approaches sharpens our awareness of the implications of our instructional practices and helps us to make our choices more consciously. By focusing on the variety of forms that group rewards can take and the conditions under which these may appropriately be used, however, we can move the debate forward to address the complexities of daily practice.□

[1]In addition to Kohn and Slavin, four other leaders in the field participated: Elizabeth Cohen, Professor of Education and Sociology at Stanford University and author of *Designing Groupwork* (1986); Spencer Kagan, known for his "structural" approach to cooperative learning and author of *Cooperative Learning Resources for Teachers* (1985); Dee Dishon, well-known consultant and staff developer and co-author (with Pat Wilson O'Leary) of *A Guidebook for Cooperative Learning* (1984); and Daniel Solomon, Director of Research of the Child Development Project in San Ramon, California, who is often cited by Kohn as an exemplar of his point of view (Kohn 1990b).

References

Clarke, J., R. Wideman, and S. Eadie. (1990). *Together We Learn*. Toronto: Prentice-Hall.
Cohen, E. (1986). *Designing Groupwork*. New York: Teachers College Press.
Dishon, D., and P. W. O'Leary. (1984). *A Guidebook for Cooperative Learning*. Holmes Beach, Fla.: Learning Publications, Inc.
Graves, T. (1990). "Are External Rewards Appropriate or Desirable in a Cooperative Classroom?" *Cooperative Learning* 11, 2: 15–17.
Kagan, S. (1985). *Cooperative Learning Resources for Teachers*. Riverside, Calif.: University of California.
Kohn, A. (1990a). "Effects of Rewards on Prosocial Behavior." *Cooperative Learning* 10, 3: 23–24.
Kohn, A. (1990b). *The Brighter Side of Human Nature: Altruism and Empathy in Everyday Life*. New York: Basic Books.
Kohn, A. (1991a). "Group Grade Grubbing Versus Cooperative Learning." *Educational Leadership* 48, 5: 83–87.
Kohn, A. (1991b). "Don't Spoil the Promise of Cooperative Learning." *Educational Leadership* 48, 5: 93–94.
Lepper, M. (1988). "Motivational Consideration in the Study of Instruction." *Cognition and Instruction* 5, 4: 289–309.
Reid, J., P. Forrestal, and J. Cook. (1989). *Small Group Learning in the Classroom*. Scarborough, Western Australia: Chalkface Press.
Schaps, E. (1990). "Response to Kohn." *Cooperative Learning* 10, 4: 17–18.
Sharan, S. (1990). "The Group Investigation Approach to Cooperative Learning: Theoretical Foundations." In *Perspectives on Small Group Learning*, edited by M. Brubacher, R. Payne, and K. Rickett. Oakville, Ontario: Rubicon Publishing Co.
Sharan, S., and H. Shachar. (1988). *Language and Learning in the Cooperative Classroom*. New York: Springer-Verlag.
Sharan, Y. (1990). "Group Investigation: Expanding Cooperative Learning." In *Perspectives on Small Group Learning*, edited by M. Brubacher, R. Payne, and K. Rickett. Oakville, Ontario: Rubicon Publishing Co.
Slavin, R. (1989). *Cooperative Learning. Theory, Research, and Practice*. Englewood Cliffs, N.J.: Prentice-Hall.
Slavin, R. (1990). "Response to Kohn." *Cooperative Learning* 10, 4: 17.
Slavin, R. (1991a). "Synthesis of Research on Cooperative Learning." *Educational Leadership* 48, 5: 71–82.
Slavin, R. (1991b). "Group Rewards Make Groupwork Work." *Educational Leadership* 48, 5: 89–91.
Solomon, D. (1990). "Cooperative Learning and the Child Development Project." *Cooperative Learning* 10, 3: 18–19.

Ted Graves is an educational consultant, staff developer, and former professor at the University of California, Los Angeles. He and Nancy Graves are Executive Editors of *Cooperative Learning* magazine and long-time members of the Executive Board of the International Association for the Study of Cooperation in Education (IASCE), which sponsors its publication. They can be reached at IASCE, Box 11582, Santa Cruz, CA 95061–1582.

Educational Leadership 48 (March 1991) 60-65

SUSAN DEMIRSKY ALLAN

Grouping and the Gifted

Ability-Grouping Research Reviews: What Do They Say about Grouping and the Gifted?

If educators are to make informed decisions based on the findings about ability grouping, they must study the *original* research and be sure that the questions they are asking are the same ones posed by the researchers.

The questions of whether, when, and how to group students according to academic ability represent some of the most difficult and frustrating challenges facing educators today. Seeking to help answer these questions, researchers have applied new techniques of research review to this subject. Two prominent sets of reviews—the meta-analyses of James Kulik and Chen-Lin Kulik of the University of Michigan (1982, 1984b) and the best-evidence syntheses of Robert Slavin of Johns Hopkins University (1986, 1990)—attempt to synthesize this information. These reviews, their techniques, and their findings are important to educators who need to make decisions about grouping that are based on accurate knowledge of its effects. This article provides both a synthesis and a critique of these research reviews of ability grouping with the aim of clarifying for practitioners how these synthetic techniques affect the results; what research questions are being asked and answered; and what is and isn't established by the research.

Understanding the Methodology

Both the meta-analytic and best-evidence techniques of research review treat all included studies as equally valid. Although the reviewers set criteria for omitting clearly inadequate studies, they give all other studies the same weight, without regard for their relative quality. The best-evidence synthesis is more selective in its criteria, but then becomes vulnerable to the charge of hand-picking the evidence. (For a description of these two methods of research review and the more traditional narrative review, see the sidebar on p. 63.)

A methodological problem that applies primarily to the gifted (the top 3–7 percent) and to a lesser degree to high-ability students (the top 33 per-

cent) is the use of standardized test scores. On most studies included in the meta-analyses, these are the main measure of achievement. The scores of gifted students usually approach the ceiling on standardized achievement tests, making it very difficult to show significant academic improvement on their part. The ceiling effect of standardized tests is also a factor—although to a lesser degree—in evaluating the improvement of high-ability students. Certainly, at the minimum, the degree of academic improvement in the studies would be much greater if it weren't masked by the ceiling effect of standardized testing.

This problem stemming from the inclusion of high-ability students may affect all the major studies. However, I have had difficulty obtaining exact data on the percentage of studies included in the analyses that use standardized test scores. James Kulik (personal communication) reports that the majority of studies in his meta-analyses used such data. In his study, Slavin (1986) reported (personal communication) that almost all studies where effect size was computed used standardized data (raw scores, grade equivalents, or standard scores). In both the meta-analyses and the best-evidence synthesis, some forms of grouping were found to improve the academic performance of gifted children, and it is likely that the real benefits were greater than could be shown by the method of measurement.

In a more recent synthesis of grouping in secondary schools, Slavin (1990) raises an additional problem concerning the use of standardized testing as a measurement of the effects of grouping on student achievement. Discussing the lack of positive evidence for grouping in his study, Slavin says, "One possibility is that the standardized tests used in virtually all the studies discussed in this review are too insensitive to pick up effects of grouping." Insensitivity of the tests is indeed one possibility. Another is the criticism commonly raised by teachers, particularly at the secondary level, that the tests don't evaluate what they are teaching. One possible check on this difficulty is to compare student progress in ability-grouped vs. heterogeneous classes using teacher-made tests. These are less commonly used in research because they are not comparable across teachers and subject areas. In fact, in both Slavin's elementary synthesis (1986) and secondary synthesis (1990), one of the criteria for inclusion of a research study was that "teacher-made tests, used in a very small number of studies, were accepted only if there was evidence that they were designed to assess objectives taught in all classes" (Slavin 1990). Clearly, if ability grouping is being used effectively, the objectives should *vary* among the different classes. Therefore, testing for the same (probably minimal) objectives will not permit any benefits of ability grouping in average- or high-ability classes to be demonstrated. A similar problem, related to differentiating instruction appropriately for the students being taught, arises again when we examine the research questions being asked.

Examining the Research Questions

The most serious difficulty with Kulik and Kulik's meta-analytic reviews and Slavin's best-evidence syntheses on grouping appears when we delve into the studies that actually make up these syntheses. The research questions actually being asked may prove very surprising to educators who have been reading general accounts of the analyses.

One question *not* asked in the Slavin research was whether programs designed to provide differentiated education for gifted or special education students were effective. Those programs were systematically omitted from Slavin's synthesis on the basis that they "involve many other changes in curriculum, class size, resources, and goals that make them fundamentally different from comprehensive grouping plans" (Slavin 1986). It is ironic that some school systems are using the Slavin best-evidence synthesis to make decisions about gifted and special education programs when

It is ironic that some school systems are using the Slavin best-evidence synthesis to make decisions about gifted and special education programs when such an application clearly is inappropriate.

such an application clearly is inappropriate. Slavin (1988) addressed such programs in a later narrative review in which he argued that the research on them was biased and the programs were ineffective. However, this subject was not researched in the systematic fashion of the best-evidence synthesis, and, logically, that synthesis cannot provide guidance on it.

Kulik and Kulik did address the effectiveness of gifted programs in their meta-analyses, including such programs when their other methodological criteria were met. Their results show clear positive gains for students in gifted programs, which they attribute to the specialized curriculum and materials used and to the training afforded teachers in such programs.[1]

The importance of the research question being asked arises again when we examine Slavin's (1986) review of regrouping in the elementary school for reading and/or mathematics. Five of seven studies in the best-evidence synthesis found that students learned more in regrouped than in heterogeneous classes, while two found negative results. However, in at least one of the studies in which students in regrouped classes failed to outperform those in heterogeneous classes (Davis and Tracy 1963), no attempt was made to provide differentiated materials to the regrouped classes. Use of the same materials for all groups also occurred in a different study, included in both Slavin's and Kulik and Kulik's analyses, where students were regrouped for reading (Moses 1966). Despite this inadequacy of educational design, Moses found weak positive evidence for regrouping.

A study by Koontz (1961), the other study with negative results noted in Slavin's synthesis, involved regrouping for three subjects (math, language, and reading) and, therefore, had as much similarity to departmentalization models as to limited regrouping. Students changed classes three to four times a day. Most significantly, in the regrouping, language arts and reading each became separate classes, a very questionable educational practice. In contrast, a study by Provus (1960) in a suburban district showed clear and

The most destructive aspect of the controversy over ability grouping is the misrepresentations of the findings, particularly those of Slavin's best-evidence synthesis, in the popular media.

sometimes dramatic gains for students who were both regrouped for mathematics and provided with ability-appropriate materials. There were cases of 4th graders who finished the year working on an 8th grade level. Importantly, however, the gains were not limited to high-ability students. There were also clear, if less spectacular, benefits for both average- and low-ability students.

It is difficult to imagine any rational disagreement that could stem from these results. It is hardly reasonable to suggest that students should be ability grouped without the use of appropriate curriculum and materials. Grouping while using the same materials and curriculum for all groups of students is not supported by any segment of the education profession. But it appears that some researchers are attempting to ask the "pure" research question of whether grouping as a single isolated factor has any effect on student achievement. The answer, not surprisingly, is mixed, although generally positive. However, this is *not* the question that educators and parents are asking. They want to know whether grouping, with appropriately differentiated instruction, has any effect on student achievement. When that question is addressed, the results provide a stronger positive answer in both math and reading for all groups of students.

Interpreting the Findings

The most destructive aspect of the controversy over ability grouping is the misrepresentations of the findings, particularly those of Slavin's best-evidence synthesis (Slavin 1986), in the popular media. Headlines such as "Is Your Child Being Tracked for Failure?" (*Better Homes and Gardens*), "The Label That Sticks" (*U.S. News and World Report*), and, the most sensational of all, "Tracked to Fail" (*Psychology Today*) distort the research findings and undermine serious discussion of an important issue. The *Psychology Today* article begins with a ridiculous comparison to the categorization of alphas, betas, and gammas in *Brave New World*! There has been too little reaction from the educational community to bring the discussion back to a substantive level. The publications cited above, as well as some general education publications, fail to take note of Slavin's very important and worthwhile distinction between types of grouping. They also paint his research as having determined that grouping is academically harmful, which is not the case. The meta-analyses of Kulik and Kulik are less frequently misinterpreted by the general media, perhaps because they are rarely cited.

In examining the actual conclusions in these research syntheses, it is essential to examine them according to type of grouping rather than as one amorphous whole. When grouping is separated into within-class, comprehensive, and between-class grouping patterns, the results become more specific and useful.

Within-class ability grouping can be accomplished in several ways and can use a variety of educational techniques. After considering programs in which students in a grade level were assigned to different groups within heterogeneous classrooms, Slavin and Karweit (1984) concluded that such grouping clearly benefits students. Kulik and Kulik (1989) separated the within-class grouping studies into those designed for all students and those designed specifically for academically talented students. The programs designed for all students showed a positive, but small effect on student achievement. This effect was

similar for high-, average-, and low-ability groups. The within-class groupings for academically talented students were found to have substantial positive academic effects.

In examining techniques used in within-class differentiation of instruction, both Slavin and Kulik and Kulik have published reviews of mastery testing, and Slavin has reviewed cooperative learning. In the area of mastery testing, Slavin (1987) finds little methodologically adequate research support for it. Kulik and Kulik (1987) find that it generally has positive effects on student learning, although those effects were more pronounced for the less able students. However, it also increased the amount of time needed for instruction. On the average, mastery testing groups require 26 percent more instructional time than conventionally taught groups. Cooperative learning was not included in the Kulik and Kulik research, but Slavin is generally supportive of the practice if groups are rewarded on the basis of the individual learning of all members.

When grouping is separated into within-class, comprehensive, and between-class grouping patterns, the research results become more specific and useful.

The practice of *comprehensive full-day grouping* of pupils into different classrooms on the basis of general ability or IQ is not supported by Slavin's best-evidence synthesis. However, it is vital to note that he did not find evidence of academic harm to students in this form of grouping—only lack of academic gain. This lack of academic gain shown among high-ability students in full-day grouping possibly is attributable to the ceiling effect of standardized testing. It also is useful to recall that gifted and special education programs were omitted from this aspect of the best-evidence synthesis, although Slavin has stated his opposition to them in other contexts (with the exception of acceleration programs, which he states may benefit gifted students). In contrast, Kulik (1985) found that students grouped in classes according to general academic ability slightly outperformed non-grouped students. The strongest positive effect size was for students in high-ability classes (0.12) with weaker effects for students in middle-level classes (0.04) and no effect for those in low-ability classes. In a separate analysis of gifted and talented programs, Kulik and Kulik (1989) found that students performed significantly better than they did in heterogeneous classes.

The practice of departmentalization was not addressed by Kulik and Kulik, and Slavin indicated that the small amount of existing research recommends against departmentalization in upper elementary and middle grades.

The final topic of direct contrast between the two reviews is that of *regrouping for specific subject areas.* This includes Joplin and non-graded plans as well as the more traditional regrouping, usually for math and language arts. Slavin (1986) concludes that such an approach can be instructionally effective, particularly when:

- it is done for only one or two subjects—students remain in heterogeneous classes for most of the day,
- it greatly reduces student heterogeneity in a specific skill,
- group assignments are frequently reassessed,
- teachers vary the level and pace of instruction according to student needs.

Slavin's conclusions raise an interesting point of conflict with Kulik and Kulik's research (1989). While they also found a positive effect on achieve-

---

Methods of Reviewing Ability Grouping Research

Three main techniques have been used to review research in the area of ability grouping: narrative review, meta-analysis, and best-evidence synthesis. Narrative review is the "traditional" method in which the reviewer surveys and comments in detail upon individual studies in the literature. While narrative review permits a great deal of evaluative commentary on the studies it includes, reviewers have always struggled with the difficulty of comparing studies with different results and different standards of measurement. Meta-analysis and best-evidence synthesis, the methods used in the two sets of reviews that form the focus of this article, were developed in order to make the results more replicable and quantifiable than the narrative technique permits.

The meta-analytic technique (used by James Kulik and Chen-Lin Kulik) requires the reviewer to locate studies of an issue through objective and replicable searches, code the studies for salient features, and describe study outcomes on a common scale. Kulik and Kulik itemized additional qualifications for the use of a study in their meta-analysis. In order for a study to be included in their review, the results had to be reported in quantitative form; the results had to be available from a conventionally instructed control group as well as from the one receiving the experimental treatment; the control group had to be similar to the experimental group in aptitude; and, very important, the studies had to take place in actual classrooms, not labs.

The best-evidence synthesis technique (used by Robert Slavin) is a combination of meta-analysis and narrative review. It has many characteristics in common with meta-analysis, including the computation of effect size[1] and the clear specification of inclusion criteria. There are, however, several crucial differences. One important difference is that studies were included whose effect size could not be computed. Such studies are characterized in the data analyses as positive, negative, or zero rather than excluded. In addition, individual studies and methodological and substantive issues are disclosed in the detail typical of narrative reviews. Finally, the Slavin review included studies that used calculations that Kulik and Kulik considered mathematically inappropriate for their meta-analytic techniques.□

[1]Effect size is computed as the difference between the mean scores of experimental and control groups, divided by the standard deviation of the control group. It provides a common scale that standardizes the various measurements used in different studies (Kulik and Kulik 1989 and Slavin 1989, 1990).

Kulik, J. A., and C.-L. Kulik. (1989). "Effects of Ability Grouping on Student Achievement." *Equity and Excellence* 23, 1–2: 22–30.
Slavin, R. E. (1989). "Grouping for Instruction." *Equity and Excellence* 23, 1-2: 31–36.
Slavin, R. E. (1990). "Achievement Effects of Ability Grouping in Secondary Schools: A Best-Evidence Synthesis." *Review of Educational Research* 60, 3: 471–499.

—Susan Demirsky Allan

---

ment for such regrouping approaches, they further observed that this effect existed even when the regrouping was not limited to only one or two subjects, did not substantially reduce student heterogeneity, and when group assignments were not frequently reassessed. In other words, Kulik and Kulik (1989) did not find evidence to support Slavin's conclusion that grouping programs are most effective when the specific criteria described above are met.

Finally, unlike Slavin, Kulik and Kulik (1982) and Kulik (1985) address the issues of attitude and self-concept.

Their findings in these areas show that grouping has minor effects and is generally positive. They found that students who were ability grouped for a specific subject had a better attitude toward that subject but that grouping did not change attitudes about school in general.

With regard to student self-esteem, Kulik and Kulik's research requires serious consideration. A major criticism of ability grouping is that it will lower the self-esteem of students in low-ability groups. Kulik and Kulik determined that, in general, effects of grouping on self-esteem were very small and somewhat dependent upon program type. Programs with high-average-low groups have a small overall effect on self-esteem, but effects tend to be slightly positive for low-ability groups and slightly negative for high and average ones. Limited studies of remedial programs (Kulik 1985) provide evidence that instruction in homogeneous groups has positive effects on the self-esteem of slow learners. Programs designed for gifted students have trivial effects on self-esteem (Kulik 1985). Why are these results counter to the prevailing expectation? Kulik (personal communication) raises an interesting point on the relative importance of the effects of labeling versus the effects of daily classroom experience. He suggests that the labeling (by placement of a student into a low-medium-high group) may have some transitory impact on self-esteem but that impact may be quickly overshadowed by the effect of the comparison that the student makes between himself or herself and others each day in the classroom. Low-ability students may experience feelings of success and competency when in a classroom with others of like ability, and high-ability students may encounter greater competition for the first time. While the data cannot, in themselves, identify the cause of these findings, the results make it clear that we must reexamine the arguments about self-esteem in light of them.

Other Issues to Consider

Kulik and Kulik's meta-analyses and Slavin's best-evidence syntheses address a number of important issues about ability grouping for academic instruction. However, other concerns should be considered in making academic grouping decisions. Issues such as the impact of adult attitudes towards grouping, the role of gifted students as role models for other students, and the impact of grouping on student behavior and teacher expectations are all crucial.

Neither of the two studies discusses the importance of teacher and parent attitudes and approaches to grouping, even though educator experience suggests that a low-key, supportive approach by all adults concerned goes a

The thorniest issue concerning grouping and the gifted is whether the gifted are needed in the regular classroom to act as role models for other students.

long way toward minimizing any emotional effects of grouping.

The thorniest issue concerning grouping and the gifted is whether the gifted are needed in the regular classroom to act as role models for other students and whether this "use" of gifted students is more important than their own educational needs. That students constantly make ability comparisons between themselves and others (Nicholls and Miller 1984) is sometimes used as the rationale for having gifted students serve as motivational models for others. While there is nothing inherently wrong with serving as a positive role model on occasion, it is morally questionable for adults to view any student's primary function as that of role model to others.

Further, the idea that lower ability students will look up to gifted students as role models is highly questionable. Children typically model their behavior after the behavior of other children of similar ability who are coping well with school. Children of low and average ability do not model themselves on fast learners (Schunk 1987). It appears that "watching someone of similar ability succeed at a task raises the observer's feelings of efficiency and motivates them to try the task" (Feldhusen 1989). Students gain most from watching someone of similar ability "cope" (that is, gradually improve their performance after some effort), rather than watching someone who has attained "mastery" (that is, can

demonstrate perfect performance from the outset). These data are compatible with Kulik and Kulik's explanation of their data on self-esteem discussed previously in this article.

A final point not considered in either of the major analyses is that teachers of high-ability classes may spend less time on discipline, spend more time interacting with students (particularly at student initiation), have students who spend more time-on-task, use better teaching techniques, and have higher expectations (Veldman and Sanford 1984). The implication is that the differences in teacher behavior may be a result of teacher bias or expectations, rather than a reaction to the behavior and needs of the students. It is questionable whether the same teacher, with the same expectations, would be able to use the same techniques with a lower ability class. However, the point is well taken that teachers need to examine whether they are "under-expecting" performance from all groups of students and thereby not providing them with the opportunity to rise to their potential.

Educators as Critical Consumers

There is a great deal to be learned from the Slavin and the Kulik and Kulik analyses of ability grouping. The separation of the data into types of grouping (comprehensive, between-class, within-class, separate program, and acceleration) is particularly valuable because it has demonstrated that the effects of grouping vary according to type of plan. However, there also has been a great deal of misrepresentation and misinterpretation of the research. Educators need to be critical consumers. I believe the following statements are supported by research results and may reasonably be applied by educators when making decisions on ability grouping.

1. Gifted and high-ability children show positive academic effects from some forms of homogenous grouping. The strongest positive academic effects of grouping for gifted students result from either acceleration or classes that are specially designed for the gifted and use specially trained teachers and

differentiated curriculum and methods. In fact, all students, whether grouped or not, should be experiencing a differentiated curriculum that provides options geared to their learning styles and ability levels.

2. Average- and low-ability children may benefit academically from certain types of grouping, particularly elementary school regrouping for specific subject areas such as reading and mathematics, as well as from within-class grouping. These benefits may be small. These students show very little benefit from wholesale grouping by general ability.

3. The preponderance of evidence does not support the contention that children are academically harmed by grouping.

4. Students' attitudes toward specific subjects are improved by grouping in those subjects. However, grouping does not have any effect on their attitudes toward school.

5. It is unclear whether grouping has any effect on the self-esteem of students in the general school population. However, effects on self-esteem are small but positive for low-ability children and slightly negative for average- and high-ability children. There is limited evidence that remedial programs have a positive effect on the self-esteem of slow learners.

I support the plea of many in the educational field that educational decisions stand upon a firm research base. The original research, however, must itself be examined rather than relying on distillations or selective, possibly biased reports in the media. Further, the questions the researcher is asking must match the questions being asked by the practitioner. Then, our decisions about ability grouping will stand on a sound research base.□

[1]R. Slavin (personal communication) suggests a distinction between enrichment and acceleration programs for the gifted. This is not always an easy distinction to make. Acceleration is clear when a 7th grader takes Algebra I or French. But is it acceleration or enrichment when a gifted program class introduces more sophisticated literature or science concepts than those used in the regular curriculum? Such material may be characteristic of that usually offered to older children but does not advance them through the instructional continuum. Many studies evaluate programs that are not clearly identifiable as being either enrichment or acceleration. Although the Kuliks did not make the enrichment/acceleration distinction in their meta-analyses on grouping, a separate meta-analysis on accelerated instruction (Kulik and Kulik 1984a) showed very strong positive benefits for acceleration. The performance of accelerated students surpassed by nearly one grade level the performance of nonaccelerates of equivalent age and intelligence. In their grouping meta-analysis, the Kuliks added an additional 24 studies on gifted children (there is only one overlap with the acceleration meta-analysis), and they obtained the positive results cited above.

References

Davis, O. L., and N. H. Tracy. (1963). "Arithmetic Achievement and Instructional Grouping." *Arithmetic Teacher* 10: 12–17.

Feldhusen, J. P. (1989). "Synthesis of Research on Gifted Youth." *Educational Leadership* 46, 6: 6–11.

"Is Your Child Being Tracked for Failure?" (October 1988). *Better Homes and Gardens*: 34–36.

Koontz, W. F. (1961). "A Study of Achievement as a Function of Homogeneous Grouping." *Journal of Experimental Education* 30: 249–253.

Kulik, C.-L. (1985). "Effects of Inter-Class Ability Grouping on Achievement and Self-Esteem." Paper presented at the annual convention of the American Psychological Association (93rd), Los Angeles, California.

Kulik, C.-L., and J. A. Kulik. (1982). "Effects of Ability Grouping on Secondary School Students: A Meta-Analysis of Evaluation Findings." *American Educational Research Journal* 19: 415–428.

Kulik, J. A., and C.-L. Kulik. (1984a). "Effects of Accelerated Instruction on Students." *Review of Educational Research* 54, 3: 409–425.

Kulik, C.-L., and J. A. Kulik. (1984b). "Effects of Ability Grouping on Elementary School Pupils: A Meta-Analysis." Paper presented at the annual meeting of the American Psychological Association, Toronto (ERIC No. ED 255 329).

Kulik, C.-L., and J. A. Kulik. (1987). "Mastery Testing and Student Learning: A Meta-Analysis." *Journal of Educational Technology Systems* 15, 3: 325–345.

Kulik, J. A., and C.-L. Kulik. (1989). "Effects of Ability Grouping on Student Achievement." *Equity and Excellence* 23, 1–2: 22–30.

Moses, P. J. (1966). "A Study of the Effects of Inter-Class Grouping on Achievement in Reading." *Dissertation Abstracts* 26, 4342 (University Microfilms No. 66–741).

Nicholls, J., and A. T. Miller. (1984). "Development and Its Discontents: The Differentiation of the Concept of Ability." In *The Development of Achievement Motivation*, pp. 185–218, edited by J. Nicholls. Greenwich, Conn.: JAI Press.

Provus, M. M. (1960). "Ability Grouping in Mathematics." *Elementary School Journal* 60: 391–398.

Rachlin, J. (July 3, 1989). "The Label That Sticks." *U. S. News and World Report*: 51–52.

Schunk, D. H. (1987). "Peer Models and Children's Behavioral Change." *Review of Educational Research* 57, 2: 149–174.

Slavin, R. E. (1986). *Ability Grouping and Student Achievement in Elementary Schools: A Best-Evidence Synthesis*. (Rep. No. 1). Baltimore, Md.: Johns Hopkins University, Center for Research on Elementary and Middle Schools.

Slavin, R. E. (1987). "Mastery Learning Reconsidered." *Review of Educational Research* 57, 2: 175–213.

Slavin, R. E. (1988). "Synthesis of Research on Grouping in Elementary and Secondary Schools." *Educational Leadership* 46, 1: 67–77.

Slavin, R. E. (1990). "Achievement Effects of Ability Grouping in Secondary Schools: A Best-Evidence Synthesis." *Review of Educational Research* 60, 3: 471–499.

Slavin, R. E., and N. Karweit. (1984). "Within-Class Ability Grouping and Student Achievement." Paper presented at the annual meeting of the American Educational Research Association, New Orleans.

Tobias, S. (September 1989). "Tracked to Fail." *Psychology Today*: 54–60.

Veldman, D. J., and J. P. Sanford. (1984). "The Influence of Class Ability Level on Student Achievement and Classroom Behavior." *American Educational Research Journal* 21, 3: 629–644.

Author's note: I conducted this review while employed by Falls Church Public Schools in Virginia and gratefully acknowledged their sponsorship and encouragement of the project.

Susan Demirsky Allan is Consultant for Gifted Education/Fine Arts, Dearborn Public Schools, Department of Instructional Services, 18700 Audette, Dearborn, MI 48124.

Educational Leadership 48 (March 1991) 68-71

ROBERT E. SLAVIN

Grouping and the Gifted

Are Cooperative Learning and "Untracking" Harmful to the Gifted?
Response to Allan

I find no evidence to support Allan's conclusion that ability grouping is worthwhile for high achievers and find much to recommend cooperative programs for these (and other) students.

In the past few years there has been remarkably rapid development in American education on two distinct but related fronts. One is the adoption of various forms of cooperative learning, and the other is the search for alternatives to traditional tracking and ability-grouping practices. Cooperative learning and "untracking" have completely different rationales, research bases, and political and practical implications. Cooperative learning can work within a completely tracked school, and untracking by no means requires cooperative learning. Yet the two movements have become intertwined in the minds of educators because cooperative learning is often offered as one means of teaching the very heterogeneous classes created by untracking and because of a widespread assumption that if homogeneous large groups are bad, then heterogeneous small groups must be good. Perhaps I have contributed to the confusion by having written in support of both practices (see, for example, Slavin 1988 and 1991).

In education, there is no fundamental change that does not generate enemies. In the case of both untracking and cooperative learning, opposition is now developing among members of the same group: researchers, educators, and parents concerned about the education of gifted children. For example, recently in *ASCD Update*, cooperative learning was cited by several researchers and educators involved in gifted education as having a detrimental effect on the gifted, both in that the cooperative learning movement has often led to abandonment of separate gifted programs and in that gifted students "report feeling used, resentful, and frustrated by group work with students of lower ability" (Willis 1990, p. 8). And in this issue of *Educational Leadership*, Susan Allan writes that "gifted and high-ability children show positive academic effects from some forms of homogeneous grouping" (see p. 64).

The questions of untracking and cooperative learning for the gifted are important for others besides the 5 percent (or so) of students who are identified as academically gifted, because arguments about the gifted are often used to defeat attempts to reduce or eliminate tracking with the remaining 95 percent of students.

What is the evidence on ability grouping and cooperative learning for gifted or other high-ability students? In this article I discuss the research and the logic around these issues of programming for very able students.

Is Untracking Bad for High Achievers?
Leaving aside the question of cooperative learning or other instructional strategies, it is important to understand what has been found in the research on ability grouping in general. Susan Allan correctly observes that the popular press has distorted the research, making ability grouping appear disastrous for the achievement of all students. She is also correct in noting that different ability grouping practices have different achievement effects (see Slavin 1988). However, I strongly disagree with her conclusion that ability grouping is beneficial to high achievers and her implication that it is therefore a desirable practice.

First, let me make a critical distinction between "high achievers" and the "gifted." In most studies, high achievers are the top 33 percent of students; "gifted" are more often the top 3–5 percent. These are very different groups, and I will address them separately.

Is ability grouping beneficial for high-ability students? My reviews of research on between-class ability grouping (tracking) found it was not. In elementary studies I found a median effect size for high achievers of +.04, which is trivially different from zero (Slavin 1987).[1] In secondary schools, the effect was +.01 (Slavin 1990a). Kulik and Kulik (1987) obtained medians of +.10 in elementary, +.09 in secondary schools —higher than mine, but still very small. Most reviewers consider an effect size less than +.20 to be educationally insignificant. In almost every study I reviewed, the achievement differences between ability-grouped and heterogeneous placement were not statistically significant for high achievers. The possibility that the failure to find educationally meaningful effects could be due to ceiling effects on standardized tests is remote; standardized tests are certainly designed to adequately measure the achievement of the top 33 percent of students.

Now let's consider the gifted, the top 3–5 percent of students. Gifted programs fall into two categories, *enrichment* and *acceleration*. In acceleration programs, students either skip a grade or take courses not usually offered at their grade level (for example, Algebra I in 7th grade). When acceleration involves only one subject, that subject is almost always mathematics. All other gifted programs, which do not involve skipping grades or courses, are called "enrichment."

Research on *acceleration* does favor

the practice (see Kulik and Kulik 1984), although this research is difficult to interpret. If one student takes Algebra I and a similar student takes Math 7, the Algebra I student will obviously do better on an algebra test. Still, studies of this type find that the accelerated students do almost as well as non-accelerated students on, say, tests of Math 7, so the extra algebra learning is probably a real benefit.

Research on *enrichment* programs, which are far more common in practice, is, to put it mildly, a mess. Most such studies compare students assigned to a gifted program to students who were not so assigned, often to students who were *rejected* from the same programs! Such studies usually control statistically for IQ or prior achievement, but these controls are inadequate. Imagine two students with IQs of 130, one assigned to a gifted program, the other rejected. Can they be considered equivalent? Of course not—the rejected student was probably lower in motivation, actual achievement, or other factors highly relevant to the student's likely progress (see Slavin 1984). A study by Howell (1962), included in the Kulik and Kulik (1982, 1987) meta-analyses, compared students in gifted classes to those rejected for the same program, controlling for nothing. The only study I know of that randomly assigned

gifted students to gifted (enrichment) or heterogeneous classes (Mikkelson 1962) found small differences favoring *heterogeneous* placement. Reviewers of the literature on effects of gifted programs (for example, Fox 1979) have generally concluded that while acceleration programs do enhance achievement, enrichment programs do not. Even if enrichment programs were ultimately found to be effective for gifted students, this would still leave open the possibility that they would be just as effective for *all* students (Slavin 1990b).

Leaving aside for a moment the special case of acceleration, nearly all researchers would agree that the achievement effects of between-class ability grouping (tracking) for all students are small to nil. What does this say to the practitioner? Since arguments for ability grouping depend entirely on the belief that grouping increases achievement, the absence of such evidence undermines any rationale for the practice. The harm done by ability groups, I believe, lies not primarily in effects on achievement but in other impacts on low and average achievers. For example, low-track students are more likely to be delinquent or to drop out of school than similar low achievers not in the low track (Wiatrowski et al. 1982). Perhaps most important, tracking works against our national ideology that all are created equal and our desire to be one nation. The fact that African-American, Hispanic, and low socioeconomic students in general wind up so often in the low tracks is repugnant on its face. Why would we want to organize our schools this way if we have no evidence that it helps students learn?

I do believe that schools must recognize individual differences and allow all students to reach their full potential, and they can do this by using flexible within-class grouping strategies and other instructional techniques without turning to across-the-board between-class grouping (see Slavin et al. 1989). In some cases (mostly mathematics), acceleration may be justified for extremely able students. But the great majority of students can and should learn together.

Is Cooperative Learning Bad for High Achievers?

In research on cooperative learning, we have routinely analyzed achievement outcomes according to students' pretest scores. Those in the top third, middle third, and low third have all gained consistently, relative to similar students in control classes, as long as the cooperative learning program in use provides group goals and individual accountability (see Slavin 1991). High achievers gain from cooperative learning in part because their peers encourage them to learn (it benefits the group) and because, as any teacher knows, we learn best by describing our current state of knowledge to others (see Webb 1985).

In preparation for writing this article, I asked my colleague, Robert Stevens, to run some additional analyses on a study he is doing in two suburban elementary schools. The two schools have been using cooperative learning in all academic subjects for many years, in which all forms of between-class ability grouping are avoided and in which special education teachers team with regular classroom teachers to teach classes containing both academically handicapped and non-handicapped students. Stevens' analyses focused on three definitions of high ability: top 33 percent, top 10 percent, and top 5 percent. The results for grades 2–5 on standardized tests are summarized in Figure 1.

Figure 1 shows that even the very highest achieving students benefited from cooperative learning in comparison to similar students in the two control schools. The only exception was on Language Mechanics, probably because the writing process approach we use does not emphasize mechanics out of the context of writing. It is important to note that the Stevens study does not involve run-of-the-mill cooperative learning in reading, writing/language arts, or mathematics, but uses Cooperative Integrated Reading and Composition or CIRC (Stevens et al. 1987) and Team Assisted Individualization (TAI) Mathematics (Slavin 1985) (also see Slavin et al. 1989/90). These programs incorporate flexible grouping within the class and there-

Fig. 1. Difference in Effect Sizes Between High Achievers in Two Cooperative and Two Control Schools

Measure	Top 33%	Top 10%	Top 5%
Reading Vocabulary	+.42	+.65	+.32
Reading Comprehension	+.53	+.68	+.96
Language Mechanics	+.28	+.11	−.14
Language Expression	+.28	+.48	+.17
Math Computation	+.63	+.59	+.62
Math Concepts & Applications	+.28	+.32	+.19

Note: These data are from Point Pleasant and Overlook Elementary Schools and two matched comparison schools in Anne Arundel County, Maryland, a Baltimore suburb.

fore differentiate instruction for students of different achievement levels. Still, no separate grouping or special program was needed to substantially accelerate the achievement of even the highest achievers (and of other students as well).

Many of the concerns expressed about high achievers in cooperative learning are based either on misconceptions or on experience with inappropriate forms of cooperative learning. First, many educators and parents worry that high achievers will be used as "junior teachers" instead of being able to move ahead on their own material. This is a confusion of cooperative learning with peer tutoring; in all cooperative methods, students are learning material that is new to all of them. A related concern is that high achievers will be held back waiting for their groupmates. This is perhaps a concern about untracking, but not about cooperative learning. In cooperative learning students are typically exposed to the same content they would have seen anyway; and in forms of cooperative learning such as CIRC and TAI, they may progress far more rapidly than they otherwise would have. Sometimes parents are concerned when their youngsters' grades are made dependent on those of their groupmates. This does happen in some forms of cooperative learning, but I am personally very opposed to the practice. Certificates or other recognition work just as well, and grades

can and should be given based on individual performance.

No Evidence in Favor of Tracking

My personal philosophy of education is that all students should be helped to achieve their full potential. I am in favor of acceleration programs (especially in mathematics) for the gifted, and I believe in differentiating instruction *within* heterogeneous classes to meet the needs of students above (and below) the class average in performance. But I see no evidence or logic to support separate enrichment programs for gifted students. Enrichment is appropriate for *all* students. I see little evidence at all for separate tracks for high achievers. The burden of proof for the antidemocratic, antiegalitarian practice of ability grouping must be on those who would group, and no one who reads this literature could responsibly conclude that this requirement has been met.

The likely impact of untracking *per se* on the achievement of high achievers is no impact at all—these students will do well wherever they are. However, with the use of effective cooperative learning programs, especially those that differentiate instruction within the class, high achievers are likely to benefit in achievement, even the very top-achieving 5 percent. Educators of the gifted should be in the forefront of the cooperative learning movement, insisting on the use of forms of cooperative learning known to benefit gifted and other able students. If these methods also happen to be good for average and below average students, so much the better!☐

[1]In this case, an "effect size" is the difference between ability grouped and ungrouped students on achievement tests divided by the test's standard deviation. Effect sizes between -.20 and +.20 are generally considered to indicate no meaningful differences.

References

Fox, L. H. (1979). "Programs for the Gifted and Talented: An Overview." In *The Gifted and Talented: Their Education and Development*, pp. 104–126, edited by A.H. Passow. Chicago: University of Chicago Press.

Howell, W. (1962). "Grouping of Talented Students Leads to Better Academic Achievement in Secondary School." *Bulletin of the NASSP* 46: 67–73.

Kulik, C-L., and J. A. Kulik. (1982). "Effects of Ability Grouping on Secondary School Students: A Meta-Analysis of Evaluation Findings." *American Educational Research Journal* 19: 415–428.

Kulik, C-L., and J. A. Kulik. (1984). "Effects of Accelerated Instruction on Students." *Review of Educational Research* 54: 409–425.

Kulik, C-L., and J. A. Kulik. (1987). "Effects of Ability Grouping on Student Achievement." *Equity and Excellence* 23: 22–30.

Mikkelson, J. E. (1962). "An Experimental Study of Selective Grouping and Acceleration in Junior High School Mathematics." Doctoral diss., University of Minnesota.

Slavin, R. E. (1984). "Meta-Analysis in Education: How Has It Been Used?" *Educational Researcher* 13, 8: 6–15, 24–27.

Slavin, R. E. (1985). "Team-Assisted Individualization: Combining Cooperative Learning and Individualized Instruction in Mathematics." In *Learning to Cooperate, Cooperating to Learn*, pp. 177–209, edited by R. E. Slavin, S. Sharan, S. Kagan, R. Hertz-Lazarowitz, C. Webb, and R. Schmuck. New York: Plenum.

Slavin, R. E. (1987). "Ability Grouping and Student Achievement in Elementary Schools: A Best-Evidence Synthesis." *Review of Educational Research* 57: 293–336.

Slavin, R. E. (1988). "Synthesis of Research on Grouping in Elementary and Secondary Schools." *Educational Leadership* 46, 1: 67–77.

Slavin, R. E. (1990a). "Achievement Effects of Ability Grouping in Secondary Schools: A Best-Evidence Synthesis." *Review of Educational Research* 60, 3: 471–499.

Slavin, R. E. (1990b). "Ability Grouping, Cooperative Learning, and the Gifted." *Journal for the Education of the Gifted* 14: 3–8.

Slavin, R. E. (1991). "Synthesis of Research on Cooperative Learning." *Educational Leadership* 48, 5: 63–74.

Slavin, R. E., N. A. Madden, and R. J. Stevens. (1989/90). "Cooperative Learning Models for the 3 R's." *Educational Leadership* 47, 4: 22–28.

Slavin, R. E., J. H. Braddock, C. Hall, and R. J. Petza. (1989). *Alternatives to Ability Grouping*. Baltimore, Md.: Johns Hopkins University, Center for Research on Effective Schooling for Disadvantaged Students.

Stevens, R. J., N. A. Madden, R. E. Slavin, and A. M. Farnish. (1987). "Cooperative Integrated Reading and Composition: Two Field Experiments." *Reading Research Quarterly* 22: 433–454.

Webb, N. (1985). "Student Interaction and Learning in Small Groups: A Research Summary." In *Learning to Cooperate, Cooperating to Learn*, pp. 147–172, edited by R. E. Slavin, S. Sharan, S. Kagan, R. Hertz-Lazarowitz, C. Webb, and R. Schmuck. New York: Plenum.

Wiatrowski, M., S. Hansell, C. R. Massey, and D. L. Wilson. (1982). "Curriculum Tracking and Delinquency." *American Sociological Review* 47: 151–160.

Willis, S. (1990). "Cooperative Learning Fallout." *ASCD Update* 32, 8: 6,8.

Author's note: This article was written under a grant from the Office of Educational Research and Improvement, U.S. Department of Education (No. OERI-R-117-R90002). However, any opinions expressed are mine and do not represent OERI positions or policies.

Robert E. Slavin is Director of the Elementary School Program, Center for Research on Effective Schooling for Disadvantaged Students, The Johns Hopkins University, 3505 N. Charles St., Baltimore, MD 21218.

Educational Leadership 48 (March 1991): 72-74

BRUCE R. JOYCE

Grouping and the Gifted

Common Misconceptions about Cooperative Learning and Gifted Students

Response to Allan

By clarifying misunderstandings about cooperative learning and high achievers, perhaps we can resolve the conflict—to the benefit of all students.

The controversy about cooperative learning in general is perplexing, because it is such a benign and beneficial innovation. Given its effects in the personal, social, and academic domains, how can anyone object to teaching students how to cooperate in learning?

When we specifically consider whether cooperative approaches to learning are suitable for gifted students, we often find the discussion clouded by questions about the wisdom of continuing GATE programs and concern about the adverse affects of tracking. The question of whether cooperative learning benefits gifted students, however, is important in its own right and needs to be settled as an issue separate from the matter of tracking. Otherwise it will persist, whether GATE programs survive or not.

Several misconceptions fuel the dispute about cooperative learning and gifted students. If we can clarify these assumptions, perhaps we can resolve the controversy.

Misconceptions about Cooperative Learning

I repeatedly hear four erroneous assumptions about cooperative learning in the arguments against its use for gifted and talented students.

Assumption No. 1: *Cooperative learning refers to only one approach to teaching.* Some objections to the use of cooperative learning are based on an

> **The issue of whether cooperative learning benefits gifted students needs to be settled as an issue separate from the matter of tracking.**

impression of *one* technique that has been overused or misused somewhere. Rejection of that technique is then extended to all cooperative approaches to learning, when, in actuality, there are *many* ways of generating cooperative activity in the classroom to achieve specific purposes (Joyce et al. 1991). For example:

● To increase attention to divergent thinking, teachers use Synectics (Gordon and Poze 1971), which combines individual and cooperative activity to teach students how to use metaphors and analogies in writing and problem solving.

● To help students take on the modes of scientific inquiry, teachers select the inductive models of cooperative activity, in which students work both separately and together to build and test hypotheses (Joyce et al. 1991).

● For the analysis of public issues and personal values, teachers use Jurisprudential Inquiry and Role Playing, which help students capitalize on individual differences in perception to

121

fuel their personal and collective investigations (Joyce et al. 1991).

● For education in cooperation itself, there are the techniques developed by Johnson and Johnson (1990), among others.

● For the study of specific academic content, there are the approaches developed by Aronson et al. (1978), Slavin (1988), and Kagan (1990).

● To teach scientific inquiry and the democratic process simultaneously, there is Group Investigation (Sharan and Shachar 1988).

All of these techniques address objectives frequently mentioned as special needs of gifted and talented students. If a teacher needs others, the catalog of publications and idea-books put out by the International Association for the Study of Cooperation in Education, now 50 pages long, includes many techniques not mentioned here (Graves and Graves 1990). The great range produced by this fertile community provides avenues that can benefit *any* student population.

Assumption No. 2: *Cooperative learning is the only type of learning approach to use.* Just because the social approaches to education are supported by a fine research base does not imply that all activity should be developed around cooperative projects. However, it *is* fundamental in all teaching to build a community of learners who use many learning tools to achieve their ends (Joyce and Weil 1986, Joyce et al. 1991). No doubt, some disseminators of cooperative approaches overclaim their research and advocate greater use of specific techniques than is reasonable, but no experts on cooperative learning suggest that any one technique will be effective all day long. Building a learning community, however, needs to be pervasive.

Assumption No. 3: *Gifted and talented students are mismatched with cooperative learning.* I simply know of no supporting evidence to uphold the belief that gifted and talented students are, as a group, immune to the benefits of cooperating in order to learn or that they possess psychic antibodies that make cooperative activity actually harmful to them. Certainly, individual students, including those thought to be

That something works well for average and below-average students should not lead to the conclusion that it must, *ipso facto*, not benefit the above-average.

gifted, respond differently to any educational environment, but that is a different question from whether they have the social skill to profit from cooperative activity (just about all students do) or whether they can or should learn those skills if they don't have them.

The literature contains stunning examples where students of a wide range of academic histories profited dramatically from the environment of a very cooperative classroom (See, especially, the findings in Sharan and Shachar 1988). The discomfort generated by learning to do unfamiliar things may, in fact, be a critical mechanism for growth (Joyce 1986/1991).

There is evidence, from the time of the early Terman studies, that manifestations of learning ability are often accompanied by general problem-solving aptitude, enabling students thus blessed to profit from a wider range of environments than many of their cohorts. That something works well for average and below-average students should not lead to the conclusion that it must, *ipso facto*, not benefit the above-average.

For example, Baveja, Joyce, and Showers (Baveja 1988) combined cooperative learning with inductive thinking strategies with students selected because of a combination of outstanding academic and athletic aptitude (talented in two areas) in a science course. The resulting effect size was 1.0 for lower-order tests, and

a mean for higher-order test items was *six times* greater than the mean of the matched control group.

In another recent study of cooperative learning—in this case, through Group Investigation—Sharan and Shachar (1988) illustrated how rapidly students of differing learning histories can accelerate their learning rates. They prepared social studies teachers to organize their students into learning communities and then compared the classroom interaction and academic achievement in these classes with classes taught by the customary "whole-class" method. In Israel, where the study was conducted, students of Middle Eastern origin generally belong to the disadvantaged population, whereas students of European-origin generally are more advantaged. Students from both origins were mixed in the classes studied.

Sharan and Shachar found that the students of Middle Eastern origin taught with Group Investigation achieved average gains nearly two-and-a-half times those of their whole-class counterparts. In fact, the "socially disadvantaged" students taught with Group Investigation learned at rates above those of the "socially advantaged" students taught by teachers who did not have Group Investigation in their repertoires. For the students of Western origin, the average gain was *twice* that of their whole-class counterparts. Thus, the model was exceptionally effective for students from both backgrounds; as it turned out, students from both backgrounds were disadvantaged in the classes where cooperative learning was not used.

Assumption No. 4: *Cooperative learning and extreme heterogeneous grouping go hand in hand.* This assumption is no doubt based on a mistaken extrapolation of a finding from the research on social models designed to make use of heterogeneity for specific purposes. An example is Synectics, where heterogeneity frequently benefits learning. But social models of teaching can be used with either specially selected *or* randomly assembled populations. Some models capitalize on heterogeneity in ability, heritage, and point of view; but in any group of students, there is enough variance to make any of the cooperative formats work to the benefit of all students. Clearly, grouping to *maximize* variance is a matter of choice rather than necessity.

Questions about variance in classrooms often get bound up with the difficult question of tracking, generating emotions that cloud important issues. Given the evidence (see, for example, Slavin 1990), it is clear that tracking is not a good thing. However, that evidence, although long-standing, has failed to influence practice. In recent years a new device for tracking, the magnet school movement—by increasing segregation by ability and social background—has been a disaster for many students in our larger cities (See *The New Improved Sorting Machine* by Moore and Davenport 1989). Thus, advocates of *all* programs for students with special needs will have to search for ways to carry them out that do not have the bad side effects that tracking has had. I have no doubt that this can be done, but the simple "track and educate" model will now have to go. Again, however, the issue about cooperative learning is a separate one.

Cooperating for Better Solutions

As we attempt to design better educational programs, giving up assumptions may be as important as developing new approaches. We have to acknowledge that individual differences exist and that they need to be accommodated much more effectively than in the past. Clinging to unwarranted assumptions in the face of evidence to the contrary will not help us in that task. But if we cooperate to develop better solutions and freely borrow from others to nourish our specialties, we should soon see success for every student—not just an avoidance of failure, but an acceleration of richness and rates of learning unanticipated even a few years ago—and for all.☐

References

Aronson, E., N. Blaney, C. Stephan, J. Sikes, and M. Snapp. (1978). *The Jigsaw Classroom*. Beverly Hills: Sage.

Baveja, Bharati. (1988). "An Experimental Study of Information Processing: Models of Teaching in Schools of India." Ph.D. thesis, University of Delhi.

Gordon, W.J.J., and T. Poze. (1971). *The Metaphorical Way of Learning and Knowing*. Cambridge: Porpoise Books.

Graves, N., and T. Graves. (1990). *Cooperative Learning: A Resource Guide*. Santa Cruz: The International Association for the Study of Cooperation in Education.

Johnson, D.W., and R.T. Johnson. (1990). *Cooperation and Competition: Theory and Research*. Edina, Minn.: Interaction Book Company.

Joyce, B. (1986/1991). "Making Discomfort Productive: The Dynamics of Disequilibrium." In *Models of Teaching*, edited by B. Joyce, B. Showers, and M. Weil, Chapter 20. Englewood Cliffs, N.J.: Prentice-Hall, Inc.

Joyce, B., and M. Weil. (1986). *Models of Teaching* Englewood Cliffs, N.J.: Prentice-Hall, Inc.

Joyce, B., B. Showers, and M. Weil. (1991). *Models of Teaching*. Englewood Cliffs, N.J.: Prentice-Hall, Inc.

Kagan, S. (1990). *Cooperative Learning Resources for Teachers*. San Juan Capistrano: Resources for Teachers.

Moore, D.R., and S. Davenport. (1989). *The New Improved Sorting Machine: Concerning School Choice*. Chicago: Designs for Change.

Sharan, S., and H. Shachar. (1988). *Language and Learning in the Cooperative Classroom*. New York: Springer-Verlag.

Slavin, R. (1988). *Cooperative Learning: Theory, Research, and Practice*. Englewood Cliffs, N.J.: Prentice-Hall, Inc.

Slavin, R. (1990). "Achievement Effects of Ability Grouping in Secondary Schools: A Best-Evidence Synthesis." *Review of Educational Research* 60, 3: 471–499.

Bruce R. Joyce is Co-Director, Booksend Laboratories, 652 Saint Andrews Dr., Rio Del Mar, Aptos, CA 95003.

The Collaborative School

In this final section we broaden our focus to the school and community. Stuart Smith defines elements of the collaborative school. Dickson Corbett and Joseph D'Amico raise questions about the image of the "hero" principal popular in the mid 1980s and suggest an alternative model of distributed leadership and organizational conditions that facilitate improvement. Karen Kent and Judith Warren Little report on the Marin County Teacher Advisor Project, an early experiment in "mentoring." A system of teacher support groups in Calgary, Alberta, is described by Mary Paquette, high school English department head.

Allan Glatthorn conceptualizes a variety of teacher peer support options under the generic term of "Cooperative Professional Development." One of these options, Peer Coaching, is described by Patricia Raney and Pam Robbins, and in another article by Ingrid Chrisco. Diana Leggett and Sharon Hoyle report on a Fort Worth, Texas, summer program that gives teachers opportunities to practice the skills of collaboration in a "lab school" setting. Next, Bruce Joyce and co-authors portray an ambitious project in Richmond County, Georgia, in which teachers learn new strategies in collegial study groups.

A final set of articles examines how collegiality relates to professionalism and school governance. Referring to a series of reports calling for more teacher autonomy and status, Ann Lieberman articulates a vision of teacher leadership. Jane David provides a synthesis of research on school-based management. Anne Ratzki and Angela Fisher describe life in their German school, where cooperation and teamwork at both staff and student levels have been the rule since 1975. Next, Richard Sagor tells how collaborative action research has enabled teachers in Washington state to answer their own questions about teaching and learning. Finally, Michael Fullan and co-authors tell how four major school districts and two higher education institutions have created a framework linking classroom instruction with teacher development and school improvement. In their partnership, cooperative learning at the classroom level is part of a broader effort to develop a facilitative school culture and manage the change process.

Educational Leadership 45 (Nov. 1987): 4-6

STUART C. SMITH

The Collaborative School Takes Shape

In collaborative schools, teachers see each other as resources for professional growth and work with the principal toward the common goal of school improvement.

Consider how the adults in two different kinds of schools interact. In school A, teachers do not discuss with one another their practice of teaching, nor do they help one another to improve their skills. They benefit little from the principal's annual visits to the classrooms to evaluate each by means of the district checklist. When administrators initiate new programs, teachers respond with apathy or are uncooperative. The faculty seldom unites around any effort to improve the school.

In contrast to the isolation and fragmentation that characterize school A, teachers in school B feel they are working toward a common goal of school improvement. Teachers observe each other's teaching and strive to help one another improve. Experienced teachers regularly share with new colleagues the practices that have worked effectively for them.

Asked why they function so well as a team, school B's teachers point to the principal, who provides the practical support they need to work together. And they point to each other as resources for solving problems. They are proud to take part in decision making; they value their control over a portion of the school's instructional budget.

Now, more than ever before, the structure of school A is being criticized. Consequently, in reforming school structures, educators are experimenting with alternatives that accord teachers greater respect as professionals while encouraging them to cooperate with one another and with administrators on school improve-

126

ment. These new practices and structures—characteristic of school B—all fit in the broad category of the *collaborative school*.

Elements of the Collaborative School

There is no one model of the collaborative school; collaboration describes a range of practices that can involve a handful of teachers or an entire faculty. Although collaboration can be encouraged by formal programs—organizational development, for instance—it cannot be imposed on a faculty. Collaboration depends on the voluntary effort of educators to improve their schools and their own skills through teamwork.

Because the collaborative school is a composite of beliefs and practices, it is easier to describe than to define. Perhaps the best way to characterize the collaborative school is to list its elements:

● the belief that the quality of education is largely determined by what happens at the school site;

● the conviction that instruction is most effective in a school environment characterized by norms of collegiality and continuous improvement (see Little 1982, Purkey and Smith 1983, Rosenholtz in press);

● the belief that teachers are responsible for the instructional process and accountable for its outcomes;

● the use of a wide range of practices and structures that enable administrators and teachers to work together on school improvement; and

● the involvement of teachers in decisions about school goals and the means for implementing them.

Although a host of other benefits may be expected to derive from collaboration—staff harmony, mutual respect between teachers and administrators, and a professional work environment for teachers—its primary rationale is instructional effectiveness. Its most important dynamic comes from teachers' working together to improve their teaching. The informal and formal interaction about instruction among teachers is what distinguishes the collaborative school from earlier models of democratic management and participative decision making.

What It Is Not

Some educators, while affirming the above characteristics as desirable for any school, may nonetheless respond negatively to the idea of collaboration. In anticipating objections that may be raised, it is therefore useful to say what the collaborative school is *not*.

It does not seek discussion for its own sake. Collaboration, some observers feel, means just a lot of talking that takes teachers away from their tasks. True, participative decision making and collegiality require a certain

investment of time. But the interaction of educators in their schools and the participation of teachers in decision making, while valuable in themselves, contribute to something of even greater value: quality education.

As Rosenholtz (in press) and Little (1982) point out, teacher interactions in themselves bear no relationship to school effectiveness. It is the content of those interactions that determines their value. Rosenholtz, for example, defines *collaboration* as "the extent to which teachers engage in help-related exchange." This definition focuses on the *kinds* of interactions believed to lead to improved teaching and learning. When teachers trade stories about problem students, they enjoy a sense of comradery; but when they also share teaching practices or critique one another's teaching, they are engaging in activities to improve their work.

It does not require school administrators to abdicate their authority. Is the collaborative school a laissez-faire approach to management in which administrators hand over the reins to

> **"Principals of collaborative schools have often discovered that power shared is power gained: teachers' respect for them grows."**

teachers? This concern lies at the root of many objections to collaboration. In actuality, strong leaders are necessary in collaborative schools, where they must halt the spread of isolationism and direct the faculty in establishing new norms of cooperation. As Alfonso and Goldsberry (1982) point out, coordinating professionals in the fluid context of collegial support is a complex task that "cannot be done through generating formal rules, or even standardized procedures." Consequently, a collaborative school requires a higher calibre of leadership than does a bureaucratic school.

However, principals must be willing to share authority. Teachers will be taking part in such tasks as setting school goals, allocating resources, and overseeing their own professional development. Nevertheless, increased responsibility for teachers need not mean decreased authority for principals. Principals of collaborative schools have often discovered that power shared is power gained: teachers' respect for them grows.

It does not reduce teachers' accountability. Efforts to give teachers more say in decisions may backfire, some observers fear, when teachers invoke "professionalism" to avoid doing what administrators or the public want them to do. But, in fact, collaborative norms reinforce traditional methods of accountability by building consensus toward school improvement. Teachers are most likely to respond favorably to the direction of an administrator if these actions conform to the expectations of their colleagues.

In the collaborative school, teachers monitor one another's performance, set limits on one another's behavior, and take responsibility for helping their colleagues to improve. These self-policing efforts are a measure of a faculty's true professionalism.

The Results of Teamwork
The collaborative school provides a climate and a structure that encourage teachers to work together and with the principal and other administrators toward school improvement and professional growth. In this setting teachers will gain respect as professionals, principals will see their efficacy increase, and all members of the school community will experience the satisfaction of accomplishing important goals through teamwork.□

References

Alfonso, Robert J., and Lee Goldsberry. "Colleagueship in Supervision." In *Supervision of Teaching*, edited by Thomas J. Sergiovanni. Alexandria, Va.: Association for Supervision and Curriculum Development, 1982, 90–107.
Little, Judith Warren. "Norms of Collegiality and Experimentation: Workplace Conditions of School Success." *American Educational Research Journal* 19, 3 (Fall 1982): 325–340.
Purkey, Stewart C., and Marshall S. Smith. "Effective Schools: A Review." *The Elementary School Journal* 83, 4 (March 1983): 427–452.
Rosenholtz, Susan J. *Teachers' Workplace: A Study of Social Organizations.* New York: Longman, in press.

Stuart C. Smith is Director of Publications, ERIC Clearinghouse on Educational Management, College of Education, University of Oregon, 1787 Agate St., Eugene, OR 97403-1215. He is co-author, with James J. Scott, of *Moving Toward the Collaborative School: A Work Environment for Effective Instruction* (1987), from which this article was adapted.

Educational Leadership 44 (Sept. 1986): 70-72

H. Dickson Corbett and Joseph J. D'Amico

No More Heroes:
Creating Systems to Support Change

Administrators can help ensure that improvement efforts
don't fall apart by providing teachers with time and
recognition for their participation, guarding projects from
competing distractions, and building new practices
into the daily routine.

Improving an educational institution—whether a school, district, or other agency—is difficult. All too often the success of improvement activities rides on the shoulders of a few heroes. If no heroes emerge, improvement may not result. This need not be the case.

Heroes and Improvement

Heroes invariably capture our attention—perhaps because hearing heroic stories enables us to join vicariously in struggles against adversity or because such tales simplify otherwise complex and seemingly inexplicable social developments. Great women and men acknowledged as the driving forces behind startling turnarounds dot the research literature and permeate the folklore of education. The wide acceptance of the hero approach to improvement is reflected in the popular belief that the school principal is the

key actor, the hero, in making a school effective. In other words, to rescue a program or turn a school around, get yourself a hero.

This simple formula has a downside, however. Heroes can move up, travel on, or burn out. A general theme in the change literature is that most improvement efforts die when special support disappears (Berman and McLaughlin 1976). Although this special support usually refers to funding, it may apply to special people as well. Unless someone steps into the void, a period of perceived and real deterioration accompanied by lowered morale often begins with the hero's departure.

Our reading of the change literature and our direct experiences in working with school improvement programs convince us that change efforts typically demand that the *majority* of staff participants become heroes since organizational conditions often impede improvement. That is, the time it takes to understand an innovation and translate it into practice conflicts with the time staff members need to perform their duties. Improvement priorities compete with one another; incentives for making changes are glaringly absent, and participants rarely see evidence of a systemwide commitment to an improvement.

Educational improvements should not have to rely on heroic efforts. We must begin to think about how to support innovation systematically. At least four organizational conditions can facilitate improvement: (1) available time, (2) cushions against interference, (3) opportunities for encouragement, and (4) recognition of the need for incorporation.

Available Time
Available time is time not already committed to official duties or to preparing for those duties. For change projects, the importance of such time cannot be overestimated. Clark (1984) argues that the availability of uncommitted time is one of seven distinguishing features of excellent schools. Available time enables staff to venture beyond the tried and true, to confer with peers about special or routine problems, to teach demonstration classes for new teachers, or to participate in change projects.

In most cases, administrators make time available either by changing schedules or altering the structure of work arrangements. For example, administrators can rearrange teachers' assignments so that improvement project participants have common planning periods. Alternatively, by recognizing that teachers usually have little opportunity to discuss instruction with their peers, administrators can create new work groups or encourage existing ones to use already available meeting times for productive discussion, for instance, rather than for catching up on paperwork. We have seen both approaches used effectively to facilitate change.

Arranging for substitutes provides project participants with available time and some flexibility, but this arrangement seldom proves satisfactory. Teachers mistrust substitutes, feel more competent than the stand-ins, and regard time away from students as time stolen from learning. Moreover, substitutes are a temporary rather than permanent means of making time available.

Cushions Against Interference
Too often principals revamp discipline policies at the same time that they revise lesson plans; superintendents standardize the curriculum *and* initiate special reading projects; state agencies launch a new testing program *while* altering graduation requirements and curriculum standards. That is, the most bothersome distraction usually comes from the system itself in the form of competing projects. Staff members have a difficult time determining what is most important and foreseeing what will last long enough to be worthwhile. They do not know where to put their already nearly depleted energies.

Fullan (1985) argues convincingly that changes in attitudes, beliefs, and understanding usually follow changes in behavior. Our experience supports this. It takes time for commitment to develop. Along with some initial ambiguity, participants experience confusion, frustration, anger, and exhaustion when they begin using new practices. Even where implementation is successful, users go through a series of steps, including:

- initial undifferentiated use and day-to-day coping;
- stepwise and disjointed use;
- initial coordination and consolidation of basic routines;
- coordinated practice and differentiated use; and
- refinement and extension.

It may take up to 18 months for staff members to achieve the higher levels of use. In the meantime, the improvement effort needs a kind of life support to give it a chance to survive early confusion and frustration.

Opportunities for Encouragement
Another element vital to success of a change effort is rewarding staff members for their participation. In the business world Peters and Waterman (1982) identify a paradox of human nature—a need to stand out and the desire to be on a winning team. In education the existence of this paradox underscores the significance of encouragement and recognition from peers, experts, and supervisors. Encouragement and recognition signal to participants that what they are doing is good for their own development and important to the institution they serve.

Such continuous incentive requires systematic, conscious effort, but it need not be time-consuming. The administrator or improvement effort leader can easily incorporate it into routine but informal staff interaction. Peters and Waterman call it "management by wandering around." Rather than relying on formal supervisory visits, the manager learns what staff members are doing and stimulates desired behavior through daily circuits around the work place. The length of an encounter is not critical, but the message given is. In excellent organizations, the message is consistently related to their core value—that is, what they want to stand for above all else.

Supportive leaders can apply this principle to school improvement efforts by frequently inquiring about the endeavor. They can routinely emphasize its priority as they interact with staff throughout the day. The heart of the activity is an informal message that the improvement effort addresses key organizational goals. Such a signal reinforces, as well as encourages, staff efforts. To use a hectic administrator's schedule to advantage requires only a conscious focus on this message. In systems where staff are routinely encouraged, giving special recognition for improvement should not present any problems; rewarding good work is a well-established habit.

Recognition of the Need to Incorporate

Ideally, new practices should survive until they are evaluated and their effectiveness is demonstrated or refuted. Realistically, changes rarely last that long. Too often they disappear through accident or neglect unless staff members continue to receive incentives for new behavior and unless the behavior is incorporated into existing policy (Corbett et al. 1984). Incorporating new practices and supporting procedures into regular school operation gives them a place in the routine and protects them if the original implementors depart. Indeed, staff turnover is one of the more calamitous events to befall a project at any level of the educational system. Because new practices require staff to rearrange what they do, the practices often have to replace, or be shoehorned in with, the old ones. Without changes in guidelines or procedures, staff members will likely view the new practices as add-ons and tend to neglect them. Unincorporated practices tend to be quickly neglected.

For these reasons, special attention should be paid, from the outset of the project, to incorporating changes into the daily operational routine to ensure that they will last. This can be done by (1) classifying the practices as rules, (2) encouraging curriculum revision, (3) establishing a training program for newcomers, and (4) supporting improvement-related activities as a line item in the school budget (rather than through special funding). The underlying theme of these strategies is that formal, substantive changes must accompany encouragement if the improvement effort is to stick. Such changes also symbolize to staff that the improvement project merits their attention. New rules, revisions, and training programs also establish an organizational climate in which systematic renewal becomes a preferred alternative to crisis-induced change.

Creating Conditions for Change

The obstacles to improvement are enormous: little available time, few cushions against interference, limited staff encouragement, and a barely acknowledged need for organizational change. Only a hero can overcome them. If no hero steps forward, the system all too frequently smothers the effort.

Alternatives to heroism exist. Rather than expecting educators to struggle to change unresponsive institutions, we can design an educational system that gives educators the time, protection, encouragement, and support they need to improve schools.☐

References

Berman, P. B., and M. W. McLaughlin. "Implementation of Educational Innovation." *Educational Forum* 40, 3 (1976): 345–370.

Clark, D. L., L. S. Lotto, and T. A. Astuto. "Effective Schools and School Improvement: A Comparative Analysis of Two Lines of Inquiry." *Educational Administrative Quarterly* 20, 3 (1984): 41–68.

Corbett, H. D., J. A. Dawson, and W. A. Firestone. *School Context and School Change: Implications for Effective Planning.* New York: Teachers College Press, 1984.

Fullan, M. "Change Processes and Strategies at the Local Level." *Elementary School Journal* 85, 3 (1985): 391–421.

Peters, T., and R. Waterman. *In Search of Excellence.* New York: Harper and Row, 1982.

H. Dickson Corbett is director of improvement studies, and **Joseph J. D'Amico** is senior research associate, both at Research for Better Schools, 444 N. Third St., Philadelphia, PA 19123.

The preparation of this paper was supported by funds from the National Institute of Education, United States Department of Education. The opinions expressed do not necessarily reflect the position or policy of NIE, and no official endorsement should be inferred. This work is based on a larger project, *Context and Change: A Training Program for School Improvement.* For additional information, contact the authors.

Educational Leadership 43 (Nov. 1985): 30-33

KAREN M. KENT

A Successful Program of Teachers Assisting Teachers

For four years, teachers in Marin County,
California, have served as advisors and
facilitators to other teachers.

As the study of new and expanded roles for teachers gains momentum, career ladder and instant master teacher programs are being created. Little has been said, however, about professional development programs to support teachers in new roles—a critical component to ensuring success.

The Teacher Advisor Project of the Marin County Office of Education was implemented five years ago as a staff development program that created two new positions for teachers: teacher advisors and peer facilitators (see Figure 1). We soon learned that professional training for the advisors and facilitators was needed, and subsequently we developed training plans to accompany these types of positions.

Now in its fifth year, The Teacher Advisor Project was developed through the collaboration of administrators of three pilot school districts, the Marin County Office of Education, Teacher Center staff members, and policy board members. It is funded for piloting by the San Francisco Foundation.

The project is based on two major beliefs:
• Teachers can and will define their own professional development needs in relation to school, system, and professional goals to improve schools and learning.
• To affect change in the classroom or school, assistance must be given onsite.

Three areas became guideposts for the success of project staff members in working with teachers: roles assumed by teacher advisors and peer facilitators as documented in contact logs, training and support needed to carry out these roles, and school readiness for change.

Roles of Advisors and Facilitators

Documented activities of advisors and peer facilitators evolved into five roles: resource linker, facilitator, trainer, colleague/coach, and supervisor.

1. *Resource Linker*. The role of resource linker includes finding or developing materials, locating speakers

or planning field trips, and linking teachers who share common interests or needs. Because teachers sometimes fill this role for each other, it required few new skills for project staff members, whose needs could be met through regular support meetings. When additional information or materials were needed, staff members could rely on each other for help. Linking resources is a good way to establish contact with teachers and prove one's reliability and ability to "deliver the goods," but it needs monitoring so that the linker's role does not become that of a "go fer."

As a result of this activity, curriculum-centered teacher networks have been created that include teachers from districts all over the county who are interested in science, computers, gifted, early childhood, or special education. A peer facilitator organizes and manages the activities of each network.

2. *Facilitator*. Project staff members learned early how to lead groups using a consensus process for planning curriculum, solving schoolwide problems, selecting materials, and sharing

teaching strategies. We employed training processes developed by a nearby county office (Baker and Scornaienchi, 1980) as well as materials from Interaction Associates (Doyle and Strauss, 1980). These skills were valuable in helping school staff members identify priorities for working together, assisting a group of teachers collaborating on implementing new strategies for teaching math, and resolving conflicts, among others. When two districts voted to consolidate, one advisor became instrumental in facilitating community, staff, and board meetings. Facilitation helped advisors and peer facilitators gain acceptance from teachers and administrators by making efficient agreements when working together.

3. *Trainer*. One of our hopes when we began this project was to involve teachers in the study of teaching. During the first year, we implemented a formal teacher training program to establish a common technical language and the project staff members' expertise. Advisors were also trained to use Madeline Hunter's theories (Wolfe, 1984) and classroom manage-

ment procedures presented in other workshops. Advisors subsequently organized material into a four-day training workshop, *Instructional Skills*, into which some of Bloom's work on mastery learning, Bloom's Taxonomy, and other teacher-effectiveness material has been incorporated during the past four years. Advisors worked together to organize the training and systematically coached each other as they began leading workshops the first summer.

Other training methods have since been developed to build on what we perceive to be the limited but basic material that makes up *Instructional Skills. Cooperative Learning* (three days), *Peer Observation* (one day), *Behavior Management* (one day), and *Models of Teaching* (one to six days) are now part of the training program. Some peer facilitators have taken on the trainer role for portions of *Instructional Skills*, but their other responsibilities to students preclude them from having the time to do much training.

All project staff members report that it is helpful for them to conduct training sessions, because other teachers then view them as persons to learn from. Their expertise is recognized by teachers throughout Marin County and by educators in other California districts who contract with advisors to conduct training sessions.

4. *Colleague/Coach.* Originally, we intended to make coaching the primary role for teacher advisors and peer facilitators. We learned that there were precedents in this role to gaining teachers' acceptance. Little (1985) clarified some factors when she studied conferences of teacher advisors with teachers. Her work resulted in the articulation of six principles of advising. The first three—common language, focus, and hard evidence—emphasize a shared technical language. The second three—interaction, predictability, and reciprocity—are termed the "social" principles of trust needed if work between advisors and teachers is to be effective.

It takes time to be accepted in this role and to develop the shared technical language and trust needed for productive observations and conferences. Advisors and peer facilitators must be able to use the technical language, model the practice, and teach the language to teachers. Training, communication, observation, and conferencing skills precede substantive in-class work with teachers. Monthly training

Figure 1. Teacher Advisor and Peer Facilitator Positions

POSITION	SALARY REMUNERATION	RESPONSIBILITIES	REQUIRED EXPERIENCE
TEACHER ADVISOR	Full- or half-time advisor	Regular teacher's salary	1. Working with staff members at two or three target schools 2. Training and facilitation	At least 5 years' teaching experi- in Marin County schools
PEER FACILITATOR	Regular classroom teacher released three days each month to work with the Teacher Advisor Project	$1,200/year stipend and released time	1. Coordinating a network or working with one school staff member 2. Some training or facilitation	Same as above

"District policy states that advisors and facilitators do not participate in teacher evaluation— a sensitive issue."

sessions for project staff members emphasize reinforcement and refining of the training described above as well as team building and communication skills. As trust develops among team members, they are able to serve as colleagues and coaches for one another in problem solving and in learning the skills needed to work with teachers.

5. *Supervisor*. Project staff members seldom venture into supervision until near the end of their second or the beginning of their third year at a school, working with the same administrator. Performing in this role requires a high degree of trust between the site administrator and advisor and between the teachers and advisor.

Teacher advisors and peer facilitators work with teachers upon their request but do not inform others of the substance of their work with a teacher in his or her classroom. District policy states that advisors and facilitators do not participate in teacher evaluation—a sensitive issue.

Issues Raised by this Program
In developing the Teacher Advisor Project, we have encountered three issues that are likely to affect the success of similar programs elsewhere.

1. *The need for additional training*. When teachers take on roles other than traditional classroom teaching, they need additional sets of skills and knowledge to work effectively with adults, implement change, and serve as curriculum or staff development consultants or researchers. Master or mentor teacher programs are sometimes based on the assumption that high quality classroom performance with students is sufficient qualification and preparation for working with other teachers. But our teacher advisors and peer facilitators say they wouldn't have lasted one year without opportunities to learn about adult learning, facilitation skills, change theory, and research on teaching. They need to have a context against which they can judge their degree of success and that shows them how to set up or change strategies when working with colleagues.

In their study of assistance personnel in three school improvement programs, Goodwin and Lieberman (1985) and Saxl and Miles (1985) confirmed this need and extended it further. Even though the assisters in their study entered these positions with impressive skills and abilities, it became clear that much new learning took place when they assumed new roles.

2. *Jealousies*. Teacher advisors and peer facilitators sometimes encounter jealousies of teachers who are not moving into new roles because of the additional training and teamwork to which they have access. In many districts, continuous learning for all teachers is not an accepted norm, as if a teacher upon graduation from college has all the professional training he or she will ever need. Further training is necessary for employees to keep up in almost every career occupation, and successful organizations allocate work time and resources for employee training. Teamwork skills in setting goals, solving problems, and keeping high morale are also valued. Traditionally, few schools have recognized that many teachers are voracious learners and capitalized on that fact as an incentive to keep classrooms and schools vital and exciting. No wonder some of our most vital, growing people leave the profession after five years!

3. *Fear of empowerment*. School districts and teachers need to re-examine their willingness for teachers to become active problem solvers participating in organizational decisions. With so many legal and public demands on schools, districts sometimes fear losing more control; teachers often are not sensitive to this.

Conversely, as teachers move into advanced career positions, they must be willing to accept some of the burden of responsibility for addressing these demands by becoming knowledgeable, committed, and active members of the organization and of the professional occupation. Teachers who choose to advance in their teaching careers must carefully consider the responsibilities that accompany empowerment.

More to Be Learned
From the beginning of the Teacher Advisor Project, we believed in the importance of collecting data and reflecting on what we were doing. The study of our work and the assistance we have received from research professionals has been critically valuable. No doubt there is much more to be learned about emerging new roles for teachers, school improvement, and an improved status of teaching. If we had not allocated time for reflection and analysis, we would not have learned what we now know.□

References
Baker, William, and Scornaienchi, August. *Problem Solving and Cooperative Planning Guide*. Alameda County, Calif.: Office of the Alameda County Superintendent of Schools, 1982.

Beckum, Leonard; Dasho, Stefan; and Bundy, Louis. "Program Evaluation of Marin Teacher Advisor Project." Report of the Far West Laboratory Evaluation Studies Unit, San Francisco, 1984.

Doyle, Michael, and Strauss, David. *How to Make Meetings Work*. Chicago: Playboy Press, 1980.

Goodwin, A. Lin, and Lieberman, Ann. "Effective Assister Behavior: What They Brought and What They Learned." Paper presented at the Annual Conference of the American Educational Research Association, Chicago, April 1985.

Little, Judith Warren. "Professional Development Roles and Relationships: Principles and Skills of 'Advising.'" Report of the Far West Laboratory for Educational Research and Development, San Francisco, 1985.

Saxl, Ellen R., and Miles, Matthew B. "The Real Thing: What Skills Do Effective Change Agents Need? Some Preliminary Findings From the Field." Paper presented at the Annual Conference of the American Educational Research Association, Chicago, April 1985.

Wolfe, Patricia R. *Instructional Skills Trainers' Manual*. Napa County, Calif.: Office of the Superintendent of Napa County, 1984.

Karen M. Kent was manager of the Teacher Advisor Project at the Marin County Office of Education when she wrote this article. She is currently Director, Region 3 Teacher Education/Computer Center, Marin County Office of Education, P.O. Box 4925, San Rafael, California 94913.

Educational Leadership 43 (Nov. 1985): 34-36

Teachers as Teacher Advisors: The Delicacy of Collegial Leadership

As they observed their own emerging relationships with teachers, Marin County teacher advisors discovered the dilemma posed by leadership among peers.

JUDITH WARREN LITTLE

Among the potentially most useful yet most demanding interactions among teachers are those that focus on actual classroom performance. Such interactions enable teachers to learn from and with one another, and to reflect on crucial aspects of curriculum and instruction. However, they also place teachers' self-esteem and professional respect on the line, because they expose how teachers teach, how they think about teaching, and how they plan for teaching to the scrutiny of peers. The challenge is to devote close, even fierce, attention to teaching while preserving the integrity of teachers.

A highly regarded Teacher Advisor Project at the Marin County Office of Education (California) presented one opportunity to examine advisor-teacher intereactions that are closely bound to observed classroom practice. Over a three-year period a cadre of experienced advisers learned not only to comment effectively on teaching but also to work reciprocally with teachers. The advisers came close to the classroom without coming close to the bone. Their direct involvement with teachers, comparable to roles envisioned for master and mentor teachers and to senior positions in career ladder plans, showed that the perspec- tives and skills of advising have broad utility.

The Skills of Advising Project

In a joint venture by the Far West Laboratory and the Marin County Teacher Advisor Project, teacher advisors, teachers, and researchers analyzed videotapes of advisor-teacher conferences based on classroom observation. Completed during the spring of 1984 by eight advisors in collaboration with fourteen teachers, the taped conferences were diverse in grade level and subject matter, but they had two crucial characteristics in common.

First, conferences were extraordinary events. Without exception, the participating teachers found the conferences stimulating, rewarding, even "an ego boost." From the point of view of the teachers, these conferences "worked," offering a professional opportunity that most would eagerly repeat.

Second, they were rare. Even in these schools where teacher advisors worked regularly, interactions that brought advisors close to teachers' thinking about teaching or to their classroom performance were infre- quent. As recorded on their routine contact logs, most advisors' work occurred outside the classroom.

For advisors, as for master or mentor teachers, the acceptance, mutual respect, and close working relations that made advisors welcome in the classroom appeared hard-won. The advisor role had neither the force of bureaucratic authority nor the weight of tradition behind it. Advisors could apply no formal sanction (for good or ill) and could wield little direct influence over teachers' future rewards or opportunities. Rather, advisors influenced teachers through informal interaction.

Drumming up business. Advisors and teachers shared the dilemma of getting started with one another. Teachers were quietly perplexed about how to proceed; some resented the hours advisors spent in the lounge (trying to drum up business) while teachers were hard at work in classrooms. Advisors' open-ended invitation to "use me" left teachers hesitant to propose anything that might cast the advisor in the role of "gofer" or aide. At the same time, advisors were hesitant to propose specific projects with teachers for fear of "stepping on toes." The result was a strange dance that transpired mostly in the teachers' lounge, mostly at a polite distance, and rarely in the more intimate environs of the classroom.

To get past the teachers' lounge, advisors recruited interested individuals on a case-by-case basis. Teachers who were interviewed felt that the first move was best made by the advisor, whose role in the school was unfamiliar and ambiguous. The advisor could make a pitch to teachers about work worth doing, but the advisor's propos-

als had to be very specific: "This is what I've done before. This is what I could do for you."

Principles and practices of advising. The generally helpful stance that advisors took toward teachers, contributing in any way they could, combined with the well-designed group training sessions, which they conducted for teachers to earn them entry to teachers' classrooms. Once there, the way advisors conducted themselves in dis-

cussions and conferences with teachers helped earn them the right to come again.

A close look at the videotaped conferences revealed six ways in which advisors and teachers successfully looked at teaching together. The six principles are presented from two points of view. First, they present the ways an advisor and teacher work together: conferences attain the greatest depth, vigor, and range as a joint

---

Figure 1. Six Principles of Advising

The "technical" principles: talk about teaching

Common Language

Skillful *pairs* agree on the importance of a common language and make a deliberate move to use shared ideas and language to describe, understand and refine teaching.

Skillful *advisors* take the lead in conveying the importance of a shared language, locating and proposing key ideas and terms, teaching them to others, and using them appropriately and creatively in their own talk.

Focus

Skillful *pairs* focus on one or two key questions, issues, situations, or problems and addresses them with depth, persistence, imagination, and good humor.

Skillful *advisors* take the lead in making observations and conferences purposeful and focused: they propose a focus or invite teachers to propose one; they draw on outside study and research as well as on their own classroom experience to discuss the topic; they tie their notes and observation records tightly to the proposed focus; without being stilted mechanical or overly rigid, they stick to the focus during conferences. They make their talk concrete and precise.

Hard Evidence

Skillful *pairs* use a record of classroom interaction as a basis for generating questions, drawing conclusions, and pursuing alternatives. They work together to invent or select the observation methods that suit their purposes.

Skillful *advisors* convey the importance of an adequate record and do a thorough job of collecting the evidence, in and out of the classroom, that will make the discussion rigorous and fruitful.

Interaction

Skillful *pairs* engage in lively interaction with one another, making the conference a vehicle for joint work on teaching and an opportunity to improve their ability to learn from one another.

Skillful *advisors* foster interaction by the way they arrange the physical setting, the introduction they give in the first two minutes, and the manner in which they use questions throughout the discussion.

Predictability

Skillful *pairs* build trust in one another's intentions by relying on a known, predictable set of topics, criteria, and methods.

Skillful *advisors* are as clear about the observation and conference criteria and methods as they expect the teacher to be about instructional aims and methods.

Reciprocity

Skillful *pairs* build trust by acknowledging and deferring to one another's knowledge and skill, by talking to each other in ways that preserve individual dignity, and by giving their work together a full measure of energy, thought and attention.

Skillful *advisors* provide a model of reciprocity by showing their own willingness to improve, by showing serious attention to teachers' knowledge and experience, and by working as hard to observe well as teachers are to teach.

Based on the Skills of Advising Study completed as a joint project of the Marin County Teacher Advisor Project and the Far West Laboratory for Educational Research and Development.

achievement of a skillful *pair* accustomed to working together on teaching. Second, they present the way an *advisor* takes the lead to build the necessary shared understandings, habits, and skills (see Figure 1).

Do advisors give advice? There are no established traditions in the teaching profession by which teachers receive advice on their teaching, or offer advice to others. However skillfully and enthusiastically conducted, the conferences described here placed teachers on unfamiliar ground with one another. Advisors were hesitant to "set themselves up as expert." They only rarely gave direct advice in their face-to-face conferences with teachers. Three explanations seemed plausible to the advisors.

1. *Knowledge.* While secure in their general grasp of curriculum and pedagogy, advisors sometimes believed they knew too little to construct useful advice about a specific teacher's intentions and practices, the observed grade or subject, or a particular classroom situation.

2. *Strategies.* Advisors were reluctant to introduce their own ideas in ways that might undermine teachers' own analyses or ignore their aspirations. To elicit commentary from teachers, they concentrated on mastering techniques of careful description, active listening, and skillful questioning.

3. *Etiquette.* In their reticence to give advice, advisors were responding to the prevailing professional etiquette among teachers: advice is not highly prized. Offering advice, especially unsolicited advice, runs counter to the valued, accepted, collegial behavior of teachers. The etiquette surrounding advice-giving appears to be one instance of a larger phenomenon, in which the reluctance to assert oneself on matters of curriculum and instruction is seen as proper restraint in the exercise of professional good manners.

Pushing the Limits of the Advisor Role

For master and mentor teachers who must live up to the honor (and title) accorded to them, the advisors' ambivalence about their position may strike a familiar chord. The advisor role can be examined from three perspectives: (1) the advisor as a *peer* who models productive professional relations, offering assistance when asked; (2) the advisor as a *staff developer or curriculum specialist* who offers training and consulting on specific topics; (3) the advisor as a *senior colleague* whose demonstrated knowledge, skill, and energy warrant the rights to initiate and lead that go with the title of advisor. The first perspective was most consistent with descriptions offered by the advisors themselves, who stressed the "facilitative" aspects of their relations with teachers. The third perspective deserves our attention in light of the recent pressure to expand career leadership opportunities and rewards.

The idea of leadership roles for teachers was attractive to advisors and teachers alike. For both, however, "facilitating" teachers was more acceptable than leading them; facilitation respects colleagues as persons and professionals, and considers their humanity and their work. Facilitative advisors should be creative and diligent in their efforts to assist teachers, eagerly joining in their work without proposing what the work should be.

A more assertive stance appeared to raise the spectre of heavyhandedness. Advisors worried that they would be seen as insensitive to teachers' preferences and blind to their talents; they feared that direct and assertive action would be interpreted as riding roughshod.

At issue was how advisors or master and mentor teachers, with the promises and claims implicit in these roles, could become leaders in the improvement of teaching. If selection as an "advisor" carried no special status or expert standing with teachers, the facilitator role necessarily would prevail: advisors would invite teachers to decide how and when to use their services; they would assist, respond, and give advice when asked.

To the extent that the teachers accepted the special status and expert standing of the advisors, however, advisors (and others in similar roles) probably would be able to propose ideas for joint work, argue topics or problems that deserve attention, raise tough questions, access more and less promising ideas straightforwardly, and offer to teach others what they knew.

These are not statements about the character or qualifications of individuals, but predictions about their actions based on the history of the profession and the organization of teaching in most schools. Facilitators are far more compatible with tradition than leaders in curriculum and instruction. In examining roles whose titles promise some professional leadership, we can reasonably ask: do their characteristic words and deeds lean more toward assertion and leadership or more toward facilitation and support?

Leadership or Facilitation?

In light of contemporary pressures—and opportunities—to expand leadership roles in the teaching profession and in schools, we have pressed the leadership issue. Deliberately exaggerating the distinction between leadership and facilitation reveals the challenges and dilemmas that the advisor role poses. In practice, the lines will be less clear, the distinctions more subtle. As we follow new efforts to invest the teaching career with richer professional opportunities, rewards, and obligations, however, we will do well to keep the less subtle construction in mind. Central to any improvement-oriented initiative that rests heavily on joint work on teaching are the principles and skills of advising. At stake are substantial gains in professional support for learning to teach, and for the steady improvement of schools.□

This article was adapted from "Professional Development Roles and Relationships: Principles and Skills of Advising" by Judith Warren Little, Priscilla Galagaran, and Rudelle O'Neal (Far West Laboratory, November 1984). The work was supported by the National Institute of Education, Contract 400–83–003.

Judith Warren Little is Senior Program Director, Far West Laboratory for Educational Research and Development, 1855 Folsom Street, San Francisco, California 94103.

Educational Leadership 45 (Nov. 1987): 36-39

MARY PAQUETTE

Voluntary Collegial Support Groups for Teachers

Teachers at a Calgary, Alberta, high school are pooling their talents and expertise within peer support groups to aid one another's professional growth.

Not only do participants in the Henry Wise Wood Development Program receive lessons on school growth models and leadership theories, but also moral support in planning their own professional growth.

139

As teachers, we invest much time, effort, and care to ensure that the right climate for growth exists in our classrooms, and that is as it should be. But it is equally important to make a similar investment in our own personal and professional growth.

The Effective Schools/Professional Development Committee of Henry Wise Wood High School in Calgary, Canada, faced the challenge of planning professional development activities for a highly trained and competent group of 93 teachers responsible for the instruction of 1,700 students. Made up of nine volunteers representing Administration, Guidance, and the Academic departments, the committee was also responsible for implementing an Effective Schools program.

In looking at professional development for our staff, we realized that while we would never think of presenting random, disconnected lessons to our students, that was precisely what we were doing in our staff development activities. The three professional days per year mandated by the Calgary Board of Education were often exciting, informative breaks in the routine of teaching; but the information they imparted was seldom directly or permanently applied to our classrooms. After much discussion and with feedback from the staff, we resolved that we needed a plan that would provide focus for both our personal and professional growth and would use our resources as a staff.

Principles of Professional Growth

Our committee established five principles that delineate our beliefs about professional growth:

1. Teachers benefit from individual, small-group, and large-group professional development activities, so each must be encouraged in the school.

2. Professional development is most effective when undertaken voluntarily by individuals.

3. Growth activities should build upon the strengths, interests, and talents of each teacher and must be relevant.

4. Professional development activities can stimulate awareness in teachers of their level of skill development, leading to celebration as well as growth.

5. Growth can be enhanced through a collegial support system that values growth activities, provides moral support, and facilitates small groups.

If the teachers at Wise Wood were truly going to make use of their talents and expertise, we had to find a way to tap the collective resources of the staff. Collegial support groups seemed to be the answer.

Details of the Program

We presented the Professional Development Program to the staff at the beginning of the 1986 school term, proposing it as a one-year pilot organized with a maximum of 30 participants divided into groups of 8 to 10 teachers. The groups would meet regularly throughout the year. Their primary role would be to provide a climate of mutual trust, respect, and support for teachers engaged in growth activities. Their content would be shaped by teachers' individual needs and would use group members' skills and talents while identifying new areas for development. We emphasized that all participants would be vital members of the group, valued as

> "We emphasized that all participants would be vital members of the group, valued as much for their support as for their talents, ideas, and participation."

"The positive response from the staff exceeded even our optimistic expectations. Within a few days, 30 teachers had volunteered."

much for their support as for their talents, ideas, and participation.

After evaluation and refinement, we said the program would be offered again in the following year. The principal, along with another committee member, would co-facilitate each group. In this way, trained facilitators would be available in subsequent years if staff demand necessitated a greater number of groups.

The positive response from the staff exceeded even our optimistic expectations. Within a few days, 30 teachers had volunteered. Groups were formed based on availability for meeting at designated times once a month. Each group consisted of teachers with a wide range of subject specialization and teaching experience, as well as department heads and administrators. Since teachers bought into time slots rather than friendship or department affiliations, the composition of the groups was quite mixed; and many people did not know one another well.

An essential part of the collegial support groups is a group member handbook we call "The Binder." This handbook includes an overview of and introduction to the Professional Development Program; a personal profile section to record data related to individual teaching careers; a professional growth section to be developed by participants according to their needs; a section for reflections, notes, and jottings; and a file section for useful articles, letters of reference, career documents, and so on. The Binder is an organizational tool as well as a diary of an individual teacher's quest. By recording professional growth within the pages of a book, we hoped to emphasize its importance.

Phases of Implementation
Our Professional Development Program was implemented in three phases.

Phase I entailed a full day of "start-up" activities—team building, self-assessment, introducing process skills, and developing the concept of individual growth and teaching improvement plans. We were fortunate to secure funding to cover substitutes for the

whole group so that activities could be held off campus at the nearby area office. Teachers' reactions to the session were overwhelmingly positive, and there was significant bonding of group members.

During *Phase II* participants met monthly for a minimum of three hours. Skills and processes such as brainstorming, problem solving, and providing feedback to colleagues developed during the initial phase were reinforced; each group formed a unique identity.

The four facilitators of the groups met before each set of sessions to discuss the development of the groups, assess group member needs and interests, and plan the agenda. Although general planning and objectives for the three groups were basically the same, facilitators were free to modify the proceedings according to the needs and personality of the groups, each of which developed a character of its own. One group, for example, tended to prefer quite practical discussions of problems or events within the school while other groups focused more upon philosophy or theory.

Each session began with refreshments contributed by a group member—we discovered many excellent cooks among our colleagues—and with a brief social interlude. A warm-up or focusing activity designed to help us get to know one another bet-

"Sharing successes as well as problems became a standard activity as members encouraged and reinforced one another's growth."

"Nothing in a school is more powerful than teachers who have achieved agreement on what is truly important. We have found the collegial support model an effective vehicle for bringing about that agreement."

ter was led by a member who had previously volunteered.

Each session in Phase II consisted of (1) the presentation of a new concept or theory that applied to the group's work, and (2) an activity that facilitated each individual's planning for personal and professional growth. For example, one session presented an explanation of the Sergiovanni Leadership Model. After a discussion of the implications of the model, teachers worked in groups to explore the applications of the model to their own classrooms and to the school as a whole, and to examine their own strengths and areas

in which they desired growth. Each session concluded with processing the day's activities and writing in Reflective Journals contained within the Binders.

As the year proceeded, group members were exposed to self-assessment strategies, theoretical material about the nature of leadership, and a model for school growth. Each teacher also created a professional growth plan, implemented it, and shared results with the group. Sharing successes as well as problems became a standard activity as members encouraged and reinforced one another's growth.

The sessions afforded teachers the opportunity to report to their groups about something exciting they had or a classroom discovery they had made. As relationships strengthened, interaction among group members in other settings increased. Small, casual collections of group members could be found in the staff room over coffee pursuing a line of thought opened up at "Group."

Phase III of the program was the wrap-up session—a time for sharing successes and joining together in celebration. Each participant assessed his or her involvement in the program and completed an evaluation to be used in refining the program.

Where Do We Go from Here?

Informal and written evaluations of the program's pilot year indicated en-

thusiasm for collegial support groups. Participants were positive about the theoretical material presented, the chance to air problems with colleagues, and the encouragement the program gave them for setting and achieving professional goals. Many felt more time was needed to pursue important issues. Much remains to be done in rewriting and polishing the program next year; there are many questions to be resolved. We are, however, convinced of the value of the collegial support group as a vehicle for professional growth within our school.

As we gain in understanding the complex process of learning and the teaching strategies that bring it about, we may become discouraged by the magnitude of our task. But there is hope in the potential within ourselves. In organizing to tap our own resources, we may help to overcome the problems plaguing our schools. Nothing in a school is more powerful than teachers who have achieved agreement on what is truly important. We have found the collegial support model an effective vehicle for bringing about that agreement.□

Mary Paquette is Chairperson of the Effective Schools/Professional Development Committee and Head of the English Dept. of Henry Wise Wood High School, 910–75 Ave., S.W., Calgary, Alberta T2V OS6.

Educational Leadership 45 (Nov. 1987): 31-35

ALLAN A. GLATTHORN

Cooperative Professional Development: Peer-Centered Options for Teacher Growth

When districts provide supporting conditions, teachers can work together in small teams, using a variety of collaborative methods, for their professional growth.

An encouraging development in instructional supervision is the widespread interest in peer-centered options such as "cooperative development" (Glatthorn 1984), "colleague consultation" (Goldsberry 1986), and "peer coaching" (Brandt 1987). *Cooperative professional development* is the inclusive term used here to embrace these and other forms of peer-oriented systems. My experience in helping numerous school districts implement such programs convinces me of the need to clarify the concept, systematize the approaches, and synthesize what has been learned about effective implementation.

Let's begin by clarifying the concept. *Cooperative professional development* is a process by which small teams of teachers work together, using a variety of methods and structures, for their own professional growth. Small teams of two to six seem to work best. The definitive characteristic is cooperation among peers; the methods and structures vary.

In systematizing the approaches, the intent is to strengthen practice by delineating the several forms that cooperative development can take. There are at least five different ways in which small teams of teachers can work together for their own professional growth (see fig. 1). A few experts in the field advocate only one approach (usually the one with which they are most closely identified), but it seems more useful to view cooperative development broadly. After all, each approach has its own special advantages. Teachers who are reluctant to observe colleagues through the processes of peer supervision or peer coaching can begin with one of the other options.

Professional Dialogue

Professional dialogue occurs when small groups of teachers meet regularly for the guided discussion of their own teaching as it relates to current developments in education. The ob-jective is to facilitate reflection about practice, helping teachers become more thoughtful decision makers. Other approaches, such as peer supervision and peer coaching, are concerned with teachers' skills, but professional dialogue puts cognition at the center. As Clark and Peterson (1986) note, three aspects of thinking play an important role in the teacher's classroom performance: the teacher's planning, both before and after instruction; the teacher's interactive thoughts and decisions while teaching; and the teacher's theories and beliefs.

Professional dialogue attempts to raise the level of all three aspects of thinking through *guided* discussion, which ensures that the process does not degenerate into unproductive verbal posturing. I have had some success with an approach derived from Buchmann's (1985) "conversation about teaching." In my own version, the process works as follows.

First, group members meet to decide basic questions about the structure of the dialogues: frequency, time and place of meetings. They lay out a tentative agenda for the first three months, identifying the leader for each discussion. In developing topics for the agenda, the group should focus on professional issues that (1) are important to them educationally; (2) are ones about which informed people seem to differ; and (3) are ones for which some background material is available. Some issues might be related to a given subject matter: the teaching of grammar in English, the use of controversy in social studies, the structure of the curriculum in art. Others might cut across the disciplines: the use of ability grouping, the importance of learning styles, the desirability of moral education.

Each session follows a three-stage format designed to make the dialogue productive. The first stage emphasizes external knowledge. The group leader begins by summarizing the views of experts and the evidence from empirical research. (I have found the syntheses of research in *Educational Leadership* especially useful for this purpose.) The members then proceed to analyze, *not* dispute, that external knowledge: To what extent do the experts agree? What are the specific issues that divide them? What evidence is available from the research reviews? To what extent is the research evidence in conflict?

In the second stage, the discussion centers on personal knowledge: What have we learned about this matter through our personal experience? In what ways does our experiential knowledge support or question the external knowledge? In this stage the teachers are encouraged to value what they have learned from teaching and to reflect in depth about that tacit knowing. The hope is that they will learn from each other through open listening. The intent here is to help teachers maintain a state of productive tension between the two kinds of knowledge—neither mindlessly accepting external knowledge nor foolishly rejecting it.

The final stage looks to the future: what are the implications of this discussion for our teaching? Here the

TYPE	FOCUS	DISTINGUISHING FEATURES
1. Professional dialogue	Reflection about practice	Guided discussion, focusing on teaching as thinking
2. Curriculum development	Production of materials	Collaborative development of curriculum, using naturalistic processes
3. Peer supervision	Analysis of teaching	Observation of instruction, followed by analysis and feedback
4. Peer coaching	Mastery of skills	Development of specific skills, usually based on models of teaching and supported with staff development
5. Action research	Solving of problems	Development and implementation of feasible solutions to teacher-identified problems

Fig. 1. Types of Cooperative Development

teachers attempt to build connections between the professional dialogue and their future practices. They examine together how the research and their shared experiential knowledge can best inform their planning and their interactive decision making. And they reflect openly about whether and to what extent their theories and beliefs have begun to change as a result of the dialogue.

"Some time should be reserved for team-developed enrichment units, which reflect the special knowledge and interests of teachers and extend the scope of the district guide in exciting ways."

Other discussion models, of course, can be used in the dialogues. Schon (1983) reports some success helping teachers use a moderately structured approach concerned with their reflection in action—how they think as professionals. The important consideration is to ensure that the dialogues have enough direction and coherence to make them professionally productive.

Although there seem to be no rigorous studies examining the effects of such dialogues, my experience indicates that they do achieve positive results. Participants report that they find the discussions useful; they note changes in their own attitudes about the issues examined.

Curriculum Development
Curriculum development, as the term is used here, is a cooperative enterprise among teachers by which they modify the district curriculum guide. While there is obviously a need for a district curriculum guide developed by curriculum specialists and expert teachers, there is also a need for teacher-generated materials that extend the district guide and in the process make it more useful.

Teachers' collaborative work can take three forms. First, when teachers *operationalize* the curriculum, they develop yearly and unit plans for teaching. They take the general district guide, which ordinarily includes only lists of objectives and recommended teaching methods, and turn it into a set of usable instructional plans. The teachers first sketch out yearly plans, indicating the general units of study and the time allocations for each unit. They then develop detailed unit plans, integrating certain areas of the curriculum, adding their own creative teaching suggestions, and including more recent materials.

Second, since most guides do not make sufficient provisions for individualization, teachers also *adapt* the district guide for special student populations. They develop materials that respond to students' varied learning styles; indicate priority objectives for the least able; include remediation activities for those who do not achieve initial mastery; and suggest instructional activities that will enable more capable students to achieve greater depth of understanding.

Finally, teachers *enrich* the district guide by developing optional enrichment units for all classes. As I have argued elsewhere (Glatthorn 1987), the district-mandated curriculum should not consume all available instructional time; some time should be reserved for team-developed enrichment units, which reflect the special knowledge and interests of teachers and extend the scope of the district guide in exciting ways. For example, one team of English teachers might develop an enrichment unit on local dialects; a social studies team could add a unit on religious cults in American history.

Obviously these curriculum development sessions make several important contributions. They increase teacher cohesiveness by bringing teachers together around a common task, enable them to share ideas about teaching and learning, and result in useful products.

Peer Supervision
Peer supervision is a process by which small teams of teachers use the essential components of clinical supervision to help each other grow professionally. Although there are several models of peer supervision, Goldsberry's (1986) "colleague consultation" approach seems to be the most systematic. (He rejects the term *peer supervi-*

"Students of coached teachers had greater achievement on a model-relevant test than did students of uncoached teachers."

sion because it seems self-contradictory: *peer* suggests equals; *supervision* connotes superiority.)

The Goldsberry model has nine key characteristics.

1. The process is observation-based: colleagues observe each other teach.
2. The observation is data-based: the observer records full information about the class observed.
3. There is collaborative assessment: each participant tries to identify patterns of teacher and learner behavior.
4. There is a concern for learner outcomes, both intended and unanticipated ones.
5. The collaborative assessment is based upon the teacher's "espoused platform," the learning goals and principles he or she subscribes to.
6. The process involves a cycle of observations and conferences.
7. The process is confidential.
8. The process has a future orientation: the goal of the consultation is to produce future benefits.
9. There is reciprocal assessment: just as the consultant helps the teacher improve practice, so should the teach-

er help the consultant improve his or her consulting skills.

Under appropriate conditions, peer supervision produces desirable results. For example, Roper and Hoffman (1986) report that the teachers involved in their program were eager to improve, had a good idea of where they most needed improvement, and learned by listening to each other and their students. When conditions were not right, however, peer supervision programs have been less than successful (see, for example, McFaul and Cooper's 1984 article and Goldsberry's critique of their research in the same issue).

Peer Coaching
Peer coaching, most clearly articulated in the work of Bruce Joyce (see Brandt 1987) and Beverly Showers (1984), is similar to peer supervision in that it includes peer observations and conferences. Yet it seems to have some crucial differences sufficient to set it apart. First, there is an assumption that peer coaching follows and builds upon staff development, in which teachers learn about the theoretical foundation of the skill, observe the skill being demonstrated, and practice the skill with feedback. Second, it seems to have a sharper focus: peer coaching teams work together to learn one of the models of teaching or to implement some specific classroom-centered improvement. Finally, the process seems to be much more intensive than most peer supervision models. Joyce (in Brandt 1987) recommends six days of staff development for the teacher to begin acquiring a new model of teaching and has found that it will take as many as 30 trials for the teacher to achieve executive control or complete command.

In her training manual for peer coaches, Showers identifies five major functions of peer coaching. The first is the provision of companionship: as teachers talk about their success and frustrations with the new model of teaching, they reduce the sense of isolation that seems endemic to the profession. Second, teachers give each other technical feedback as they practice the new model of teaching. The

Programs in cooperative professional development will enjoy a greater chance of success when the following conditions prevail.

1. There is strong leadership at the district level: a district administrator or supervisor coordinates and monitors the school-based programs.
2. There is strong leadership at the school level: the principal takes leadership in fostering norms of collegiality, in modeling collaboration and cooperation, and by rewarding teacher cooperation.
3. There is a general climate of openness and trust between administrators and teachers.
4. The cooperative programs are completely separate from the evaluation process: all data generated in the cooperative programs remain confidential with the participants.
5. The cooperative programs have a distinct focus and make use of a shared language about teaching.
6. The district provides the resources needed to initiate and sustain the cooperative programs.
7. The school makes structural changes needed to support collaboration: the use of physical space facilitates cooperation; the school schedule makes it possible for teachers to work together; staff assignment procedures foster cooperation.

Fig. 2. Conditions Supporting Cooperative Professional Development

feedback is objective, not evaluative, and is confined to observations about the execution of model-relevant skills. Third, there is a continuing emphasis upon analyzing the application of the new model of teaching, to help participants extend executive control. The goal is not to employ the model only once in a somewhat uncertain trial but to internalize it so that its use becomes spontaneous and flexible. Fourth, the peer coach helps the teacher adapt the

"Collaborative research ... can close the gap between 'doing research' and 'implementing research findings.'"

teaching model to the special needs of the particular students involved. The coach assists the teacher in analyzing student responses and modifying the model accordingly. Finally, the coach facilitates early trials of the model by providing support.

Preliminary studies suggest that peer coaching achieves the results intended. In one carefully designed study, Showers (1984) found that, with a relatively brief period of training, peer coaches were able to provide follow-up training to other teachers, who came to regard them as helpful and professional in their conduct. Second, peer coaching did increase transfer of learning. And, perhaps most important of all, the students of coached teachers had greater achievement on a model-relevant test than did students of uncoached teachers.

Action Research
Action research is a collaborative effort by teams of teachers to identify an important problem and to develop a workable solution. As a means of solving school problems, action research was first recommended by Stephen Corey (1953). After languishing for a few decades as a research approach, it seems to be enjoying a revival of interest.

As with most collaborative approaches, action research takes several forms. A very useful model has been

developed and tested by Lieberman (1986) and her colleagues, who modified a process used initially by Tikunoff, Ward, and Griffin (1979). In general the process works as follows.

1. Collaborative research team members identify a problem they would like to research.
2. They make collaborative decisions about the specific research questions and the methodology.
3. They carry out the research design, attending sufficiently to the complexities of the classroom.
4. They use the research results to design an intervention to be implemented in the school.

While noting that collaborative research has both successes and failures, Lieberman reports that the process can:
- facilitate reflection about teaching,
- unite teachers and promote collegial interaction,
- close the gap between "doing research" and "implementing research findings,"
- give teachers an opportunity to assume new roles and gain a sense of empowerment, and
- legitimate teachers' practical understanding and professional concerns.

Implementing Cooperative Professional Development
How can a school district implement a cooperative development program? The answer involves both a general set of supportive conditions and a specific process of implementation. The general conditions needed for successful implementation, summarized in Figure 2, have been drawn from a review of literature on the several forms of cooperative development. Since the research has been limited in extent and uneven in quality, those conditions should be viewed as tentative guidelines.

If these conditions are generally present, then what specific process should be used? Clearly, several implementation strategies can work. The process explained below derives from my experience in working with numerous school districts in establishing such programs.

1. A district planning team composed of district administrators, supervisors, principals, and classroom teachers establishes guidelines to apply to all district schools. Those guidelines specify such matters as: which program options may be offered at the school level; which teachers will be eligible to participate in the cooperative programs; how schools may provide time for the cooperative programs; how the programs may be evaluated; how the program will be administered and coordinated at the district level.

2. Under the leadership of their principal, each school's faculty members review the guidelines and analyze the various collaborative options. They determine how many and which of the collaborative programs they wish to undertake, then work out the specific details of implementing those programs. One school might decide to begin with only peer coaching. Another might choose to have some teachers experience professional dialogues, while others collaborate in action research. These decisions are summarized in a proposal submitted to the district planning team.

3. The district planning team reviews the proposals, suggests modifications, develops a budget to support the school-based proposals, and makes appropriate plans for any required districtwide staff development.

4. Each school implements its own program, providing the specific staff development needed for the options

chosen and conducting its own evaluation.

The implementation process, like the programs themselves, is collaborative, involving cooperation between the district and the member schools and between administrators, supervisors, and teachers.

Less a Job, More a Profession

There are, then, several ways by which teams of teachers can profitably work together to facilitate their professional growth. There is little "hard" evidence that such approaches will result in better student achievement, but there is a growing body of evidence that they are making teaching less a job and more a profession.☐

References

Brandt, R. S. "On Teachers Coaching Teachers: A Conversation with Bruce Joyce." *Educational Leadership* 44, 5 (1987): 12–17.

Buchmann, M. "Improving Education by Talking: Argument or Conversation?" *Teachers College Record* 86 (1985): 441–453.

Clark, C. M., and P. L. Peterson. "Teachers' Thought Processes." In *Handbook of Research on Teaching*, 3d ed., edited by M. C. Wittrock, pp. 255–296. New York: Macmillan, 1986.

Corey, S. M. *Action Research to Improve School Practices*. New York: Teachers College Press, Columbia University, 1953.

Glatthorn, A. A. *Differentiated Supervision*. Alexandria, Va.: Association for Supervision and Curriculum Development, 1984.

Glatthorn, A. A. *Curriculum Renewal*. Alexandria, Va.: Association for Supervision and Curriculum Development, 1987.

Goldsberry, L. F. "Reality—Really?" *Educational Leadership* 41, 10 (1984).

Goldsberry, L. F. "Colleague Consultation: Another Case of Fools Rush In." Paper presented at the annual meeting of the American Educational Research Association, San Francisco, April 1986.

Lieberman, A. "Collaborative Research: Working With, Not Working On … " *Educational Leadership* 43 (February 1986): 28–32.

McFaul, S. A., and J. M. Cooper. "Peer Clinical Supervision: Theory vs. Reality." *Educational Leadership* 41 (April 1984): 4–9.

Roper, S. S., and D. E. Hoffman. *Collegial Support for Professional Improvement: The Stanford Collegial Evaluation Program*. Eugene: Oregon School Study Council, University of Oregon, 1986.

Schon, D. A. *The Reflective Practitioner: How Professionals Think in Action*. New York: Basic Books, 1983.

Showers, B. *Peer Coaching: A Strategy for Facilitating Transfer of Training*. Eugene: Center for Educational Policy and Management, University of Oregon, 1984.

Tikunoff, W., B. Ward, and G. Griffin. "Interactive Research and Development on Teaching: Final Report." San Francisco: Far West Laboratory for Educational Research and Development, 1979.

Allan A. Glatthorn is Visiting Professor at North Carolina State University and Professor of Education at East Carolina University. He can be reached at 102A Speight, East Carolina University, Greenville, NC 27834.

Educational Leadership 46 (May 1989): 35-38

PATRICIA RANEY AND PAM ROBBINS

Professional Growth and Support through Peer Coaching

In a Sonoma County, California, school district, the
spirit of companionship and experimentation
created during coaching training has
spilled over into daily life.

In 1985 the Old Adobe Union School District, in Sonoma County, California, implemented a peer coaching program to provide support to newly hired teachers and to offer leadership roles to experienced teachers.[1] The need for such a program first became evident when, after 10 years of declining enrollment, the district suddenly faced an increase that allowed the hiring of additional teachers. With enrollment increasing, the principals did not have time to give the new teachers the support they deserved and needed. As a result, many were overwhelmed by classroom demands. When one of them resigned after two months, citing undue stress as the reason, district administrators began searching for a solution.

At the time, Old Adobe District had in place a long-range plan to train teachers in instructional strategies. Between 1982 and 1985, all teachers had attended five-day workshops based on the Hunter model of teaching. Teachers and administrators therefore had a common language for talking about teaching; but there had been no follow-through to help them maintain their new skills, and they had found few opportunities to talk about teaching.

In 1983 another event had encour-

aged district officials to take action; California had enacted Senate Bill 813, requiring school districts to address the needs of probationary teachers. Old Adobe District elected to try to meet all these different needs—those of new teachers, those of probationary teachers, and those of experienced teachers—through peer coaching.

Being able to laugh and joke about mistakes facilitated shared examination of teaching, opportunities for reflection, self-analysis, and growth.

Becoming Peer Coaches

In spring 1986, 11 teachers volunteered to become the first peer coaches. An additional 14 teachers received training the following spring. Under the direction of Pam Robbins, the training addressed seven major content areas (see fig. 1). On the first day, Robbins defined *colleague coaching* and presented its rationale and research base. She asked teachers and principals to envision colleague coaching, or peer coaching, in its ideal state—what it would look like, sound like, feel like. Their recorded responses became the ground rules that governed ensuing peer coaching activities and that eventually culminated in the program's being renamed "Peer Sharing and Caring."

Participants received intensive training in Cognitive Coaching (Costa and Garmston 1985), one of the exemplary models they surveyed. In Cognitive Coaching, during the preconference, the teacher makes explicit for the observer the intended purpose of the lesson, expected student outcomes and behaviors, planned teaching behaviors and strategies, any concerns about the lesson, and the desired focus of the observation. During the observation, the observer collects information about the instructional/curricular elements identified by the teacher. After the observation, the two discuss what actually happened during the lesson, as opposed to what was planned. The observer facilitates this analysis by asking questions that prompt the teacher to reflect on the lesson, recalling actual teacher and student behaviors. An integral part of the postconference is a discussion of what the observer did that facilitated or hindered the learning process for the teacher. Together they learn, each from a different perspective, about the business of teaching, observing, and supporting one another.

During the session, "Factors Influencing Peer Coaching Relationships," participants examined various elements (cognitive styles, educational beliefs, modality preferences) that influence what they value, how they communicate, and what they look for

during observations. From this exploration, the teachers gained an appreciation for the diverse ways a lesson can be planned, delivered, thought about, and discussed. They later reported that the session helped build trust and acceptance and increased their ability to concentrate on the *practice* of teaching, separate from the *person* doing the teaching.

Throughout all the sessions, the presenters provided theory, demonstration, practice opportunities, and feedback. Then the participants planned how they would implement the new strategies back in their schools. After practicing in groups of two or three to perfect their coaching skills, each experienced teacher was assigned a new teacher to coach.

Sharing and Caring
In the follow-up meetings, the teacher-coaches shared successes and grap-

pled with challenges, and a spirit of companionship and experimentation emerged. As they realized that others experienced the same frustrations and doubts, they became comfortable talking about difficult issues. Light-hearted humor was an integral part of every meeting. Being able to laugh and joke about mistakes facilitated shared examination of teaching, opportunities for reflection, self-analysis, and growth.

Coaching new teachers also sensitized the coaches to their own daily interactions with students. At one workshop, a teacher shared this experience:

During the presentation of new concepts, I caught myself in the middle of a monologue that went something like: "Matt, you *still don't understand*. I can't believe you don't get it. I've explained it three different ways, it's written on the board, and everyone else understands."

Suddenly, I became painfully aware that I was putting the student down. I caught my breath and said, "It's okay. This is really hard stuff. No one understands it. I don't know why I'm teaching it. I don't understand it—that's it." I threw the chalk down and said, "Let's go to recess."

The laughter shared over this reflection was very different from the nervous laughter that sometimes occurs in groups where the members do not allow themselves to be vulnerable for fear of being judged less competent than others. By modeling that it is okay to experiment and not to be perfect, Robbins had set a tone of trust and acceptance; and the group had maintained the feeling "we're all in this together."

As the project progressed, the teachers expressed the idea that the term *coaching* implied an unequal relationship. Thus, they unanimously supported changing the name of the program from "Peer Coaching" to "Peer Sharing and Caring," which implied equality, safety, and support.

Making Peer Coaching Work
In Old Adobe, several factors were critical to the success of Peer Sharing and Caring. Participation was, of course, voluntary, and the training empowered teachers as well as equipping them with an expanded repertoire of coaching skills. Further, the training was ongoing; the coaches continued to meet as a group to learn from each other. Above all, the atmosphere was

Session 1:
- Overview of the research on peer coaching
- A context for peer coaching
  — collaborative goal structures in schools
  — peer coaching, school norms, and culture
  — social and technical principles of coaching
  — organizing for peer coaching
- Exemplary peer coaching models

Sessions 2, 3:
- Overview of observation instruments for coaching: from mirroring to coaching
  — interaction analysis
  — time-off-task
  — drop-in observation
  — cognitive coaching
  — script-taping
  — checklists

Session 4:
- Factors influencing peer coaching relationships: how we look, what we value
- A model of factors influencing teacher thinking and behavior
  — modality preferences
  — educational beliefs
  — cognitive style

Session 5:
- Advanced conferencing skills
  — preconferencing
  — observing
  — postconferencing

Session 6:
- Fine-tuning communication skills
  — mediational questions
  — probing for specificity
  — identifying and staying aware of presuppositions

Session 7:
- Change theory and effective staff development practices
  — what the research says
  — implications for peer coaching
  — planning for maintenance

Fig. 1. Overview of Peer Coaching Training Sessions

supportive, so that teachers felt they could take risks. As one teacher said, "Anything worth doing is worth doing poorly, at first."

Beyond the training itself, financial and logistical support from the district was essential. Our superintendent and principals allocated funds for training, released time, and follow-up activities. To solve the problem of conflicts between meetings, for example, in 1987-88 the district scheduled peer coaching meetings monthly on faculty meeting days. And the principals agreed not to schedule staff meetings on the second Wednesday of each month to free that time for peer coaches from all four schools to meet together.

Further, the principals provided direction for the program by attending workshops with the coaches, modeling coaching behaviors, and responding to coaches' concerns. They also "ran interference" to free up time for teachers to coach and to be observed and saw that agreements and timelines were established and that coaches followed through on commitments.

Reaping the Benefits

The spirit that characterized the training environment has now become a part of the school culture. Coaching—or "Peer Sharing and Caring"—is a norm in Old Adobe. Each new teacher is assigned a coach who assists with instruction and introduces him or her to the way things are done at the school. Twenty-one new and probationary teachers have served since the program was initiated.

Prior to the program, parents as well as experienced teachers and the staff had voiced concerns about newly hired teachers. The overall impression was that, as a result of lack of experience, new teachers were covering the material too fast, that they were not assigning appropriate amounts of homework, and that the children were not achieving their potential. As peer coaches began spending time with the new teachers, these complaints decreased, and the new teachers also reported feeling less overwhelmed and stressed.

As a result of Peer Caring and Sharing, topics of conversation in the staff room are less often about personal matters and more frequently about the

Off to a Good Start in Peer Coaching

Aurora Chase and Pat Wolfe

"Peer coaching lets me take greater risks in teaching—now I can try out new strategies and get feedback on whether they're working."

"If the support for peer coaching were to end tomorrow, I guess we'd just continue it subversively."

"We have a lot of activities now that get teachers together, focusing on what goes on in the classroom."

In schools across the nation, teachers and administrators are singing the praises of peer coaching. This innovation promises to reduce teachers' isolation, to create a collegial and professional environment in the school, and to promote the transfer of skills from training to the workplace. To help peer coaching achieve these results, educators may find these guidelines useful.

• *Know what peer coaching is and what it is not.* Peer coaching is a confidential arrangement between peers that includes a focused classroom observation and feedback on that observation. It is not evaluation; it does not certify a teacher's effectiveness. Instead, coaching provides teachers a means of examining and reflecting on what they do in a psychologically safe environment where it is all right to experiment, fail, revise, and try again.

• *Develop a clear understanding of the various forms of peer coaching.* The interaction between teacher and observer generally falls into one of three categories: mirroring, in which the coach records but does not interpret classroom action; collaborative coaching, in which the observer collects and helps analyze the data; or expert coaching, in which the observer gives feedback to help the teacher learn or refine particular skills. Typically, too, peer coaching models follow the familiar steps of preconference, classroom observation, collection of data, data analysis, and postconference.

• *Assess your school's culture.* Each school has its own set of conditions, norms, values, and beliefs. Consequently, a peer coaching program that has succeeded in a neighboring district may be inappropriate for your school. Trust levels, administrative support, the history of past change efforts, the role of the teachers' union, the experience of the staff, the size of the school—all will influence a program's acceptance and growth.

• *Design your program and its implementation around the characteristics of your school.* Begin planning with knowledge of your school's culture in mind, and build in flexibility and sensitivity to staff needs so that changes can be made as the program evolves. Extend your planning by looking at practical matters. Your budget, for example, will influence how much training you can provide and how much time you can free up for observations and conferences. Staff size and number of grade levels will affect coaching arrangements. Trust levels will influence the composition and selection of coaching teams, and the history of past efforts will influence the kinds of support required.

Whatever their differences from school to school, successful peer coaching programs share these conditions: verbal and tangible support from administrators, adequate training in coaching skills, trust among participants, and program adjustments responsive to the changing needs of staff members. Successful programs help new teachers learn the norms of professionalism and help all teachers develop collegiality.

Like many innovations, peer coaching is more complex than it appears at first glance, but a well-grounded, flexible program based on a match between coaching models and each school's needs offers unparalleled support to teachers in their efforts to find new and better ways to educate children.

Aurora Chase is a Staff Development Specialist, Fairfax County Public Schools, 7423 Camp Alger Ave., Falls Church, VA 22042. **Pat Wolfe** is an Educational Consultant, 555 Randolph St., Napa, CA 94559.

act of teaching and classroom management. Many teachers say they have been able to let go of "having to be perfect," realizing that it is okay to let their rough edges show. There is an atmosphere of experimentation and openness to new ideas. Teachers eagerly consult their colleagues for assistance and share their own expertise. "In our diversity," one teacher remarked, "we are richer and can offer more to each other and to our students."

In addition to promoting collegiality and providing new teachers the support they so urgently need, the program has had beneficial effects on experienced teachers. The act of coaching gives the teacher-coach an opportunity to observe a classroom from an objective perspective. The insights a teacher gains during these observations often have applicability to his or her own classroom. In one teacher's words: "I learned more from my observation of others than I did from being observed and receiving feedback."

Exploring New Avenues

Peer Sharing and Caring has opened up avenues of communication between teachers from different grade levels and schools, between specialists and classroom teachers. Talking about teaching—reflecting on how they do what they do—has helped teachers develop a genuine appreciation and acceptance of others. Feelings of isolation and passivity have given way to an environment of collaboration and professional growth. In short, the norm has changed from "What others do is not my business" to "What we do here at school is everybody's business, and *business is booming*."□

1. The Old Adobe Union School District based its peer coaching program on the research of Joyce and Showers (1982), Little (1982), and Showers (1982, 1984, 1985).

References

Costa, A., and R. Garmston. (February 1985). "Supervision for Intelligent Teaching." *Educational Leadership* 42, 5: 70-80.
Joyce, B., and B. Showers. (October 1982). *Educational Leadership* 40, 1: 4-10.
Little, J.W. (1982). "Norms of Collegiality and Experimentation: Workplace Conditions of School Success." *American Education Research Journal* 19, 3: 325-340.
Showers, B. (1982). *Transfer of Training, The Contribution of Coaching*. Eugene, Oreg.: Center for Educational Policy and Management.
Showers, B. (1984). *Peer Coaching and Its Effects on Transfer of Training*. Eugene, Oreg.: Center for Educational Policy and Management.
Showers, B. (April 1985). "Teachers Coaching Teachers." *Educational Leadership* 42, 7: 43-48.

Patricia Raney is Principal, Miwok Valley Elementary School, Union School District, 1010 St. Francis Dr., Petaluma, CA 94952.
Pam Robbins is Director, Special Projects and Research, Office of the Superintendent, Napa County Schools, 4032 Maher St., Napa, CA 94558-2296.

Educational Leadership 46 (May 1989): 31-32

INGRID M. CHRISCO

Peer Assistance Works

By learning from one another, teachers can improve communication and foster professional growth.

We are forever in pursuit of connections. When these connections happen between people, we feel less isolated. For the past two years, teachers in the English department at Brattleboro Union High School in Brattleboro, Vermont, have been making connections by defining and shaping their own peer assistance program. This grass roots effort has succeeded for three reasons: (1) it is voluntary; (2) it has received administrative support; and (3) it has been allowed to evolve slowly and naturally.

Beginnings

Traditionally, in the English department we spend the last meeting or two of the year focusing on goals for the approaching school year. Three years ago in one of those meetings, we started to talk about formal evaluation and assistance—and the differences between the two. This was an important distinction for us. It didn't take us long to realize that we really wanted to talk about professional support: assistance, guidance, and insight from our peers. We were not interested in evaluative exchanges that could affect whether or not we kept our jobs, yet we knew these exchanges might influence whether or not we *wanted* to keep our jobs. What we wanted was

professional growth in a nonthreatening atmosphere.

In September 1986, following our initial discussions, a department member suggested that each of us try to observe, and be observed by, one colleague, by the end of October. This was a realistic goal: flexible enough to work, yet visible enough to encourage us to try. At this point, we were also

> **Our administrators' support was crucial to ensure that the time spent in peer assistance was not *time added* to what we were already doing, but rather *time that added* to the quality of what we were doing.**

able to hire a substitute teacher to cover noninstructional duties while we observed other teachers.

What began to evolve, even this early in the process, was a three-stage approach: a preconference, the observation, and a postconference. For some teachers, the preconference was a couple of minutes together in the hallway. Others discussed the lesson in depth, for 20-30 minutes. We allowed ourselves the license to define these stages as we thought best. Some teachers chose to summarize their observations in writing. Others chose to discuss what was observed. A few did both. Later we were delighted when our department head adopted this three-step model in his formal evaluative observations.

The Second Year

One year later, to provide more time for peer assistance, our department hired a full-time paraprofessional, releasing us from such noninstructional tasks as lunch duty, study hall, and corridor duty.

During the second year, new definitions of peer assistance began to surface. One teacher taught another to use a word processing program. Another asked a colleague to observe just the first 10 minutes of a series of

Photograph by Diana Powell, 8th grader at Brattleboro Union High School, Brattleboro, Vermont

When Cynthia Payne (third from right) and Ingrid Chrisco (the author of this article) collaborated in teaching, they discovered they could become helping professionals to each other, just as they had long been to their students.

classes in order to get feedback on a new vocabulary program. A 7th grade teacher and a 12th grade teacher cooperatively taught a novel to their respective classes. The 7th and 12th graders were reading the same novel and writing back and forth to one another in response journals. The teachers were assisting each other in teaching; the students, in learning. A few teachers engaged in a longitudinal study: they observed the same class several times throughout the year and reported on its development. The more we explored our needs, and the more of our own resources we contributed, the more potential for peer assistance we discovered.

At the end of the second year, we decided to record in print what the program had meant to us. Several teachers in the department organized this effort. Our publication, the "blue book," included teachers' impressions and personal histories as well as a history of the program—"everything you've always wanted to know about peer assistance but didn't know whom to ask."

Why It Has Worked

Brattleboro's program has worked, in part, because those who participate truly want to. Although we didn't articulate this willingness at first, intuitively we knew it. To some degree, all 16 members of our department have participated.

A second reason for the program's success is administrative support. We were encouraged to explore the differences between peer assistance and formal evaluation. Equally important, we were given time to participate in the program. Many department meetings were devoted to the topic, and a substitute teacher was hired to enable us to visit each other's classrooms.

Our administrators' support was crucial to ensure that the time spent in a peer assistance relationship was not *time added* to what we were already doing, but rather *time that added* to the quality of what we were doing.

The third reason the program has been successful is the way we chose to spend our time together. We didn't adopt an established model. We allowed the shape of our program to evolve slowly and naturally, in harmony with what we ourselves saw that we needed and wanted to do.

Benefits

Peer assistance has had at least three major benefits for us. They relate to communication, rehearsal, and awareness.

First, the program has helped us reestablish communication among the members of our department. According to Robert Kramsky, a teacher, "the greatest strength of the peer assistance project has been to initiate and encourage dialogue between professionals about teaching, about education. I think the program has made us all aware of our peers as resources, as a great wealth of experience and information to be shared."

A second way peer assistance has helped us has been with rehearsal. In the preconference, teachers talk about teaching style, methods, content, and the role the observer is to play. By talking about what will happen in the lesson, the teacher has an opportunity to run through the lesson—a kind of dress rehearsal. This procedure clarifies for both teacher and observer what is intended and why it is important. The more we examine what we are teaching and why we are teaching it, the better we will perform.

The third way the peer assistance program has helped us is with aware-

ness. We have been able to bring what we do instinctively to the conscious level. Our professional instincts are usually strong and accurate, yet many of us teach without being consciously aware of the strategies and techniques we employ. That doesn't mean that we don't stop to assess what we are doing— we do, but it can be a lonely monologue. When we grapple with a problem or situation and work it through with others, we don't feel alone, and we arrive at a better understanding.

Zeke Hecker, one of the teachers, supports this: "Peer assistance and observation have made me a better teacher because they have made me a more conscious teacher, more aware of what I'm actually doing, more aware of what others are doing, more aware of alternatives. . . . I believe the effect is cumulative. The more you observe and the more you are observed, the more conscious you become of your technique, and the better you get at it."

A Different Kind of Accountability

Our peer assistance program has made us aware of a different kind of professional accountability—not the accountability measured in a formal evaluation by an administrator, but the kind that recognizes our responsibility for helping each other grow and improve. We can help each other challenge our own limits, and we can challenge the isolation that imposes artificial limits. We are recognizing that school can be much more than a place where we shut our classroom doors and teach as we please. The English teachers in Brattleboro are making connections that are leading to what Carl Rogers calls "unconditional positive regard" for one another. In essence, we are expanding our roles: we are becoming helping professionals for each other, just as we are for our students.□

Author's note: As a testimony to the strength and validity of this program, the Windham Southeast Supervisory Union has adopted this approach as a valuable form of professional development and support. As a result, more than 100 teachers districtwide are now participating in peer assistance.

Ingrid M. Chrisco is an English Teacher at Brattleboro Union High School, Fairground Rd., Brattleboro, VT 05301.

Educational Leadership 45 (Nov. 1987): 58-63

DIANA LEGGETT AND SHARON HOYLE

Preparing Teachers for Collaboration

At Fort Worth's summer "Lab School," teachers learn to facilitate collegial efforts back in their schools.

Photographs by Sharon Hoyle

Observation and feedback are key components of collegiality. Charlsa Stewart, far right, collects data on the teaching methods of summer school teacher Lamar Favors.

The principal's role in a supportive environment is well known, but teachers, too, can initiate and facilitate collaboration in their schools. In settings where "collegiality and experimentation" are the norm, teachers themselves engage in certain "critical practices" (Little 1981). These teachers prepare and review curriculum units and lesson plans together. Further, they talk about and test new ideas and persuade others to try them. They extend collaboration into their classrooms by observing each other and inviting others to observe them.

Fort Worth Independent School District, an ethnically diverse district of approximately 65,000 students, has targeted, through its Keystone Project, the critical practices of colleagueship that Little describes. This project, funded by the Sid Richardson Foundation, trains teachers in the use of effective instructional strategies including mastery learning and the writing process. Peer coaching and collaborative learning are two elements of this training.

The staff of the Keystone Project believe that collegiality does not just happen, it must be nurtured and developed. Teachers can learn to share in the planning and delivery of instruction. They can become change agents as they work collaboratively to improve their schools.

Lab School

The Keystone Project staff offer teachers the skills necessary for collaboration in "Lab School," a special four-week program overlapping a regular summer school for middle school students. Lab School participants learn how to work together in planning and implementing curriculum, in teaching other teachers, and in observing and coaching each other.

A spirit of comradery as well as a higher level of teaching skills is often the result of collaboration.

Teachers who apply for admission to Lab School are selected on the basis of a writing sample, an interview, an actual teaching tape, and their willingness to work and share with each other. In 1984, 30 teachers participated in the first Lab School. In 1985, 18 teachers returned, and 10 new ones were selected. Participation jumped drastically in 1986 to include 15 returning participants and 43 new ones. By the summer of 1987, Lab School included 43 returning participants and 39 new ones. Teachers who complete the four-week program are committed to return to their schools to assume either a formal role as a Cadre Trainer or an informal one as a Demonstration Teacher in promoting a supportive

"Lab School participants learn how to work together in planning and implementing curriculum, in teaching other teachers, and in observing and coaching each other."

"Teachers' increased sense of efficacy has helped them overcome their isolation and open their classrooms to the potential of professional sharing."

school climate. Both options encompass one or more of the critical practices of colleagueship.

Cadre Trainers

Cadre Trainers are practicing teachers who conduct staff development sessions after school on selected weekdays and on Saturdays for other teachers at the district or building level. Teachers who wish to become Cadre Trainers must first internalize the district's staff development curriculum by using in their own classrooms the strategies they will eventually present in workshops. Keystone Project staff determine the degree to which a teacher has internalized the concepts by assessing tapes of teaching epi-

sodes, which are a prerequisite to admittance to Lab School.

Once selected for the Lab School, a Cadre Trainer chooses a workshop segment from the existing staff development curriculum and prepares a presentation for a variety of settings. A trainer first makes a presentation to a small group of peers, then to the workshop consultant, and finally in the actual workshop setting to an audience of 30–40 people. Constructive feedback from peers is processed at each step. After making a sufficient number of presentations to assure internalization of the concept, the trainer selects a new concept and begins again. Because this procedure is extensive and time consuming, Cadre

Laura Carson trains Lab School participants to plan and implement curriculum and to observe and coach other teachers.

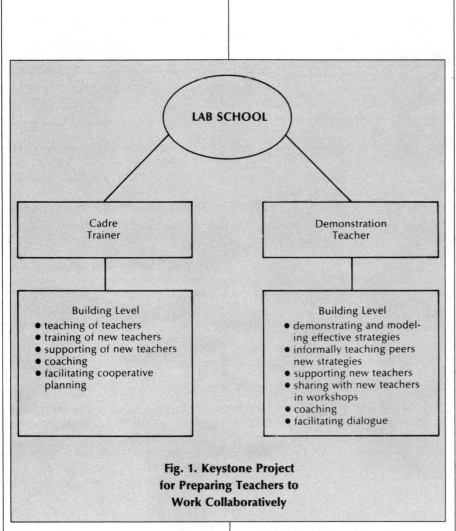

**Fig. 1. Keystone Project
for Preparing Teachers to
Work Collaboratively**

aration during the school year with 30 hours of individualized follow-up training that focuses on aspects of the curriculum they did not address during Lab School. In this way the group finds common ground for exploration during the next Lab School and school year, thereby extending opportunities for members to support each other through discussion of new instructional strategies and techniques.

Throughout Lab School and the school year, Demonstration Teachers plan and implement curriculum together, try new ideas, talk to others about them, and informally teach others—setting in motion the elements for change. Their willingness and openness to share within their schools is instrumental in developing a supportive environment.

Additional Support

The roles of Cadre Trainer and Demonstration Teacher help diminish teachers' feelings of isolation in other important ways. For example, teachers in both roles actively support new

> **"Each Cadre Trainer . . . is also responsible for maintaining contact with new teachers in the group. Such a lifeline when they really need it establishes a 'sense of community' for inexperienced teachers."**

Trainers continue their training during the school year with at least 30 hours of released time seminars. The role of Cadre Trainer itself ensures that teachers engage in some of the critical practices of colleagueship: publicly talking about new ideas, persuading others to try them, and formally and informally teaching others.

Demonstration Teachers

Another option that prepares teachers to facilitate collegiality is the more informal role of Demonstration Teacher. Again, persons who select this role must be willing to adapt the concepts learned in the Lab School to the levels of their students and to share those adaptations by allowing others to observe. These observations are usually conducted as part of some coaching model being implemented at the building level, but a Demonstration

Teacher may also model use of a particular concept for an individual teacher. After any observation, formal or informal, the Demonstration Teacher asks for feedback and helps the observer(s) analyze what has been seen. In addition to observations, the Demonstration Teacher is available for collaboration in planning and developing content, curriculum, and instructional strategies.

While Cadre Trainers feel comfortable instructing a large group, Demonstration Teachers prefer sharing information and knowledge informally as discussion leaders or small-group facilitators in workshop settings. Demonstration Teachers provide grade-level examples and models that clarify the content being presented and relate it to the needs of workshop participants. As with Cadre Trainers, Demonstration Teachers continue their prep-

Lab School participants discuss how to give nonevaluative feedback during a coaching conference.

teachers in the district. Before school begins each year, Keystone Project staff schedule a Classroom Management Workshop for the district's 200–300 new teachers. As a result of attending Lab School, Cadre Trainers and Demonstration Teachers have learned to share classroom management strategies and to facilitate these new teachers' small-group discussions during the workshop. Also, each Cadre Trainer or Demonstration Teacher is responsible for maintaining contact with new teachers in the group. Such a lifeline when they really need it establishes a "sense of community" for inexperienced teachers (Gray and Gray 1985).

Another form of new teacher sup-

port is the New Teacher Buddy system. During Lab School each participant devises a plan that outlines the kinds of information new teachers will need to function in the classroom and to feel a part of the faculty. New Teacher Buddies also develop a yearly timeline to offer new teachers support at critical points—at grading periods, before and after vacation, at opening and closing of school—instead of only once or twice a year.

Coaching

One of the critical practices of collegiality is observing and being observed by other teachers. During Lab School, Demonstration Teachers and Cadre Trainers learn to work with teachers

back at their schools who are interested in establishing coaching teams. This training equips them with skills basic to peer coaching—data collection, observation, and giving nonevaluative feedback—and prepares them to schedule and coordinate peer coaching. As these teachers work to create and maintain comradery among teachers in a given building, school climate improves.

Lab School participants also play a key role in implementing other models of peer coaching in the district. For example in the Group Guided Practice Model (Leggett et al. in press), teachers attend district training that includes implementation of the steps in planning for mastery and basic peer

inar Coaching Model (Leggett et al. in press) in which teachers are relieved by substitutes to attend half- or full-day seminars conducted by Cadre Trainers. Again, Demonstration Teachers exemplify the strategy being discussed. These participants, who register for the seminar as partners, are prepared to return to their buildings and coach each other on the new strategies learned. Again, this model extends the support of Lab School participants to their fellow teachers by preparing them to help each other try out new ideas and observe and be observed by their colleagues.

Breaking Down the Barriers

As Demonstration Teachers and Cadre Trainers complete the Lab School program and share their enthusiasm for collaboration in their respective buildings, school climate noticeably improves. Dialogue about the planning and delivery of instruction increases, and teachers share instructional strategies. New teachers are assimilated more quickly, and teachers are involved in peer coaching. In short, the Keystone Project has helped foster in Fort Worth's teachers the practices that are critical to collegiality, which in turn leads to positive change. Teachers' increased sense of efficacy has helped them overcome their isolation and open their classrooms to the potential of professional sharing.□

References

Gray, W., and M. Gray. "Synthesis of Research on Mentoring Beginning Teachers." *Educational Leadership* 43, 3 (1985): 37–43.

Leggett, Diana, et al. *Peer Coaching Manual*. Fort Worth: Fort Worth Independent School District, in press.

Little, J. W. *School Success and Staff Development: The Role of Staff Development in Urban Desegregated Schools, Executive Summary*. Washington, D.C.: National Institute of Education, 1981.

Diana Leggett is Coordinator for the Keystone Project, Fort Worth Independent School District, 3320 W. Cantey, Fort Worth, TX 76109. **Sharon Hoyle** is Mastery Learning Specialist for the Keystone Project, at the same address.

coaching training. At this point, teachers who are interested in follow-up practice in coaching can visit the classroom of a Demonstration Teacher along with a more experienced coach to practice the skills of observing, gathering data, and delivering technical feedback. The Demonstration Teacher, who has been prepared for this role in Lab School, can then serve as an example of how a teacher who is receiving technical feedback can obtain the most from a peer conference. In this way, small groups of teachers learn from guided practice before selecting a partner and practicing in their own classrooms.

Another form of support that leads to coaching is the Released Time Sem-

Educational Leadership 47 (Nov. 1989): 70-77

BRUCE JOYCE, CARLENE MURPHY, BEVERLY SHOWERS, AND JOSEPH MURPHY

School Renewal as Cultural Change

When teachers in Richmond County, Georgia, were organized into study groups to help them learn new teaching strategies, their students' achievement and behavior improved markedly.

During the past two years we and our colleagues have developed a school improvement program based on principles derived from research on:
- the culture of the school and the process of innovation,
- the ways teachers learn new teaching strategies,
- the ways teachers transfer new skills into the classroom, and
- models of teaching and teaching skills.

Our design restructured the workplace—organizing teachers into collegial study groups, providing regular training on teaching, and inducing faculties to set goals for school improvement and strive to achieve them.

We can now begin to report the degree of change that occurred and the lessons we learned in the process. Some of the effects have been dramatic. For example, in one middle school only 30 percent of the students reached promotion standards the year before the program began. That number rose to 72 percent during the first year of the program and 94 percent during the second year. However, be-

cause the effects have not been uniform, we have begun to learn what factors explain the varying degrees of success. For example, achievement rose more rapidly in social studies and science than in the language arts. This finding prompted us to inquire into

the reasons and to try to reorient future work for more rapid across-the-board results.

In addition, while virtually all the teachers learned to use the teaching strategies to a mechanical level of competence, some reached much

Under the guidance of their teacher, Lisa Annis, 4th grade students work cooperatively on an inductive thinking lesson.

higher levels of skill, and these differences were reflected in the achievement of their students. On portions of the Iowa Tests of Basic Skills, the median students of teachers who reached the higher levels of skill fell between the 85th and 90th percentiles of the students whose teachers reached only mechanical levels of use. This finding led us to search for ways to improve training to ensure that *all* teachers reach the level of skill that will provide their students with expert instruction.

In this first report of our work, we describe the shape of the project, its results in the three schools involved from the beginning, and the first steps in our search to refine and improve our procedures.

An Organic Approach

We adopted an organic approach to school renewal, restructuring the workplace and introducing training to bring the study of research-based teaching strategies into the regular workday of teachers.

We subscribe to Fullan's (1982) thesis that it is the bond of shared understandings and common language that sustains innovations and reduces the stress of change. Also, we designed our training around the theory-demonstration-practice-coaching paradigm that has been found to bring about high levels of skill and implementation (Joyce and Showers 1987). We used a "peer-coaching" process: the teachers were organized into study groups and the faculties into problem-solving groups. The content of our training has focused on teaching strategies that increase students' learning by affecting their aptitude to learn (Joyce and Weil 1986).

We intended that the development of shared understandings would develop vertical and horizontal social cohesiveness, thereby reducing administrator-teacher divisions while increasing cooperation between classrooms and teams of teachers. Our training paradigm was intended (a) to enable teachers to develop high levels of skill in the content of the program, and (b) to bring teachers and admin-

Our training paradigm brought teachers and administrators together in study groups committed to implementing instructional changes.

istrators together in study groups committed to implementing instructional changes and achieving goals for school improvement. Another effect of the study groups was to contribute to faculty cohesiveness and, thus, to reduce isolation.

The models of teaching we selected had a research history indicating that they could bring about fairly rapid improvement in student learning. The initial models included cooperative learning, mnemonics, concept attainment, inductive reasoning, and synectics. The teachers studied how to organize classrooms into study teams, how to use link words to assist memorization, how to classify information into categories, learn concepts, build and test hypotheses, and use analogies to reconceptualize problems and generate solutions to them. All of these models addressed student learning problems characteristic of the schools involved in the initial phases of the project.

These planned changes in the workplace are easy to describe and, on the surface, easy to implement. Organizing staffs into study groups, providing regular training in models of teaching, and making concerted efforts to achieve specific goals are

changes that hardly call for radical rhetoric. For many of the teachers and administrators, however, these changes required difficult adaptations in patterns of behavior and ways of thinking. In negotiating these changes, we have learned much about problems that must be solved during the period of change.

Context and Planning

We implemented our program in Richmond County, Georgia, where 50 schools and 1,800 teachers serve 33,000 students. The school district serves the city of Augusta and the surrounding county, with a combined population of about 200,000 people. The principal industries of the region are chemical processing, pulp processing, textile manufacturing, metalworking, brick and clay manufacturing, and food processing. The major employers are Fort Gordon, the Medical College of Georgia, and the Savannah River Plant located in neighboring South Carolina. Many of the students in the district are economically disadvantaged. In the three participating schools, over two-thirds of the students received subsidized meals.

Low student achievement had long frustrated many of the schools in the district. Despite Chapter One and special education programs, a variety of programs for at-risk students, regular revision and upgrading of curriculum and instructional materials, and 14 years of staff development, many students remained in academic difficulty. In the middle school mentioned above, half of the students were receiving attention from special programs, yet 70 percent of the student body was achieving below the levels set by the state and district for promotion on merit.

We began our planning in January 1987 with intensive seminars for cabinet level staff. By March, district administrators had decided on the general dimensions of the project. During the first two years, the consultants (Joyce and Showers) would provide most of the training, but a cadre of

The development of the district cadre symbolized the intent to make permanent changes in the workplace.

teachers and administrators would be trained to offer service to other teachers and administrators—to bring other schools into the project on a regular basis in the future.

The development of the district cadre was critical to the project and to the relationship between the district and the consultants; it symbolized the intent to make permanent changes in the workplace. It made concrete the need for district personnel to possess the expertise of the consultants and to take over the functions of the consultants.

Our efforts during the first year (phase one) concentrated on three schools and the initial preparation of the cadre. During the second year (phase two), we added four more schools and prepared the cadre to add other schools during the following year. During the third year, two more entire faculties will be added; and teams from 10 other schools will begin training to become leaders of the process in their schools. The cadre provides follow-up training throughout the school year, for study teams cannot be left to maintain themselves. Regular training will become embedded in the workplace.

Schools competed to participate in the first three phases. We asked principals to poll their staffs to determine interest in summer training and a closely monitored implementation effort throughout the academic year. We asked principals to submit letters of application if faculty interest was high. The first year, 12 of the 13 schools invited to participate submitted applications. The superintendent's cabinet and the department directors selected one middle school and two elementary schools for phase one and one high school and three middle schools for phase two. Each faculty member in these schools had made a written commitment to:

- attend summer training,
- practice the new teaching strategies with peers regularly throughout the summer and share plans for implementation during the fall,
- employ the new strategies regularly throughout the 1987-1988 academic year,
- work with peer study groups during the academic year in planning lessons and visiting one another in classrooms,
- participate in regular training activities during the school year,
- make videotapes of their teaching on a regular basis,
- participate in a similar program in the summer of 1988 and during the 1988–89 school year.

The summer programs included two weeks of intensive training, followed by six weeks of practice and design of lessons for the fall, and the organization of study groups. We asked all participants to practice the teaching strategies no less than 30 times apiece during September and October and to strive to incorporate them into their active repertoires by the end of October. The study groups were to meet weekly; between meetings, members were to visit one another in their classrooms to study the children's responses to the teaching strategies and plan to teach the students to respond more powerfully. Our intent was to involve the faculties immediately in collective action that would have rapid effects on student learning.

Initiation and Initial Response

The training, practice, organization of study groups, development of short-run school goals, and initial classroom use of the teaching strategies occurred more or less as planned.

Learning to work together. Participants planned lessons they would teach, then shared their plans—and their skepticism about whether the plans were practical. The models of teaching were new to almost all the teachers and their students; they required substantial amounts of new learning. Administrators scheduled time for study groups to meet; they also practiced the strategies in classrooms, as did counselors and supervisors. Some study groups were comfortable planning and sharing, while others were anxious. New teachers hired at the last minute had to be integrated into the process.

The success of the study groups depended on the leadership of teachers. Because leadership was uneven—

We asked all participants to practice the teaching strategies no less than 30 times apiece during September and October.

some groups had several energetic leaders while others had none—we reorganized the groups several times to distribute initiative throughout the schools. At the end of the second year, the study groups still depended on the leadership of a relatively small number of teachers and the stimulation of the cadre to help them learn new teaching techniques.

We asked the study groups to concentrate on teaching their students how to respond to the models of teaching they were learning. They had been told that, although the students might respond immediately to the new cognitive and social tasks presented by those models, it would take about 20 practices before students would become really proficient. The initial goal for student skill would be attained when a trainer could enter the classroom, announce the model to be used in a lesson, and students could respond efficiently and comfortably. The goal for teachers was to bring students to that level of proficiency as rapidly as possible. The study groups gradually learned to track student progress and design ways of accelerating learning.

As we had hoped, there were immediate and positive effects on students. Especially visible was the reduction in disciplinary referrals. Many teachers reported that their students liked the new teaching strategies and that classroom management was easier. Some of the teachers became very excited about the increase in cooperative activity and the positive responses of their students. Some were anxious as they altered their familiar classroom routines; they worried because they could not predict how their students would respond until both they and their students had experience with the new procedures.

Academic year training. At six-week intervals during the first and second years we provided regular assistance to the faculties, derived from our observations of the staff. Through direct observation and the examination of videotapes, we gathered information about implementation and devised demonstrations and practicums to ad-

Changing the workplace climate to one of cooperative study and decision making was a complex process marked by uneven progress.

dress the needs we saw. With the supportive relationship among the staff development director, consultants, and the principals of the schools, problems could be identified and approached.

Progress. By stages, the new teaching strategies became familiar and the study groups learned to function together. By the beginning of the second year, the operation in the phase one schools was relatively smooth. Each faculty had a few members who still hoped the project would go away, but teacher leadership within the faculties was dominant in maintaining and extending the study groups and practice.

The cadre. During the winter and spring of 1988, we selected candidates for the cadre. The candidates, who were teachers and administrators from throughout the district, submitted applications and videotapes of classroom teaching to demonstrate their competence with the models of teaching they had practiced.

Cadre training included assisting with the introductory workshops for the phase two schools. By the end of

July, they had designed courses and workshops to be offered at the district level during the 1988-89 school year. They also provided assistance to phase one and two study teams, prepared training materials, developed videotaped demonstrations of teaching, and studied research on training and teaching.

Formative Evaluation

Throughout the project, we have collected information about changes in the workplace, the implementation of the models of teaching, and effects on students. Our analysis of this information guides the reshaping of the training and the orientation of new schools and provides estimates of the extent to which the goals are being achieved. Now we will discuss the general picture for the phase one schools.

The workplace. Changing the workplace climate to one of cooperative study and decision making was a complex process marked by uneven progress (as described by Sudderth 1989, Black 1989). All three schools showed the individualistic organization that Lortie considered typical of American schools (Lortie 1975), and two of them had histories of very high staff turnover (about one-third annually), typical of schools with reputations for being troubled. Few teachers sought the leadership of other teachers—most were oriented toward their *own* classrooms. For these faculties, increasing collegial interaction was quite an innovation.

After a few weeks, some teachers emerged as the leaders in the transfer process. They developed "executive control" over the models and applied them appropriately in their teaching and learned to share lessons and demonstrate for their peers. They also instigated concerted efforts to teach the students to respond to the models. Some who developed executive control eschewed leadership, however, wishing to avoid conflict with resistant colleagues. By the end of two years, the number of teacher/leaders who have emerged is just enough to keep the study groups going; and the teacher/leaders need continual assistance from the cadre.

Schoolwide objectives for teaching the students to respond to the models of teaching were very important. For example, administrators led the teachers in establishing "cooperative learning days," "writing days," "number facts days," and other schoolwide efforts. Although administrators' teaching skill and experience played an important role, more important was their "cheerleading" function and their willingness to "carry the flag" prominently.

Schoolwide objectives for improving the social climate of the schools were established only with difficulty, although two schools have made great progress. In both cases the schools had relied heavily on quasi-legal methods of control, chiefly suspensions. In one elementary school, there were nearly 200 incidents of suspension per year (in a student population of about 550). When disciplinary referrals began to drop, apparently as a result of students' increased involvement in learning, the building administrators seized the opportunity to induce the staff to reflect on the dynamics of management and the relationship between instruction and classroom control. Consequently, the staff worked hard to use instruction as the major mechanism of control and, during the second year of the project, only six students were suspended. The school had moved from massive reliance on suspension to minimal use, in extreme cases only. Nearly 1,000 days of lost instructional time were thus recovered, and management became a much less obtrusive feature of the school. The middle school had a similar problem and, although it still uses an in-house suspension program, out-of-school suspensions have dropped from about 150 per semester (again in a population of about 550 students) to about 35.

The faculties are still individualistic in many ways but show their increasing willingness to attack common problems. The services of process-oriented consultants would perhaps be timely, to enable the faculties to capitalize more fully on the collegial settings.

The extent of change in the workplace has affected the degree of implementation by individuals. The concerted implementations that occurred when building administrators generated "whole-school" goals became enthusiastic collaborations as faculties generated mnemonics to be employed throughout the school, or gave concentrated energy to "metrics," or otherwise worked together. Concerted efforts helped teachers learn that they can be effective as a faculty. However, unified efforts continue to be a function of the active leadership of the building administrators and lead teachers. Only by being *very* active can they maintain collective activity.

> **Although administrators' teaching skill and experience played an important role, more important was their willingness to "carry the flag" prominently.**

Implementation of the Teaching Models

The administrators observed their teachers on a regular basis and collected records of their use of the teaching strategies. Predictably, use of the models of teaching varied widely, from tentative and minimal use to regular and appropriate use. Administrators reported extensive use by about three-fourths of the faculty members, with moderate use by most of the others. From each school six teachers were selected randomly and observed and interviewed regularly throughout the year to determine quality of use (see Showers 1989). The 18 teachers were also videotaped near the end of the school year, and we analyzed those tapes to determine the level of skill they had achieved.

The training and use of the study group format were designed to ensure that 75–90 percent of the teachers would reach a mechanical level of use of at least two of the teaching strategies by the end of the first year. This goal was achieved during the first year. About one-third of the teachers developed a high level of skill in using three or four models of teaching. Another third learned to use at least two of them with a satisfactory level of competence. About half of the remainder were able to use one or more of them to a mechanical but not fluid level.

During the second year, the phase one teachers have continued to develop and consolidate skills. They are much more comfortable with the addition of new models but continue to struggle with new skills until they have practiced them about 20 times. The study groups and the use of peer coaching continue to be important as new models are introduced. More than 50 videotapes have been made to demonstrate aspects of the teaching strategies where the teachers have had difficulty. These, together with dozens of "live" demonstrations, have helped greatly, but the road to executive control is a rocky one for many of the teachers. Because the reading and language curriculums of the district are tightly prescribed, most "legitimate" use of the models of teaching has been

Disciplinary referrals began to drop, apparently as a result of students' increased involvement in learning.

in the social studies, mathematics, and, in the middle school, the sciences. In these curriculum areas the opportunity for use has been greatest; therefore, we understand the impact on student achievement that we have found there.

Student Learning

Our study of student learning has had two objectives: (1) to learn whether differences in teacher skill in using the new strategies is associated with student learning; and (2) to learn whether our effort narrowed the gap between students from poor families and their wealthier counterparts.

The clearest test of the first question was in the elementary schools where, in self-contained classrooms, individual teachers have instructional responsibility for curriculum areas other than reading. To determine whether any differences in achievement were a function of developed ability to learn, we used reading level as an indicator of general competence. We compared the classes of the teachers who had reached executive control with those of the teachers who performed at the mechanical level, with respect to reading level. We found them to be about equal in both mean and range.

The social studies tests from the Iowa Tests of Basic Skills battery was

administered to the 5th grade students at the end of the second year. The achievement of the classes whose teachers had reached executive control was compared with the classes whose teachers used them mechanically (and, thus, generally less than they could be used appropriately).

When the two distributions are compared, the median student in the "executive control" classes is between the 85th and 90th percentiles of the "mechanical use" classes. Compared to national norms, the median student of the "executive control" classes was at the 76th percentile, compared to the 44th percentile for the "mechanical use" classes. At the time the tests were given, the median grade-equivalent score for the national sample was 5.8. The median grade-equivalent scores for the "executive control" classes range from 6.5 to 7.9, or from 0.7 to 2.1 above the national median. For the "mechanical use" classes, the range was from 5.0 to 6.1. The distributions

of the extreme classes barely overlap. Figure 1 depicts the comparison between the "executive control" and "mechanical use" classes in grade-equivalent terms.

The message is clear. Skillful implementation of these research-based teaching strategies can have a substantial impact on student achievement. However, to reach their full potential, these models must be used with considerable skill and frequency. The "mechanical use" classes are not achieving badly in normative terms—in fact they are above average for schools equivalent in socioeconomic status—but their students could have learned much more. Thus, we need to find ways of increasing the impact of training. We have many clues about how to achieve this, particularly for providing more explicit training for those teachers who require it; some of our previous research on the relationship between conceptual level of teachers and need for structure in

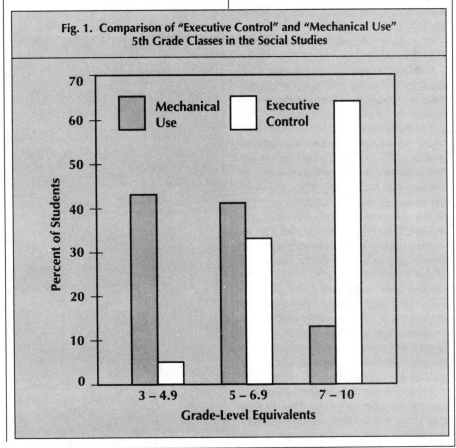

Fig. 1. Comparison of "Executive Control" and "Mechanical Use" 5th Grade Classes in the Social Studies

Now most of these students will not be wiped out in the economic marketplace, as appeared to be their destiny.

training will be useful here (Joyce et al. 1981).

The best answer to our second question—whether we narrowed the achievement gap between the children of the poor and their economically advantaged counterparts—lay in the study of the middle school. The promotion rate for the school rose from 30 percent before the project began to 70 percent at the end of the first year and 94 percent at the end of the second year, using the same standards for promotion. The magnitude of the increase certainly indicates that student learning is on the rise.

Because the school district administrative staff and, reportedly, members of the board of education place more credence in "standard tests" than on local tests and teacher judgment of achievement, the district's staff development unit administered the ITBS battery in science, social studies, mathematics, and one language test at the end of the second year to attempt to confirm the standards used for promotion in normative terms. This testing also provided us with the opportunity to explore whether the 8th grade stu-

dents, who had been exposed to the program for two years, had gained on their wealthier counterparts.

The analysis, which compared 6th and 8th grade students, dealt with our question about whether the students had nonetheless continued to fall behind "middle class" students. It confirms our impression that the majority of the students are now making "normal" progress.

The social studies scores of the 6th grade students indicate that, through the first six years of their schooling, the average student had been achieving the equivalent of about seven months of growth for each year in school (10 months of growth being, by definition, the average for the national sample). The mean score on the social studies test for the 6th grade was 1.5 grade equivalents below the national mean (5.3 compared with 6.8 for the national sample). If the students continued at that rate of growth, we would expect that in the 8th grade the mean would be 6.7. However, the 8th grade

mean was 7.3 for social studies, still below the national average but six months higher than their past rate of growth had been (see fig. 2).

Their probable rate of growth was about average for the national sample. The mean grade equivalent was 7.5 for science and 7.7 for mathematics. In the 6th grade, only five 6th grade students scored as high as 7.0. By contrast, 13 8th grade students scored 10.0 or higher, indicating that the school had become an environment that would support above-average achievement.

Given the educational history of the school, it is quite an accomplishment for it to become a place where average achievement is now normal. Much remains to be done, of course, especially to increase the executive level use of the teaching models and to drive toward equality in overall achievement. However, if the current levels of achievement can be sustained, most of these students will not be wiped out in the economic marketplace, as appeared to be their destiny before the

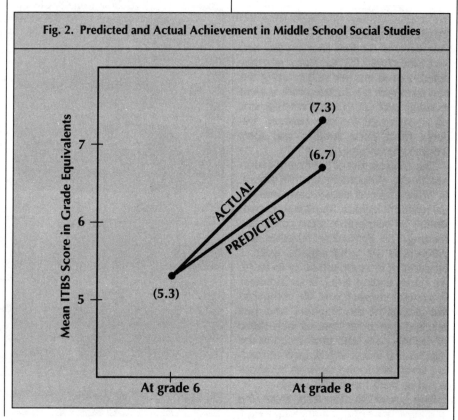

Fig. 2. Predicted and Actual Achievement in Middle School Social Studies

Mean ITBS Score in Grade Equivalents

(7.3)

(6.7)

ACTUAL

PREDICTED

(5.3)

At grade 6   At grade 8

program was initiated. Moreover, if the students can increase their learning rates as much as they appear to have done, there is no good reason why they cannot be helped to increase them still further.

From Anxiety to Pleasure
This project relies on staff development to reorganize the workplace and help teachers learn teaching strategies. Hence, it is different from a curriculum or technological innovation where a new program of study or learning device is "put into place" and its effects are studied. In our project, as appropriate implementation is achieved, effects are expected to be gradual but eventually large. The district has been able to bring about large changes in the workplace, and the cadre development has been splendid. The phase one teachers have practiced unfamiliar strategies until many of the teachers have reached a good level of skill with them. The study groups are functioning, and the school faculties as a whole are making concerted efforts to advance student achievement in specific areas. The students are learning more, and social control is more a function of instruction than of coercion.

The phase two schools are in about the same developmental stage as were the phase one schools a year ago, with uneven implementation and a great deal of skepticism on the part of many teachers. The pessimistic attitudes of many teachers about the possibility of improving student learning are not intractable, but success by peers has little apparent effect on it. The practice of collective action does have effect, albeit gradual, provided the workplace is changed to make cooperative behavior the norm.

We do not believe that success in improving student learning will sustain the collaborative activity. Success makes it easier to reiterate the purpose for changing the workplace, but the schools will surely return to their previous states fairly rapidly unless they are well tended. Also, success in some schools does not inspire most teachers in other schools. The most

> **Collective action does have effect, albeit gradual, provided the workplace is changed to make cooperative behavior the norm.**

active resistors fight the cadre as actively as they fight consultants from outside the district—and the cadre have less experience in dealing with resistance.

However, the changed organism offers many satisfactions—and the concerted schoolwide efforts are rewarding to those teachers who experience the power of working together and the real and immediate effects on the students. Better-planned lessons are more satisfying to teach, and borrowing the ideas and materials of others becomes a pleasurable source of success.

The collegial setting is least satisfying to the least-prepared teachers, whose shaky hold on subject matter and uninspired teaching is unmasked in the collegial environment. This is necessary but sad; and it takes a long time to remedy, for the least competent teachers learn both subject matter and teaching practices more slowly than do the others. It is natural that they would want to hide in their classrooms. Nevertheless, the charisma of the most inspired teachers should dominate the environment. Where it does, the learning climate can change

quite rapidly—far more so than conventional wisdom would predict.

In the few schools we have been discussing, hundreds of students are daily experiencing success and can expect promotion rather than failure and, just as important, know they have earned that promotion. Social control is becoming an effect of instruction rather than "management." Teachers are learning from one another and are welcoming the fruits of research into their repertoires. It is a pleasure to watch their transition from anxiety to pleasure in the company of their colleagues.□

References

Black, J. (1989). "Building the School as a Center of Inquiry: A Whole-School Approach Built Around Models of Teaching." Doctoral project, Nova University, Fort Lauderdale, Florida.
Fullan, M. (1982). *The Meaning of Educational Change*. New York: Teachers College Press.
Joyce, B., and B. Showers. (1987). *Student Achievement Through Staff Development*. White Plains, N.Y.: Longman, Inc.
Joyce, B., L. Peck, and C. Brown, eds. (1981). *Flexibility in Teaching*. White Plains, N.Y.: Longman, Inc.
Joyce, B., and M. Weil. (1986). *Models of Teaching*. Englewood Cliffs, N.J.: Prentice-Hall, Inc.
Lortie, D. (1975). *Schoolteacher*. Chicago: University of Chicago Press.
Showers, B. (1989). "Research-Based Training and Teaching Strategies and Their Effects on the Workplace and Instruction." Paper delivered at the annual meeting of the American Educational Research Association, San Francisco.
Sudderth, C. (1989). "The Social Battleground of School Improvement." Paper delivered at the annual meeting of the American Educational Research Association, San Francisco.

Bruce Joyce and **Beverly Showers** are Directors of Booksend Laboratories, 3830 Vine Maple Dr., Eugene, OR 97405. **Carlene Murphy** is Director of Staff Development for the Richmond County Schools. She can be reached at the Staff Development Center, 804 Katharine St., Augusta, GA 30904. **Joseph Murphy** is Dean of the Faculty of Education at Augusta College, Augusta, GA 30910.

Educational Leadership 45 (Feb. 1988): 4-8

Ann Lieberman

Expanding the Leadership Team

The recent shift in dialogue about reform calls for reshaping the role of teachers to give them greater autonomy, responsibility, and status.

Teacher leaders provide potent models of professionalism to other teachers when they share expertise on a consultative basis.

Although it has been more than four years since the country was shocked by a report declaring the "nation at risk," the pressure for educational reform has continued unabated. Recently, however, a shift in the discussion has become evident. Where earlier reports stressed adding courses, changing requirements, and rethinking curriculum and instruction (particularly in the high school), current reports focus on the teaching force itself. This "second wave of reform" raises issues of fundamental change in the way teachers are prepared, inducted into teaching, and involved in leadership and decision making at the school level. Affecting the very structure of schools themselves, teachers are assuming new roles with far more discretion, autonomy, and responsibility than they have ever had before.

Perhaps the most influential reports are those of the Holmes Group (1986) and the Carnegie Task Force on Teaching as a Profession (1986). The former raises the necessity for reforming teacher preparation, restructuring the teaching force, and developing professional schools; the latter focuses on the role of "lead teachers," who work collaboratively with colleagues and principals at the local school level. These reports have moved discussion of the reform movement in a new direction, indicating, among other things, that people in higher education are trying to understand the implications of these reforms for their own institutions as well as for the field (Soltis 1987). It is also of great significance that, perhaps for the first time, teachers themselves are being asked their views (Cohn et al. n.d.). We are just beginning to get reports on what some of the new roles look like, what the changed relationships are, and what organizational arrangements appear necessary to complement these changes (Lieberman et al. in press, Little in press, Rosenholtz in press).

What has caused this shift of attention from more courses, testing, and monitoring systems to restructuring schools and the roles of teachers? What are school districts doing because of it? What tensions and dilemmas are surfacing as a result of changes in the roles and relationships of teachers and principals? What are we learning about the possibilities of expanding the leadership team in schools? Answering these questions will, we hope, move the discussion along so that we can better understand the leap that we must make if we are to go from report to action, from the theoretical possibility to the actual process.

Changing Conditions of Teachers and Teaching

Growing teacher shortages in many areas of the country have helped to cause the shift in discussion about reform to a focus on restructuring the roles of teachers (Wise et al. 1987, Theobald 1987). The reasons for the teacher deficit are complex, including political, social, and economic trends. As teachers hired during the '50s approach retirement, there is concern that there will be fewer competent and talented teachers to replace them (Darling-Hammond 1984). In some areas—for example, New York City—the crisis is already here (Warren 1986). (It is important to note that at a time when, in urban districts, "minorities" are becoming the majority of students, very few "minority" students are going into teaching.)

Teaching has historically been a female occupation, but the women who were always there are not there anymore. The last two decades have seen more and more younger women move into what were traditionally male occupations, with fewer entering education. Better working conditions, higher status positions, greater recognition, higher salaries, greater autonomy, and more control over working conditions have attracted women to other fields of endeavor. In contrast, those women remaining in schools have seen their own workplaces become even more bureaucratized. They are increasingly feeling the absence of support, inadequate facilities and resources, low status, and the ever-present lack of control over their work. This bureaucratization, mated with paternalism, continues to keep women in subordinate positions (Schlechty 1987). Experienced teachers, the very ones needed to help in the development of new teachers, are leaving the profession in increasing numbers.

In addition, teachers are bearing the brunt of changing family structures and the unwillingness or inability of government and private agencies to respond to these changes. For many teachers, the social and economic changes in our society are sharply felt through the attitudes of parents and students, manifested by apathy on one hand and lack of respect on the other (Cohn et al. n.d.).

Meanwhile, business groups have begun to issue reports calling for many of the same kinds of changes recommended by educators (Committee for Economic Development 1987). Voicing their desire to improve education now to provide an educated workforce later, business groups are promoting changes that go beyond the holding of higher expectations or adding more courses to the redefining of how the work itself gets accomplished.

What we see, then, is the coming together of important and disparate social and political forces with a common interest in reforming the nation's schools: governors making education the number one priority in their states; universities calling for massive reform of teacher preparation in their own institutions; business concerned with reform because of the need for better-educated workers; and teacher associations recognizing that they must play a significant role in restructuring and professionalizing teaching if they are to influence the direction of change. This is an unprecedented, if uncoordinated, coalition of forces calling for structural reforms.

Changes Occurring in the Schools

The reports keep coming, and there is no question that the rhetoric of "restructuring schools" is catching on. Changes are appearing in varied forms. School site management, for

"Working in collaborative situations exposes teachers to new ideas, to working on problems collectively, and to learning from the very people who understand the complexity of their work best—their own colleagues."

"As teachers and principals renegotiate the terms of their work, creating these new roles and structures will undoubtedly produce conflicts over turf, rewards, and responsibilities. No movement grows without this kind of struggle for a redefinition of rights and responsibilities."

example, in its most advanced form, shifts control of the money from the district office to the school. Parents, teachers, administrators, and students form a planning group to decide the emphasis for schoolwide goals, the needs for professional development, and the general means for running the school. Some districts provide development activities to help people at the school make such decisions. In South Bend, Indiana, they are replacing retiring district-level content specialists with teacher specialists.

Teacher centers, now in their second or third iteration, have reappeared as a strong vehicle both for professionalizing the staff and working with new teachers. Teachers with specific expertise are now participating in a variety of leadership roles. For example, in a district in Washington, teachers provide professional development for other teachers in their specific subject area; after two years they are replaced by other subject matter specialists and return to their classrooms.

Some schools are experimenting with flextime. In one situation, when husband and wife, both outstanding teachers, decided to quit teaching, the district asked them to share one position; now one works in the morning, the other in the afternoon.

In California, a statewide program funding mentor teachers is expanding the role of teacher to mean not only teaching students but teaching colleagues as well. They teach children part-time and work part-time with other teachers. The powerful appeal of this option is that teachers receive recognition for the help they give their peers while gaining important learnings for themselves. Even the untouchable element—time—is being negotiated.

In Maine, a principal and his staff are restructuring their school. They have "broken the back of the schedule" and plan to group 80 students with 4 teachers for the equivalent of 4 periods a day. Students will spend the rest of their time in electives in the related arts. Teachers will spend the remainder of their day in preparation, team planning, and staff development.

The New York City Teacher Center Consortium, functioning for over eight years under the leadership of Myrna Cooper, is perhaps the most fully developed model of teacher leadership (Miles et al. in press). In studying the roles of these teacher leaders, we found that they provide powerful models of professionalism for their peers, afford leadership in a variety of content areas, and help create a positive climate in extremely difficult environments. By observing how they actually work in schools, we have produced materials that can be used by others in similar situations (Saxl et al. in preparation). We found that a teacher in an expanded leadership role becomes involved in a comprehensive series of actions, which include:

- building trust and rapport
- making an organizational diagnosis
- building skill and confidence in others
- using resources
- dealing with the change process
- managing the work

Inherent in each of these "skill clusters" are strategies teacher leaders use to build structures for collaborative work with their peers. Finding ways to create structures for teachers to work together, to focus on the problems of their school, to enhance their repertoires of teaching strategies—all are part of the work of teachers who work with other teachers.

Another subject for study has been the development of collegial relations in schools, both what they look like and how to create them. Rosenholtz (in press) found differences between "collaborative" settings and "isolated" ones. In schools characterized by collaborative relationships, teachers seek each other out for help; and principals support the idea that any problem of any teacher can be worked on collectively. Teachers in collaborative settings assist colleagues who need help; in isolated settings, teachers feel that they must learn everything on their own. Because "isolated" teachers turn inward, they have little access to knowledge of alternative ways of working and little peer support for trying to gain or apply such knowledge.

In her landmark study, Judith Warren Little (1986) documents the process by which norms of collegiality and experimentation were built in some schools. She describes the collaborative arrangements that developed as teachers worked together toward common goals. In time allotted during the school day, shared work on curriculum units made possible the growth of teachers who developed the skills necessary to carry out their plans. Teachers had time to discuss the details of their work with each other and, in so doing, fashioned new ways of working together. Principals in these schools helped by providing resources and support.

Expanding the leadership team in schools, then, means not just creating a few new roles or giving the principal some help, but finding new ways of organizing schools to create an open, collaborative mode of work to replace teacher isolation. Such changes do not come easily.

Tensions in Creating Teacher Leadership Roles

The process of changing the roles and responsibilities of school people will stir up and disturb some deeply rooted beliefs, not because current arrangements are effective, but because "that is the way things are." It will take vision and courage to break clear of these beliefs and engage states and local communities in changing the way schools are organized.

The "egalitarian ethic" (that a teacher is a teacher no matter how experienced, how effective, or how knowledgeable) has long been held by teachers. Part of the norm is that teachers must spend all their time with students in classrooms. A major source of tension, then, comes from the conflict of values in teachers themselves. They do not trust the intervention of other adults (including their own peers), who may come between the

teachers and their major source of rewards—their students. However, working in collaborative situations exposes teachers to new ideas, to working on problems collectively, and to learning from the very people who understand the complexity of their work best—their own colleagues.

Another source of tension exists because principals and teachers often work in a parent-child relationship rather than as peers. As in any large family, some children make it, some children rebel, and some continue to respond dutifully to being told what to do. Parents, like principals, differ too. Some control inappropriately, even when their "kids" are 35 years old. Some parents let go and even learn from their children as everyone in the family grows up together; others hold tightly to some things and are laissez-faire with others. The analogy ends when we realize that, even as relationships change over time, parents will always be parents. It is possible, however, to conceive of principals and teachers moving away from the parent-child relationship to a far more collaborative, shared view in which principals and teachers can all be leaders in the school.

The past decade has exacerbated the growth of adversarial relationships among all levels of the school community. However, organizing to protect one's rights and privileges, although historically an effective vehicle for change, now stands in the way of building the very collaborative structures needed to support teacher leadership. Somehow, a new dialogue must take place; and a new set of organizational arrangements must be created so that all members of the school community can be involved in building a collaborative culture. But those involved in such creations must realize that time, perseverance, and courage will be needed to work out these new forms.

Most of us who work in organizations know that it is easier to do things by ourselves than to work with others. Still, if we are to institutionalize new leadership roles for teachers and build a healthier organization for the adults

" . . . we may indeed have a real opportunity to change the teaching profession profoundly. . . . [to] provide greater recognition and status for teachers, who have suffered too long from mythological and oversimplified definitions of their work; . . . [to] reshape teaching as an occupation to encourage young people to become teachers and more experienced teachers to share their expertise."

as well as the students, we must learn to take collective responsibility. This will cause tension, too, as it will inevitably make necessary new forms, new time arrangements, and new ways of carrying out the work. The process of organizational change is not well understood by most of us, and learning to do things differently is not comfortable for any of us. Although we read articles about this process (and write them too), threat, discomfort, and uneasiness are not conditions that we happily accept. As teachers and principals renegotiate the terms of their work, creating these new roles and structures will undoubtedly produce conflicts over turf, rewards, and responsibilities. No movement grows without this kind of struggle for a redefinition of rights and responsibilities—nor will this one.

Possibilities for a Restructured Profession

From the early descriptions of attempts to provide new, expanded roles for teachers, we see that we may indeed have a real opportunity to change the teaching profession in profound ways. The possibilities include:

● building colleagueship among teachers who have long been isolated from one another so they can share common problems and collective solutions;

● providing greater recognition and status for teachers, who have suffered too long from mythological and oversimplified definitions of their work;

● enlarging the reward structure to allow for choice, renewal, and opportunities to grow and learn—for teachers as well as students;

● building a school structure that permits autonomy, flexibility, and responsibility, and provides resources for teaching and learning;

● reshaping teaching as an occupation to encourage young people to become teachers and more experienced teachers to share their expertise. (As better working conditions increase teacher satisfaction, education will compete more favorably as a career choice with other professions); and

> **"As better working conditions increase teacher satisfaction, education will compete more favorably as a career choice with other professions."**

● building a professional culture in the schools that will broaden the way they function and enable them to become more sensitive to the communities they serve.

Reform movements are born out of crisis. The so-called second wave of reform in education is no exception. We now have a real opportunity to do more than tinker with a few courses or follow another short-term fad. We have the potential to change the structure of the school itself and, in so doing, the nature of American education. □

References

Carnegie Forum on Education and the Economy. *A Nation Prepared: Teachers for the 21st Century*. Report of the Carnegie Task Force on Teaching as a Profession. Washington, D.C.: Carnegie Forum, May 1986.

Cohn, Marilyn, et al. "Teachers' Perspectives on the Problems of Their Profession: Implications for Policy Makers and Practitioners." Washington, D.C.: Office of Educational Research and Improvement, U.S. Department of Education, n.d.

Committee for Economic Development. *Children in Need: Investment Strategies for the Educationally Disadvantaged*. New York: Committee for Economic Development, 1987.

Darling-Hammond, Linda. *Beyond the Commission Reports: The Coming Crisis in Teaching*. Santa Monica, Calif.: The RAND Corporation, 1984.

The Holmes Group. "Tomorrow's Teachers, A Report of the Holmes Group." East Lansing, Mich.: The Holmes Group, Inc., 1986.

Lieberman, Ann, et al. "Teacher Leadership: Ideology and Practice." In *Building a Professional Culture in Schools*, edited by Ann Lieberman. New York: Teachers College Press, in press.

Little, Judith Warren. "Seductive Images and Organizational Realities in Professional Development." In *Rethinking School Improvement: Research, Craft, and Concept*, edited by Ann Lieberman. New York: Teachers College Press, 1986.

Little, Judith Warren. "Assessing the Prospects for Teacher Leadership." In *Building a Professional Culture in Schools*, edited by Ann Lieberman. New York: Teachers College Press, in press.

Miles, Matthew B., Ellen R. Saxl, and A. Lieberman. "What Skills Do Effective 'Change Agents' Need?: An Empirical View." *Curriculum Inquiry*, in press.

Rosenholtz, Susan J. *Schools, Social Organization, and the Building of a Technical Culture*. New York: Longman Publishing, in press.

Saxl, Ellen R., Matthew B. Miles, and Ann Lieberman. *ACE—Assisting Change in Education* (a set of modules to use in training professional assisters, teachers, leaders, etc.). Alexandria, Va.: Association for Supervision and Curriculum Development, not available, in preparation.

Schlechty, Philip. From a speech delivered at a conference on Building Collegiality in Schools given at the University of Washington for the Puget Sound Educational Consortium, May 8, 1987.

Soltis, Jonas F., ed. *Reforming Teacher Education: The Impact of the Holmes Group Report*. New York: Teachers College Press, 1987.

Theobald, Neil. "Who Shall Teach Our Children?" A report issued by the Puget Sound Educational Consortium, the University of Washington, and the State Superintendent for Public Instruction, Olympia, Washington, 1987.

Warren, Constancia. "Teaching in New York City, 1986: A Profession in Crisis." Unpublished paper, 1986.

Wise, Arthur, et al. "Effective Teacher Selection: From Recruitment to Retention." Monograph prepared for the National Institute of Education. Santa Monica, Calif.: The RAND Corporation, January 1987.

Ann Lieberman is Executive Director, Puget Sound Educational Consortium, University of Washington, M215 Miller Hall, DQ-12, Seattle, WA 28195.

Educational Leadership 46 (May 1989): 45-53

JANE L. DAVID

Synthesis of Research on School-Based Management

Although school-based management has a chameleon-like appearance, we can learn about it by listening to practitioner testimony and by examining the research on relevant topics such as school improvement and organizational change.

Dade County, Florida, has made front-page headlines with its pilot School-Based Management/Shared Decision Making Program. The Montgomery County School Board in Maryland has approved a similar plan for spring 1989. In Baton Rouge, Louisiana, school-based management is coupled with parental choice as part of an unusual desegregation strategy. Santa Fe, New Mexico, is implementing school-based management with teacher-led school improvement teams. The list goes on.

"School-based management" is rapidly becoming the centerpiece of the current wave of reform. The growing number of districts "restructuring" their schools, as well as commentary from the National Governors' Association, both national teachers' unions, and corporate leaders—all make reference to some form of increased school autonomy.

Yet there is surprisingly little empirical research on the topic. Searches of education indexes yield numerous references for school-based management, but virtually all are conceptual arguments, how-to guides, and testimonials from practitioners. There is, nevertheless, an abundance of rele-

vant research. Topics ranging from school improvement to corporate innovation bear directly on school-based management. Their relevance can be seen when we look at why districts are turning to school-based management today.

Under school-based management, professional responsibility replaces bureaucratic regulation.

School-Based Management Today

In the 1960s and 1970s, certain forms of school-based management, usually called *decentralization* and *school-site budgeting*, had a wave of popularity. These were adopted in order to give political power to local communities, increase administrative efficiency, or offset state authority (e.g., Wissler and Ortiz 1986). In the late 1980s, however, school-based management is a focus of attention for quite different reasons. Districts are implementing school-based management today to bring about significant change in educational practice: to empower school staff to create conditions in schools that facilitate improvement, innovation, and continuous professional growth (e.g., Goodlad 1984, Carnegie Forum 1986). Current interest is a response to evidence that our education system is not working, and, in particular, that strong central control actually diminishes teachers' morale and, correspondingly, their level of effort (Meier 1987, Corcoran et al. 1988).

Bolstered by analogous research findings in corporations, districts are turning to management structures that delegate more authority and flexibility to school staff (e.g., Kanter 1983). Under school-based management, professional responsibility replaces bureaucratic regulation; districts increase school autonomy in exchange for the staff's assuming responsibility for results (Cohen 1988). Two specific accountability mechanisms often accompany school-based management proposals and practices. One is an annual school performance report. The other is some form of parent choice or open enrollment; schools that do not produce results lose enrollment (Garms et al. 1978, Raywid 1988).

Delegating authority to all schools in a district distinguishes school-based management practices from school improvement programs. Both approaches share a school-based, schoolwide orientation to improvement and, usually, a mechanism for shared decision making (David and Peterson 1984). But school-based management has a broader scope; it represents a change in how the district operates—how authority and responsibility are shared between the district and its schools. It not only changes roles and responsibilities within schools but has implications for how the central office is organized and the size and roles of its staff (Elmore 1988). School improvement programs, on the other hand, usually have no special authority, do not have a separate budget, and involve only a small

Without autonomy, shared decision making within schools has little meaning.

number of schools (although they can be districtwide).

Once school-based management is understood in the context of empowering school staff to improve education practice through fundamental change in district management functions, the relevant research topics are easy to identify. They include school improvement programs, organizational change, efforts to stimulate innovation, participatory decision making, and effective practices in many areas, from teacher selection to staff development. Next I draw on the literature on these topics, as well as the handful of studies of school-based management itself, to describe (1) how school-based management works in theory and in practice, and (2) the connections between changing man-

agement structures and achieving improvement goals.

School-Based Management = Autonomy + Shared Decision Making

The rationale for school-based management rests on two well-established propositions:

1. The school is the primary decision-making unit; and, its corollary, decisions should be made at the lowest possible level (e.g., Smith and Purkey 1985).

2. Change requires ownership that comes from the opportunity to participate in defining change and the flexibility to adapt it to individual circumstances; the corollary is that change does not result from externally imposed procedures (e.g., Fullan 1982).

In practice, these propositions translate into two policies that define the essence of school-based management: (1) increasing school autonomy through some combination of site budgetary control and relief from constraining rules and regulations; and (2) sharing the authority to make decisions with teachers, and sometimes parents, students, and other community members (e.g., Garms et al. 1978).

School Autonomy
The backbone of school-based management is delegation of authority from district to schools; without autonomy, shared decision making within schools has little meaning. Analysts of school-based management describe autonomy as decision-making authority in three critical arenas: budget, staffing, and curriculum (Garms et al. 1978, Clune and White 1988). In practice, these distinctions blur because (1) staffing is by far the largest part of a school's budget, and (2) decision-making authority is a matter of degree, constrained by district, union contract, state, and even federal rules and regulations (as well as historical practice).

Budget. Under school-based management, schools receive either a lump-sum budget or some portion of the budget, usually for equipment, materials, supplies, and sometimes other categories such as staff development. Because money usually equals

Key Elements of Site-Based Management

Gordon Cawelti

A large number of districts across the country are experimenting with site-based management, usually by selected schools responsive to the idea of having their authority and responsibility increased in an attempt to improve accountability and productivity. Here are some key elements emerging from their work:
- Various degrees of site-based budgeting affording alternative uses of resources
- A team operation affording groups to expand the basis of decision making
- School-site advisory committees with key roles for parents and students at the high school level
- Increased authority for selecting personnel who are assigned to the school
- Ability to modify the school's curriculum to better serve their students
- Clear processes for seeking waivers from local or state regulations that restrict the flexibility of local staffs
- An expectation for an annual report on progress and school improvement

Gordon Cawelti is Executive Director, Association for Supervision and Curriculum Development, 1250 North Pitt St., Alexandria, VA 22314-1403.

authority, budgetary authority sounds like the most important manifestation of granting authority to schools. But this is misleading because whether or not school-site budgeting equals autonomy depends on how much freedom from restrictions is allowed. For example, a school can receive a lump-sum budget for all expenditures including staff, yet have no decision-making authority because of rules governing class size, tenure, hiring, firing, assignment, curriculum objectives, and textbooks.

Beyond allotments for staffing (see below), the budgets that districts delegate to schools are typically discretionary funds based on a per-pupil allocation (Clune and White 1988). With staffing, building repairs, and textbook costs removed, each school's budget is the small amount left for materials and supplies, sometimes augmented by district funds for staff development and related categories. Exceptions are found in districts with a large number of federal and state programs that can be passed on to schools without restrictions (David 1989).

Staffing. Typically, schools receive budgets for staffing in terms of "staffing units," which are based on the average cost of a teacher, including benefits. There are two very different types of decision making about staff: defining positions and selecting people to fill them. Once the number of certificated teachers is determined on the basis of enrollment, school staff can choose to spend residual dollars (usually very few) on another teacher, several part-time specialists, instructional aides, or clerical support. Some districts achieve the same effect by allocating one full-time equivalent to each school to be used at the school's discretion (David 1989).

The second area of discretion lies in filling vacancies due to retirements, transfers, or increasing enrollment. Under school-based management, the principal and the teachers select from among applicants, often from a pool screened by the district (Clune and White 1988). Officially, the principal makes a recommendation with advice from teachers; the district still does the hiring. This practice, however, is not

---

To Shift to School-Based Management, Districts Should:

- Build strong alliances with the teachers' union
- Delegate authority to schools to define new roles, select staff, and create new learning environments
- Demonstrate and promote shared decision making
- Communicate goals, guiding images, and information
- Create direct communication links between school staff and top leaders
- Encourage experimentation and risk taking
- Provide for waivers from restrictive rules
- Motivate principals to involve teachers in school-site decisions
- Promote creation of new roles in schools and central office
- Create new forms of accountability with school staff
- Provide broad range of opportunities for professional development
- Provide time for staff to assume new roles and responsibilities
- Reduce size of central office
- Promote role of central office as facilitator and coordinator of school change
- Match salaries to increased responsibilities

---

limited to districts with school-based management, and is, in fact, a characteristic of effective teacher selection practices (Wise et al. 1987).

Curriculum. Under school-based management, teachers are encouraged to develop curriculum and select or create instructional materials, usually within a framework of goals or core curriculum established by the district or the state (David 1989). Clearly, this cannot occur in districts with highly prescribed curriculums, required textbooks, and mandated testing. On the other hand, because students move

---

Although school-based management takes many forms, the essence is school-level autonomy plus participatory decision making.

---

from school to school, some degree of coordination across schools is required. Districts with a history of decentralization have established effective lines of communication among schools and between schools and the district; and they tend to reflect an ebb and flow regarding control of curriculum. Delegating control of curriculum to schools stimulates the creation of new ideas and materials, which in turn requires new lines of communication and districtwide committees of teachers to coordinate curriculum (David 1989, Wissler and Ortiz 1988).

Most teachers have neither the desire nor the time to create or adapt curriculum beyond what they normally do within their classrooms. Nor does typical participation require formal school-based management. Many districts have committees of teachers who play an active role in choosing textbooks and defining curriculum; more comprehensive curriculum development usually occurs over the summer by paid staff (e.g., David 1989, Sickler 1988). Under school-based management and other forms of decentralization, the primary difference is that school staff, instead of district staff, initiate and lead the efforts (Guthrie 1986). For example, one highly decentralized district, which does not characterize its practices as school-based management, has formally transferred control of curriculum to teachers. The district funds 10 districtwide subject area committees, with representatives from each school, and a Curriculum Master Plan Council composed of the elected heads of each committee. The Curriculum Council makes final decisions on new curriculums subject to the school board's approval (Sickler 1988).

Beyond Budget, Staffing, and Curriculum

Authority to make decisions about budget, staffing, and curriculum goes only part way toward school-based management's goal of empowering staff to create more productive workplaces and learning environments. The images guiding today's reforms and the rhetoric of school-based management include, for example, schools characterized by teacher collegiality and collaboration, schools within schools, ungraded classes, and creative uses of technology. These images require changes beyond staffing and curriculum, such as the school calendar, scheduling, criteria for pupil assignment and promotion, the allocation and use of space, and the roles of staff—what Cuban (1988) calls "second-order" changes.[1]

When the extra time and energy demanded by planning and decision making are balanced by real authority, teachers report increased satisfaction, even exuberance.

Under school-based management, authority to make changes in areas beyond those explicitly designated is typically granted by some type of waiver process. Districts vary in the complexity of the process and the scope covered by waivers (e.g., Casner-Lotto 1988). Usually, a waiver process is the result of

agreements between the district and teachers' union that expand the scope beyond what a district can allow on its own. In a few cases, districts may also have agreements with their states that permit waivers from state rules as well (David 1989).

Shared Decision Making

In the context of school-based management, "shared decision making" refers generally to the involvement of teachers in determining how the budget is spent, who is hired, and whatever other authority has been delegated to the school. The phrase can also refer to students, their parents, and other community members; in fact, in many proposals for school-based management, parents are the primary focus—but in an advisory capacity only (e.g., Garms et al. 1978).

Typically, a school forms a school-site council with representatives of each constituency. How participants are selected and what their responsibilities are varies considerably, across and within districts (Clune and White 1988). Some councils are composed of teachers elected schoolwide, or by grade level or department; others are composed of representatives from pre-existing committees. In some schools, the entire faculty is the council. In others, the budget is simply divided among teachers (David 1989).

Findings from School-Based Management Studies

School-based management encompasses a wide variety of practices. Most manifestations have one or more of the following: some marginal choices about staffing; a small discretionary budget for materials or staff development; a mechanism for teachers to be involved in certain decisions; an annual performance report; and a role for parents, either through an advisory group, membership on a decision-making group, or through some form of parent choice.

Although school-based management takes many forms, the essence is school-level autonomy plus participatory decision making. In districts that practice school-based management essentials, research studies find a range of positive effects, from increased

Highlights of Research on School-Based Management

Varieties of school-based management—decentralization and school-site budgeting—were used in the '60s and '70s to achieve political and administrative goals. In contrast, school-based management today is viewed as a way to transform schools into effective learning environments by providing school staff with the authority, flexibility, and resources they need to implement change.

Research on school-based management and related practices points to these conclusions:

• School faculties make different decisions about elements of staffing, schedules, and curriculum when they are given actual control over their budgets and relief from restrictions.

• Teachers report increased job satisfaction and feelings of professionalism when the extra time and energy demanded by planning and decision making are balanced by real authority; conversely, marginal authority coupled with requirements for site councils, plans, and reports results in frustration.

• School-based management affects the roles of district as well as school staff; to change their roles and relationships, teachers and administrators need extra time and a range of opportunities to acquire new knowledge and skills.

• The leadership, culture, and support of the district have a far greater impact on the success of school-based management than its operational details.

• Implementing school-based management involves a lot of pieces and takes a long time, from 5 to 10 years; it is premature to pass final judgment on districts in the early stages.

—Jane L. David

teacher satisfaction and professionalism to new arrangements and practices within schools. These findings apply to districts with decentralized systems whether or not they carry the "school-based management" label (e.g., David 1989, Sickler 1988).

When the extra time and energy demanded by planning and decision making are balanced by real authority, teachers report increased satisfaction, even exuberance (Clune and White 1988, David 1989, Raywid 1988). There is evidence that there are greater differences among schools under a system of school-based management than under one of centralized management. For example, schools make different choices about staff (choosing a part-time music teacher instead of a full-time aide), curriculum (selecting a different textbook), and discretionary funds (spending more on supplies and less on field trips or vice versa) (Garms et al. 1978, Casner-Lotto 1988).

There are a few examples of second-order change, schools that have altered the daily schedule to allow more time for teachers to work together or to increase time devoted to reading (Clune and White 1988, Casner-Lotto 1988). This is not surprising, since studies of school improvement find that school councils rarely tackle even instructional issues, let alone second-order change; dealing with such issues is much more difficult than creating a new discipline policy or decorating the entranceway (David and Peterson 1984, Berman and Gjelten 1984).

That there are few examples of second-order change, and, indeed, of districts that have implemented the essential elements of school-based management, can be explained in part by the paucity of empirical research and the fact that many efforts are quite new. However, studies of successful school-based management and the much larger literature on school improvement and organizational change identify two related pitfalls, each of which can undermine school-based management practices: (1) substituting shared decision making for authority, and (2) delegating authority without strong leadership and support.

A real shift in management responsibility from the district to the school requires everyone to change roles, routines, and relationships.

Substituting Participation for Authority

Shared decision making does not necessarily bring benefits to those involved. It depends on what the decision concerns and who participates, in what capacity, for what reason, and at what stage (Miles 1981). When schools are given only marginal authority (e.g., a small discretionary budget) and are asked to form site councils, develop annual plans, and prepare annual reports, teachers perceive these requests as yet another set of top-down demands. This perception is intensified when districts retain tight control over accountability (Corcoran et al. 1988).

In practice, teacher input in decision making often substitutes for delegated authority, which contributes to the blurring of labels between school improvement programs, shared decision making, and school-based management (Kolderie 1988). When the authority and resources to act are not provided, district efforts can actually backfire (Meier 1987). Asking people to participate in decisions about which they have no information is frustrating, not empowering; participating in planning committees, in contrast to action committees with specific agendas, increases alienation because it uses up

time and energy with no visible results (Kanter 1983).

The Need for Leadership and Support

A real shift in management responsibility from the district to the school requires everyone to change roles, routines, and relationships. Research on school improvement and organizational change is strong on this point: such change does not happen without leadership and support (Fullan 1982, Smith and Purkey 1985). Studies of successful school-based management practices reach the same conclusion. Successful practices have less to do with management details—size of budget, type of decision-making body, amount of control over staffing or curriculum—and more to do with the leadership and culture of the district and the moral and material support it offers school staff (David 1989, Sickler 1988). Hence, some of the most striking examples of second-order change are in districts without formal school-based management that have facilitated the development of schools within schools through leadership and extensive professional development opportunities (David 1989).

Districts that have successfully delegated substantial authority to their schools are characterized by leadership that empowers others, a small central administration, support for experimentation, communication channels, and opportunities for continuous professional growth for principals and teachers (David 1989, Sickler 1988, Casner-Lotto 1988). Similarly, studies of school improvement programs find that when changes occur, they are the result of district support, site leadership, and opportunities for staff development (David and Peterson 1984, Berman and Gjelten 1984). This conclusion is also supported by studies of Australia's school decentralization, which find the absence of understanding and training to be major roadblocks (Chapman and Boyd 1986).

When districts delegate authority to schools, four elements are important. The first is access to new knowledge and skills. Real authority comes from knowledge as well as from delegated authority and waiver provisions; historical practices, myths about requirements, and the absence of known alternatives block change as much as actual requirements (Wissler and Ortiz 1986).

Second, school-based management intensifies the need for leadership from the principal, who functions like a chief executive officer (Guthrie 1986). Ultimately, the degree to which school-level authority is shared and how it is shared are in the hands of the principal. Districts with a history of successfully decentralizing authority are characterized by strong superintendents who use training, hiring and evaluation criteria, and incentives to develop strong site managers (David 1989). These superintendents send clear signals to principals that they value and reward those who involve teachers in decision making.

Third, school staff need time to acquire new knowledge and skills and, equally important, time to put them to use. Successful district practices incorporate plans for reducing teachers' workloads; providing extra time for professional development; and, at the school level, reorganizing schedules to free teachers to participate in decision making and other collegial activities (David 1989, Johnson 1988). Finally, salary levels communicate the value attached to the new roles and responsibilities (Guthrie 1986).

The Future of School-Based Management

School-based management is not a fixed set of rules. It is the opposite of prescription; in fact, by definition it operates differently from one district to the next and from one school to the next and from one year to the next. And that is the point—the goal is to empower school staff by providing authority, flexibility, and resources to solve the educational problems particular to their schools.

> **The goal of school-based management is to empower school staff by providing authority, flexibility, and resources to solve the educational problems particular to their schools.**

Research on school-based management, school improvement, and organizational change tells us that schools are unlikely to change without increased autonomy. But research also tells us that, in the absence of district leadership and support for change, school-based management is not enough. Autonomy can be increased in many ways—through granting control over budgets, through allowing policy-setting authority, through providing waivers—but it is primarily increased by the norms and culture established by district leaders, including the superintendent, the school board, and the teachers' union.

From the research we also know that school-based management takes a long time to implement; districts that have successfully decentralized have done so over a period of 5 to 10 years (Wissler and Ortiz 1986, Casner-Lotto

1988, Sickler 1988, David 1989). School-based management also raises some complicated issues that research has not addressed; for example: the relationship between parent choice and school-based management; the tension between school autonomy and collective bargaining and alternative models; issues regarding the legal authority of the district versus the school; and the role of the state. Although theory can inform some of these issues, most of the unanswered questions will be answered as districts experiment with new structures. We will all learn from their mistakes and their successes.□

1. Cuban (1988) calls these "second-order" change. "First-order" change is like an engineer's quality control solution; it accepts existing goals and structures and aims to correct deficiencies. Examples of first-order change include recruiting better teachers, selecting better texts, and marginal changes to the curriculum. Second-order change is more complex and of wider scope, akin to redesigning a system; it alters roles, routines, and relationships within an organization.

References

Berman, P., and T. Gjelten. (1984). *Improving School Improvement: A Policy Evaluation of the California School Improvement Program, Volume 2: Findings*. Berkeley, Calif.: Berman, Weiler Associates.

Carnegie Forum on Education and the Economy. (1986). *A Nation Prepared: Teachers for the 21st Century. Report of the Carnegie Task Force on Teaching as a Profession*. Washington, D.C.: Carnegie Forum.

Casner-Lotto, J. (1988). "Expanding the Teacher's Role: Hammond's School Improvement Process." *Phi Delta Kappan* 69: 349-353.

Chapman, J., and W.L. Boyd. (1986). "Decentralization, Devolution, and the School Principal: Australian Lessons on Statewide Educational Reform." *Educational Administrative Quarterly* 22: 28-58.

Clune, W.H., and P.A. White. (1988). *School Based Management: Institutional Variation, Implementation, and Issues for Further Research*. Madison, Wis.: Center for Policy Research in Education.

Cohen, M. (1988). *Restructuring the Education System: Agenda for the 1990s*. Washington, D.C.: National Governors' Association.

For Information

To obtain copies of *Resource Materials on School-Based Management* (September 1988) by Paula A. White, contact: Center for Policy Research in Education, Eagleton Institute of Politics, Rutgers, The State University of New Jersey, New Brunswick, NJ 08901; attention: Publications. Phone: (201) 828-3872. Also available is *School-Based Management: Institutional Variation, Implementation, and Issues for Further Research* (September 1988) by William H. Clune and Paula A. White.

Corcoran, T.B., L.J. Walker, and J.L. White. (1988). *Working in Urban Schools*. Washington, D.C.: Institute for Educational Leadership.

Cuban, L. (1988). *The Managerial Imperative and the Practice of Leadership in Schools*. Albany, N.Y.: State University of New York Press.

David, J.L. (1989). *Restructuring in Progress: Lessons from Pioneering Districts*. Washington, D.C.: National Governors' Association.

David, J.L., and S.M. Peterson. (1984). *Can Schools Improve Themselves?: A Study of School-Based Improvement Programs*. Palo Alto, Calif.: Bay Area Research Group.

Elmore, R.F. (1988). "Early Experiences in Restructuring Schools: Voices from the Field." Washington, D.C.: National Governors' Association.

Fullan, M. (1982). *The Meaning of Education Change*. New York: Teachers College Press.

Garms, W.I., J.W. Guthrie, and L.C. Pierce. (1978). *School Finance: The Economics and Politics of Public Education*. Englewood Cliffs, N.J.: Prentice-Hall.

Goodlad, J.I. (1984). *A Place Called School*. New York: McGraw-Hill.

Guthrie, J.W. (1986). "School-Based Management: The Next Needed Education Reform." *Phi Delta Kappan* 68: 305-309.

Johnson, S.M. (1988). "Pursuing Professional Reform in Cincinnati." *Phi Delta Kappan* 69: 746-751.

Kanter, R.M. (1983). *The Change Masters*. New York: Simon & Schuster.

Kolderie, T. (1988). "School-Site Management: Rhetoric and Reality." Minneapolis: Humphrey Institute, University of Minnesota. Unpublished manuscript.

Meier, D. (Fall 1987). "Success in East Harlem: How One Group of Teachers Built a School that Works." *American Educator*: 36-39.

Miles, M. (1981). "Mapping the Common Properties of Schools." In *Improving Schools: Using What We Know*, edited by R. Lehming and M. Kane. Beverly Hills, Calif.: Sage Publications.

Raywid, M.A. (1988). "Restructuring School Governance: Two Models." Hempstead, N.Y.: Hofstra University. Unpublished manuscript.

Sickler, J.L. (1988). "Teachers in Charge: Empowering the Professionals." *Phi Delta Kappan* 69: 354-358.

Smith, M.S., and S.C. Purkey. (1985). "School Reform: The District Policy Implications of the Effective Schools Literature." *Elementary School Journal* 85: 352-390.

Wise, A.E., L. Darling-Hammond, and B. Berry. (1987). *Effective Teacher Selection: From Recruitment to Selection*. Santa Monica, Calif.: The RAND Corporation.

Wissler, D.F., and F.I. Ortiz. (1986). "The Decentralization Process of School Systems: A Review of the Literature." *Urban Education* 21: 280-294.

Wissler, D.F., and F.I. Ortiz. (1988). *The Superintendent's Leadership in School Reform*. Philadelphia: The Falmer Press.

Jane L. David is Director of the Bay Area Research Group, 3144 David Ave., Palo Alto, CA 94303.

Educational Leadership 47 (Dec. 1989-Jan. 1990): 46-51

ANNE RATZKI AND ANGELA FISHER

Life in a Restructured School

For 14 years, cooperation and teamwork have been a way of life at Holweide School in Cologne, Germany.

Photographs by Monika Kliemann

Unlike the high school in the U.S. or the comprehensive school in Britain, one school for all children is still the exception, not the rule, in Germany. We have a class-based system that dates from the 19th century, from the *Kaiserreich*. Beginning at age 10, students are sorted out and tracked. Children from the upper class—and the most able from other social classes—go to the Gymnasium in preparation to enter the university. Middle-class students attend the *Realschule*. And the children of the lower class, including many immigrant children, go to the *Hauptschule* until age 15 or 16, when they join the work force.

Since 1969, however, a net of *Gesamtschulen* (high schools, comprehensive schools) has been established side by side with the old system, and they have developed different concepts to educate all children in one school. At the Gesamtschule in Cologne (Köln)-Holweide, teachers and students have been operating under a special framework since the mid-70s. For example:

• teachers no longer work as isolated individuals but as part of a team of six to eight teachers;

• each team constitutes a small independent school within the larger framework of the big school;

- teachers and students stay together for six years;
- children and youth feel socially accepted in a cooperative group and in an environment that supports them in making friends, in learning, and in growing up.

Something in the Air

We started out by trying to answer the question, "How can we adequately 'educate' children of all social classes and learning abilities in *one* school?" In the 1970s, this question had not—and has not yet—been raised generally in Germany, as it has in other countries. Only in 1965, with the publication of *The German Educational Disaster* (by Georg Picht, Olten, 1965), was attention drawn to the deficiencies of the country's system, which was not producing enough qualified students for the needs of modern industry, science, and technology. So many potentially talented students were labeled at age 10 for Hauptschule or Realschule that Germany was sending fewer students to universities than were most other industrialized countries. Its economy would soon pay the price.

To respond to the educational dilemma, in the late '60s a national commission was set up to create schools for children from all social classes and of all abilities. The first Gesamtschulen opened in 1968. Today a network of them exists side by side with the traditional system. The early Gesamtschulen were huge uninviting buildings, housing more than 2,000 students. It wasn't long before they earned a reputation as concrete jungles of alienated students and teachers.

The Holweide Gesamtschule in Cologne, begun in 1975, was supposed to be one of the largest schools in the country—and it still is—with a nine-form entry and roughly 2,000 pupils and 200 teachers. Every year, we have many more applicants than we can take in. About a quarter of our students are immigrant children, especially Turks (the biggest ethnic minority in Germany). The Holweide school had formerly been a Gymnasium with a selected population of middle- and upper-class children. When we decided to turn comprehensive, we observed closely how the first comprehensive schools had fared and developed an approach we called the "Team-Small-Group Plan." Teachers from another comprehensive school in Germany, in Göttingen, independently developed the same plan; there was obviously something "in the air."

The Team-Small-Group-Plan

In developing the plan, we hoped (1) to diminish the anonymity of a big school, and (2) to design a way of teaching in which students of very different abilities and backgrounds could reach their potential by working together. To achieve these aims, we divided the big school into small units called "teams." A small and stable group of teachers, usually six, are responsible for about 90 students, in three units called "classes." This smaller design is intended to enable teachers and pupils to get to know each other well. They stay together for six years, from grade 5 through grade 10, up to the first leaving certificate.

Next we extended the team idea to the students by organizing them in small heterogeneous "table-groups" of 5 or 6 pupils. To establish a close relationship and enable the students to help each other with their work, they generally work with their same cooperative table-group for at least a year, often longer. The table-group concept has become the school's core instructional idea.

Our school is run as a team primarily by the head teacher, together with his or her two deputies and a governing panel of senior colleagues, some of whom are elected with others appointed by the authorities. The roles of the head teacher and the members of the governing panel, about 20 in Holweide, are quite different from the traditional ones of control and supervision. They are *coordinators*, supporting the teachers in their difficult work, monitoring the school's progress, and recognizing problems in time to discuss ways of solving them.

A small and stable group of teachers, usually six, are responsible for about 90 students, in three units called "classes."

An important duty of the head teacher is to provide teachers the freedom to do their work by contending with the authorities who distrust team-based decision making. Another of the head teacher's principal responsibilities is to find sufficient well-qualified new teachers for the school and to bargain with the authorities to hire them.

Teaching Teams

Teachers in Holweide have a great deal of autonomy. Between them, they teach all the subjects and are responsible for the education of three groups of 28 to 30 students. They form their own teams of 6 to 8 members; devise schedules for the coming year; choose who will teach which subjects in which classes; decide how the curriculum will be taught (in a single period or a longer block of time, for example); cover for absent colleagues; and organize lunchtime activities, parents involvement, field trips, and many other concerns. They also decide among themselves which two people will work together as *class tutors* (home class, or homeroom, teachers) in a given class.

To ensure continuity and progress in their work, the teachers set aside every second Tuesday afternoon for regular team meetings. (See "Sample Team Meeting Agenda" for an agenda from one of last year's meetings.) The team I (Angela Fisher) am involved in decided from the outset that we wanted to have our meetings once a week rather than every fortnight. To create a more pleasant atmosphere, we combine these meetings with an evening meal, taking turns cooking and playing host so that no one has too much work to do. In that the teachers must work together closely and consult each other constantly on all aspects of their work, the demands upon them are considerable. In reality, the practice may fall considerably short of the ideal; therefore, a limited reshuffling of the teams sometimes takes place at the end of the school year.

Though the teams have a great deal of autonomy, there is nevertheless a framework to ensure consistency in the academic standards of all the pu-

The table-group concept has become the school's core instructional idea.

pils. For instance, all teams send a delegate to *curricular conferences*, where the necessary decisions are made. Each team also sends a delegate to weekly *counseling conferences* with the school psychologist. At these meetings, general problems affecting the school are discussed, as well as students' problems that prove too difficult for the team to work with or that are of exemplary value. In addition, the norms of the school—for example, the principle of "social learning"—are discussed, surveyed, and developed within the framework of the conference.

About the Students

We assign students to table-groups of five or six members integrated by sex, ability, and ethnic origin. Within these "social unit" groups, the children tutor and encourage each other. The difference between our groups and cooperative learning groups is that our children stay in these same groups for every subject, normally for at least a year. The aim is to promote stable groups in which the members learn to work together despite their individual differences. To achieve good group results, each member is responsible not only for his or her own work but also for that of the other members. If the work of one child in the group is unsatisfactory or his or her behavior a problem, then we try to discuss the issue with the individual child as well as the group. Here we give them assistance in coping with difficult situations and characters.

Each table-group meets once a week to discuss any problems or to suggest improvements in their everyday working situations. For example, a group may decide that because two boys constantly annoy one another during lessons, it would be better to arrange the seating differently. Or if one child feels unhappy within his or her group, the group then tries to discover what the reasons are and to resolve the issue. Usually the students need a lot of help from the tutor here.

During lessons, except for free learning periods, the group practices and works things out *together*. Students who are more able are expected to help the other members in their group. Since the teacher's time is limited, this *helper system* is of great benefit. Sometimes during an English lesson, for example, I (Angela) have given the groups a text to read aloud and then to practice together. Later, when they are ready, I hear and assess each group. Quite often one or two groups ask for a little extra time because, "We haven't finished with Hans yet!" Because the students are keen to achieve good results for their groups, a considerable amount of *personal coaching* takes place. Working in this way, the better students reinforce their knowledge through repetition and the necessity of transmitting their knowledge to others. Less able children have the chance to practice and pose questions they would otherwise be too shy or unsure to ask.

Key Program Concepts

To support the awareness of being in a group and the techniques required for working together as a group, we have incorporated several key concepts into our program. First, we try to maintain a regular group training program during the school week, for example, by having a second teacher take one group out of the regular lesson for this purpose. The students are made aware of the most favorable methods to adopt when working together; that is, making sure that everyone in the group has understood what the task at hand actually is—how to divide up a given task sensibly and allocate parts to the various group members. As a result, the group work becomes more effective and efficient.

Second, twice a year we set aside a day for group consultation. On this day the groups come one at a time to talk to the tutors for an hour about their progress during the previous weeks. They assess their own positions and contributions to the group work and hear comments from the other group members. When these meetings take place at a tutor's house, they are often combined with an extended breakfast. We have found these meetings very rewarding and often notice that the students talk much more freely in an informal setting away from school.

During the school year there are also certain days, such as parents' consulting day or inservice training days, when regular lessons do not occur. On such days each table-group in a team thinks of a common activity for the whole group—for example, a visit to an exhibition or a museum—which they will then pursue and report on the following day in a discussion circle. They may even find something so interesting that they recommend it as worthy of a visit by the whole team. These special days are an important factor in stabilizing the groups because it is essential that they have experiences away from the tables and away from school. In doing so, they often realize that it is great fun doing things together. Other days are set aside for *project work*. Students themselves select the activities they undertake. For example, they may leave

Each table-group meets once a week to discuss any problems or to suggest improvements in their everyday working situations.

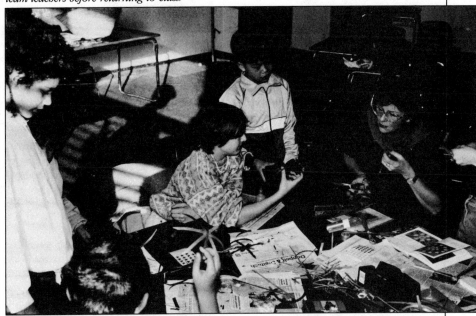

After a 20-minute lunch, these students have plenty of time for a group activity led by one of the team teachers before returning to class.

their school to find out about certain aspects of their suburb—playgrounds, the living conditions of elderly people, and so on—or they may work on improving environmental problems like replanting the banks of a stream to give bird life a new chance.

Because students and their ways of learning are different, we have also developed individual learning strategies in addition to the table-groups. For example, we hold "learning how to learn" to be extremely important. That is, we believe that our pupils should share in decisions about what they want or need to learn or practice, as well as the way they want to learn and whether to study individually or in groups.

Discussion Groups and Weekly Plans

Each school week begins with a discussion circle. For this event, the students move their tables aside, and those who wish to can tell about something special or interesting that happened to them over the weekend. After these remarks, the tutors announce any special events in the coming week. Next, the tutors present the weekly plan, which structures each student's work for the upcoming days. They also write the individual obligatory tasks for their subjects on the board, which the students copy into their plan books. Each student then checks his or her plan for the previous week and copies any unfinished exer-

---

Sample Team Meeting Agenda

● A visit to an exhibition as part of the social studies class—how and when will we organize this?
● The table groups in one of the classes—how can we help two of the groups with their problems?
● Parents' consulting day—what activities will we give the table groups on that day? What aspects do we find particularly important for the talks with parents?
● Problems with the behavior of one particular child—how can we best deal with them? How can the groups help?
● Free learning and the plan for the week—how can we improve the effectiveness here?

cise into the new plan. As teachers for other subjects come into the classroom, the plans are added to.

In addition to being involved in decision making about organization, our students also choose many individual learning tasks as well; for example, what they can do during free learning periods. These periods can be used in a very personal and differentiated way; that is, a less able student may be told that he or she need only complete certain parts of the plan, whereas a very bright student is either given extra work or can choose extra tasks.

The circular discussion group format is also used for certain lessons. For example, during *tutorial lessons*, students discuss any problems with the tutors and how these can be solved. The students themselves determine the agenda for these lessons; the teacher plays a passive role. Each person in the discussion group who has just spoken in turn chooses the next speaker, irrespective of whether students or teachers have expressed their wish to voice an opinion. Coming from traditional schools, where teachers have an almost absolute right to speak whenever they wish, many

teachers find that this format requires some getting used to. My first few weeks of classroom discussions were punctuated by children sighing and saying, "Angela, it's not your turn!" I was surprised how quickly the students themselves, who also came from traditional German schools, got used to their new way of discussing things. They stuck to the rules much better than, for example, me. In retrospect, I supposed the reasons are clear: students are used to waiting to speak; teachers are not!

Parent Activities

Our students' parents, whom we consider a very important part of our school community, are involved in our work in Holweide in many ways. For example, the parents in each class elect five parents to a council, which provides a link between team-teachers and the other parents. The council members discuss issues and problems facing the team as a whole—ranging from topics that parents want their children to learn to their priorities for selecting the next team trip or questions of evaluation and career. In addition, every few weeks the team parents arrange a regular but informal

meeting, often in a nearby pub. At these functions, any parents and teachers who have time gather to get to know one another in a more relaxed atmosphere.

We also invite parents to the school to see teachers and students at work. They have been of great help in starting a fund-raising activity for students who are unable to cope with a field trip financially. Some parents accompany younger students on research trips when they do project-work. They have also always supported us in any disagreement with the authorities. Further, we devote a great deal of attention to ways we can present our work to the parents, since they cannot be expected to feel actively involved in their child's learning unless they experience regular insights into what is actually being done. For example, one year we had an autumn festival at which students shared their schoolwork with their parents. The table-groups presented the topics they had been working on in project lessons. Students drew pictures, told stories, presented a little play in English, demonstrated dances they had worked out for themselves in P.E., and so forth. Everyone—teachers, parents, and students—benefited from the event.

A number of parents have become more involved in school life by taking charge of lunchtime activities. After the first 20 minutes of our 80-minute break, set aside for eating lunch, students are free to participate in a variety of lunchtime activities. Teachers, as part of their schedules, lead many of these efforts—such as music, sports, and mask-making—but by involving parents as well, we find that teachers' workloads are a little lighter and students are exposed to a greater variety of activities. For example, last year, parents led groups in cooking and calligraphy and helped put on a play. In addition, some older students direct lunchtime activities for younger ones.

We encourage and welcome parent involvement, but it would be untrue to say that we have no problems with parents and that differences of opinion do not occur. However, in our experi-

Five or six students working together over time is the school's core instructional concept. Here members of a table-group select the information they will need to complete a task.

The parents associated with our school have a much closer relationship with the teachers than in a traditional school.

ence, any issues that arise are much more easily solved in our setting than in other schools. This may be due to intervention by other parents or merely because the parents concerned do not feel so powerless and have a much closer relationship with the teachers than in a traditional school.

The Costs and the Benefits

Holweide is a democratically run school where every group in the school community—teachers, students, parents—is actively involved in decision making and participates in

school life. The most obvious problem in the system, however, is the matter of time. Cooperation within the school, within the year group, and within the team itself is vital. Without extra meetings to promote cooperation, though, chaos would soon predominate. Thus, it is more time-consuming to work in Köln-Holweide than in a traditional school. At the same time, however, it is more enjoyable to work in an atmosphere where you are involved in decision making than it is to follow rules and ideas thought up by others, to be completely alone in a classroom situation, and to be caught up in the mood of helpless resignation felt by many teachers today.

Being a student at our school is more rewarding and more fun too. Because of the group learning format, students can get special help when they need it. Their self-confidence increases, which leads to other positive outcomes. Our dropouts are under 1 percent, and about 60 percent of our students score sufficiently well to be admitted to the three-year college that leads on to the university (the German average is 27 percent).

Effective Self-Government

Reared in a world of hierarchy, teachers in Germany have not found it easy to come to terms with team structures. Relying on a "leader" is much more convenient than making one's own decisions and taking responsibility for the results. Teachers in Holweide have had to learn the hard way: by doing, making mistakes, and trying again. Yet, despite many conflicts and difficulties, the team idea has convinced practically everybody. Our experience of 14 years demonstrates that responsibility and decision making by the teachers themselves, as well as school as a form of self-government are not only possible but also beneficial and deeply satisfying.□

Authors' note: Quite a few other schools in Germany have adopted the team-small-groups plan and on these principles have developed their own individual program: schools in Cologne, Berlin, Kassel, Hagen, Ludwigshafer, The Saarland.

Anne Ratzki is Headmistress of Köln-Holweide and a teacher in a team of grade 6, Kuckelbergweg 13, 5000 Cologne 80, West Germany. **Angela Fisher** is a teacher in a team of grade 7, Schneider-Clauss-Str. 12, 5000 Cologne 60, West Germany.

Educational Leadership 48 (March 1991): 6-10

RICHARD SAGOR

What Project LEARN Reveals about Collaborative Action Research

With "critical friends" to assist them, teachers in 50 schools in Washington are researching the answers to their own questions about teaching and learning.

Looking at the surface of things, we might believe that the last 20 years of educational research have provided us all the insights we need to improve our schools. We have seen the effective schooling correlates validated in study after study; we have been given rich descriptions of the workplaces where teachers are motivated and self-actualized; and we have seen evidence that certain instructional strategies enhance the achievement of students regardless of their socioeconomic status.

With each report of a school's success, we want to believe that we, too, can show comparable levels of performance if only we can replicate those factors in our schools. Yet all too often we find the anticipated growth in performance still eluding us. This repeated cycle of high hopes followed by our inability to replicate results continues to produce cynicism among teachers.

Enter Project LEARN

To break this cycle of hope and despair, Washington State University and the faculties of more than 50 schools have collaborated on Project LEARN (League of Educational Action Researchers in the Northwest). Our project is grounded in the belief that education's past failures have resulted not from incorrect data or lack of commit-

ment but from an inadequate understanding of the process of change.

Rather than focusing on adopting "proven" practices, Project LEARN fosters school improvement by enhancing the professional lives of teachers. We accomplish this by working with the staffs of schools and districts who have expressed an interest in initiating school improvement (defined as "enhancing the quality of teaching and learning") by engaging in action research.

Rather than focusing on adopting "proven" practices, Project LEARN fosters school improvement by enhancing the professional lives of teachers.

Project LEARN's hope is that meaningful practitioner research will lead to improved classroom practice and become a stimulus for both the cultural transformation of schools and the restructuring of the teaching profession. To accomplish those twin purposes, the project discourages individualistic initiatives, encouraging instead the participation of a "critical mass" of collaborating teachers from each member school.

The Project LEARN cycle begins with the formation of action research teams, teachers who will work together on a problem for at least one full academic year. To prepare for their work, the teams participate in a two-day workshop on the basic steps of conducting action research: identifying problems and collecting data. Teams from several schools and localities receive the training together at a central location so they can create networks with colleagues who are addressing similar problems. At the end of this initial training period, each action research team completes a written action plan, specifying the problem, the data collection techniques, and any anticipated technical or logistical needs.

Next, the teams begin conducting their research. During this period the project offers assistance through a cadre of trained "critical friends." Crit-

The Project LEARN cycle begins with the formation of action research teams, teachers who will work together on a problem for at least one full academic year.

ical friends are educators with research experience who volunteer to help project teachers by giving their independent viewpoints. Many school districts participating in Project LEARN train their supervisors to serve as critical friends for action research teams both inside and outside the district. The current cadre of 20 critical friends consists of school administrators, teachers, university professors, and independent consultants. Project LEARN teachers can request the help of these critical friends whenever they feel the need for feedback from a colleague with a fresh perspective on their particular teaching or research problems. To ensure that the critical friends work to support the research rather than to direct it, their efforts are governed by a set of ethical and procedural guidelines (see fig. 1).

In mid-January of each year, approximately four months after the basic training, the teams attend a one-day follow-up workshop. The purpose of this meeting is to address difficulties encountered during the data collection phase and to provide instruction for conducting the data analysis and action planning portions of the cycle.

Then each spring, Project LEARN hosts a two-day International Symposium on Action Research, where project participants as well as action researchers from elsewhere in the United States, the United Kingdom, and Canada can present both the process and the results of their school-based research. The annual International Symposium completes the first-year Project LEARN cycle; however, since many teams will continue to conduct research, we have created a program to serve them. The major purpose of the continuing program is to provide networking training in advanced methods and access to future symposiums.

A First-Cycle Experience

For example, some middle school math teachers at the fall Project LEARN training session began to wonder: If writing is a window into thinking and if the act of writing helps improve comprehension, why not try it in middle school math classes?

The teachers began a collaborative inquiry into the role of writing in the development of computational skills. To test their hypothesis that writing can improve those skills, they decided to use an experimental design. They constructed, then administered tests to their math students during the first nine weeks of school to gather baseline data. They used the results to split the four 7th grade math classes into two groups: two performing well and two below expectations. Then they made the lower-achieving classes the treatment group; and the higher achievers, the control group.

During the second quarter the teachers continued to instruct the students in the control group as before, while they gave the lower-achieving students the opportunity to write about the math concepts they were learning, on the day before each examination. In every other respect they provided the two groups of students the same educational experience: the same amount of time for instruction and independent study (minus the writing time for the experimental group) and the same exams.

When the data were analyzed at the January workshop, the teachers found that writing had indeed made a substantial difference in concept acquisition. The experimental sections actually outperformed their (previously higher-achieving) classmates on each test.

With the experimental work out of the way, the project team turned to the "action" stage of the action research process. They presented the data to their colleagues (and to the International Symposium) and made plans to revise their middle school's math curriculum. This year all math classes in this school include "writing about computation."

Will it continue to make a difference? The teachers think so, but they are sure of one thing: "data-driven" teaching has become a way of life for them. They don't ever intend to give up the search for a "better mousetrap."

Fig. 1. Project LEARN Guidelines for Critical Friends

A critical friend is chosen according to the needs and desires of the project participants. The critical friend will not hold a "stake" or "ownership" in the problem being addressed or in the outcome of the project unless such is granted by the participants.

- A critical friend is a positive friend, whose primary agenda is to assist the project toward success.
- A critical friend may have a personal agenda complementary to the project's. The critical friend will share with the participants his or her motives/intents at the time of the first interaction.
- A critical friend is a visitor and participates only at the continued invitation of the project.
- A critical friend will respond and act honestly at every juncture.
- It is the critical friend's obligation to declare any conflict of interest or conflict of values with the project focus or methods.
- A critical friend will assume that the project's interactions, work, and findings are confidential unless the project directs otherwise.
- The project participants are expected to assist the critical friend by fully informing him or her of all agendas prior to each consultation.

Factors in Our Success

It all began in the fall of 1989, when administrators from eight districts in two states were invited to send teams to participate in Project LEARN's inaugural training program. These districts/schools were invited because of their history of commitment to school improvement and their willingness to support the project financially.

It didn't surprise us that more than 130 teachers from more than 20 separate schools enrolled in that first year program. What was surprising, however, were their comments after their first two days of training. This comment from one teacher was typical: "It's about time someone asked teachers to help set their own school improvement agenda!" Had those comments come from faculty in schools led by top-down dictatorial principals, we wouldn't have been the least bit surprised. Yet, when we repeatedly heard those statements from the lips of teachers who had been participating in organized school improvement projects for years, we had to ask ourselves, *What is it about collaborative action research that has teachers perceiving it as so different from other school improvement programs?* After analyzing preliminary data, we have identified five factors that have facili-

tated the success of our work. We believe these factors have implications for anyone designing school improvement programs.

1. The importance of volition. Teachers have come to expect that their school improvement agendas will be set for them. Thus, participants in Project LEARN appeared genuinely surprised when they found the focus of their projects could be any issue they deemed both important and perplexing. The only preconditions were that the problems being investigated had to impact student learning and be under their control. Further, the reflective interviewing process we used to tease out topics turned out to be a surprise in itself. Apparently, being granted the uncommon luxury of 20 uninterrupted minutes of dialogue with colleagues on instructional concerns was as foreign to participants as it was refreshing. Furthermore, reflective interaction about what is important resulted in common goals for the team. Clearly, people are more committed to goals they have formulated themselves than to those which are imposed upon them.

Ironically, the set of topics that emerged from these teachers weren't much different than we'd expect from a traditional administrator-led process

> # Clearly, people are more committed to goals they have formulated themselves than to those which are imposed upon them.

(see fig. 2). The only differences were slight: for example, a site administrators' second priority might have emerged as the teachers' first, or vice versa. That's a small price for management to pay in exchange for enhanced ownership and commitment.

2. Availability of critical friends. One major difference in this project was the availability of "critical friends." Throughout the year, this cadre volunteered to lend their expertise to the action research teams. Ethical guidelines were developed to assure that ownership of the research would reside with the practitioners. Those who used critical friends liberally praised their assistance as giving a substantial boost to their projects. Apparently, having high-quality, free consultant help available on demand was not only a new experience for these teachers, but it gave them the psychological freedom to venture into territory where their interests, if not their confidence, led them.

3. A first-class environment. At the outset we decided to hold our training sessions in the large banquet rooms of centrally located first-class hotels where the training time could be divided equally between large group presentations and small group work. Although this format was originally chosen for its efficiency, it ended up paying unforeseen dividends. Our participants repeatedly told us that the quality of the catering, the service, and the surroundings reinforced the perceived importance placed on the tasks at hand—as did the energy generated by dozens of colleagues actively and visibly involved in the same work.

Fig. 2. A Selection of Project LEARN 1989–1990 Projects

1. What factors influence student achievement in our school? What can we do to improve achievement?

2. Will group retellings of literature be a useful tool for K-5 teachers to accurately describe a student's comprehension ability and improve the instructional program?

3. Evaluate the student management system (discipline) and give direction for any subsequent changes.

4. How can we effectively and efficiently conduct group parent/teacher conferences?

5. Is the integrated elementary special education model better for "resource" students than a traditional pull-out approach?

6. Identify variables common to academically at-risk students in order to provide better intervention techniques.

7. How can we increase the articulation of our Language Arts program through 6th, 7th, and 8th grades?

8. Is our delivery of support services helping to maintain or improve student progress in academics, social environment, and language?

9. Develop, implement, and assess effective strategies for at-risk students.

10. How can we create a teaching environment that uses thematic instruction and meaningful activities to bring focus and inspiration to teaching academics while maintaining academic accountability?

4. Public affirmations. Several times in numerous ways, each team was invited to tell all the other teams about the status of their initiatives, their needs, and their goals. The sharing provided a supportive environment for risk-taking and experimentation in which people could generate ideas, network with each other, and become collegial. Apparently, enthusiasm and success are contagious: the positive, successful teams provided hope, encouragement, and inspiration to faltering colleagues.

The public affirmations not only facilitated sharing across schools, but they also created a certain amount of peer pressure to follow through with the upcoming tasks of data collection, analysis, and action planning.

*5. Strategic scheduling.*Teachers are very busy people. The constant demands from students, administrators, and parents can be so overwhelming that an optional project, regardless of how meritorious, often falls to the bottom of a "to-do" list. Fortunately for us, we made several strategic and logistical decisions that provided just the requisite amount of extrinsic pressure for participants.

The initial training, held during the last week in September, coincided with the time of year in which the pressures of getting school started had largely subsided while all the school-opening enthusiasm was still in bloom. Even so, many participants' best intentions went unfulfilled until December, when they realized that the January follow-up training was just around the corner. The knowledge that they were expected to have locally derived data to work on at this session apparently was just enough of an incentive to get them moving on their projects.

Likewise, the need to conclude and polish the projects in time for presentation at the International Symposium (late April) provided just the push that several teams needed to stay on task. Apparently, our inservices not only provided training but strategically orchestrated support and encouragement throughout the year.

Making Good Schools Better

It would be nice to say that every team that participated in Project LEARN

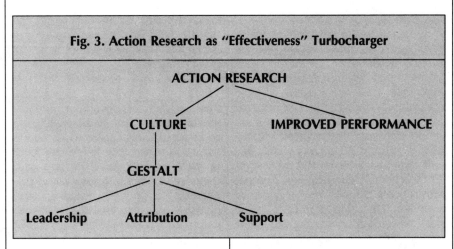

Fig. 3. Action Research as "Effectiveness" Turbocharger

ACTION RESEARCH

CULTURE   IMPROVED PERFORMANCE

GESTALT

Leadership   Attribution   Support

completed its research, that the culture of all the schools underwent positive transformations, and that student learning dramatically improved at each site. Unfortunately, that didn't happen, at least not everywhere. However, our preliminary data did suggest certain sharp distinctions between the work environments of the teams that thrived and those that faltered.

When asked to identify which factors enabled or constrained progress on the projects, the responses of Project LEARN participants produced an interesting pattern. Those who had been part of successful teams credited the nature of their projects (the importance of the topic being researched and the action research process itself), external support (released time, administrative encouragement, and the help of their critical friends), and the nature of their colleagues (their drive, commitment, and "chemistry") with keeping the projects on track. Likewise, teachers on the teams that failed to carry through cited the nature of their projects (not important enough to justify the energy necessary), the absence of extrinsic support (lack of resources and released time), and the nature of their collegial work group (divisive and leaderless) as the chief reasons for dropping their projects.

Our analysis of these data led us to conclude that schools with productive cultures (a habit of focusing on important issues, norms of leadership, collegiality, and support) are the ones that will get the most out of action research

(Saphier and King 1985). Conversely, schools where these norms are weak will probably not find action research to be a particularly productive strategy (although the evidence suggests it will do no harm). Those findings brought us to conceptualize "action research" as a cultural turbocharger (see fig. 3).

A Promising Tool

So far, our search for the perfect school improvement strategy hasn't turned up the magic potion which will turn any frog into a prince. As powerful a tool as collaborative inquiry appears to be, it will not transform a school in the absence of leadership, collegial respect, and technical and logistical support for the professional work of teachers.

But in an atmosphere of support, trust, and collegiality, collaborative action research has great potential for focusing a school's attention on the correlates of effective schooling. Offering such a tool to school faculties may prove to be one of the most promising actions we can take to improve our schools.□

Reference

Saphier, J., and M. King. (March 1985). "Good Seeds Grow in Strong Cultures." *Educational Leadership* 42, 6: 67–74

Richard Sagor is Assistant Professor, Washington State University, 1812 E. McLoughlin Blvd., Vancouver, WA 98663–3597.

Educational Leadership 47 (May 1990): 13-19

MICHAEL G. FULLAN, BARRIE BENNETT, AND CAROL ROLHEISER-BENNETT

Linking Classroom and School Improvement

Through their Learning Consortium, four school districts and two higher education institutions in the greater Toronto area created a framework that drives their efforts to support the sustained development of educators.

Educators have learned a great deal about classroom and school improvement recently, and this new knowledge has provided us with much valuable information to make more informed decisions. Yet the amount and complexity of that information is raining down on our heads so hard that it is very difficult to understand and implement what we know about classroom and school improvement.

We need a powerful framework to assist our efforts to achieve lasting and substantial change—one like the framework we derived from our work in the Learning Consortium. This three-year experiment began in February 1988 as a partnership among four major school districts and two higher education institutions in the greater Toronto area.[1] The four districts are large, ranging in size from 45,000 students (90 schools) to 60,000 students (150 schools).

The Learning Consortium brings together teachers, administrators, and professors in a collegial partnership that focuses on the sustained development of educators. This, in turn, is directed at improving students' experiences and learning. All activities undertaken by the Learning Consortium are invested with the spirit of inquiry.

We make use of previous research and produce new research findings of our own in our "living laboratory" environment. Two of our most important concerns include curriculum and instruction priorities of school boards and issues pertaining to the management of change. We work with the assumption that classroom improvement, teacher development, and school improvement must be systematically linked if substantial progress is to be achieved.

Systemic and cultural change in schools as workplaces and in teaching as a profession are intimately linked; and these links represent a powerful route to educational reform.

Creating an Action Framework for Better Schools

Specifically, we are interested in the question of how classroom and school improvement might be linked.[2] The framework evolving from our attempts to make sense of and guide our improvement efforts in the Consortium is shown in Figure 1. A word is necessary about the imagery of gears and cogs.[3] Taken literally, this imagery is misleading—teaching is not mechanistic, and one cog does not necessarily start another. Nor do the framework's components simply move in one direction or the other. Different and contradictory initiatives affect different parts, moving them in different directions at the same time—indeed, this is part of the complexity.

Nonetheless, the overall metaphor of movement is important and useful. The different elements of classroom and school development do affect one another, and in effective schools they do work together in the same direction in an interactive, dynamic way. The diagram in Figure 1 can also serve as an "advance organizer," illustrating how ideas are interrelated. Although the purpose of the framework is not to indicate where to start, it does assist educators to inquire into the current condition of their school or classroom situation and predict what factors might need consideration. For example, before a staff decides to implement a process that breaks down norms of isolation and builds norms of collaboration—perhaps through a peer coaching or mentoring program—teachers and administrators might consider what factors in the classroom and school will support or militate against such programs. The framework, in other words, points to the main components of improvement—all of which must be addressed.

We did not develop the framework and then apply it in the Learning Consortium. Over a number of years we had been working separately on different parts of this schematic in other activities. The Consortium provided us with an opportunity to work together on developing a more comprehensive conceptual framework. Our goal has become to understand classroom improvement on the one hand, school improvement on the other, and then to identify systematic links between the two.

For classroom improvement, we and others have found that teachers work simultaneously (but not at the same pace) on all four inner cogs: content, classroom management, instructional skills, and instructional

strategies. For both teachers and students, the capacity to integrate these four components is essential. *Content* encapsulates areas such as the teacher's knowledge of curriculum, child development, and learning styles. *Classroom management* includes what teachers do to prevent and respond to student misbehavior. *Instructional skills* are less complex teacher behaviors such as providing wait time after asking a question and framing questions at different levels of complexity. Although less complex than instructional strategies, they are essential behaviors in a teacher's instructional repertoire. *Instructional strategies*, such as concept attainment and cooperative learning, are more complex processes of teaching that are based on models of learning. When all four of these inner cogs function in partnership, the chances of designing a classroom environment that promotes student learning are dramatically increased.

The inner cogs at the far right of Figure 1 relate to school improvement. The basic features of school improvement (as distinct from a list of effective schools characteristics) are these: shared purpose, norms of collegiality, norms of continuous improvement, and structures representing the

Photograph by Carol Rolheiser-Bennett

University of Toronto preservice teachers (from left to right) Mary Loree, Cathy Bernatt, Brad Boehmer, and Diane Bakarich prepare to work in classrooms of Summer Institute participants, who will help train them in cooperative learning techniques.

Innovations should be seen as points of departure or catalysts, rather than as things to be implemented.

organizational conditions necessary for significant improvement (Little 1989, Rosenholtz 1989).

Shared purpose includes vision, mission, goals, objectives, and unity of purpose. It refers to the shared sense of purposeful direction of the school relative to major educational goals. Shared purpose is, of course, not static and does not arise by itself. The other three cogs in interaction constantly generate and (re)shape purpose.

Norms of collegiality refers to ways in which mutual sharing, assistance, and joint effort among teachers is valued and honored in the school. However, as Little (1989) has stressed, there is nothing particularly virtuous about collaboration *per se*: It can serve to block change or put down students, or it can elevate learning. Thus, collegiality must be linked to *norms of continuous improvement* and experimentation in which teachers are constantly seeking and assessing potentially better practices inside and outside their own schools (and contributing to other people's practice through dissemination).

Structure refers to organizational arrangements, roles, and formal policies which explicitly create working conditions that support and inspire movement in the other cogs. Examples of school-level structural changes that are conducive to improvement include creating time for joint planning, developing joint teaching arrangements and staff development policies, establishing new roles such as the mentor function, and establishing school improvement procedures. (Restructuring, of course, has much to do with this cog, although no single component by itself can make much of a difference.)

The teacher-as-learner concept is the centerpiece linking classroom and school improvement. In this instance the term includes anybody at the school level who is a professional educator, for example, classroom teachers, teacher leaders, head teachers, vice-principals, and principals.

The teacher-as-learner centerpiece serves two critical uses. The first concerns the four aspects of teacher as learner—the technical, the reflective, the research, and the collaborative. The mastery of a *technical repertoire* increases instructional certainty; *reflective practice* enhances clarity, meaning, and coherence; *research* fosters investigation and exploration; *collaboration* enables one to receive and give ideas and assistance. Each aspect has its separate tradition of research and practice, and each has made important contributions in its own right. The important question is how to integrate and establish the strengths of each of these four traditions in the individual

teacher as learner. Rarely have all four received intensive attention in the same setting.

The second critical use of the teacher-as-learner centerpiece is as a method to distinguish between specific and generic levels of the development of the teacher as learner. By *specific* we mean how particular improvements are experienced and designed. For example, in the Learning Consortium we began with a technical instructional innovation, cooperative learning, and found it had consequences for all four aspects of the teacher as learner. Similarly, others could begin with any of the other three inner cogs—an inquiry research

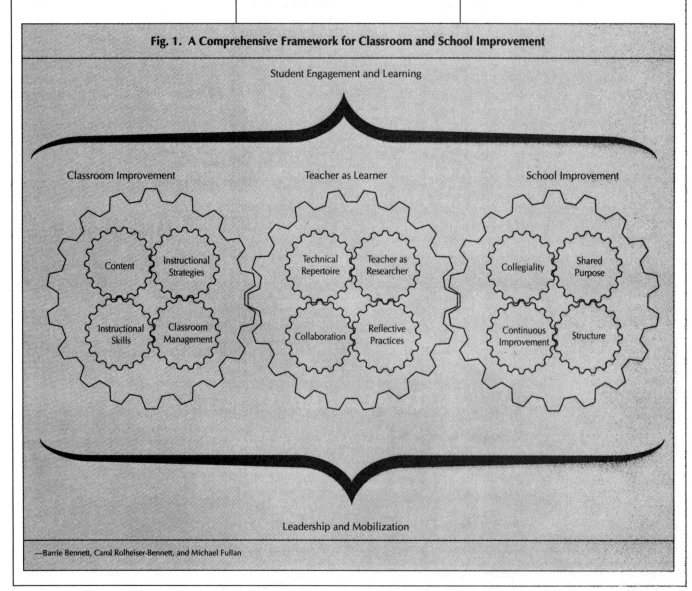

Fig. 1. A Comprehensive Framework for Classroom and School Improvement

Student Engagement and Learning

Classroom Improvement

Teacher as Learner

School Improvement

Content

Instructional Strategies

Instructional Skills

Classroom Management

Technical Repertoire

Teacher as Researcher

Collaboration

Reflective Practices

Collegiality

Shared Purpose

Continuous Improvement

Structure

Leadership and Mobilization

—Barrie Bennett, Carol Rolheiser-Bennett, and Michael Fullan

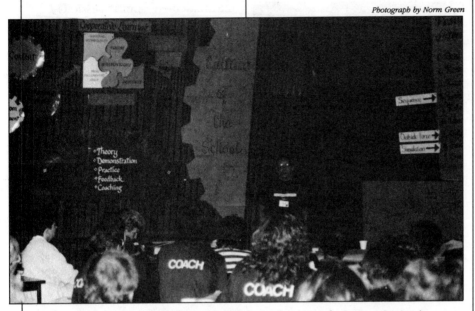

Photograph by Norm Green

School administrator Don Real shares his plans for implementing the Summer Institute's cooperative learning and peer coaching model with participants in the seven-day retreat.

project, for example—and proceed to incorporate the development of the technical, reflective, and collaborative components. Or a group could try to work on all four aspects from the start.

It is, however, the generic point that is more fundamental; that is, teachers can come to develop their *generic capacities* in all four aspects. This would mean not just being good at cooperative learning, but at an array of instructional models; not just being involved in a reflective practice project, but being a reflective practitioner; not participating in a research investigation, but conducting constant inquiry; not being part of a peer coaching project, but being collaborative as a way of working. In short, teachers gradually internalize these ways of being so that it becomes second nature to be learners. The point is not that the four aspects are valuable separate elements of the teacher as learner, but that they must become part and parcel of a natural seamless fabric of what it means to be a professional educator.

Now, it is precisely when every teacher in the school develops this generic capacity that classroom improvement and school improvement entirely overlap. Such an ideal will rarely be achieved of course, but one can immediately deduce how power-

ful the bridge can become when a school experiences a significant increase in the proportion of staff who are learners.

Two other elements of the framework revolve around the issue of what drives the framework. One of these is the presence of student engagement and learning—a preoccupation that pervades the framework. In our model, impact on all students is central to each and every cog and to interrelationships among the cogs. Constant valuing of and attention to student engagement and learning is a powerful motivating force, the ultimate purpose of the efforts represented in Figure 1.

The second driving force for change is leadership and mobilization. We explicitly rejected the idea that leadership be a particular component of the framework. Leadership comes from different sources in different situations and from different sources in the same situation over time: the principal, key teachers, the superintendent, parents, trustees, curriculum consultants, governments, universities, and others. Further, once the model is fully functioning, leadership can and does come from multiple sources simultaneously. Certainly the principal, for example, is key, but leadership must be mobilized

on multiple fronts if development is to continue. Finally, we want to acknowledge that the framework is not intended to incorporate all variables that impinge on students, teachers, and schools. The teacher as learner, for example, is shaped by a variety of personality and career factors that make up "the total teacher" (Fullan and Hargreaves, forthcoming).

The comprehensive model just described is both guiding and emerging from the Learning Consortium's activities. Two major initiatives undertaken by the Learning Consortium since its inception are the Summer Institute and the Cadre of Trainers, both discussed below. Each of them seeks to link classroom and school improvement.

Initiatives of the Consortium

The Summer Institute. The first Summer Institute brought together approximately 90 educators from the Consortium's four school districts and two higher education institutions in the summer of 1988. Participants (the majority were teachers and principals or vice-principals, with a few central office administrators and professors) attended a seven-day residential workshop. The workshop emphasized cooperative learning and coaching and the management of the change process, including plans for follow-up implementation of the summer program.

The planning group chose cooperative learning because of the evidence that it stimulates *student* learning. Coaching and mentoring were emphasized as vehicles for sharing expertise and for encouraging collaboration in schools. And the concept and process of coaching and mentoring were also introduced in the training process because of their effect on stimulating *teacher* learning.

Participants spent the first four days learning about cooperative learning and peer coaching. Their training included learning the basic theory, observing and participating in live and videotaped demonstrations, and practicing in microteaching situations. Then they received three days of instruction on the variables that would affect implementation of the cooperative learning model and peer coaching in their classrooms and schools. Videotapes, focused reading, small- and large-group instruction, and task-related implementation planning enabled individuals and groups to get started on their follow-up plans.

The districts had committed themselves to follow-up support in the classroom, but because of different agendas and limited time, they chose a range of support strategies—some participants worked alone, some with colleagues and administrators, and some received in-class support from the summer institute instructors.

To increase the chances that the teachers would successfully transfer their new learning to the classroom, we built the program to include certain elements. First, a powerful model of teaching was employed: cooperative learning (see Johnson et al. 1981, Johnson and Johnson 1989, Rolheiser-Bennett 1986, Sharan 1980, Slavin 1980, 1988). Second, we used an effective training strategy that provided follow-up support—the skill training model (see Bennett 1987, Joyce and Showers 1988, Joyce and Weil 1986). Third, we combined cooperative learning training with instruction on implementing change (see Fullan 1985, Fullan in press). And fourth, volunteer participants were selected to participate on the basis of their interest in instructional improvement. Subsequently, data collected from classroom visits, interviews and conversations, and analyses of videotapes of classroom practice showed that teachers did effectively implement the cooperative learning strategies.

During the first six months of follow-up, while the instructors, peers, and administrators supported and observed the teachers as they developed their thinking and their ability to apply that thinking to cooperative learning, we noticed development in two dimensions. One dimension was the movement toward fidelity to training content. Teachers' confidence in their ability to transfer their learning to the classroom increased, and we gained confidence that our staff development program was working. The other dimension, more fascinating because of

Sustained, cumulative improvements at the classroom and school level, by each and every teacher in the school, are required to meet the challenge of our collective vision of the potential of schools.

its richness and insight into a new and possibly powerful line of inquiry, was the variety of patterns of implementation, as well as the variety of learning outcomes reported by the teachers.

The Cadre of Trainers Program. One goal of the Consortium is to have school staffs assume responsibility for their professional development while concomitantly developing networks between and among schools and districts. The Cadre of Trainers Program was designed to facilitate this goal. Each school district and the faculty of education selected approximately 8 educators to attend 10 one-day workshops spaced 2–3 weeks apart from January to June 1989. Of these 40 participants, about one quarter had also attended the previous Summer Institute.

We developed the content of the program around both classroom teaching skills and training skills, so that participants could become workshop leaders for other educators. The teaching skills component included adding or refining classroom management skills, instructional skills, and instructional strategies to the cadre members' repertoires. The training component focused on ways to plan

and implement similar sessions back in the workplace.

Team members from each board attending the Cadre program were asked to practice the skills and strategies back in their district after each session. However, they were encouraged not to feel pressured to do any inservice work during the remainder of the school year, so that they could feel free to practice their skills and experiment with learning. The only inservice work required was that the teams meet back in their districts to practice thinking through and designing workshops that integrated the content and process of effective training sessions. Thus, the Cadre program focused on developing the capacity of the individuals and the districts to work more effectively with the components contained in the framework.

Growing into the Future
Other activities taking place and being planned by the Learning Consortium include:
- districtwide inservice led by Summer Institute and Cadre graduates;
- a second Summer Institute held in 1989 with 100 participants, all of whom attended in teams, as well as a third Summer Institute to be held in 1990;
- new field-based apprenticeship and preservice programs for student teachers in the one-year teacher certification program at the Faculty of Education, with Summer Institute and Cadre participants acting as mentors or providing inservice to mentors;
- school leadership programs for principals and vice-principals on instructional improvements, the management of change, and the role of school leaders in establishing collaborative work cultures;
- induction programs for first-year teachers;
- the establishment of professional development schools.

Some of these are formal programs of the Consortium, some involve two or three districts, others are individual district initiatives that build on Consortium activities. Each district in its own way is forging connections and achieving synergy of effort as one activity supports or integrates with another. When integration does occur, we see powerful multiplier effects on classroom, school, and system development.

Only the Beginning

So ... where does one begin? We started with teachers and administrators learning an instructional strategy or model of teaching selected because of its effect on student learning. As we continued, we integrated that learning with other needs, such as classroom management and peer coaching. Then concepts related to the culture of the school and the management of change helped guide our efforts.

We do not know the best place for others to begin. Individual classroom, school, and district needs and conditions will generate a variety of options. But regardless of where they start, districts will find it helpful to attend to all the components in Figure 1. Systemic and cultural change in schools as workplaces and in teaching as a profession are intimately linked; and these links represent a powerful route to educational reform. We are striving to put innovations and reforms in proper perspective, which means day-to-day improvements in the work and learning lives of teachers and students. In this sense, innovations should be seen as points of departure or catalysts, rather than as things to be implemented. Moreover, fixing on particular innovations is less important than paying attention to the potential ways in which classrooms and schools can improve. Innovations, even major reforms, because they are by definition temporary, can be diversions rather than aids to fundamental, long-term change. The problem of seeking innovations as solutions is acute because decision makers are so vulnerable to "quick fixes," given the political and time pressures under which they work.

What we have described here is only our beginning.[4] Progress cannot be sustained by individuals working alone no matter how energetic and skilled they may be. Systematic links must be made across classrooms. Progress cannot be measured by the successful implementation of a valuable innovation or even by having a good year. Sustained, cumulative improvements at the classroom and school level, by each and every teacher in the school, are required to meet the challenge of our collective vision of the potential of schools.☐

[1]The Consortium's school districts include the Dufferin-Peel Roman Catholic Separate School Board, the Durham Board of Education, the Halton Board of Education, and the North York Board of Education. The two higher education institutions are the Faculty of Education, University of Toronto, and The Ontario Institute for Studies in Education.

[2]In this paper we concentrate on classroom and school improvement. In other work we are also examining the link between school improvement and school district coherence, as well as the impact of the partnership on the higher education institutions (Fullan and Watson, forthcoming). In our view, the greatest problem faced by school districts is not resistance to innovation, but the fragmentation, overload, and incoherence resulting from the uncritical acceptance of too many different innovations which are not coordinated.

[3]We use the term *cogs* instead of *gears* because we feel it more appropriately portrays the metaphor of movement and connection points.

[4]Future reports will document the various activities and results of the Consortium (see Fullan, Bennett, and Rolheiser-Bennett 1989, Watson et al.1989, and Fullan and Watson, forthcoming).

Authors' note: We would like to thank our many academic and school-based colleagues who contributed to this article.

References

Bennett, B. (1987). "The Effectiveness of Staff Development Training Practices: A Meta-Analysis." Doctoral diss., University of Oregon.

Fullan, M. (1985). "Change Processes and Strategies at the Local Level." *The Elementary School Journal* 85, 3: 391–421.

Fullan, M. (In press). *The Meaning of Educational Change.* 2nd ed. New York: Teachers College Press; Toronto: OISE Press.

Fullan, M., B. Bennett, and C. Rolheiser-Bennett (1989). "Linking Classroom and School Improvement." Invited address to the American Educational Research Association.

Fullan, M., and A. Hargreaves. (Forthcoming). *What's Worth Fighting For in Your School.* Toronto: Ontario Public School Teachers' Federation.

Fullan, M., and N. Watson. (Forthcoming). "Beyond School-University Partnerships." In *Teacher Development and Educational Change*, edited by M. Fullan and A. Hargreaves. United Kingdom: Falmer Press.

Johnson, D.W., and R.T. Johnson (1989). *Leading the Cooperative School.* Edina, Minn.: Interaction Book Company.

Johnson, D.W., G. Maruyama, R.T. Johnson, D. Nelson, and L. Skon. (1981). "Effects of Cooperative, Competitive, and Individualistic Goal Structures on Achievement: A Meta-Analysis." *Psychological Bulletin* 89, 1: 47–62.

Joyce, B., and B. Showers. (1988). *Student Achievement Through Staff Development.* White Plains, N.Y.: Longman, Inc.

Joyce, B., and M. Weil. (1986). *Models of Teaching.* Englewood Cliffs, N.J.: Prentice Hall.

Little, J. (1989). "The Persistence of Privacy: Autonomy and Initiative in Teachers' Professional Relations." Paper presented at the annual meeting of the American Educational Research Association.

Rolheiser-Bennett, C. (1986). "Four Models of Teaching: A Meta-Analysis of Student Outcomes." Doctoral diss., University of Oregon.

Rosenholtz, S. (1989).*Teachers' Workplace: The Social Organization of Schools.*White Plains, N.Y.: Longman, Inc.

Sharan, S. (1980). "Cooperative Learning in Small Groups: Recent Methods and Effects on Achievement, Attitudes, and Ethnic Relations." *Review of Educational Research* 50, 2: 241–271.

Slavin, R.E.(1980). "Cooperative Learning." *Review of Educational Research* 50, 2: 315–342.

Slavin, R.E. (1988). "Cooperative Learning and Student Achievement." *Educational Leadership* 46, 2: 31–33.

Watson, N., C. Rolheiser-Bennett, B. Bennett, and D. Thiessen. (1989). *The Learning Consortium: Year 1 of A School/ University Partnership.* Symposium presented at the Canadian Society for Studies in Education.

Michael G. Fullan is Dean, Faculty of Education, University of Toronto, 371 Bloor St. West, Toronto, Ontario M5S 2R7, Canada. **Barrie Bennett** is a researcher and consultant for the Learning Consortium, Toronto, Canada. **Carol Rolheiser-Bennett** is Assistant Professor, Education Dept., University of Toronto.

Cooperative Learning:
An Annotated Bibliography

Compiled by Toni Sills and Samuel Totten

I. Cooperative Learning Strategies

A. Overviews

Brandt, R. (December 1989-January 1990). "On Cooperative Learning: A Conversation with Spencer Kagan." *Educational Leadership* 47, 4: 4-7.

Discusses Kagan's "structural approach" to cooperative learning and its effect on competitive behavior and racial relations as well as how it differs from other cooperative methods. Also describes "Numbered Heads Together" strategy.

Clarke, J., R. Wideman, and S. Eadie. (1990). *Together We Learn.* Scarborough, Ontario, Canada: Prentice-Hall Canada, Inc.

Developed by a team of Canadian educators, and designed as "a practical how-to' handbook to help teachers implement cooperative learning strategies in all subject areas and at all grade levels across [Canada]."

Davidson, N., and P.W. O'Leary. (February 1990). "How Cooperative Learning Can Enhance Mastery Teaching." *Educational Leadership* 47, 5: 30-3.

Discusses how the blending of cooperative learning with mastery teaching (variously referred to as the U.C.L.A. model, the Hunter model, PET or Program for Effective Teaching, ITD or Instructional Theory into Practice) makes for a richer classroom instruction and learning environment. Delineates the basics of mastery teaching, principles of cooperative learning, and ways to enhance lesson design and strengthen learning principles.

Guskey, T. R. (September 1990). "Cooperative Mastery Learning Strategies." *The Elementary School Journal* 91, 1: 33-42.

Describes the basics of cooperative learning and mastery learning, and then explains how these strategies are "naturally complementary to one another."

Johnson, D. W. (1970). "Cooperation, Competition, and Conflict Resolution." In *The Social Psychology of Education*, by D. W. Johnson. New York: Holt, Rinehart and Winston, Inc.

Discusses the general nature of conflict and types of conflict occurring in the classroom. Explains that conflicts can occur both in cooperative and competitive learning contexts. Cites research, Deutsch in particular, in arguments that cooperative learning is a more facilitative environment for conflict resolution. In a cooperative classroom, more communication between members is likely to take place and disagreements and conflicting interests are more likely to be viewed as mutual problems requiring cooperative solutions.

Johnson, D. W., R. T. Johnson, and E. J. Holubec. (1986). *Circles of Learning: Cooperation in the Classroom (Revised).* Edina, Minn.: Interaction Book Company.

Presents a general overview of cooperative learning, including a comprehensive definition of cooperative learning and an explanation of goal structures, learning processes, and instructional outcomes. The teachers role, how to create positive interdependence, how to teach students cooperative skills, and how to generate cooperation among teachers are subjects of other chapters. This easy-to-read book ends with a chapter on misinformation about cooperative learning and reflections on the nature and future of cooperative learning. Classroom teachers will find *Circles of Learning* provides a solid introduction to cooperative learning.

Johnson, R. T., D. W. Johnson, and E.J. Holubec, eds. (1987). *Structuring Cooperative Learning: Lesson Plans for Teachers 1987.* Edina, Minn.: Interaction Book Company.

Features cooperative learning lesson plans by teachers who have used cooperative learning in their classrooms; also provides sample lessons for grade levels K-12 and various subject areas, including reading, language arts, mathematics, science, and social studies. Materials in the book (except those for which reprint permission must be obtained from the primary sources) may be freely reproduced for education/training activities with the addition of an acknowledgement on all reproductions.

Kagan, S. (1989). *Cooperative Learning: Resources for Teachers.* San Juan Capistrano, Calif.: Resources for Teachers.

A general manual containing a wide variety of materials for implementing Jigsaw, detailed steps for introducing Co-op Co-op, a streamlined version of Group Investigation, and a synthesis of Jigsaw and Co-op Co-op. Includes forms, examples, and step-by-step instructions. A highly practical and helpful resource for teachers.

Kagan, S. (December 1989-January 1990). "The Structural Approach to Cooperative Learning." *Educational Leadership* 47, 4: 12-15.

Discusses the structural approach, which is based on the "creation, analysis, and systematic application of structures, or content-free ways of organizing social interaction in the classroom. . . . An important corner stone of the approach is the distinction between 'structures' and 'activities.'" Discusses competitive vs. cooperative structures, and ways for school to effectively handle the structural approach. Includes an overview of selected structures.

Slavin, R. E. (1986). *Using Student Team Learning.* Baltimore, Md.: Center for Research on Elementary and Middle Schools, The Johns Hopkins University.

Provides an outstanding overview of student team learning. Includes an overview of research on student team learning methods, a separate discussion of Student Teams-Achievement Divisions (STAD) and Teams-Game-Tournament (TGT). Includes suggestions on how to make worksheets and quizzes for STAD and TGT and brief overview of the following cooperative learning strategies: Team Accelerated Instruction, Cooperative Integrated Reading and Composition (CIRC), Jigsaw II, Co-op Co-op, and Group Investigation. Also discusses the Johnsons' methods, informal cooperative learning methods, student team learning and mastery learning, cooperative classroom management, team building, and troubleshooting.

Slavin, R. E. (1990). *Student Team Learning: An Overview and Practical Guide.* 2d ed. Washington, D.C.: National Education Association.

Second edition of a popular and useful guide to cooperative learning. Especially useful for teachers working with diverse groups of students. Contains games, scoring sheets, and lesson plans.

Toni Sills is Assistant Professor, Department of Elementary and Secondary Education, Murray State University, Murray, Kentucky.

Sam Totten is Assistant Professor of Curriculum and Instruction, University of Arkansas-Fayetteville.

B. Cooperative Integrated Reading and Composition (CIRC)

Madden, N. A., R. E. Slavin, N. L. Karweit, B. Livermon, and R. J. Stevens. (1987). *Success for All: Teacher's Manual for Reading.* Baltimore, Md.: Johns Hopkins University, Center for Research on Elementary and Middle Schools.

Partly focuses on the role of Cooperative Integrated Reading and Composition (CIRC) in the Success for All Program, a model of elementary school organization that incorporates much of what is known about effective programs for students at risk.

Madden, N. A., R. E. Slavin, and R. J. Stevens. (1986). *Cooperative Integrated Reading and Composition: Teacher's Manual.* Baltimore, Md.: Johns Hopkins University Center for Research on Elementary and Middle Schools.

Teacher's manual for a teaching strategy that uses a combination of mixed-ability cooperative groups and skill-based reading groups to teach reading, language arts, and writing in the upper elementary grades.

Stevens, R. J., N. A. Madden, R. E. Slavin, and A. M. Farnish. (1989). *Cooperative Integrated Reading and Compostion: A Brief Overview of the CIRC Program.* Baltimore, Md.: Center for Research on Elementary and Middle Level Schools, Johns Hopkins University.

Discusses composition of teams, basal-related activities, partner reading, story grammar and story related writing, word mastery list, word meaning, story retell, spelling, partner checking tests, direct instruction in reading comprehension, integrated language arts and writing, independent reading, and program evaluation. Concludes with lists of resources and materials available for implementing such a program.

C. Structured Controversy

Holubec, E. J., D. W. Johnson, and R. T. Johnson. (In press). "Structuring Controversy in a Cooperative Context: Studying Civil Disobedience." In *Social Issues in the English Classroom: Theory and Practice,* edited by C. M. Hurlbert, and S. Totten. Urbana, Ill.: National Council of the Teachers of English.

Explains how English teachers can use "structured controversy," a cooperative learning strategy, to teach about civil disobedience. This strategy can be used across the curriculum to address any controversial issue.

Johnson, D. W., and R. T. Johnson. (1988). "Critical Thinking Through Structured Controversy." *Educational Leadership* 46, 8: 58-64.

Explains a cooperative learning model (structured controversy) for engaging students in academic conflicts. Discusses how to structure controversy in the classroom as well as prerequisites for providing constructive controversy, and benefits gained by students. Includes an excellent chart on the differences between controversy, debate, concurrence-seeking, and individualistic learning processes as well as a schematic diagram of the structured controversy process.

Johnson, D. W., and R. T. Johnson. (1989). "Controversy and Learning." In *Cooperation and Competition: Theory and Research*, edited by D. W. Johnson and R. T. Johnson. Edina, Minn.: Interaction Book Company.

Examines the nature of controversy, some of its outcomes, and how it can be used constructively as a learning experience. Controversy arises in cooperative situations when group members feel committed to an issue being discussed. Controversy within the cooperative group may be constructive if the group is heterogeneous, knowledgeable, and have good communication and conflict skills.

Nijhof, W., and P. Kommers. (1985). "An Analysis of Cooperation in Relation to Cognitive Controversy." In *Learning to Cooperate, Cooperating to Learn*, edited by R. Slavin, S. Sharan, S. Kagan, R. Hertz-Lazarowitz, C. Webb, and R. Schmuck. New York: Plenum Press.

Dutch researchers discuss a study that focused on an analysis of the cognitive functioning of students within small groups. The two basic questions examined were: Is the level of communication influenced by group composition or prior knowledge of a task domain? and What is the shift in perspective of the individual members of a group due to a cooperative learning experience?

D. Co-op Co-op

Kagan, S. (1985). "Co-op Co-op: A Flexible Cooperative Learning Technique." In *Learning to Cooperate, Cooperating to Learn*, edited by R. Slavin, S. Sharan, S. Kagan, R. Hertz-Lazarowits, C. Webb, and R. Schmuck. New York: Plenum Press.

Presents a thorough overview of the philosophy, elements, and effects (cognitive and affective) of Co-op Co-op. Appendices include "Elicited Student Comments About Co-op Co-op," and a list of "Spontaneous Student Comments."

Wyatt, F. (1988). "Rethinking the Research Project Through Cooperative Learning." *Middle School Journal* 20, 1: 6-7.

Describes research projects that engage the students in an adapted version of Co-op Co-op, a cooperative learning strategy developed by Spencer Kagan. The key difference, Wyatt says, is "the strategy described here focuses on group rather than individual mini-topic presentations as described by Kagan." The unit of study discussed here is Energy. One of the primary goals for this project was to involve students in a different approach to research. Students form research questions using specific data collection techniques which help focus on research questions, synthesizing this information, and sharing findings through group interaction.

E. Group Investigation (GI)

Sharan, S., and R. Hertz-Lazarowitz. (1979). "A Group-Investigation Method of Cooperative Learning in the Classroom." In *Cooperation in Education*, edited by S. Sharan, P. Hare, C. D. Webb, and R. Hertz-Lazarowitz. Provo, Utah: Brigham Young University Press.

Provides an overview of the theoretical underpinnings and purposes of the Group Investigation method (e.g., it "attempts to combine in one teaching strategy, the form and dynamics of the democratic process and the process of academic inquiry"), describes the stages of implementation of the strategy (identifying the topic, organizing pupils into research groups, planning the learning task, carrying out the investigation, preparing a final report, presenting the final report, and evaluation), and a discussion of research and a plan for future development of the model.

Sharan, S., and H. Shachar. (1988). *Language and Learning in the Cooperative Classroom.* New York: Springer-Verlag.

Reports the findings of a study of the Group-Investigation method that was implemented in eighth grade classrooms with a multi-ethnic Jewish population. Explored types of achievement and extent of verbal interactions among the ethnic groups.

Sharan, Y., and S. Sharan. (December 1989-January 1990). "Group Investigation Expands Cooperative Learning." *Educational Leadership* 47, 4: 17-21.

Provides an overview of the group investigation approach, including stages of implementation. This is an approach that attempts to "combine in one teaching strategy the form and dynamics of the democratic process and the process of academic inquiry." Includes a sample worksheet.

F. Jigsaw

Aronson, E., N. Blaney, C. Stephan, J. Sikes, and M. Snapp. (1978). *The Jigsaw Classroom*. Newbury Park, Calif.: Sage Publications.

Outlines the Jigsaw method for cooperative learning and teaching. Designed for use with grades four and up. Classrooms are divided into groups which all study segments of a subject area. Expert groups then share their knowledge with "home" groups.

Clarke, J., and R. Wideman. (1985). *Cooperative Learning: The Jigsaw Strategy*. Scarborough, Ontario: Board of Education.

An account of the Jigsaw method and strategy. Includes five sample lessons in the content areas.

Male, M. (1986). "Cooperative Learning for Effective Jigsaw Mainstreaming." *Computing Teacher* 14, 1: 35-37.

Based upon research that supports the effectiveness of "students teaching each other, the opportunity to be successful, the support and interaction with teammates, and the amount of actual engaged time with the task at hand." Gives practical classroom examples of Jigsaw and Teams-Games-Tournaments (TGT) strategies that can be used effectively to mainstream handicapped students. Concludes by offering suggestions for creating a cooperative competitive classroom for mainstreaming.

G. Student Teams Achievement Divisions (STAD)

Bejarano, Y. (1987). "A Cooperative Small-Group Methodology in the Language Classroom." *TESOL Quarterly* 21: 483-504.

Discusses the results of a study designed to test the effects of cooperative learning techniques, including Discussion Groups and Student-Teams-Achievement Divisions (STAD), upon the achievement of students enrolled in English as a Foreign Language class. Concludes that "both small-group methods proved superior to the whole-class method on these scales, and the two group methods emerged as equally effective."

Ross, J. A., and D. Raphael. (1990). "Communication and Problem Solving Achievement in Cooperative Learning Groups." *Journal of Curriculum Studies* 22, 2: 149-164.

Using a version of Student-Teams-Achievement Divisions (STAD) researchers attempted to find out if what students talk about in cooperative groups is related to their learning of complex cognitive tasks. Results showed strong correlations between achievement and communication. Large group differences in communication patterns were found between the two classes used in the study. Students in the class which implemented a highly structured version of the cooperative learning program did not learn as much as did students in the class that rejected the task structure. Unknown and pre-existing differences among teachers and students affected the quality of inferences to be made about results. An interesting article highlighting teacher researcher interactions. The teacher who rejected the treatment did so in the interest of her students and did achieve better results. Authors hypothesized that, in the case of the class which completed the highly structured treatment, the students may have become bored with doing similar activities repeatedly, and that the STAD design itself was not at fault.

Slavin, R. E. (1986). "Getting Started With STAD." *American Educator: The Professional Journal of the American Federation of Teachers* 10, 2: 10-11.

Briefly discusses each step involved in using Student-Teams-Achievement Divisions (STAD). Steps explained are assigning students to teams, determining base scores, preparing resources, scheduling activities, teaching the material, monitoring team study, testing, computing improvement scores, computing team scores, recognizing team accomplishment, and assigning final grades.

H. Team-assisted Individualization (TAI)

Slavin, R. E. (1985). "Team-Assisted Individualization: A Cooperative Learning Solution for Adaptive Instruction in Mathematics." In *Adapting Instruction to Individual Differences*, edited by M. C. Wang and H. J. Walberg. Berkeley, Calif.: McCutchan Publishing Corporation.

Provides a solid overview of the strategy entitled Team-Assisted individualization (TAI), and its role in regard to adaptive instruction. Briefly discusses the research on TAI, including that which is concerned with academic achievement, attitudes, race relations, and effects on academically handicapped students.

Slavin, R. E. (1985). "Team-Assisted Individualization: Combining Cooperative Learning and Individualized Instruction in Mathematics." In *Learning to Cooperate, Cooperating to Learn*, edited by R. Slavin, S. Sharan, S. Kagan, R. Hertz-Lazarowitz, C. Webb, and R. Schmuck. New York: Plenum Press.

Addresses the principle features of Team-Assisted Individualization (TAI), describes a series of experiments involving TAI, and presents a summary of results.

Slavin, R. E. (November 1987). "Cooperative Learning and Individualized Instruction." *Arithmetic Teacher* 35: 14-16.

Details principal elements of the Team-Assisted Individualization (TAI) program: teams, placement tests, curriculum materials, team-study method, team scores and team recognition, teaching groups, tests, and whole-class units. Cites findings from several studies on TAI and concludes that, in addition to increased achievement, "positive effects have been found on such varied outcomes as students' self-esteem in mathematics, liking of mathematics, acceptance of mainstreamed classmates, and race relations."

Slavin, R. E., N. A. Madden, and R. J. Stevens. (December 1989- January 1990). "Cooperative Learning Models for the 3 R's." *Educational Leadership* 47, 4: 22-28.

Provides a strong overview of Team-Assisted Individualization (e.g., principal features and research on TAI) and Cooperative Integrated Reading Composition (e.g., principal features of CIRC and research). Argues that these cooperative learning strategies can be "used successfully as the primary instructional method in reading, writing, and mathematics."

I. Teams Games Tournaments (TGT)

DeVries, D. L., R. E. Slavin, G. M. Fennessey, K. J. Edwards, and M. M. Lombardo. (1980). *Teams-Games-Tournaments: The Team Learning Approach*. N.J.: Educational Technology Publications.

A well-written, comprehensive practical resource for teachers who want to use Teams-Games-Tournament (TGT) in their classrooms. The first chapter discusses TGT, explains when it is most effective, and tells why the strategy has positive effects upon student achievement, student satisfaction, and cross-racial cooperation.

Wodarski, J. S. (1988). "Teams-Games-Tournaments: Teaching Adolescents About Alcohol and Driving." *Journal of Alcohol and Drug Education* 33, 3: 46-57.

Presents a brief review of variables that influence adolescent drinking habits. Seeking alternatives to traditional approaches, the author presents an in-depth discussion of Teams-Games-Tournaments (TGT) by summarizing an alcohol education program tested in Georgia. The comprehensive article concludes that TGT is an effective strategy through which to teach facts about alcohol and its effects upon driving behaviors.

Wodarski, J. S. (1987). "Teaching Adolescents about Alcohol and Driving: A Two-Year Follow Up." *Journal of Drug Education* 17, 4: 327-344.

The author used the "Teams-Games-Tournaments" (TGT) program as a method for teaching students about drinking and driving. Two years later, students in the TGT group reported remembering and enjoying the learning experience, and reported maintaining the knowledge and attitudes formed during the instruction. Students in TGT scored substantially better on a test of alcohol knowledge than either of the control groups.

Wodarski, L. A., C. L. Adelson, M. T. Todd, and J. S. Wodarski. (1980). "Teaching Nutrition by Teams-Games-Tournaments." *Journal of Nutrition Education* 12, 2: 61-65.

Two Teams-Games-Tournament units were developed to test the effect of cooperative learning on the teaching of nutrition. Results of student responses to questionnaires indicated significant increases in nutrition knowledge for both elementary and high school students. Teachers, in addition to students' improvement in knowledge of nutrition, felt students reinforced reading, math, spelling, and measurement skills. Some teachers felt middle and lower ability students benefited more than higher ability students. Higher ability students sometimes seemed frustrated when they received lower scores than they were used to.

II. Subject Areas

A. Computers

Davies, D. (1988). "Computer-Supported Co-Operative Learning Systems: Interactive Groups." *Programmed Learning and Educational Technology.* 25: 205-215.

Presents the view that learning is a group process and examines computer-assisted co-operative learning. Offers some techniques for the design of computer-supported cooperative learning environments.

Fazio, R. P., and F. J. Berenty. (1983). "Everybody Wins in Group Computing." *The Science Teacher* 50: 56-58.

Discusses a cooperative computer learning curriculum in earth science used in the Fairfax County Public Schools in Virginia. Development of the innovative curriculum became necessary when the high school received one computer to be used with twenty-five to thirty students.

Johnson, D. W., and R. T. Johnson. (1985). "Cooperative Learning: One Key to Computer Assisted Learning." *The Computing Teacher* 13, 2: 11-13.

Based upon the assumption that "the teaching of computers and the interpersonal interaction promoted by cooperative learning provides complimentary strengths." Offers practical cooperative learning activities for teachers to use in a computer course.

Concludes with two sample lesson plans for use in elementary classrooms.

Johnson, R. T., R. W. Johnson, and M. B. Stanne. (1985). "Effects of Cooperative, Competitive, and Individualistic Goal Structures on Computer-Assisted Instruction." *Journal of Educational Psychology* 77, 6: 668-677.

The study involving eighth graders compared the relative efficacy of computer-assisted cooperative, competitive, and individualistic learning in promoting high achievement, oral interaction among students, perceptions of status, and positive attitudes toward subject area and instructional methods. The results indicated that computer-assisted cooperative instruction promotes greater quantity and quality of daily achievement, more successful problem solving, and higher performance on factual recognition, application, and problem-solving test items than did the computer-assisted competitive or individualistic learning.

The authors were particularly concerned that the competitive condition seemed to be detrimental to the achievement of girls. "If educators wish to promote girls' success in using computers and positive attitudes toward working with computers, computer-assisted cooperative learning situations should be emphasized."

Johnson, R. T., D. W. Johnson, and M. B. Stanne. (1986). "Comparison of Computer-Assisted Cooperative, Competitive, and Individualistic Learning." *American Educational Research Journal* 23: 382-392.

Cooperative learning computer-assisted instruction was found to promote greater quantity and quality of daily achievement, more successful problem solving, more task related student-student interaction, and increased perceived status of female students.

MacGregor, S. K. (1988). "Structured Walk-Through." *The Computing Teacher* 15, 9: 7-10.

Describes the results of a project using the "structured walk-through" procedure designed to improve students' programming practice. Outcomes of the project were positive. Students' programming performance and attitude toward programming improved. Provides a strong research base for using a collaborative learning environment. Stresses that cooperative learning promotes "more and better work, more successful problem solving, and higher performance on factual recognition, applications, and problem solving tasks." Points out that in a cooperative situation, students must have a clearly defined cooperative goal structure to maximize achievement. Concludes by addressing some of the major concerns of teachers who implement cooperative learning strategies.

Male, M., R. T. Johnson, D. W. Johnson, and M. Anderson. (1985). *Cooperative Learning and Computers: An Activity Guide for Teachers.* Minneapolis, Minn.: Cooperative Learning Project.

Includes the following chapters: An Introduction to Cooperative Learning and Computers; Essential Ingredients of Cooperative Computer Lessons; General Design Principles for Three Cooperative Learning Strategies (Learning Together, Jigsaw, and Teams-Games-Tournaments); Sample Lessons: Learning Together, Sample Lessons: Jigsaw; Sample Lessons: Teams-Games-Tournaments; Software Descriptions and Simplified Reference Cards; and Suggestions for Dividing Students into Teams. The appendices include a lesson plan guide, sample team recognition certificates, sample observation forms, and sample scoring systems.

McDonald, P. (1989). *Cooperation at the Computer-A Handbook for Using Software with Cooperative Learning Groups.* Quincy, Ill.: Looking Glass Learning Products.

A useful resource for teachers of all disciplines. Contains a wide variety of lesson plans, including suggestions for cooperative learning activities, effective establishment of groups, and follow-up activities.

Reglin, G. L. (1990). "The Effects of Individualized and Cooperative Computer Assisted Instruction of Mathematics Achievement and Mathematics Anxiety for Prospective Teachers." *Journal of Research on Computing in Education* 22, 4: 404-412.

> Study found that prospective minority teachers who worked cooperatively significantly outperformed those who worked individually in mathematics achievement. Math anxiety scores did not significantly increase or decrease for either group. Females, however, significantly increased their anxiety scores.

B. Language Arts

Reading, Composition, and Spelling

Augustine, D. K., K. D. Gruber, and L. R. Hanson. (December 1989-January 1990). "Cooperative Spelling Groups." *Educational Leadership* 47, 4: 6.

> A five-part procedure for using cooperative learning to teach spelling.

"Cooperative Learning in English." (October 1990). *English Journal* 79, 6: 74-77.

> The editors solicited a response from public school English teachers in regard to this question: "How are you using collaborative or cooperative learning in your classroom?" Eight short responses are included.

Duin, A. H. (May 1984). "Implementating Cooperative Learning Groups in the Writing Curriculum: What Research Shows and What You Can Do." Paper presented at the Annual Meeting of the Minnesota Council of Teacher of English, Mankato, Minn. (ERIC Document Reproduction Service No. ED 251 849).

> Duin reviewed the results of over 800 studies of cooperative learning. She found that students who studied in cooperative learning groups—as compared to competitive or individualized learning—achieve more academically, have more positive attitudes toward school, subject areas, and teachers, are more positive about each other, regardless of ability, race, or handicap, and are more effective interpersonally. Students who learn cooperatively actively discover knowledge and direct their own learning. Cooperative learning strategies can help student writers practice invention techniques, share writing, revise, edit, and discuss material. Discusses the requirements for cooperative learning (group interdependence and individual accountability) and explains their implementation in the composition class. Appendices include several activities adapted for group use.

Duin, A. H. (1986). "Implementing Cooperative Learning Groups in the Writing Curriculum." *Journal of Teaching Writing* 5: 315-323.

> Based upon the hypothesis that students who work cooperatively experience greater achievement than students who work competitively and individually, the article outlines cooperative learning activities designed to teach the writing process. Concludes by challenging writing instructors to incorporate cooperative learning activities in their curriculum as a means of achieving "better communication and better writing skills."

Kelly, P., M. P. Hall, and R. C. Small, Jr. (1984). "Composition Through the Team Approach." *English Journal* 73, 5: 71-74.

> Writing teachers used Slavin's Student Teams-Achievement Division (STAD) cooperative learning technique to improve composition. A step-by-step explanation is given for setting up a unit in composition using teams. When compared with other classes who did not use the STAD approach, yet who studied the same content and wrote the same papers, teachers found that STAD students improved their writing twice as often. In addition to improving writing skills, students and teachers both said they enjoyed class more. Teachers felt the team approach was no more

difficult to manage than a traditional class once the routine was established.

Stone, J. (1990). *Cooperative Learning and Language Arts: A Multi-Structural Approach*. San Juan Capistrano, Calif.: Resources for Teachers.

> Provides field-tested, step-by-step multi-structural lessons for kindergarten through eighth grade students.

English as a Second Language (ESL)

Pierce, L.V., ed. (1987). *Cooperative Learning: Integrating Language and Content-Area Instruction*. Wheaton, Md.: National Clearinghouse for Bilingual Education. (ERIC Document Reproduction Service No. 291 245).

> A review of research on language minority students' academic success precedes the presentation of a bilingual, content-based curriculum which uses cooperative learning techniques. The Finding Out/Descubrimiento Approach (FO/D) developed by Edward A. De Avila, S.E. Duncan, and Cecelia J. Navarrete is described and its curriculum outlined. FO/D is an integrated language skills program for oral and written communication mastery in English and Spanish within a cooperative learning environment used in second to fifth grades, it is designed to involve students with diverse cultural, academic, and linguistic backgrounds in learning by focussing on their natural interest in how the world works. Introduction to social aspects of cooperative learning and supervised content-learning activities comprise the two phases of the program. Methods and materials for program implementation are discussed and several specific activities are explained in detail.

General Language Arts Skills

Maring, G. H., G. C. Fruman, and J. Blum-Anderson. (1985). "Five Cooperative Learning Strategies for Mainstreamed Youngsters in Content Area Classrooms." *The Reading Teacher* 39, 3: 310-317.

> The authors recommend placing students of different abilities together. Rules should be given for group behavior. Several strategies for learning are discussed: the Jigsaw method, "list-group," "small group structured overview," "survey, predict, read, revise" method, and "translation reading."

Uttero, D. A. (1988). "Activating Comprehension Through Cooperative Learning." *The Reading Teacher* 41, 4: 390-394.

> The author discusses three phases for implementing cooperative learning. In connection, the first phase, the students work in small groups, brainstorming, categorizing, and comparing and contrasting. In the second phase, students read independently, answer questions, outline and paraphrase. In the follow-up phase, they prepare to take test using summarization and nmemonic strategies. Benefits of this approach include helping evaluate progress during learning stage and promoting positive attitudes.

C. Mathematics

Andrini, B. (1990). *Cooperative Learning and Mathematics: A Multi-Structural Approach*. San Juan Capistrano, Calif.: Resources for Teachers.

> Provides field-tested, step-by-step multi-structural lessons for kindergarten through eighth grade students.

Artzt, A. F., and C. M. Newman. (1990). *How to Use Cooperative Learning in the Mathematics Classroom*. Reston, Va.: National Council of Teachers of Mathematics.

A manual, which was developed under the auspice of the National Council of Teachers of Mathematics, on how to incorporate various cooperative learning strategies in mathematics classrooms across the grade levels.

Artzt, A. F., and C. M. Newman. (September 1990). "Cooperative Learning." *Mathematics Teacher* 83, 6: 448-452.

This article is comprised of the following sections: "What is cooperative learning," "Why use cooperative learning," "How are Groups Formed," "How can cooperative learning be incorporated in the mathematics class," and "Why do students like cooperative learning."

Bryant, R. R. (1981). "Effects of Team-Assisted Individualization on the Attitudes and Achievement of Third, Fourth and Fifth Grade Students on Mathematics." University of Maryland. *Dissertation Abstracts International* 43, 70A.

Discusses an eight-week study designed to evaluate the effects of Team-Assisted Individualization (TAI) that combined student team learning and individualized interaction and Rapid Progress Mathematics (RPM) upon the mathematical achievement of elementary school children. Students in the TAI experimental group revealed greater achievement than did students in the RPM groups. Both experimental groups experienced more achievement than did students in the control group.

Davidson, N. (1990). "Introduction and Overview." In *Cooperative Learning in Mathematics: A Handbook for Teachers*, edited by N. Davidson. New York: Addison-Wesley Publishing Company.

In his introduction, Davidson provides a detailed discussion about the place and use of cooperative learning in math courses from elementary through introductory college courses.

Davidson, N., ed. (1990). *Cooperative Learning in Mathematics: A Handbook for Teachers*. New York: Addison-Wesley Publishing Co.

A major resource on cooperative learning in mathematics. Includes the following essays: "The Math Solution: Using Groups of Four" by Marilyn Burns; "Finding Out about Complex Instruction: Teaching Math and Science in Heterogeneous Classrooms" by Rachel A. Lotan and Joan Denton; "Student Team Learning and Mathematics" by Robert E. Slavin; "Using Cooperative Learning in Math" by David and Roger Johnson; "Cooperative Learning and Computers in the Elementary and Middle School Math Classroom" by Mary Male; "Cooperation in the Mathematics Classroom: A User's Manual" by Roberta L. Dees'; "Small-Group Learning in the Secondary Mathematics Classroom" by Calvin D. Crabill; "Real Maths in Cooperative Groups in Secondary Education" by Jan Terwell; "Integrating Computers as Tools in Mathematics Curricula (Grades 9-13): Portraits of Group Interaction" by Charlene Sheets and M. Kathleen Heid; "Cooperative Learning Using a Small-Group Laboratory Approach" by Julian Weissglass; "The Small-Group Discovery Method in Secondary- and College-Level Mathematics" by Neil Davidson; and "Implementing Group Work: Issues for Teachers and Administrators" by Laturel Robertson, Nancy Graves, and Patricia Tuck.

Gilbert-Macmillan, K., and S. J. Leitz. (1986). "Cooperative Small Groups: A Method for Teaching Problem Solving." *The Arithmetic Teacher* 33, 7: 9-11.

The authors discuss methods for training a small group (ideally four children) to work well together. The goals of the group must be specified, the individual talents of each member must be made use of, the responsibilities of listening, encouraging and participating must be emphasized, and this training should proceed gradually as the children experience working together. They also point out that children must be allowed to talk through extra information in a problem in order to facilitate the development of problem solving skills.

Good, T. L., B. J. Reys, D. A. Grouws, and C. M. Mulryan (December 1989-January 1990). "Using Work-Groups in Mathematics Instruction." *Educational Leadership* 47, 4: 56-62.

A descriptive analysis of "how teachers who use work-groups actually employ these formats and to explore, in a preliminary way, the possible advantages and disadvantages of using these groups." Includes practical lesson examples, including possible problem areas.

Johnson, D. W., and R. T. Johnson. (1989). "Cooperative Learning in Mathematics Education." In *New Directions for Elementary School Mathematics*, edited by P. R. Trafton and A. P. Shulte. Reston, Va.: The National Council of Teachers of Mathematics.

A very broad overview that addresses the nature of cooperative learning, a few basic concerns vis-a-vis cooperative learning and learning mathematics, basic elements of cooperative learning, and the teacher's role in implementing cooperative learning.

Pagni, D. L. (1989). "A Television Programming Challenge: A Cooperative Group Activity That Uses Mathematics." *Arithmetic Teacher* 36, 5: 7-9.

Designed for junior high students to apply mathematical principles to the real world, the Television Programming Challenge consists of the following tasks: to conduct a survey of junior high school students to determine how much television they watch, the types of shows that they watch, and the types of advertisements that captured their attention; to prepare a report of the survey; and to prepare a suggested week of television shows. To complete the assignment, students were divided into cooperative groups. The article details the instruction and procedures for the project.

Robertson, L., N. Graves, and P. Tuck. (1990). "Implementing Group Work: Issues for Teachers and Administrators." In *Cooperative Learning in Mathematics: A Handbook for Teachers*, edited by N. Davidson. New York: Addison-Wesley Publishing Company.

Discusses issues affecting the use of cooperative learning in mathematics with an emphasis on teachers' decision making and factors affecting implementation.

Rosenbaum, L. J., K. J. Behounek, L. Brown, and J. V. Burcalow. (1989). "Step Into Problem Solving with Cooperative Learning." *Arithmetic Teacher* 36, 7: 7-11.

Offers suggestions about using small, cooperative groups to teach problem solving to primary-level students. Gives practical classroom activities for use in cooperative groups and lists five tricks for success: Teach strategies, rehearse technique, involve everyone, cooperate to solve problems, keep groups small, and share ideas.

Slavin, R. E. (1985). "Team-Assisted Individualization: A Cooperative Learning Solution for Adaptive Instruction in Mathematics." In *Adapting Instruction to Individual Differences*, edited by M. C. Wang and H. J. Walberg. Berkeley, Calif.: McCutchan Publishing Corporation.

Provides a solid overview of the strategy entitled Team-Assisted Individualization (TAI), and its role in regard to adaptive instruction. Briefly discusses the research on TAI, including that which is concerned with academic achievement, attitudes, race relations, and effects on academically handicapped students.

Slavin, R. E. (1987). "Cooperative Learning and Individualized Instruction." *Arithmetic Teacher* 35: 14-16.

Discusses Team-Assisted Individualization (TAI), which applies principles of cooperative learning to an individualized program. Examines team composition, placement tests, curriculum materials, team scores and recognition, and teaching groups. Concludes that "Research on TAI has amply justified our expectation that if the management, motivational, and direct instructional problems of individualized instruction can be solved, the approach could considerably improve students' mathematics achievement. In six carefully controlled studies in grades 3-6, TAI classes gained an average of twice as many grade equivalents as control classes on standardized tests. Results in mathematic concepts and applications have been less dramatic but are still positive as are results on such varied outcomes as students' self-esteem in mathematics, liking of mathematics, acceptance of mainstreamed classmates, and race relations."

D. Science

Bonnstetter, R., and J. Pedersen. (1990). "S/T/S for Students." *Science Scope* 13, 4: 49.

Presents an interesting, effective method for using cooperative controversy to teach science, technology, and societal issues. Written as a conversation between a son and his mother, the article provides good reading for any teacher or parent interested in cooperative learning.

Hannigan, M. R. (December 1989-January 1990). "Cooperative Learning in Elementary Science." *Educational Leadership* 47, 4: 25.

Discusses "Science for Life and Living: Integrating Science, Technology, and Health," a new science program for elementary students that emphasizes concrete experiences and is one in which cooperative learning is a central strategy.

Johnson, R. T., and D. W. Johnson. (1986). "Action Research: Cooperative Learning in the Science Classroom." *Science and Children* 24, 2: 31-32.

Emphasizes the need for studies testing the effectiveness of cooperative learning activities within science classrooms. Written for teachers who desire to conduct research, the article discusses three types of studies that can be done by classroom teachers: replication, refining, and extending. Concludes that teachers who do cooperative learning research will gain valuable experience and knowledge that will enhance their teaching skills.

Lazarowitz, R., R. L. Hertz, J. H. Baird, and V. Bowlden. (1988). "Academic Achievement and On-Task Behavior of High School Biology Students Instructed in a Cooperative Small Investigative Group." *Science Education* 72, 4: 475-487.

A modified Jigsaw method combined with the investigative group approach was used to teach two biology units (cells and plants) to tenth graders. Authors concluded that while academic results were inconclusive, improvement in time-on-task behaviors caused by cooperative learning may lead to better attitudes toward science, less absenteeism, and higher student expectations.

Okebukola, P. A. (1985). "The Relative Effectiveness of Cooperative and Competitive Interaction Techniques in Strengthening Students' Performance in Science Classes." *Science Education* 69, 4: 501-509.

Compared the effectiveness on students' performance in science classes of two "pure" cooperative (Johnsons' technique and jigsaw), two cooperative-competitive (Teams-Games-Tournament and Student Teams-Achievement Division), and one "pure" competitive learning technique (student has own set of learning materials, studies independently, and competes for first, second, and third place within the class).

Results showed that cooperative-competitive methods had greater positive effects on student performance when compared to "pure" cooperative and "pure" competitive methods. STAD and TGT techniques also caused students to perform significantly better on higher cognitive skills. Okebukola concluded that a combination of cooperation and competition may be considered to be the best method of instruction in science classes to increase student achievement.

Sachse, T. P. (1989). "Making Science Happen." *Educational Leadership* 47, 3: 18-21.

Discusses how cooperative learning strategies are outstanding for use with "constructivist teaching" and an ideal way to engage students in "interactive learning."

Sherman, L. W. (1989). "A Comparative Study of Cooperative and Competitive Achievement in Secondary Biology Classrooms: The Group Investigation Model Versus an Individually Competitive Goal Structure." *Journal of Research in Science Teaching* 26, 1: 55-64.

This study was done in a mainly white middle class rural school. It explores the success of GI (Group Investigation). Over a 35 day period, the children participated in small groups, researching a topic. The children divided the work among themselves. Pretests showed that the experimental group was similar to the control group, taught by the traditional methods. The study found that both groups showed gains and that neither one was superior to the other. The author suggests that the way in which the study was carried out may have had bearing on the results. Not everyone in the cooperative group participated fully and the time in the school year may have had some effect.

E. Social Studies

Bump, E. (1989). "Utilizing Cooperative Learning to Teach Social Studies in the Middle School." *Social Science Record* 26, 2: 32-36.

A social studies supervisor's insight as to why and how cooperative learning can be used in middle school social studies programs to attempt to meet the needs of "transcents" and to make the study of social studies more interesting.

Ferguson, P. (1988). "Modernization in Meiji Japan: A Jigsaw Lesson." *Social Education* 51: 393- 394.

Provides a step-by-step procedure for teaching a jigsaw lesson on modernization in Meiji, Japan. It also provides the actual information and directions needed by the students in order to complete the jigsaw exercise.

Lyman, L. K., and H. C. Foyle. (1988). "Cooperative Learning: Experiencing the Constitution in Action." Paper presented at the Rocky Mountain Regional Conference of the National Council for the Social Studies, Salt Lake City, Utah. (ERIC Document Reproduction Service No. ED 293 791).

Ten basic steps for implementation of cooperative learning are identified. Sample cooperative learning lesson plans include "Creating a Classroom Bill of Rights" for 4-6th graders and "The United States Constitution: Powers of Congress" for 7-12th graders. Encourages use of cooperative learning by social studies teachers because it motivates students and encourages social and academic interaction among students.

Palmer, J. J. (1988). "The Electoral College: A Jigsaw Lesson." *Social Education* 52: 306-307.

A jigsaw lesson for high school students. Addresses what the electoral college is and how it works.

F. Students with Special Needs

Bina, M. J. (1986). "Social Skills Development Through Cooperative Group Learning Strategies." *Education of the Visually Handicapped* 18, 1: 27-40.

Describes the use of cooperative learning strategies with visually handicapped (VH) students in order to improve socialization skills and integration with nonhandicapped peers. Looks at reasons for poor social skills of handicapped students: 1.

inadequate time to teach social skills; 2. over reliance on individualized or competitive learning; 3. social skills not assigned a high priority by teachers. Contains a brief overview of cooperative learning and various cooperative learning strategies, then reports how it has been used effectively with visually impaired students. Gives concrete and useful suggestions for implementing cooperative learning with handicapped students. Discusses potential problems in implementation with visually handicapped students and offers solutions.

Guinagh, B. (1980). "The Social Integration of Handicapped Children." *Phi Delta Kappan* 62, 1: 27-29.

Argues that integration of handicapped children into the mainstream of schooling should not be left to chance, and suggests that cooperative learning activities make social integration more likely. Discusses research of Johnson and Johnson and their associates, and Slavin and his associates.

Johnson, D. W., and R. T. Johnson. (1981). "The Integration of the Handicapped Into the Regular Classroom: Effects of Cooperative and Individualistic Instruction." *Contempory Educational Psychology* 6: 344-353.

Details a study that compares the effects of cooperative and individualist learning experience on interpersonal attraction between handicapped and nonhandicapped fourth grade students. Results indicated that "cooperative learning experiences, compared with individualistic ones, promote more cross-handicapped interaction during both instructional and free-time situations and more interpersonal attraction between handicapped and nonhandicapped students." Concludes that cooperative learning activities are effective when handicapped students are mainstreamed into the regular classroom.

Johnson, D. W., and R. T. Johnson. (1989). "Cooperative Learning: What Special Education Teachers Need to Know." *Pointer* 33, 2: 5-10.

Paper seeks to identify what cooperative learning is and the basic factors within it that make cooperative learning effective. Also examines the importance of the teacher in constructing cooperative learning groups, various ways groups may be utilized, how the learning outcome is affected by cooperation, and teaching methods which can be used in placing handicapped and non-handicapped students in the same groups.

Johnson, R. T., and D. W. Johnson. (1981). "Building Friendships Between Handicapped and Nonhandicapped Students: Effects of Cooperative Learning and Individualistic Learning." *American Educational Research Journal* 18: 415-423.

The results of the study involving third graders indicate that cooperative learning experiences, compared with individualistic ones, "promote more cross-handicapped interaction during instruction; promote interaction characterized by involving handicapped students in the learning activities, giving them assistance, and encouraging them to achieve; promote more cross-handicap friendships; and promote more cross-handicap interaction during post instructional free-time."

Johnson, R. T., D. W. Johnson, N. DeWeerdt, V. M. Lyons, and B. Zaidman. (1983). "Integrating Severely Adaptively Handicapped Seventh-Grade Students Into Constructive Relationships with Nonhandicapped Peers in Science Class." *American Journal of Mental Defciency* 87, 6: 611-618.

Cooperative learning and individualistic learning modes were compared on interactions and relationships between severely handicapped and nonhandicapped seventh grade students. Results of the cooperative learning condition showed: 1. achievement of nonhandicapped students was unaffected; 2. handicapped students did not withdraw from interaction with nonhandicapped peers; 3. handicapped students participated in more tasks, management, and social interactions with nonhandicapped than in the individualistic condition; and 4. handicapped felt they "belonged" more.

Authors recommend cooperative learning procedures be used when mainstreaming severely handicapped students, but warn that nonhandicapped students must be given instruction in strategies to effectively work with them and must give nonhandicapped students feedback as to how well they are working with handicapped students.

Lew, M., D. Mesch, D. W. Johnson, and R. T. Johnson. (1986). "Positive Interdependence, Academic and Collaborative-Skills Group Contingencies, and Isolated Students." *American Educational Research Journal* 23: 476-488.

Investigated the effects of opportunities to interact with classmates, positive goal interdependence, positive goal and positive reward interdependence, and positive goal and reward interdependence with an added contingency for the use of collaborative skills. The results indicate that both positive goal and reward interdependence are needed to maximize student achievement and the interpersonal attraction between socially withdrawn and nonhandicapped students.

Madden, N. A., R. E. Slavin. (1983). "Effects of Cooperative Learning on the Social Acceptance of Mainstreamed Academically Handicapped Students." *The Journal of Special Education* 17, 2: 171-182.

An attempt to discover if the social acceptance of mildly-academically handicapped children enrolled in regular classes would improve as a result of cooperative learning. An adaptation of Students Teams-Achievement Division (STAD) was used as the cooperative intervention. In the control condition, students studied individually and were given feedback individually.

While cooperative learning did not result in increased friendships between academically handicapped and normal-progress children, it did cause a significant decrease in rejection of handicapped students. Both groups showed greater academic achievement and self concept as a result of cooperation. The authors believe that if cooperation had been used for a longer time period, friendships may also have grown between the two groups.

Madden, N. A., R. E. Slavin, N. L. Karweit, and B. J. Livermon. (1989). "Restructuring the Urban Elementary School." *Educational Leadership* 46, 5: 14- 1 8.

Discusses how the "Success for All" program has improved achievement of students at an inner-city elementary school by producing immediate intensive interventions when learning problems occur. Briefly touches on the strategy called "Cooperative Integrated Reading and Composition" (CIRC), which "provides cooperative learning activities built around story structure, prediction, summarization, vocabulary building, decoding practice, writing, and direct instruction in reading comprehension and language skills."

Madden, N. A., R. E. Slavin, N. L. Karweit, B. J. Livermon, and L. Dolan. (1988). *Success for All: Effects on Student Achievement, Rententions, and Special Education Referrals.* Baltimore, Md.: Johns Hopkins University, Center for Research on Elementary and Middle Schools.

Discusses a model of elementary school organization that incorporates much of what is known about effective programs for students at risk. This model makes solid use of such cooperative learning strategies as Team-Assisted Individualization (TAI), and Cooperative Integrated Reading and Composition (CIRC). The Success for All program was initially piloted and evaluated at one Baltimore City elementary school during the 1987-1988 school year, and has been expanded to additional schools in subsequent years.

Male, M., and M. A. Anderson. (1990). *Fitting In: Cooperative Learning in the Mainstream Classroom.* Arlington, Va.: Majo Press.

Authors envision classrooms where differences are viewed as strengths to draw on, with cooperative learning strategies as the catalyst for allowing each student to discover a place to fit in. Text includes lessons and worksheets for grades K-12 in language arts, math, science, health, and social studies.

Margolis, H., and E. Schwark. (1989). "Facilitating Mainstreaming Through Cooperative Learning." *The High School Journal* 72: 83-88.

Broad overview as to why the use of cooperative learning may facilitate mainstreaming. Also provides suggested guidelines for implementation.

Maring, G. H., G. C. Fruman, and J. Blum-Anderson. (1985). "Five Cooperative Learning Strategies for Mainstreamed Youngsters in Content Area Classrooms." *The Reading Teacher* 39, 3: 310-313.

Highlights learning strategies for implementing cooperative learning techniques for main-streamed youngsters in content area classrooms. Small groups of students (4-8) at various instructional levels are placed in a non-competitive environment of working together toward a common goal. Describes effective cooperative strategies such as jigsaw strategy, list-groups-label strategy, small group structures, survey, predict, read, revise, and translation writing in developing cooperative learning strategies for mainstreamed students.

Reynolds, M. C. (1989). "Students with Special Needs." In *Knowledge Base for the Beginning Teacher*, edited by M. C. Reynolds. New York: Pergamon Press.

Under a section entitled "Positive Interdependence Among Students," Reynolds suggests that the use of cooperative group strategies for part of the day may be a way to achieve a decent environment for students who "show wide diversity in characteristics." Discusses achievement advances when cooperative learning is used with inner city pupils, children from low-income families, black students, mentally retarded, and others. Also discusses "gains in appreciation and acceptance among students who are diverse in racial and ethnic backgrounds and children with handicaps."

Robinson, A. (1990). "Cooperation or Exploitation? The Argument Against Cooperative Learning for Talented Students." *Journal for the Education of the Gifted* 14, 1: 9-27.

Reviews the following disadvantages of using cooperative learning with academically talented students: 1. limiting instruction to grade level materials, 2. presenting information to meet the needs of grade-level students, and 3. using basic skills measures to evaluate student achievement. Also points out problems with the existing research base and its applicability to talented students. Among the problems discussed are sampling, treatment comparisons, contradictory results for higher level outcomes, and overgeneralization. Concludes that cooperative learning does produce positive outcomes, but that the strategy should be used cautiously to avoid exploiting gifted students for the benefit of the other students.

Robinson, A. (1990). "Cooperation, Consistency, and Challenge for Academically Talented Youth." *Journal for the Education of the Gifted* 14, 1: 31-36.

In her response to Robert Slavin's article "Ability Grouping, Cooperative Learning and the Gifted," the author discusses areas of agreement with Slavin and offers suggestions for understanding and using cooperative learning with talented students.

Schniedewind, N., and S. J. Salend. (1987). "Cooperative Learning Works." *Teaching Exceptional Children* 19: 22-25.

Presents special education teachers with practical guidelines for designing and implementing cooperative learning strategies. Illustrates how these guidelines are used by teachers in mainstreamed, resource room, and self-contained classroom settings. Topics discussed include: Selecting a cooperative learning format, establishing guidelines for cooperating activities, forming cooperative groups, arranging the classroom, developing cooperative skills, and confronting problems. Even though the article targets special education teachers, it will serve as a valuable resource for all teachers interested in cooperative learning.

Slavin, R. E. (1990). "Ability Grouping, Cooperative Learning and the Gifted." *Journal for the Education of the Gifted* 14, 1: 3-8.

Points out that "it is possible to reduce the use of tracking and of separate enrichment programs for the gifted, increase the use of cooperative learning, and meet the learning needs of gifted students better than in traditionally organized classes." Reviews research findings that support the effectiveness of cooperative learning with accelerated groups. Concludes by emphasizing that the best way to meet the needs of all learners, including the gifted, is to modify the structure of traditional classrooms.

Slavin, R. E. (1990). "Cooperative Learning and the Gifted: Who Benefits?" *Journal for the Education of the Gifted* 14, 1: 28-30.

A response to Ann Robinson's article "Cooperation or Exploitation? The Argument against Cooperative Learning for Talented Students." Agrees that the research base for application of cooperative learning to gifted classes is "virtually nonexistent." Points out that many studies have reported the benefit of using cooperative learning for high achievers and that the "extrapolation to accelerated programs seems straightforward."

Slavin, R. E., and N. A. Madden. (1989). "Effective Classroom Programs for Students At Risk." In *Effective Programs for Students at Risk*, edited by R. E. Slavin, N. L. Karweit, and N. A. Madden. Boston: Allyn and Bacon.

Includes a section entitled "Cooperative Learning" (pp. 39-42) that discusses Team Accelerated Instruction (TAI) and Cooperative Integrated Reading and Composition (CIRC).

Slavin, R. E., and N. A. Madden. (1989). "What Works for Students At Risk: A Research Synthesis." *Educational Leadership* 46, 5: 4-13.

A section of this article (pp. 8-10) examines the value of cooperative learning strategies in regard to the student at risk. The researchers found four strategies to meet the inclusion criteria applied in the synthesis: Team Accelerated Instruction, Cooperative Integrated Reading and Composition, Student Teams-Achievement Divisions, and Companion Reading.

Slavin, R. E., N. A. Madden, and N. L. Karweit. (1989). "Effective Programs for Students At Risk: Conclusions for Practice and Policy." In *Effective Programs for Students At, Risk*, edited by R. Slavin, N. L. Karweit, and N. A. Madden. Boston: Allyn and Bacon.

Briefly discusses how Cooperative Integrated Reading and Composition (CIRC) and Team-Assisted Individualization (TAI) have been incorporated into a model of elementary school organization and "Success for All," an effective educational program for students at risk.

Tateyama-Sniezek, K. M. (1990). "Cooperative Learning: Does it Improve the Academic Achievement of Students with Handicaps?" *Exceptional Children* 56: 426-437.

Presents a review of the research on the effects of cooperative learning on the achievement of handicapped students. To be included in this review, studies must have included handicapped students as part of the sample. In addition, achievement had to be the dependent variable and cooperative learning the independent variable. As a result, only twelve studies met the criteria and were included for review purposes. Findings were inconsistent among the twelve studies, indicating a need for more research in this area before teachers are encouraged to use cooperative learning methods with mainstreamed special education students.

G. Vocational Education

Bell, J., V. Clark, E. Gebo, S. Lord. (1989). "FHA: Achieving Excellence Through Cooperative Learning." *NASSP Bulletin* 73: 114-117.

Reviews the findings of studies on cooperative learning conducted by Johnson and Johnson. Explains ways in which vocational student organizations, especially Future Homemakers of America, teach these skills in conjunction with academic content of courses. Outlines a five-step planning process involved in establishing cooperative activities. Concludes with suggestions for administrators about how to support and encourage increased cooperation.

Johnson, D.W. (1987). *Human Relations and Your Career: A Guide to Interpersonal Skills*, 2d ed. Englewood Cliffs, N.J.: Prentice-Hall, Inc.

Designed to teach students in career training programs the interpersonal and group skills they need to be successful. Experiential learning procedures are used to help students learn practical interpersonal skills. Each chapter begins with a questionnaire introducing the terms, concepts, and skills to be learned. Exercises are followed by relevant theory in social psychology to help students reach conclusions about their experiences.

The role of the teacher is explained and instruction and suggestions given for organizing students into cooperative groups. Students use learning contracts and participate in competitive tournaments. Evaluation and grading are explained. An informative, readable, practical book. If not used as a class text, should be included in a career education teacher's professional library.

III. General

A. Classroom Climate and Social Needs of Students

Carson, L., and S. Hoyle. (December 1989-January 1990). "Teaching Social Skills: A View From the Classroom." *Educational Leadership* 47, 4: 31.

A useful piece by two high school teachers on effective methods for teaching social skills—modeling the skill, taking social skills one at a time, easing students into using social skills, and rewarding groups in which all members in the group practice/display the social skill.

Johnson, D. W., and R. T. Johnson. (1989). "Social Interdependence and Self-Esteem." In *Cooperation and Competition: Theory and Research*, edited by D. W. Johnson and R. T. Johnson. Edina, Minn.: Interaction Book Company.

Defines self-esteem and explains its importance. The authors argue that a relationship exists between self-esteem and cooperation, competition, and individualism. Findings indicate that higher self-esteem is promoted in the cooperative situation than in the competitive or individualistic. Along with the cooperative situation come self-acceptance and greater self-esteem, whereas in the competitive situation, self-esteem is conditional and in the individualistic, self-esteem is turned to self-rejection.

Johnson, D. W., and R. T. Johnson. (December 1989-January 1990). "Social Skills for Successful Group Work." *Educational Leadership* 47, 4: 29-33.

An excellent piece on the value of teaching social skills and methods for doing so. Includes sections on teaching cooperative learning skills, using bonus points, long-term outcomes, and a discussion as to why teaching social skills is as important as teaching academic content.

Johnson, R. T., and D. W. Johnson. (1985). *Cooperative Learning: Warm-Ups, Grouping Strategies, and Group Activities*. Edina, Minn.: Interaction Book Company.

An activity booklet filled with exercises designed to reinforce and build on previous ideas for group work activities. Contains a wide assortment of lessons including warm-ups, grouping strategies, and cooperative group activities.

Kagan, S. (1985). "Learning to Cooperate." In *Learning to Cooperate, Cooperating to Learn*, edited by R. Slavin, S. Sharan, S. Kagan, R. Hertz-Lazarowitz, C. Webb, and R. Schmuck. New York: Plenum Press.

A fascinating essay on the need to incorporate cooperative, prosocial socialization experiences in schools especially in light of "the modern socialization void, the negative consequences of this void, and projected and economic needs."

Schultz, J.L. (December 1989-January 1990). "Cooperative Learning: Refining the Process." *Educational Leadership* 47, 4: 43-45.

Emphasizes the crucial need for teachers to give adequate attention to monitoring and teaching social skills if they are to introduce cooperative learning successfully. Addresses the author's initial difficulty and final triumph after some reflection, monitoring, and adjustment on his part.

B. Comparisons of Learning Conditions (Cooperative, Competitive, Individualistic)

Azmih, M. (1988). "Peer Interaction and Problem Problem Solving: When Are Two Heads Better Than One?" *Child Development* 59: 87-96.

Addresses the findings of three questions: 1. Does group work and cooperative activities lead to greater learning than independent study? 2. Does group and/or cooperative team learning generalize to later independent situations? 3. What characteristics of group interaction facilitate learning? Azmita found that preschool children are "more likely to acquire cognitive skills when they work with a more expert partner, only novices who worked with an expert generalized their skills to the individual post-test," and "observational learning and guidance by an expert mediated learning."

Griffin, R. (1988). "Cooperation, Competition, Individualism—Students Need All Three." *Clearing House* 62: 52.

A short article that presents the necessity, as well as the merits, of providing students a wide range of learning activities, including cooperative, competitive, and individual learning activities.

Johnson, D. W., and R. T. Johnson. (1985). "The Internal Dynamics of Cooperative Learning Groups." In *Learning to Cooperate, Cooperating to Learn*, edited by R. Slavin, S. Sharan, S. Kagan, R. Hertz-Lazarowitz, C. Webb, and R. Schmuck. New York: Plenum Press.

In their discussion of "the internal processes within cooperative learning groups that mediate or moderate the relationship between cooperation and productivity as well as interpersonal attraction among students," the Johnsons address the following: Theory of social interdependence, their research efforts and procedures, social interdependence and achievement, social interdependence and relationships among students, and various variables that illustrate internal dynamics of cooperative learning groups (e.g., type of task, quality of learning strategy, controversy versus concurrence seeking, time on task, cognitive processing, peer support, active mutual involvement in learning, ability levels of groups members, psychological support and acceptance, attitudes toward subject areas, and fairness of grading).

Johnson, D. W., and R. T. Johnson. (1989). "Motivational Processes." In *Cooperation and Competition: Theory and Research*, edited by D. W. Johnson and R. T. Johnson. Edina,   Minn.: Interaction Book Company.

Discusses motivation and its determinants which cause different levels of achievement. Results indicate that in the cooperative condition, achievement levels are high and positive in regards to success expectation, commitment, persistence, incentive to achieve, curiosity, and interest. In the competitive and individualistic conditions, results were low or negative in all areas except ability.

C. Cultural and Ethnic Differences

Cohen, E. G. (1986). *Designing Groupwork: Strategies for the Heterogeneous Classroom*. New York: Teachers College Press.

A guide for designing and encouraging participation in group activities regardless of race, sex, academic achievement, or socioeconomic class. The book may be an effective tool in teaching bilingual classes. Not specifically cooperative learning, but includes adaptable material.

Johnson, D. W., and R. T. Johnson. (1981). "Effects of Cooperative and Individualistic Learning Experiences on Inter-Ethnic Interaction." *Journal of Educational Psychology* 73, 3: 444- 449.

Results of the study involving fourth graders, indicate that cooperative learning experiences, compared with individualistic experiences, promote greater interaction between minority and majority students during instruction. This interaction is characterized by greater perceived helping between minority and majority students and stronger beliefs that students encourage and support each others efforts to learn, that students know each other and are friends, that students think through the rationale for their answers and apply and use what they know in new situations, that students work together and help each other, and that students do not work alone, without interacting with other students.

Findings also provide behavioral evidence that the cross-ethnic relationships created in cooperative learning groups do generalize to free-time, free-choice situations.

Kagan, S., G. L. Zahn, K. F. Widaman, J. Schwarzwald, and G. Tyrrell. (1985). "Classroom Structural Bias: Impact of Cooperative and Competitive Classroom Structures on Cooperative and Competitive Individuals and Groups." In *Learning to Cooperate, Cooperating to Learn*, edited by R. Slavin, S. Sharan, S. Kagan, R. Hertz-Lazarowitz, C. Webb, and R. Schmuck. New York: Plenum Press.

The express purpose of this essay is to present empirical evidence that addresses the hypothesis that "classroom structures common in the U.S. public schools discriminate against the achievement, the cultural values, and well-being of Mexican-American and black students (or the structural bias hypothesis)." Discusses the theory of structural bias, the (University of California's) Riverside Cooperative Learning Project, empirical evidence of structural bias, and conclusions.

Little Soldier, L. (1989). "Cooperative Learning and the Native American Student." *Phi Delta Kappan* 71, 2: 161-163.

Discusses how cooperative learning can be used to upgrade the quality of education for Native American children while remaining sensitive to cultural issues. Claims that cooperative learning matches traditional Indian values and behaviors such as respect for the individual, development of an internal locus of control, cooperation, sharing, and harmony. Also provides a discussion of how to use cooperative learning, mentions a few research studies, and potential benefits of cooperative learning for Native American students.

Sharan, S., P. Kuffell, R. Hertz-Lazarowitz, Y. Bejarano, S. Raviv, and Y. Sharan. (1985). "Cooperative Learning Effects on Ethnic Relations and Achievement in Israel: Junior-High School Classrooms." In *Learning to Cooperate, Cooperating to Learn*, edited by R. Slavin, S. Sharan, S. Kagan, R. Hertz-Lazarowitz, C. Webb, and R. Schmuck. New York: Plenum Press.

Describes a field experiment conducted in desegregated junior high schools in Israel that compared the effects of three teaching models (Group-Investigation, Student-Teams Achievement Divisions, and traditional whole-class instruction) on the pupil's academic learning, cooperative behavior, and attitudes toward peers of their own and of the other ethnic group. Describes the three teaching methods, the teachers and pupils, sources of teachers' resistance to the new strategies they were required to implement, the teacher training program, processes of implementation, dependent variables, academic achievement in English and literature, cooperative behavior that took place, and impact on social relations.

Strickland, D. S., and E. J. Cooper, eds. (1987). *Educating Black Children: America's Challenge*. Washington, D.C.: Bureau of Educational Research. (ERIC Document Reproduction Service No. ED 298 1 88).

A series of papers on effectively educating black children. In Section II, Robert E. Slavin ("Cooperative Learning and the Education of Black Students") discusses the use of cooperative learning as a successful strategy for increasing student achievement in both desegregated and majority-black schools. He finds that cooperative learning methods seem to be particularly effective for black students regardless of achievement level, possibly because black students are known to be more favorable toward cooperation with their peers than are white students. In addition to increased achievement, cooperative learning also causes students to have improved attitudes toward their classmates, particularly those of different ethnicities. Slavin emphasizes that the students themselves can be the most powerful, free instructional resource available in any school, when effectively involved in cooperative learning activities.

Towson, S. (1985). "Melting Pot or Mosaic: Cooperative Education and Interethnic Relations." In *Learning to Cooperate, Cooperating to Learn*, edited by R. Slavin, S. Sharan, S. Kagan, R. Hertz-Lazarowitz, C. Webb, and R. Schmuck. New York: Plenum Press.

Explores the idea that research on the use of cooperative learning as a teaching strategy "to facilitate positive interethnic relations has been profoundly affected by the two ideologies that have dominated North American thought on this issue: the melting pot and the mosaic—or, more prosaically, assimilation and pluralism."

D. Teacher Educational/ Staff Development

Aronson,E., and Goode, E. (1980). "Training Teachers to Implement Jigsaw Learning: A Manual for Teachers." In *Cooperation in Education*, edited by S. Sharan, P. Hare, C. D. Webb, and R. Hertz-Lazarowitz. Provo, Utah: Brigham Young University Press.

An overview of why and how the jigsaw strategy was developed as well as the "jigsaw classroom" (including how to implement team-building, constructing the jigsaw materials, teaching it to students, and a question and answer section on the jigsaw), and information about teacher training workshops on the jigsaw.

Bernagozzi, T. (February 1988). "The New Cooperative Learning." *Learning* 88: 38-43.

First hand account about the year Bernagozzi and his third grade class spent as part of a Johns Hopkins pilot program in cooperative learning. Discusses setting up teams, managing the scoring system, teaching cooperative skills, using cooperative learning to teach reading and writing, and pitfalls and benefits.

Bohlmeyer, E. M., and J. P. Burke. (1987). "Selecting Cooperative Learning Techniques: A Consultative Strategy Guide." *School Psychology Review* 16: 36-49.

A comprehensive article that presents "a classification scheme for cooperative learning techniques. This scheme can be utilized by consulting psychologists when collaborating with teachers to select cooperative learning techniques that are compatible with their styles of teaching and specific instructional objectives. " Included in the article are detailed descriptions of each category within the classification scheme: type of subject matter, nature of student interdependence, interaction among cooperative groups, method of grouping students, basis for evaluation and reward, and practical requirements for implementation. Nine cooperative learning strategies (Jigsaw, Group Investigation, STAD, TGT, Jigsaw II, Co-op Co-op, Circles of Learning (Learning Together), Small Group Mathematics, and TAI) are discussed and classified according to the classification scheme. Concludes with general guidelines for implementing cooperative learning. This is an article that anyone interested in cooperative learning should read.

Edwards, C., and J. Stout. (December 1989-January 1990). "Cooperative Learning: The First Year." *Educational Leadership* 47, 4: 38-41.

Two elementary teachers who use cooperative learning offer practical suggestions (e.g., pacing the program, assigning groups, determining group size, forming new groups, group responsibilities, and deciding when to use cooperative learning) to other educators.

Ellis, S. (1985). "Introducing Cooperative Learning Groups: A District-Wide Effort." *Journal of Staff Development* 6: 52-59.

Ellis describes the efforts of the Greenwich, Connecticut, public school system to train administrators and teachers in the use of cooperative learning strategies. She describes the components of the staff development program, the specific cooperative learning strategies that were taught, and the impact on the students and teachers vis-a-vis the use of such strategies.

Ellis, S. (December 1989-January 1990). "Introducing Cooperative Learning." *Educational Leadership* 47, 4: 34-37.

Discusses a successful teacher training program in cooperative learning. Addresses issues such as local support, district support, expanded opportunities for training, indistrict expertise, and tips on implementing cooperative learning.

Ferguson, P. (Winter 1989-1990). "Cooperative Team Learning: Theory Into Practice for the Prospective Middle School Teacher." *Action in Teacher Education* XI, 4: 24-28.

Discusses why and how cooperative learning is ideal for use with middle level students, describes an effort to employ a cooperative learning strategy (Jigsaw) as a vehicle for helping prospective middle school teachers enrolled in a social studies methods course translate theory into practice, and makes recommendations for the broader implementation of cooperative learning in middle school teacher education programs.

Glass, R. M., J. W. Putnam. (1988-1989). "Cooperative Learning in Teacher Education: A Case Study." *Action in Teacher Education* 10: 47-52.

This case study describes several ways in which cooperative learning can be used in teacher education courses as well as how students view their own learning and performance during cooperative learning activities. In doing so, it discusses the following: Definitions of cooperative learning; why and how cooperative learning can be used in teacher education programs; an overview of such cooperative learning strategies as Jigsaw, informal resource groups, study teams, group projects; and an analysis of a cooperative learning survey the authors administered to a sampling of their undergraduate and graduate students at the University of Maine, Farmington.

Johnson, D. W., R. T. Johnson. (1984). "Cooperative Small-Group Learning." *Curriculum Report* 1: 1-6.

A brief but detailed overview of the theory and practice of cooperative learning. Initially defines key elements of cooperative learning and then delineates principles of implementation along with nineteen specific steps of implementation. Also provides guidelines and tips in regard to how principals can most successfully promote and support cooperative learning in their schools. Concludes with descriptions of two district-wide cooperative learning programs.

Johnson, D. W., and R. T. Johnson. (1987). "Implementing Cooperative Learning: The Teachers' Role." In *Structuring Cooperative Learning: Lesson Plans for Teachers 1987*, edited by R. T. Johnson, D. W. Johnson, and E. J. Holubec. Edina, Minn.: Interaction Book Company.

Explains five sets of strategies included in the teacher's role when implementing cooperative learning: 1. clearly specifying objectives for the lesson; 2. making decisions about placing students in groups before teaching the lesson; 3. clearly explaining the task, goal structure, and learning activity to students; 4. monitoring effectiveness of groups and intervening to provide task assistance or to increase students' interpersonal and group skills; and 5. evaluating students' achievement and helping students discuss success with elaboration. The strategies are broken down into eighteen practical steps which elaborate upon and detail a procedure for structuring cooperative learning.

Johnson, D. W., R. T. Johnson, and E. J. Holubec. (1987). "Getting Started with Cooperative Groups." In *Structuring Cooperative Learning: Lesson Plans for Teachers 1987*, edited by R. T. Johnson, D. W. Johnson, and E. J. Holubec. Edina, Minn.: Interaction Book Company.

Discusses the stages teachers often go through as they learn to implement cooperative learning in their classrooms. Contains practical suggestions and advice on assigning students to learning groups and quick cooperation starters. Outlines the jigsaw method and lists a variety of roles which may be assigned to student working in groups. Also includes a skills checklist for students, a checklist for teachers' role in cooperative learning, an observation form, and two generic cooperative lesson plan forms. A section on structuring academic controversies in the classroom wraps up the article.

Johnson, R. T., and D. W. Johnson. (1985). "Student-Student Interaction: Ignored but Powerful." *Journal of Teacher Education* 34: 22-26

Reviews the research on three goal structures (cooperative, competitive, and individualistic) and discusses the implications for teacher education programs. Argues that "research indicates that cooperation should be the dominant interaction pattern in the classroom and researchers cite advantages of a predominantly cooperative setting over a predominantly competitive or individualistic setting."

Johnson, R. T., and D. W. Johnson. (1987). "Monitoring Groups Effectively." In *Structuring Cooperative Learning: Lesson Plans for Teachers 1987*, edited by R. T. Johnson, D. W. Johnson, and E. J. Holubec. Edina, Minn.: Interaction Book Company.

Explains the tasks related to monitoring students as they work cooperatively. Providing task assistance, collecting data on students' behavior in the groups, and intervening to teach specific cooperative skills were identified as the three most important monitoring tasks for teachers. Simple rules for intervening in groups are suggested.

Joyce, B., B. Showers, C. Rolheiser-Bennett. (1987). "Staff Development and Student Learning: A Synthesis of Research on Models of Teaching." *Educational Leadership* 45, 2: 11-23.

The authors assert that it is now possible "to design staff development programs around teaching approaches with potential for increasing student learning." The section on social models discusses cooperative learning at some length (pp. 14-17). The authors state that "Cooperative learning approaches, representing social models of teaching, yield effect sizes from modest to high. The more complex the outcomes—higher order thinking, problem solving, social skills and attitudes—the greater are the effects."

Kagan, S. (1990). *Cooperative Learning Workshops for Teachers*. San Juan Capistrano, Calif.: Resources for Teachers.

For teachers who want to put together workshops on cooperative learning. Over 100 pages of background material and suggestions.

Lyman, L. and H.C. Foyle. (1990). *Cooperative Grouping for Interactive Learning: Students, Teachers, and Administrators*. Washington D.C.: National Education Association.

This volume in the NEA School Restructuring Series presents a plan for extending cooperative learning throughout a school, from students to administrators. Includes specific strategies and plans for implementation with useful examples and activities.

Prescott, S. (Winter 1989-1990). "Teachers Perceptions of Factors that Affect Successful Implementation of Cooperative Learning." *Action in Teacher Education* XI, 4: 30-34.

A thought-provoking article that examines comments from 30 elementary and twenty-one secondary teachers in regard to factors that contribute to and interfere with successful implementation of cooperative learning. Among the factors discussed are the following: reward systems, composition of team members, teaching/management skills, activity design, readiness phase, student evaluation, and student characteristics.

Pusch, L., J. McCabe, and W. Pusch. (1985). "From Awareness to Personalized On-Site Coaching." *The Journal of Staff Development* 6: 88-92.

Discusses the role and importance of peer coaching in cooperatively structured settings. Outlines one six-month staff development program implemented for the purpose of helping teachers "to acquire the basic theoretical background of the cooperative-learning method of teaching, of being able to demonstrate the cooperative-learning teaching strategies in the classroom, and of viewing peer coaching "as a valuable process for assisting transfer of a new teaching model into the classroom." Reports that the objectives were satisfactorily met mainly because of the peer coaching element.

Sapon-Shevin, M., and N. Schniedewind. (December 1989-January 1990). "Selling Cooperative Learning Without Selling it Short." *Educational Leadership* 47, 4: 63-65.

Urges teachers to be more reflective vis-a-vis their use of cooperative learning and to consider such issues as: Reflecting on content, making content and process compatible, coordinating the approach with other classroom values, giving teachers and students a voice, eliminating competition, and promoting cooperative learning appropriately.

Sharan, Y., and S. Sharan. (November 1987). "Training Teachers For Cooperative Learning." *Educational Leadership* 45, 3: 20-25.

Focuses on how creating a cooperative learning situation/classroom for themselves in a workshop setting is valuable preparation for teachers who wish to foster norms of helping and sharing among their students. At the outset the Sharans, professors in Israel and noted researchers/proponents of cooperative learning, discuss the "experiential learning model" and then cogently delineate how to design and implement a cooperative learning experiential workshop.

Thew, D. (1980). "Teacher Education for Cooperative Learning." In *Cooperation in Education*, edited by S. Sharan, P. Hare, C. D. Webb, and R. Hertz-Lazarowitz. Provo, Utah: Brigham Young University Press.

Describes a plan for assisting elementary preservice teachers to acquire the skills to promote inter-student cooperative learning.

Tyrrell, R. (January 1990). "What Teachers Say About Cooperative Learning." *Middle School Journal* 21, 3: 16-19.

Argues that cooperative learning is an ideal strategy that builds on the learning styles of early adolescents and one that lends itself to a climate that is more conducive to the needs of such students. Also discusses how and why the training of teachers in cooperative learning was implemented in the Program of Studies for Teachers of Emerging Adolescents at Cleveland State University as well as the outcomes that ensued.

E. Academic Achievement

Johnson, D. W., and R. T. Johnson. (1987). "The High Achieving Student in Cooperative Learning Groups." In *Structuring Cooperative Learning: Lesson Plans for Teachers 1987*, edited by R. T. Johnson, D. W. Johnson, and E. J. Holubec. Edina, Minn.: Interaction Book Company.

Gives several practical suggestions for encouraging high ability students to work cooperatively in groups. Cites research showing improved grades, higher-level reasoning strategies, higher creativity, development of friendships and social skills.

Johnson, D. W., and R. T. Johnson. (1989). *Cooperation and Competition: Theory and Research*. Hillsdale, N.J.: Lawrence Erlbaum.

A comprehensive review of cooperative learning studies. Three hundred and fifty-two studies have been meta-analyzed and the results reduced to a single analysis. When all studies were included in the analysis, the average student in a cooperative situation performed at about 2/3 a standard deviation above average students in a competitive learning situation and 3/4 a standard deviation above average students in an individualistic situation. When the results of "pure" cooperative learning strategies were compared with "mixed" strategies (i.e. original Jigsaw, Teams-Games-Tournaments, Team-Assisted Instruction, and Student-Teams Achievement Divisions), "pure" operationalizations consistently produced significantly higher achievement. Results of the meta-analysis are reported and discussed for a number of other areas, including motivation, emotional involvement in learning, achievement and productivity, social skills, attitudes, and critical thinking competencies. Discusses limitations of many of the studies.

Johnson, D. W, R. T. Johnson, and S. Yager. (1985). "Oral Discussion, Group-to-Individual Transfer, and Achievement in Cooperative Learning Groups." *Journal of Educational Psychology* 77: 60-66.

In the first study noted, students were placed in one of three groups: conventional classroom, cooperative learning (CL) groups, and CL groups with 5 minutes of "group processing" at the end of each lesson. Scores on a retention test given three weeks after the unit were as follows (pretest average: 50 percent): conventional class scored 65 percent, CL groups scored 75 percent, and CL groups with group processing scored 87 percent. In addition, the gap between scores of students of different "ability" levels decreased.

In a second study, discussion was "structured" with students assuming a role of "learning leader" or active questioner. Retention scores for conventional , CL, and structured discussion CL groups were 49 percent, 70 percent, and 95 percent respectively.

Lambiotte, J. G., D. F. Dansereau, T. R. Rocklin, B. Fletcher, V. I. Hythecker, C. O. Larson, and A. M. O'Donnell. (1987). "Cooperative Learning and Test Taking: Transfer of Skills." *Contemporary Educational Psychology* 12: 52-61.

> Discusses a study designed to test effects of cooperative learning upon studying and test taking. Four treatments were used: Cooperative learning/cooperative testing, cooperative learning/individual testing, individual learning/cooperative testing, and individual learning/individual testing. Results indicate that cooperative learning positively affects recall performance and accuracy.

Slavin, R. E. (October 1988). "Cooperative Learning and Student Achievement." *Educational Leadership* 46, 2: 31-33.

> A highly significant article. Slavin notes that over the years numerous and impressive claims have been made about the effectiveness of cooperative learning. While many of these are true, the research shows that to produce achievement gains, cooperative learning methods must include both group goals and individual accountability. He also provides a succinct, but informative discussion about the achievements gained when using various cooperative learning methods.

Slavin, R. E. (1990). *Ability Grouping and Student Achievement in Secondary Schools: A Best-Evidence Synthesis.* Baltimore, Md.: Johns Hopkins University, Center for Research on Elementary and Middle Schools.

Slavin, R. E. (Fall 1990). "Achievement Effects of Ability Grouping in Secondary Schools: A Best-Evidence Synthesis." *Review of Educational Research* 60, 3: 471-499.

> Under a section entitled "Alternatives to Ability Grouping" (pp. 492-493), Slavin discusses various types of cooperative learning methods (e.g., he cites Cooperative Integrated Reading and Composition or CIRC and Team Assisted Individualization or TAI as particularly effective for use in middle schools) that have been found to be effective alternatives to ability grouping.

F. Cooperation and Cooperative Learning: General Information

Augustine, D. K., K. D. Gruber, and L. R. Hanson. (December 1989-January 1990). "Cooperation Works!" *Educational Leadership* 47, 4: 3.

> A testimonial to the effects of cooperative learning by three teachers (grades 6, 3, 4, respectively). Discusses effects on achievement, use with gifted students, and dramatic changes they have witnessed regarding perspectives on both teaching and learning.

Brandt, R. (November 1987). "Is Cooperation Un-American?" *Educational Leadership* 45, 3: 3.

> Discusses the current popularity of cooperative learning in classrooms across the U.S., cites research by Johnson and Johnson, Slavin, and Joyce in regard to the benefits of using cooperative learning, and concludes that while Americans "have always prized individuality" we also need teamwork.

Brandt, R. (November 1987). "On Cooperation in Schools: A Conservation with David and Roger Johnson." *Educational Leadership* 45, 3: 14-19.

> An informative interview with two of the main researchers and proponents of cooperative learning. The following issues are discussed: how widespread cooperative learning is at the classroom level, the empirical support for cooperative learning, various outcomes that result when cooperative learning is used correctly, the five elements (positive interdependence, face-to-face interaction, individual accountability, group process, and social skills) it takes to make cooperative learning work, and the type of support system teachers need in order to successfully implement this strategy.

Bregman, G. (October 1989). "Cooperative Learning: A New Strategy for the Art Room." *School Arts*: 32-33.

> Discusses how art teachers can combine a traditional ceramics project with cooperative learning to bring about a more powerful learning experience. Briefly describes components of cooperative learning, and explains how to set up the ceramics/cooperative learning project and how to evaluate the learning exercise.

Brubacher, M., R. Payne, and K. Pickett, eds. (1990). *Perspectives on Small Group Learning.* Oakville, Ontario: Rubicon Publishing Co.

> Includes the following chapters on cooperative learning: Shlomo Sharan's "The Group Investigation Approach to Cooperative Learning: Theoretical Foundations"; David and Roger Johnson's "What is Cooperative Learning?"; David and Roger Johnson's "Cooperative Classrooms"; Yael Sharan's "Group Investigation: Expanding Cooperative Learning"; Laurel Robertson's "Cooperative Learning Ala CLIP"; Spencer Kagan's "Cooperative Learning for Students Limited in Language Proficiency"; and Ioane Coucian's "Cooperative Learning and Second Language Teaching." Many of the other articles (e.g., "The Role of the Teacher in Small Group Learning," "A Climate for Small Group Learning," and "Using Group Process to Transform the Educational Experience") should also be of interest to educators working with cooperative learning.

Carnegie Council on Adolescent Development. (1989). *Turning Points: Preparing Youth for the 21st Century.* New York: Carnegie Council on Adolescent Development.

> A major report on the educational needs of young adolescents and a clarion call vis-a-vis the need for special organization of schools and programs for this age (10-14 year olds) child. Among the many recommendations posited herein is the need "to focus once again on the goal that ranking sought to achieve in the first place: effectively teaching students of diverse ability and differing rates of learning." (p. 50). One such method, the authors report, for reaching such a goal is cooperative learning. On page 51, a section entitled "Mathematics Students Cooperate to Accelerate" includes a discussion of Team-Accelerated Instruction (TAI).

Cohen, E. G. (1986). *Designing Group-Work: Strategies for the Heterogeneous Classroom.* New York: Teachers College Press. (Foreword by John I. Goodlad)

> Discusses and illustrates how students can more actively contribute, share, and learn when group-work is integrated into the classroom. Acknowledges the problems and successes of group-work and provides numerous useful suggestions for remedying such problems. Intended for use by elementary and secondary school teachers, this volume combines easy to understand theory and teaching suggestions. Individual chapters address the following: why it's worthwhile to use groups, the problems one faces when using groups, planning strategies, etc. Chapter 4 is entitled "Preparing Students for Cooperation," and focuses on training for cooperation, and cooperation and prosocial behavior.

Cohen, E. G. (October 1990). "Continuing to Cooperate: Prerequisites for Persistence." *Phi Delta Kappan* 72, 2: 134-138.

> An engaging article by a proponent of cooperative learning who initially states: "I greatly fear that—unless developers, disseminators, and practitioners realize that establishing a cooperative learning program requires more than attending a few workshops and attempting to assist one another in developing materials and managing classrooms—we will quickly see both teachers and students burn out on these new techniques" (p. 135). She then cogently examines the following issues: "The Need for New Materials," "Treatment of Status Problems" (e.g., "the problem of unequal participation in groups"), and "Changes in the Organization of Teaching."

Deutsch, M. (1949). "A Theory of Co-operation and Competition." *Human Relations* 2: 129-152.

A landmark article on the subject of cooperation. "The purpose of this article is to sketch out a theory of the effect of co-operation and competition upon small (face-to-face) group functioning." Deutsch addresses the following issues and concepts: definitions of "co-operation" and "competition," basic concepts in the theory of co-operation and competition, implications resulting from a study of the basic concepts, psychological implications inherent in various types of social situations, hypotheses that test the effects of co-operation and competition upon group processes, and relationships of group concepts. He also states 34 hypotheses designed to test the effects of co-operation upon self-esteem, substitutability, cathexis, individuality, helpfulness, organization motivation, communication, group productivity, and interpersonal behavior.

Deutsch, M. (1962). "Cooperation and Trust: Some Theoretical Notes." In *Nebraska Symposium on Motivation*, edited by M. R. Jones. Nebraska: University of Nebraska Press.

An important document on cooperation, the paper is divided into three sections: 1. the psychological consequences of cooperation and competition; 2. the conditions necessary to establish cooperative situations; and 3. the relationships between trust and cooperation. A key finding is that "a cooperative orientation primarily leads the individual to make a cooperative choice and results in mutual gain, while a competitive orientation primarily leads the individual to make a non-cooperative choice and results in mutual loss." The article is necessary reading for anyone interested in the concepts of cooperation and competition.

Graves, N. B., and T. D. Graves, eds. (1987). *Cooperative Learning—A Resource Guide*. (Available from the International Association for the Study of Cooperation in Education, 136 Liberty Street, Santa Cruz, CA 95060.)

This bibliography is comprised of 120 titles and references on various aspects of cooperative learning. The major sections of the bibliography are: Specific Cooperative Learning Strategies, Creating a Cooperative Classroom Climate, Cooperative Outdoor Education, Cooperative Learning and Science Education, Cooperative Learning and Mathematics, Cooperative Learning and Computers, Cooperative Learning and Social Studies, Cooperative Learning and Language Arts, and Second Language Learning.

Johnson, D. W., and R. T. Johnson. (1984). *Cooperation in the Classroom*. Edina, Minn.: Interaction Book Company.

The manual used by the Johnsons in their cooperative learning workshops. Contains practical suggestions for teaching collaborative skills to students. The seven chapters: "What Is Cooperative Learning," "The Teacher's Role in Cooperation," "Research Evidence on Cooperative Learning," "Creating Positive Interdependence," "Teaching Students Collaborative Skills," "Processing for Effective Cooperative Learning Groups," "Building a Climate for Acceptance of Differences," provide an excellent overview in the use of cooperative learning methods. Practical suggestions and clear explanations of activities will allow teachers to immediately implement introductory cooperative learning activities into their classes.

Johnson, D. W., and R. T. Johnson. (1985). "Cooperative Learning and Adaptive Education." In *Adapting Instruction to Individual Differences*, edited by M. C. Wang and H. J. Walberg. Berkeley, Calif.: McCutchan Publishing Corporation.

At the outset of the chapter the Johnsons define adaptive instruction and discuss how cooperative learning is an excellent adaptive learning strategy. Under the discussion of cooperative learning they discuss the following: critical components of cooperative learning, achievement paradox, social interdependency and achievement, internal dynamics of cooperative learning groups, other achievement-related outcomes, structuring adaptiveness into cooperative learning groups, and socialization paradox.

Johnson, D. W., and R. T. Johnson. (1985). "The Internal Dynamics of Cooperative Learning Groups." In *Learning to Cooperate, Cooperating to Learn*, edited by R. Slavin, S. Sharan, S. Kagan, R. Hertz-Lazarowitz, C. Webb, and R. Schmuck. New York: Plenum Press.

In their discussion of "the internal processes within cooperative learning groups that mediate or moderate the relationship between cooperation and productivity as well as interpersonal attraction among students," the Johnsons address the Theory of social interdependence, their research efforts and procedures, social interdependence and achievement, social interdependence and relationships among students, and various variables that illustrate internal dynamics of cooperative learning groups (e.g., type of task, quality of learning strategy, controversy versus concurrence seeking, time on task, cognitive processing, peer support, active mutual involvement in learning, ability levels of groups members, psychological support and acceptance, attitudes toward subject areas, and fairness of grading).

Johnson, D. W., and R. T. Johnson. (1987). *Learning Together and Alone: Cooperative, Competitive, and Individualistic Learning*. Englewood Cliffs, N.J.: Prentice-Hall.

Discusses methods for systematically using cooperative, competitive, and individualistic learning in the classroom. Chapter one compares the use of the three types of instruction with an emphasis on developing interdependence among students. Chapter two discusses the importance of peer relationships, student interaction patterns, and instructional outcomes of cooperative, competitive, and individualistic learning. Chapters three, four, and five explain the structuring of each of the three types of learning. Additional chapters discuss "student acquisition of collaborative skills," how to create positive interdependence, and explain group processing. Chapter nine is devoted exclusively to teacher concerns such as classroom management, high and low achievers, and cooperation among teachers. An epilogue stresses the importance of cooperative learning to the future of education.

Johnson, D. W., and R. T. Johnson. (1989). *Leading the Cooperative School*. Edina, Minn.: Interaction Book Company.

Focuses on using cooperative learning strategies to enable teachers and administrators to work together to achieve shared goals. "What is good for students, is even better for faculty." While recognizing that most teachers work independently or even competitively and are often reluctant to interrupt the status quo, the Johnsons have written a book encouraging and outlining a systematic change of attitudes toward and adoption of cooperative working environments in the schools. A research-based rationale supporting cooperating learning is included along with practical strategies for structuring cooperative faculty teams. The book is a valuable aid for administrators interested in restructuring their schools to a cooperative learning and teaching format. The Johnsons have included an excellent summary of their recent meta-analysis of the research on cooperative, competitive, and individualistic research.

Kohn, A. (1987). "It's Hard to Get Left Out Of A Pair." *Psychology Today* 21: 53-57.

An interesting and informative profile of David and Roger Johnson, two of the leading researchers, teacher trainers, and advocates of cooperative learning. They discuss why they are such keen advocates of cooperative learning, explain what cooperative learning is, and talk about their research on cooperative learning, and the practical aspects of that research.

Miel, A. (1952). *Cooperative Procedures in Learning*. New York: Bureau of Publications, Teachers College, Columbia University.

An early and significant volume on the value and place of cooperation in the classroom as well as a discussion of procedures teachers can use to implement cooperation in the class. It reports the findings of classroom teachers and other school people who worked with the staff of the Horace Mann-Lincoln Institute of

School of Experimentation (at Teachers College, Columbia University) in an effort to learn more about cooperative procedures in schools.

Pepitone, E. A., ed. (1980). *Children in Cooperation and Competition.* Lexington, Mass.: Lexington Books.

Part I, which was written by Pepitone, covers the following: Major Trends in Research on Competition and Cooperation, 1897-1980; theoretical orientation on competition and cooperation; and the research methodology used in a majority of the studies presented in Part II. Part II is comprised of a series of research reports on competitive, cooperative, and collaborative interactions among students. Concludes with a lengthy list of useful references (pp. 413-439).

Poirier, G. A. (1970). *Students as Partners in Team Learning Through Diagnostic and Individualized Teaching.* Berkeley, Calif.: Center of Team Teaching.

Poirier's team learning approach was a predecessor of the cooperative learning strategies later developed by Slavin, et al. Various chapters describe the team learning concept, team learning activities, and methods for rating, scoring, and rewarding.

Rath, J. (October 1987). "Enhancing Understanding Through Debriefing." *Educational Leadership* 45, 2: 24-27.

In this general overview on the value of debriefing, Rath notes that "the recent work in cognitive psychology and cooperative learning supports the claim that debriefing enhances learning. Yeager, Johnson and Johnson (1985) assert that recent meta-analysis demonstrate that intermittent summarizing or recalling increase students' ability to remember what they learned." "Cognitive rehearsal," the process that occurs when students talk about what they have learned, is viewed as "one of the most promising of the mediating variables' examined to account for the success of cooperative learning."

Schaps, E., D. Solomon, and M. Watson. (December 1985-January 1986). "A Program that Combines Character Development and Academic Achievement." *Educational Leadership* 43, 4: 32-35.

Discusses the Child Development Project of San Ramon, California, which claims to produce intellectual gains while also influencing students' prosocial behavior. The purpose of the project is to "refine, increase, and coordinate five types of activities that most teachers or parents already do to some degree," including engaging children in cooperative activities and promoting social understanding. Presents an overview of the program, discusses research that has examined how the projects works, and discusses the effects that the program has had. Also includes a sidebar entitled "Cooperative Learning in Action" (p. 34) which presents a scenario of children in a second grade class using cooperative learning.

Schmuck, R, and P. A. Schmuck. (1983). *Group Processing in the Classroom.* Dubuque, Iowa: William C. Brown Company Publishers.

A guide for teachers who wish to implement a cooperative classroom curriculum. Topics include cohesion, communication, and conflict.

Schniedewind, N., and E. Davidson. (1987). *Cooperative Learning, Cooperative Lives: A Sourcebook of Learning Activities for Building a Peaceful World.* Dubuque, Iowa: William C. Brown Company Publishers.

Among the chapters in this volume are the following: "Why Cooperative Learning and Living"; "The Nuts and Bolts of Implementing Cooperative Learning"; "Joining Together at School"; and "Working Together for Worldwide Interdependence and Peace." It also includes a section of resources (e.g., "Teaching formats for Cooperative Learning," "Evaluation Formats for Cooperative Learning," "What Would You do if . . .?" and "Teacher and Students Say . . .?"), and a detailed bibliography.

Sharan, S., P. Hare, C. D. Webb, and R. Hertz-Lazarowitz., eds. (1980). *Cooperation in Education.* Provo, Utah: Brigham Young University Press.

Based on the proceedings of the first International Conference on Cooperation in Education, this highly informative volume is comprised of 25 essays on various aspects of cooperative learning. Section 1 ("Life in Schools and "Classrooms") includes essays of small group methods, school programs, and research. Section 2 is entitled "Professional Training," and Section 3 is entitled "School-Community Relations." Includes pieces by such noted cooperative learning specialists as Elliot Aronson, Spencer Kagan, Shlomo Sharan, and Robert E. Slavin. Pertinent essays in this volume are separately annotated in this bibliography.

Sharan, S., and Y. Sharan. (1976). *Small-Group Teaching.* Englewood Cliffs, N.J.: Prentice Hall.

A comprehensive overview of small-group teaching. Includes chapters on a rationale for using small groups and describes how small groups work, types of small groups, and organizing small-group learning.

Sharan, Y., and S. Sharan. (December 1989-January 1990). "How Effective is Group Investigation?" *Educational Leadership* 47, 4: 18.

Discusses research findings on the group investigation method vis-a-vis academic achievement, social interaction, and teacher reaction to implementation of a new teaching strategy.

Slavin, R. E. (1983). *Cooperative Learning.* New York: Longman.

An outstanding text that thoroughly integrates research findings with the author's analysis of cooperative learning. Addresses the following: definition of key concepts, discussion of various cooperative learning strategies, a review and analysis of the literature regarding cooperative learning and its impact on student achievement and intergroup relations, a section on mainstreaming academically handicapped students, and a presentation of evidence of the effects of cooperative learning on non-cognitive outcomes such as self-esteem and classroom behavior. One of the most interesting and provocative conclusions is "that the effects of cooperative learning . . . are primarily motivational effects, not process effects; cooperative incentive structures explain the effects of cooperative learning on achievement."

Slavin, R. E. (October 1987). "A Visit to a Cooperative School." *Educational Leadership* 45, 2: 11.

Provides a scenario of what a "cooperative school" (one in which cooperative learning is used in the 3 R's and across every grade level, and where teachers are working cooperatively to help students to learn) would look like if such a program were implemented.

Slavin, R. E. (October 1987). "Cooperative Learning and the Cooperative School." *Educational Leadership* 45, 2: 7-13.

Slavin claims that with "cooperative learning programs capable of being used all year in the 3 R's, it is now possible to design an elementary school program based upon a radical principle: students, teachers, and administrators can work cooperatively to make the school a better place for working and learning." Among the issues he discusses are: "What is cooperative learning and why does it work?"; "Under what conditions is cooperative learning effective?"; "Comprehensive cooperative learning models"; and "The cooperative school today."

Slavin, R. E. (1988). "Research on Cooperative Learning: Why Does it Matter?" *Newsletter. The International Association for the Study of Cooperation in Education* 9, 3-4: 3.

Slavin's statements emphasize the importance of continuing research into cooperative learning. His first reason for continuing research is to ensure that cooperative learning achieve the status of a practical, effective method so that it cannot simply go out of style with the next "back-to-basics" movement. Secondly, Slavin wishes to establish a clear set of elements "essential" to cooperative learning, so that teachers may add their own modifications while understanding what is essential, to use cooperative learning for greatest effectiveness (for example, team scores are cited as an essential part of Student Team Learning, and it is noted that many cooperative strategies are equal in effectiveness to whole-class methods). Finally, the ethical aspect is noted.

Slavin, R. E. (1988). "The Cooperative Revolution in Education." *The School Administrator* 45: 9-13.

Speaks about the popularity and pervasiveness of cooperative learning in U.S. schools, describes cooperative learning, and briefly discusses key research findings. Also talks about how it is possible to design a school based "on the radical principle that students, teachers, and administrators can work cooperatively to make the school a better place for learning in the classroom, integration of special education and remedial services, peer coaching, cooperative planning, building-level steering committee, and cooperation with parents and community members."

Slavin, R. E., ed. (1989). *School and Classroom Organization*. Hilldale, N.J.: Lawrence Erlbaum Associates, Publishers.

Contains an entire chapter on cooperative learning (Slavin's "Cooperative Learning and Student Achievement") and brief discussions of Team Assisted Individualization in two other chapters (Slavin's "A Theory of School and Classroom Organization" and Leinhardt's and Bickel's "Instruction's the Thing Wherein to Catch the Mind that Falls Behind").

Slavin, R. E. (December 1989-January 1990). "Here to Stay or Gone Tomorrow?" *Educational Leadership* 47, 4: 3.

A powerful and insightful article on the dangers of widespread adoption of cooperation learning by large numbers of teachers who only have "half-knowledge" about the strategies.

Slavin, R. E. (1990). *Cooperative Learning: Theory, Research, and Practice*. Englewood Cliffs, N.J.: Prentice Hall.

An outstanding handbook for elementary and secondary school teachers, it includes up-to-date research findings, a host of practical ideas (including step-by-step advice for implementing various cooperative learning strategies), and resources (including sample worksheets, quizzes, and award certificates). One of the most unique and valuable components of the volume are the section entitled "Teachers on Teaching," where practicing teachers comment on their experiences concerning various aspects of cooperative learning. The seven chapters are: An Introduction to Cooperative Learning, Cooperative Learning and Student Achievement, Cooperative Learning and Outcomes Other Than Achievement, STAD and TGT, TAI and CIRC, Task Specialization Methods, and Other Cooperative Learning Methods and Resources. Also includes a lengthy bibliography.

Slavin, R. E., N. L. Karweit, and N. A. Madden. (1989). *Effective Programs for Students at Risk*. Boston: Allyn and Bacon..

Three chapters (Chapter 2, Slavin et al.'s "Effective Classroom Programs for Students at Risk"; Chapter 10 Larrivee's "Effective Strategies for Academically Handicapped Students in the Regular Classroom"; and Chapter 12, Slavin et al.'s "Effective Programs for Students at Risk: Conclusion for Practice and Policy") in this volume briefly discuss Cooperative Integrated Reading and Composition (CIRC) and Team Assisted Individualization (TAI), and the role they have and can play in addressing the needs of students at risk.

Strother, D. B. (October 1990). "Cooperative Learning: Fad or Foundation for Learning." *Phi Delta Kappan* 72, 2: 158-162.

A thought-provoking and outstanding article that all teachers who use or plan to use cooperative learning need to read. Using the insights of such luminaries as Deutsch, Slavin, Sharan, and others, she addresses the following factors: "What makes it work,"

"Factors that lead to failure," the usefulness of specific cooperative learning models, and the issue as to how much training is needed before one can be proficient in the use of a model.

IV. Research on Cooperation

Johnson, D. W. (1989). *Cooperation and Competition: Theory and Research*. Edina, Minn: Interaction Book Company.

Over 500 studies were included in this meta-analysis. Studies were analyzed and coded for: sample size, group size, length of study, subject area, control condition, random assignment, teacher rotation, curriculum same, conditions checked, study's methodological quality.

Sharan, S., ed. (1990). *Cooperative Learning: Theory and Research*. New York: Praeger.

Contains the following essays: George Knight and Elaine Bohlmeyer's "Cooperative Learning and Achievement: Methods for Assessing Causal Mechanisms"; David and Roger Johnson's "Cooperative Learning and Achievement"; Norman Miller and Hugh Harrington's "A Situational Identity Perspective on Cultural Diversity and Teamwork in the Classroom"; Rachel Hertz-Lazarowitz and Hana Shachar's "Teachers' Verbal Behavior in Cooperative and Whole-Class Instruction"; Gordon Wells, Gen Ling M. Chang and Ann Maher's "Creating Classroom Communities of Literate Thinkers"; Reuven Lazarowitz and Gabby Karsenty's "Cooperative Learning and Students' Academic Achievement, Process Skills, Learning Environment, and Self-Esteem in Tenth-Grade Biology Classrooms"; Gunter Huber and Renate Eppler's "Team Learning in German Classrooms: Processes and Outcomes"; Shlomo Sharan and Ada Shaulov's "Cooperative Learning, Motivation to Learn, and Academic Achievement"; Elizabeth Cohen, Rachel Lotan, and Lisa Catanzarite's "Treating Status Problems in the Cooperative Classroom"; Daniel Solomon et al.'s "Cooperative Learning as Part of a Comprehensive Classroom Designed to Promote Prosocial Development"; Robert Slavin's "Comprehensive Cooperative Learning Model: Embedding Cooperative Learning in the Curriculum and the School"; and Shlomo Sharan's "Cooperative Learning: A Perspective on Research and Practice."

Solomon, D., M. Watson, V. Battistich, E. Schaps, P. Tuck, J. Solomon, C. Cooper, and W. Ritchey. (1985). "A Program to Promote Interpersonal Consideration and Cooperation in Children." In *Learning to Cooperate, Cooperating to Learn*, edited by R. Slavin, S. Sharan, S. Kagan, R. Hertz-Lazarowitz, C. Webb, and R. Schmuck. New York: Plenum Press.

Describes a project whose purpose was to develop and evaluate the effectiveness of a comprehensive school- and home-based program (Child Development Program) to enhance pro-social tendencies in young children. Discusses the theoretical model used, the program, evaluation of the program, significance of the program, and future directions.

Totten, S., T. Sills, A. Digby, and P. Russ. (1991). *Cooperative Learning: A Guide to Research*. New York: Garland Press.

This volume contains 818 annotations vis-a-vis the following subjects and topics on cooperative learning: various cooperative learning strategies (Co-op Co-op, Group Investigation, Jigsaw, Structured Controversy, Student Assisted Instruction (TAI), Student Teams Achievement Divisions (STAD), Teams Games Tournaments (TGT)); specific strategies germane to specific subject areas (art, computers, language arts, mathematics, science); classroom climate and social needs of students; comparisons of learning conditions (cooperative, competitive, and individualistic); cultural and ethnic differences; teacher education and staff development; academic achievement; research on cooperation and cooperative learning; book reviews; films and videos; newsletters; and organizations.

VI. Film/Videos

CIRC (Videotape) Available from Dissemination Office, Center for Research on Elementary and Middle Schools, Johns Hopkins University, 3503 N. Charles St., Baltimore, MD 21228.

Describes the CIRC (Cooperative Integrated Reading and Composition Program) while showing it being implemented in a classroom. The video is useful for providing awareness of CIRC to staff members.

Cooperative Learning (videotape). Available from Teaching Inc., P.O. Box 788, Edmonds, WA 98020.

This video is includes many practical ideas. Several elementary classroom clips highlight the following: the importance of cooperative learning, the type of classroom routines and the necessary social skills that need to be taught. Includes a complete lesson with a master teacher demonstrating how to set up a cooperative lesson for a writing assignment."

Johnson, D. W., R. T. Johnson. (writers and producers). *Controversy in the Classroom* (videotape). (1979). Interaction Book Company, 7208 Cornelia Drive, Edina, MN 55435.

Written and produced by Roger and David Johnson in 1979, this film presents fifth and sixth grade students reenacting a "structured cooperative controversy." The film is intended for use in courses on conflict.

Johnson D. W., and R. T. Johnson. (writers and producers). *Belonging* (1981). Interaction Book Company, 7208 Cornelia Drive, Edina, MN 55435.

This film presents the experiences of a special education student who is mainstreamed into a classroom via cooperative learning.

Johnson, D. W, and R. T. Johnson. (writers and producers). *Circles of Learning* (videotape). (1983). Interaction Book Company, 7208 Cornelia Drive, Edina, MN 55435.

The primary focus of this film is on the teaching and learning of social skills needed in cooperative learning settings.

Slavin, R. E., R. T. Johnson, and D. W. Johnson. (program consultants). *Cooperative Learning* (videotape). (1990). Alexandria, Va.: Association for Supervision and Curriculum Development.

A five-tape set of video tapes designed to communicate to staff, school board members, and parents how cooperative learning increases student achievement and enhances the development of social skills. Step-by-step procedures are demonstrated for turning existing lessons into cooperative learning lessons.

Tape 1 explains the value of cooperative learning by showing institutions and businesses where cooperation and teamwork have become vital for success. Explains why teamwork must be structured and planned, why individual accountability increases in small-group work, why social skills must be taught, and why cooperative learning improves students' abilities to become better learners. Tape 2 shows teachers implementing cooperative learning in the classroom. Demonstrates the basic elements of any cooperative learning lesson and a five-step lesson planning process which includes adaptation of existing lessons to cooperative learning lessons and how to make decisions about group size and

composition. Tape 3 demonstrates the steps involved in teaching students the social skills they need for effective small-group work. Tape 4 illustrates three proven cooperative learning strategies: Student Teams Achievement Divisions (STAD), Teams Games Tournaments (TGT), and Jigsaw II. Tape 5 shows a teacher modeling the cooperative learning process in a full-length lesson.

A comprehensive Facilitator's Manual comes with the tape set. Viewing time is over three hours. Priced at $980 (ASCD members) and $1,180 (nonmembers). Individual tapes can be purchased. The set may also be rented and an overview of the program is available for previewing.

VII. Games

DeVries, D. L., and K. J. Edwards. (1973). "Learning Games and Student Teams: Their Effects on Classroom Process." *American Educational Research Journal* 10: 307-318.

The study examines the effects of using a learning game (EQUATIONS), student teams, and the games-teams combination on classroom process variables in seventh grade mathematics classes. Results indicated that "using the game created greater student peer tutoring, less perceived difficulty, and greater satisfaction with the class. Using student teams positively altered classroom process by creating greater student peer tutoring, and greater perceived mutual concern and competitiveness in the classroom. The games-teams combination resulted in greater peer tutoring than either games or teams alone." This research was later used, in part, by researchers to develop the cooperative learning strategies known as Teams-Games-Tournaments and Students-Teams Achievement Divisions.

Edwards, K. J., D. L. DeVries, and J. P. Snyder. (1972). "Games and Teams: A Winning Combination." *Simulation and Games* 3: 247-269.

Discusses the results of a study designed to test the effects of the combined use of nonsimulation games and student teams upon student achievement. Concludes that combining nonsimulation games with cooperative team competition had a significant positive effect upon mathematical achievement when compared to traditionally taught classes.

VIII. Newsletters

Cooperation Unlimited Newsletter. (Available from Educational Excellence, P.O. Box 68, Portage, MI 49081).

Issued six times a year, it includes information by experts, practical tips by classroom teachers, lists of resources, and sample lesson plans.

Cooperative Learning: The Magazine for Cooperation in Education. (Available from the International Association for the Study of Cooperation in Education (IASCE), 136 Liberty St., Santa Cruz, CA 95060).

A practitioner-oriented magazine. Each issue features: tips by and for teachers on how to implement cooperative learning; a feature cover story on an experienced cooperative learning teacher; cooperative learning lesson plans in a variety of content areas; a column by leaders in the field on major controversies within cooperative learning; regular columns on staff development, computer applications, and research; networking on cooperative learning programs around the world; reviews of new cooperative learning resources; and thematic articles by leaders in the field.

Our Link: Cooperative Learning Newsletter. (Available from the Cooperative Learning Center, University of Minnesota, 202 Patee Hall, 150 Pillsbury Drive, Minneapolis, MN 55455).

Addresses all aspects of cooperative learning. Often includes short lesson plans, handy hints, and listings of resources.

IX. Organizations

Center for Social Organization of Schools, The Johns Hopkins University, Department L88, 3005 N. Charles St., Baltimore, MD 21218.

Key research center headed up by Robert Slavin that keys in on cooperative learning. Also publishes research findings, teachers' guides, and classroom materials on cooperative learning.

Cooperation Unlimited, P.O. Box 68, Portage, MI 49081.

Provides various workshops on cooperative learning (a 1/2 day awareness session on cooperative learning strategies, and a 4-day "in-depth training workshop").

Cooperative Learning Center, 202 Pattee Hall, University of Minnesota, Minneapolis, MN 55455.

Directed by David and Roger Johnson, it conducts research into various aspects of cooperative learning, conducts inservice programs on cooperative learning, and publishes research findings, texts, and classroom materials.

International Association for the Study of Cooperation in Education (IASCE), 136 Liberty St., Santa Cruz, CA 95060.

Initiated in 1979, this organization's mission is "to study all aspects of educational cooperation, including teachers working together to support and coach each other, and to develop and share curriculum materials." It sponsors international conferences on cooperative learning, and publishes *Cooperative Learning: The Magazine for Cooperation in Education.*

These abstracts are from *Cooperative Learning: A Guide to Research* (1991, Garland Publishing) by Samuel Totten, Toni Sills, Annette Digby, and Pamela Russ. Several abstracts have been revised for brevity. Selections for this ASCD annotated bibliography were made by Samuel Totten and Toni Sills. Revisions to the Garland abstracts were made by Toni Sills.

Acknowledgements: Thanks to Annette Digby, University of Arkansas, and Pamela Russ, Tulane University, for their cooperative efforts in compiling *Cooperative Learning: A Guide to Research* and for permitting their work to appear in this briefer selection.

DATE DUE

SEP 0 1 1998

Demco, Inc. 38-293